Excel

Get the Results You Want!

SmartStudy 8

Mathematics

Allyn Jones

PASCAL PRESS

Reprinted 2015, 2017, 2018, 2019, 2020, 2022, 2023, 2024, 2025

ISBN 978 1 74125 474 7

Pascal Press
PO Box 250
Glebe NSW 2037

www.pascalpress.com.au
Publisher: Vivienne Joannou
Project editors: Rosemary Peers and Mark Dixon
Edited by May McCool, Grant Bailey and Rosemary Peers
Proofread by Chris Greef
Answers checked by Peter Little
Cover, page design and typesetting by DiZign Pty Ltd
Printed by Vivar Printing/Green Giant Press

Students
All care has been taken in compiling this book, but please check with your teacher about the exact requirements of the course as these can change from year to year.

TABLE OF CONTENTS

TAKE THESE REVISION STEPS TO SUCCESS!

Step 1 Study Notes

- This section contains valuable **suggestions**, **tips** and **essential points** about the topic.
- When reading this section, **highlight** the points that are new to you or that you consistently forget. You could also **rewrite** these points so that you are making a summary of the Study Notes. Keep this summary in a prominent place at home—you could stick it on a mirror, wall or door.
- Work carefully through the **checklist** at the end of the section to ensure that you have mastered each of the listed skills.
- If there is something that you are **not sure about**, take time out to read through your class notes, textbooks or another relevant ***Excel*** book. (Check our website at www.pascalpress.com.au for more titles.)

Step 2 Skills Check

- Check that you know the **basic skills** you need to successfully complete the topic.
- Once you have completed the check, **mark your work** quickly by looking at the answers at the bottom of the page. This is **instant feedback** for you. The **worked solutions** are located at the back of the book if you want to check the working of any answer.
- If you have **scored less than 50%** in this section then you should revise your basic skills.

Step 3 Intermediate Test

- This test has very similar questions to the ones you will get in your **class test** or **exam**.
- Look carefully for the **Hints** which are provided for the trickiest questions—these appear at the bottom of the page.
- **Marks** are allocated for each question. These are similar to the marks in your tests.
- Time yourself—**check** how much **time** you have got to complete the test. Also look at the **total marks** of the test to calculate approximately how much time you should spend on each question. For example, if there are twenty marks in total and twenty minutes have been allocated for completion of the test, then spend about one minute on each mark. If you cannot complete all the questions within the suggested time, you may need to revise the topic.
- Fill in the **Your Feedback** panel once you have marked your work in order to calculate your percentage mark. Then complete the **Test & Exam Results** on page 177 to keep a running total of all your test marks.

Step 4 Advanced Test

- This test features only **extension questions** such as problem–solving questions.
- This test is not like a class test, as all the questions in it are challenging. There are no easier questions in it. Mastery of questions in this test, however, will ensure you gain top marks in your class tests and exams, and will also prepare you for the Mathematics you will learn next year.
- **Marks** are allocated for each question. These are similar to the marks in your tests.
- Time yourself—**check** how much **time** you have to complete the test. Also look at the **total marks** of the test to calculate approximately how much time you should spend

on each question. For example, if there are forty marks in total and forty minutes have been allocated for completion of the test, then spend about one minute on each mark.

- Fill in the **Your Feedback** panel once you have marked your work in order to calculate your percentage mark. Then complete the **Test & Exam Results** on page 177 to keep a running total of all your test marks.

Step 5 Check Your Solutions

- **Worked solutions** to all questions are found at the back of the book. Work through the solutions to any questions that you got wrong.
- **Longer questions** are usually worth two or more marks and will involve some working. You should set out all your working, because in Maths you may get some marks for your working even if your answer is wrong.
- The **ticks** that appear in the worked solutions indicate those parts of the working which receive marks. Therefore, even if your answer is wrong, you may be entitled to some marks for what you have written. Compare the worked solution to your own working to find out whether you are entitled to any marks for the question.
- If you still **cannot understand** how the correct answer was obtained, revise that part of the topic and, if necessary, refer to your class notes or ask your teacher for help. It is important to learn from your mistakes.

Step 6 Test & Exam Results

- Go to the **Test & Exam Results** section on page 177 to record your test score as a percentage. When you have completed all topics you will be able to determine your areas of weakness and your areas of strength.
- It is important that you know which **areas need further work**—to 'know what you don't know'. The more you prepare for the topic tests, the more successful you will be and the more you will remember when you sit your end-of-term/semester/year test or exam.

Step 7 Tips for the Sample Exam Papers

- These **useful tips** appear on page 88. Read them before you start one of the Sample Exams (see Step 8 below).

Step 8 Sample Exam Papers

- Three **Sample Exam Papers** are provided at the end of the book. These are of three levels of difficulty: Average, Above Average and Difficult. The Above Average paper will be very similar to your final examination.
- Before attempting the Sample Exam Papers, make sure that you have completed all of the **Tests** and have worked through the solutions to all questions that you answered incorrectly.
- Set aside the **time allowed** for the paper and complete it under **exam conditions**—no sneaking a look at your notes or textbooks! That way you will be better prepared for your final exam.
- **Worked solutions** to the Sample Exam Papers are found at the back of the book. Work through the solutions to any questions that you got wrong. Carefully note the **ticks** in the worked solutions and remember to give yourself marks for correct working. Write down your total marks for each section in the **Your Score** boxes at the end of each part of the paper, then add them up to get a total percentage for each test.

HOW TO USE THIS BOOK TO STUDY FOR A CLASS TEST, HALF-YEARLY OR END-OF-YEAR EXAM

Depending on your teacher or school, you will be given a variety of tests and exams each year. There may be a single-topic test, a test that covers a number of topics, a semester test or exam, or even a half-yearly or yearly exam.

Step 1

Find out which topics will be covered in the class test.

- To do this, look at your class workbook/textbook, laptop/tablet or online study program, and ask your teacher.
- For example, your class test may be on Number, Fractions, Decimals, Percentages and Using your Calculator.

Step 2

Match the topics that your test is on to the topics in this book.

- For example, the first three units in this book cover Number, Fractions, Decimals, Percentages and Using your Calculator.

Step 3

Use this book to study the topics being tested.

- For example, the first three units in this book contain the topics you will study for your class test!

Note:

- When you are using this book to study for a **half-yearly** test, follow the same steps as above—the only difference being that you will have more topics to revise of course!
- When you are using this book to study for an **end-of-year** test, you will more than likely need to study the whole book!

NUMBER, FRACTIONS AND DECIMALS

Number and Algebra

STUDY NOTES

1 Multiples and factors. Let's look at some examples:

a Is 246 divisible by 3?
As 2 + 4 + 6 = 12,
and 12 is divisible by 3,
$\therefore$ 246 is divisible by 3

b $\sqrt{144}$

144 → 12, 12

$\therefore 144 = 12 \times 12$

i.e. $\sqrt{144} = \sqrt{12^2} = 12$

c $276 \div 41$

$$\begin{array}{r} 6\frac{30}{41} \\ 41\overline{)276} \\ 246 \\ \hline 30 \end{array}$$

$\therefore 6\frac{30}{41}$

2 Order of operations. Let's look at some examples:

a $5 + 2 \times 3 = 5 + 6$
$= 11$

b $2(8 + 4 \div 4) = 2 \times (8 + 1)$
$= 18$

c $\frac{5 + 4}{2 + 1} = \frac{9}{3}$
$= 3$

3 Fractions. Let's look at some examples:

a $\frac{27}{4}$ as a mixed number
$= \frac{24}{4} + \frac{3}{4} = 6\frac{3}{4}$

b $1\frac{2}{7}$ as an improper fraction
$= \frac{7 + 2}{7} = \frac{9}{7}$

c Reciprocal of $\frac{2}{3} = \frac{3}{2}$
$= 1\frac{1}{2}$

d $2\frac{1}{2} + 3\frac{1}{4} = 5 + \frac{2 + 1}{4}$
$= 5\frac{3}{4}$

e $1\frac{1}{2} \times 2\frac{1}{3} = \frac{\cancel{3}^{1}}{2} \times \frac{7}{\cancel{3}_{1}}$
$= \frac{7}{2} = 3\frac{1}{2}$

f $5\frac{1}{4} \div \frac{3}{4} = \frac{\cancel{21}^{7}}{\cancel{4}_{1}} \times \frac{\cancel{4}^{1}}{\cancel{3}_{1}}$
$= \frac{7}{1} = 7$

4 Decimals. Let's look at some examples:

a $\frac{5}{7}$ as a decimal:
$= 5 \div 7$

$$= 7\overline{)5.0^{1}0^{3}0^{2}0^{6}0^{4}0^{5}0^{1}0^{3}0^{2}0} \quad \text{quotient } 0.7\,1\,4\,2\,8\,5\,7\,1\,4\,2\ldots$$

$= 0.\dot{7}1428\dot{5}$

b 0.048 as a fraction:
$= \frac{48}{1000}$
$= \frac{6}{125}$

c 37.6028 correct to 2 decimal places:
$= 37.60$

d $4.76 \times 100 = 476$
[decimal point 2 places →]

e $305.7 \div 1000 = 0.3057$
[decimal point 3 places ←]

f $9.5 \div 10^4 = 0.00095$
[decimal point 4 places ←]

g $2.93 + 0.317$
$= 2.930 + 0.317$
$= 3.247$

h 4.21×0.3
$= 1.263$
[maintain number of decimal places]

i $5.05 \div 0.5$
$= 50.5 \div 5$
$= 10.1$

5 Directed numbers. Let's look at some examples:

a $-12 - 8 = -20$

b $-4 - (-3) = -4 + 3$
$= -1$

c $2 \times 4 - 3 \times 5 = 8 - 15$
$= -7$

Checklist

Can you:

1 *Recognise and use basic number concepts and rules from Year 7?* ☐

NUMBER, FRACTIONS AND DECIMALS

Number and Algebra

SKILLS CHECK

Note: Complete all of these questions *without the use of a calculator*.

1 By the use of a factor tree, find the value of $\sqrt{576}$.

2 Evaluate:

a 42×26 b $667 \div 21$

3 True or false?

a 23 431 is divisible by 6 b 7614 is a multiple of 3 c 5 is a factor of 37 615

4 Evaluate:

a $12 - 36 \div 9$ b $\dfrac{\sqrt{12 + 4}}{5 - 3}$ c $4(21 - 3 \times 5)$

5 a Rewrite $\dfrac{16}{5}$ as a mixed numeral. b Rewrite $3\dfrac{9}{11}$ as an improper fraction.

c Find the reciprocal of $1\dfrac{2}{3}$ d Simplify $\dfrac{75}{90}$

6 Write as a decimal:

a $\dfrac{17}{25}$ b $\dfrac{5}{8}$ c $\dfrac{5}{11}$

7 Simplify:

a $\dfrac{3}{4} - \dfrac{2}{5}$ b $1\dfrac{2}{3} + 3\dfrac{4}{5}$ c $2\dfrac{7}{8} - 1\dfrac{1}{3}$

d $\dfrac{2}{5}$ of $3\dfrac{1}{3}$ e $\left(\dfrac{3}{8}\right)^2$ f $1\dfrac{1}{5} \div 1\dfrac{1}{2}$

8 Evaluate:

a 32.415×100 b $809.1 \div 1000$ c 0.321×10^4

9 Simplify:

a $2 - 0.034$ b $3.604 - 1.8$ c 2.9×3

d 1.04×0.06 e $4.239 \div 0.02$ f $(0.04)^2$

10 Simplify:

a $1.8 - 4 \div 10$ b $0.1(4.5 - 1.06)$ c $\dfrac{0.4 \times 0.2}{0.4 \div 0.2}$

11 Simplify:

a $11 - 18$ b $-3 - (-5)$ c $-3 - 2 \times 4$

PAGE 111

Answers 1 24 2 a 1092 b $31\frac{16}{21}$ 3 a F b T c T 4 a 8 b 2 c 24 5 a $3\frac{1}{5}$ b $\frac{42}{11}$ c $\frac{3}{5}$ d $\frac{5}{6}$
6 a 0.68 b 0.625 c $0.\dot{4}\dot{5}$ 7 a $\frac{7}{20}$ b $5\frac{7}{15}$ c $1\frac{13}{24}$ d $1\frac{1}{3}$ e $\frac{9}{64}$ f $\frac{4}{5}$ 8 a 3241.5 b 0.8091 c 3210
9 a 1.966 b 1.804 c 8.7 d 0.0624 e 211.95 f 0.0016 10 a 1.4 b 0.344 c 0.04 11 a −7 b 2 c −11

NUMBER, FRACTIONS AND DECIMALS

Number and Algebra

INTERMEDIATE TEST

Part A Multiple Choice

1 Which of the following has a factor of 6? *Hint 1*

A 4371 B 8144 C 2094 D 2168 (1 mark)

2 Evaluate $28 - 24 \div (4 \times 2 + 4)$.

A $\frac{1}{3}$ B 6 C 26 D 1 (1 mark)

3 What fraction is halfway between $\frac{1}{3}$ and $\frac{1}{5}$?

A $\frac{4}{15}$ B $\frac{1}{4}$ C $\frac{1}{15}$ D $\frac{2}{5}$ (1 mark)

4 A recipe to serve 4 people requires $\frac{2}{3}$ cup of milk. If 10 people will be present at the meal, how many cups of milk will be required? *Hint 2*

A $1\frac{2}{3}$ B 2 C $2\frac{2}{3}$ D $1\frac{1}{3}$ (1 mark)

5 The quotient of $2\frac{2}{5}$ and $\frac{5}{8}$ is:

A $1\frac{1}{2}$ B $2\frac{17}{20}$ C $3\frac{21}{100}$ D $3\frac{21}{25}$ (1 mark)

6 Which of the following is equal to 0.4?

A $\frac{3.2}{0.8}$ B $\frac{1.2 \times 0.4}{12}$ C $\sqrt{1.6}$ D reciprocal of $2\frac{1}{2}$ (1 mark)

7 The average of four numbers is -2. If three of the numbers are 4, -5 and 2, the other number is:

A -9 B 4 C 2 D -1 (1 mark)

Part B Short Answer

8 Evaluate:

a $4 - (2 + 5)$ b $15 - 4 \times 3$ c $-3 - (3 - 3 \div 3)$ (6 marks)

9 In a race Jenny covers three-fifths of the distance in the first hour and a third of the distance in the second hour. If the race was 45 km, how far does she still need to run? (2 marks)

10 A water tank is $\frac{3}{4}$ full and presently holds 2700 litres.

How much will the tank hold when full? (2 marks)

11 Simone bought 42 litres of petrol and paid $1.60 per litre.

a Find the cost of the petrol. (1 mark)

b If Simone is able to travel 540 km with the 42 litres of petrol, find the fuel consumption rate, correct to 2 decimal places, expressed as L/100 km. (2 marks)

Hint 1: Use divisibility tests.
Hint 2: Use unitary method approach—i.e. find for one person, then for 10 people.

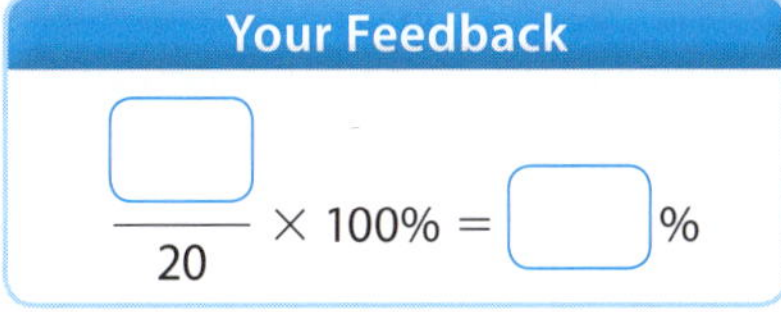

PAGE 111
PAGE 177

NUMBER, FRACTIONS AND DECIMALS

Number and Algebra

ADVANCED TEST

1 Here is a list of numbers. (1 mark each)

53 78 120 184 205 368

How many numbers in the list are:

a multiples of 6? b divisible by 8?

2 At a display booth at a trade show, sample bags are handed to customers. Some of the bags have special items. Every second bag has a key-chain, every fourth bag has a flashlight and every fifth bag has a voucher. How often will a bag contain all three items? (2 marks)

3 Two music classes are combined for a special lesson. 8MUW has 24 students and 8MUH has 30 students. The students are to divide into groups of the same size. Each small group needs to have the same number of students from 8MUW. What is the most number of groups possible? (2 marks)

4 A bag contains 20 balls numbered from one to 20. What fraction of the balls in the bag are:

a even? b multiples of 3?

c prime? (1 mark each)

5 Evaluate:

a $12 - 4 \times 2$ b $(21 \div 7 + 4 \times 2)^2$

c $\dfrac{16 - 4 \times 2}{2(3 + 1)}$ (1 mark each)

6 What fraction is:

a 20 cents of $3? (1 mark)

b 500 millimetres of 10 kilometres? (1 mark)

c 2 litres of 2 megalitres? (1 mark)

d 40 seconds of 4 hours? (1 mark)

7 Evaluate:

a $\dfrac{\frac{2}{3} + \frac{1}{2}}{\frac{2}{3} - \frac{1}{2}}$ b $\dfrac{4}{5} \times 1\dfrac{2}{3} - \dfrac{5}{6} \div \dfrac{2}{3}$

(1 mark each)

8 A tank is three-eighths full of water. A storm adds 1330 litres of water and the tank is two-thirds full. What is the total capacity of the tank? (2 marks)

9 Jackson has decided to give part of his stamp collection away. He gives $\frac{1}{4}$ of the stamps to his brother, and then $\frac{2}{3}$ of the remaining to his sister. If he has 48 stamps remaining, how many stamps did Jackson have in his original collection? (2 marks)

10 One-third of Jasmine's weekly wage is used to pay for the rent, while she spends one-fifth of the remainder on food. She saves one-quarter of the rest of the money. If she still has $360 left, how much was Jasmine originally paid? (2 marks)

11 Evaluate:

a $0.35 \div 0.05 + 0.4 \times 0.8$ b $1 - (0.6)^2$

c $\dfrac{2.4 + 0.6}{1.2 - 0.6}$ (1 mark each)

12 Jo, Mo and Flo shared equally the cost of their restaurant meal. If the total cost was $217.20, how much did each pay? (1 mark)

13 On her second birthday, Lisa's parents measured her height as 0.83 metres. Sixteen years later Lisa's height was 1.7 metres. How much did she grow? (1 mark)

14 A DVD case is 1.5 cm thick. Bryce's stack of DVDs is 94.5 cm high. How many DVDs are in his stack? (1 mark)

15 The table shows the approximate mass of water, petrol and diesel fuel at 4 °C.

Liquid	Quantity (L)	Mass (kg)
Tap Water	1	1
Petrol	1	0.72
Diesel	1	0.82
Sea Water	1	1.02

a What is the mass of 32.4 L of petrol? (1 mark)

b How many litres of diesel have a mass of 16.4 kg? (1 mark)

c Minh put $75 worth of petrol into her car. The cost of petrol was $1.50 per litre. What was the additional mass of her car? (2 marks)

d Liam is comparing the mass of tap water and sea water. How much heavier is a megalitre of sea water than tap water? Give your answer in tonne. (2 marks)

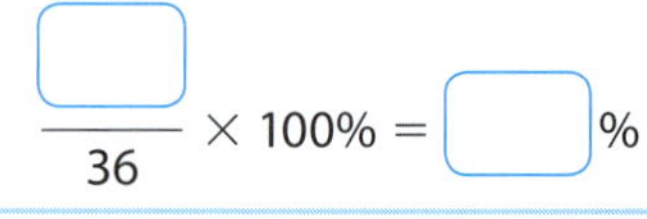

PERCENTAGES
Number and Algebra

STUDY NOTES

1 A fraction with a denominator of 100 can be written as a **percentage.**

2 **One whole** is written as **100%**.

3 **Conversions involving percentages**

- **fraction to a percentage: multiply by 100%**

For example, convert to a percentage:

a $\frac{17}{100}$

$\frac{17}{100} \times \frac{100}{1}\% = 17\%$

b $\frac{3}{25}$

$\frac{3}{25} \times \frac{100}{1}\% = 12\%$

- **decimal to a percentage: multiply by 100%**

For example, convert to a percentage:

a 0.09

$0.09 \times 100\% = 9\%$

b 1.6

$1.6 \times 100\% = 160\%$

- **percentage to a fraction: divide by 100 (put number over 100)**

For example, convert to a fraction:

a 12%

$12\% = \frac{12}{100}$

$= \frac{3}{25}$

b $7\frac{1}{2}\%$

$\frac{7\frac{1}{2}}{100} = \frac{15}{200}$

$= \frac{3}{40}$

- **percentage to a decimal: divide by 100**

For example, convert to a decimal:

a 28%

$28 \div 100 = 0.28$

b $14\frac{1}{2}\%$

$14.5 \div 100 = 0.145$

4 To find **a percentage of a quantity,** we write the percentage as a decimal (or fraction) and multiply by the quantity.

For example, find:

a 8% of $4000

As $0.08 \times 4000 = 320$

∴ $320

b 27% of $300

As $\frac{27}{100} \times \frac{300}{1} = 81$

∴ $81

5 Writing **one quantity as a percentage of another,** we first check that both are of the same units, then write as a fraction before converting to a percentage. For example:

a Rewrite 14 out of 20 as a percentage.

$\frac{14}{20} \times \frac{100}{1}\% = 70\%$

b Express $2.40 as a percentage of $4.

$\frac{240}{400} \times \frac{100}{1}\% = 60\%$

Checklist
Can you:

1 *Convert between fractions, decimals and percentages?* ☐

2 *Find a percentage of a quantity?* ☐

3 *Express one quantity as a percentage of another?* ☐

PERCENTAGES
Number and Algebra

SKILLS CHECK

1 Convert to a percentage:

a $\frac{71}{100}$ b $\frac{3}{100}$ c $\frac{7}{25}$

d $\frac{3}{5}$ e $\frac{17}{20}$ f $\frac{3}{8}$

g $\frac{2}{3}$ h $1\frac{1}{4}$ i $\frac{7}{1000}$

2 Express as a fraction:

a 16% b 6% c 95%

d $12\frac{1}{2}\%$ e $5\frac{1}{4}\%$ f $\frac{3}{5}\%$

3 Express as a mixed numeral:

a 111% b 186% c 550%

4 Express as a percentage:

a 0.4 b 0.07 c 0.019

d 1.6 e 1.05 f 0.125

5 Write as a decimal:

a 32% b 6% c 120%

d 8.5% e 12.5% f 7.25%

6 Find:

a 16% of \$700 b 8% of \$72 c 104% of \$280

d 125% of \$4000 e $3\frac{1}{2}\%$ of \$4900 f $5\frac{3}{4}\%$ of \$680

7 Find:

a 6% of 3 metres b 30% of 2 minutes c 108% of 12 mm

d 21% of 14 kg e 135% of 42 km f $4\frac{1}{2}\%$ of 2 L

8 Express the first quantity as a percentage of the second quantity:

a \$14, \$56 b 20 minutes, 2 hours

9 What percentage is:

a \$4.20 of \$21? b 15 seconds of 2 minutes?

PAGE 113

Answers **1 a** 71% **b** 3% **c** 28% **d** 60% **e** 85% **f** $37\frac{1}{2}\%$ **g** $66\frac{2}{3}\%$ **h** 125% **i** $\frac{7}{10}\%$ **2 a** $\frac{4}{25}$ **b** $\frac{3}{50}$ **c** $\frac{19}{20}$ **d** $\frac{1}{8}$ **e** $\frac{21}{400}$ **f** $\frac{3}{500}$ **3 a** $1\frac{11}{100}$ **b** $1\frac{43}{50}$ **c** $5\frac{1}{2}$ **4 a** 40% **b** 7% **c** 1.9% **d** 160% **e** 105% **f** 12.5% **5 a** 0.32 **b** 0.06 **c** 1.2 **d** 0.085 **e** 0.125 **f** 0.0725 **6 a** \$112 **b** \$5.76 **c** \$291.20 **d** \$5000 **e** \$171.50 **f** \$39.10 **7 a** 18 cm **b** 36 s **c** 12.96 mm **d** 2940 g **e** 56.7 km **f** 90 mL **8 a** 25% **b** $16\frac{2}{3}\%$ **9 a** 20% **b** 12.5%

PERCENTAGES

Number and Algebra

20 MINUTES

INTERMEDIATE TEST

Part A Multiple Choice

1 1.06 written as a percentage is:

A 106% B 10.6% C 1.06% D 0.0106% (1 mark)

2 18% of \$51 equals:

A \$9.18 B \$9.20 C \$9180 D \$9174 (1 mark)

3 What percentage of a revolution is 120°?

A 3% B 30% C $33\frac{1}{3}\%$ D 40% (1 mark)

4 42% is closest to:

A $\frac{2}{5}$ B $\frac{43}{100}$ C 0.042 D 4.2 (1 mark)

5 Part of the rectangle has been shaded. The percentage shaded is: *Hint 1*

0 1 2 3 4

A 24% B 60% C 64% D 83% (1 mark)

6 A bus is carrying 50 passengers of which 24 are females. The percentage that is male is:

A 12% B 24% C 48% D 52% (1 mark)

Part B Short Answer

7 An election was held and the results put into a table as illustrated. If there were 200 votes, then:

Students	Votes
Brown	64
Black	
Green	48
White	70

a how many votes did Black receive? (1 mark)

b who received the most votes? (1 mark)

c what percentage of the voters selected Green? (1 mark)

8 One hundred and sixty boys who play Saturday sport were surveyed and the results were displayed in the horizontal bar graph at right.

Soccer	Rugby Union	Rugby League	Aust. Rules

a How many boys played Australian Rules? (2 marks)

b What percentage of the boys played soccer? (2 marks)

9

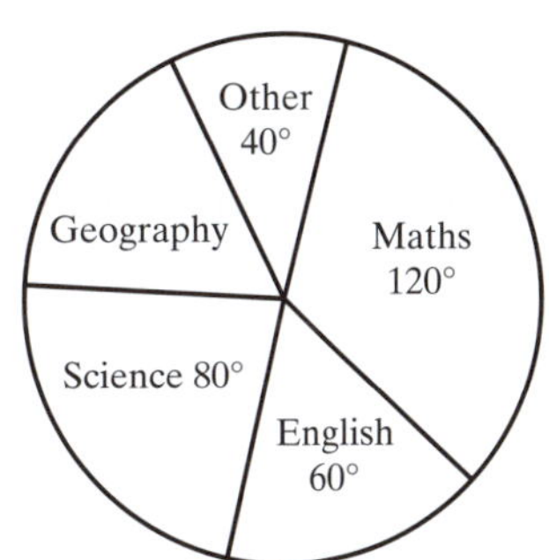

Ninety students were asked for their favourite school subjects and the results were recorded in the sector graph at left.

a What angle is represented by geography? (2 marks)

b What percentage of students selected:

i mathematics? ii science? (4 marks)

Hint 1: Measure the bar graph and find the percentage.

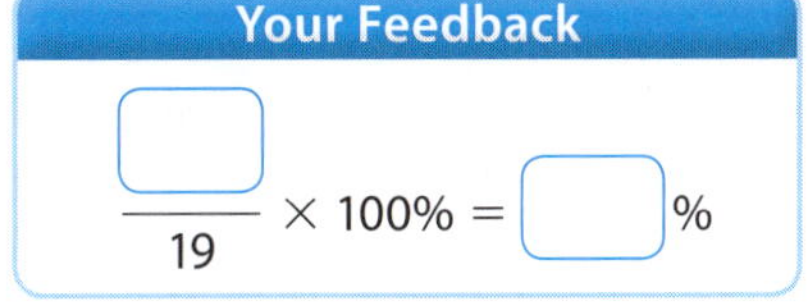

PERCENTAGES

Number and Algebra

45 MINUTES

ADVANCED TEST

1 Change the following to percentages:

a $\frac{37}{40}$ b $2\frac{21}{25}$

c $\frac{17}{1000}$ d $\frac{3}{500}$

e 1.003 f 0.0009 (1 mark each)

2 Rewrite as a simplified fraction:

a $\frac{3}{4}\%$ b $7\frac{4}{5}\%$

c 15.5% (1 mark each)

3 Rewrite as a decimal:

a 270% b 0.03%

c 5.05% d $17\frac{3}{5}\%$

e $20\frac{17}{20}\%$ (1 mark each)

4 What percentage is:

a 20 cents of \$1.60? (1 mark)

b 3 litres of 1 kilolitre? (1 mark)

c 15 marks out of a possible 40? (1 mark)

d $\frac{1}{2}$ of 2? (1 mark)

e $2\frac{1}{5}$ of 10? (1 mark)

f 15 months of 2 years? (1 mark)

g a millimetre of a kilometre? (1 mark)

h half a dozen of 10 dozen? (1 mark)

5 Find:

a 23% of \$400 b $12\frac{1}{4}\%$ of \$800

c 120% of 60 d 95% of 200

e 16% of 3 mg (1 mark each)

6 A bronze alloy contains 75% copper, 16% tin and the remainder zinc. The alloy is used to make a statue with a total mass of 65 kg. What is the mass of zinc in the statue? (2 marks)

7 Tenille is paid \$960 per week. If her pay increases by 4%, what is the increase in her pay? (2 marks)

8 Chi scored 80% in a maths test. If the test had 40 questions, all of equal value, how many questions did he get incorrect? (2 marks)

9 Sixty per cent of the players in a mixed netball club were females. If there were 24 males at the club, what was the total membership? (2 marks)

10 A hockey team played 20 games in a season. They won 11 games, lost 5 games and drew the remainder.

a In what percentage of the games did the team draw? (2 marks)

b Of the games the team drew, three were nil-all results. In what percentage of the drawn games did the team score? (2 marks)

11 Each week a group of runners increases the distance they run by 20%.

a If last week Craig ran 2.4 km, how much further will he run this week? (1 mark)

b If Jess runs 4.8 km this week, how far did she run last week? (2 marks)

c If next week Ian increases the distance by 1.6 km, how far will he run the week after. (2 marks)

12 A school has 132 students in year 12. If this represents 11% of the school's population, how many students are not in year 12? (2 marks)

13 The table shows the votes received by five candidates in a recent election.

Candidate	Votes
Anderson	160
Bradshaw	630
Connors	720
Delaney	450
Edden	40

What percentage of the total votes did Delaney receive? (2 marks)

14 Fenton has a coin collection. Eloise has three times as many coins in her collection as Fenton. Jaydyn has twice as many coins in his collection as Eloise. What percentage of the total coins is in Jaydyn's collection? (2 marks)

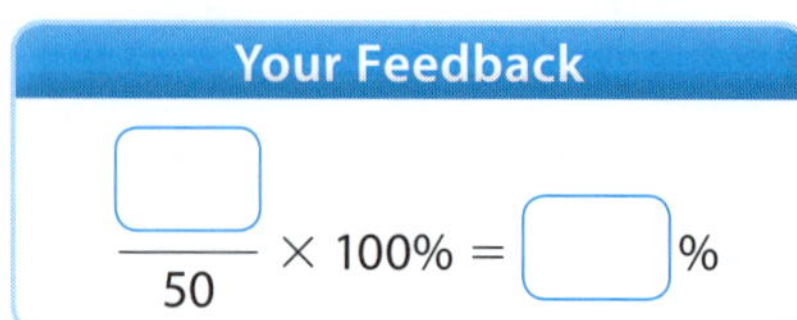

PAGE 114
PAGE 177

USING THE CALCULATOR

Number and Algebra

STUDY NOTES

1 The scientific calculator is programmed for **correct order of operations**, including multiplication between brackets. For example, a calculator will correctly process the following:

a $14 - 6 \times 2 = 2$ b $3 \times (2 + 5) = 21$ c $4 \times (24 \div 12 \times 2) = 16$

2 The **brackets keys** (and) can be used to group parts of the numerical expression. For example, evaluate:

a $\frac{12 - 4}{3 + 5}$
$= (12 - 4) \div (3 + 5)$
$= 1$

b $\sqrt{15 - 2 \times 3}$
$= \sqrt{(15 - 2 \times 3)}$
$= 3$

c $\frac{3 \times 4 + 4}{\sqrt{6 - 2}}$
$= (3 \times 4 + 4) \div \sqrt{(6 - 2)}$
$= 8$

Make sure you press the equals sign = at the end of each expression to display the correct answer.

3 The **exponent key**, y^x is used for indices, e.g. $2^7 = 2\,y^x\,7 = 128$.

For example, evaluate:

a 13^5

$13\,y^x\,5 = 371\,293$

b $(3.4 - 3.2)^4$

$(3.4 - 3.2)\,y^x\,4$
$= 0.0016$

c $\frac{\sqrt{1.44}}{(0.1)^4}$

$\sqrt{1.44} \div (0.1\,y^x\,4)$
$= 12\,000$

4 **Directed numbers** are entered using the +/− key. For example, evaluate:

a $-3 - 5$
$= -8$

b $-5 - (-2)$
$= -3$

c $6 + (-3)$
$= 3$

5 The $a\frac{b}{c}$ key is used in numerical expressions involving **fractions**. For example:

a Rewrite $\frac{27}{6}$ as a mixed numeral.

$27\,a\frac{b}{c}\,6 = 4\frac{1}{2}$

b $\left(\frac{3}{5} - \frac{1}{2}\right)^2 = (3\,a\frac{b}{c}\,5 - 1\,a\frac{b}{c}\,2)\,y^x\,2 = \frac{1}{100}$

c $3\frac{1}{2} + 1\frac{7}{8} = 3\,a\frac{b}{c}\,1\,a\frac{b}{c}\,2 + 1\,a\frac{b}{c}\,7\,a\frac{b}{c}\,8 = 5\frac{3}{8}$

6 The DMS key, or ° ' " key, is the '**degrees, minutes, seconds**' key but it can be used for calculations involving time. For example:

a Find the average of 1 h 42 min, 3 h 18 min, 58 min and 2 h 16 min.

Average = (1 DMS 42 + 3 DMS 18 + 0 DMS 58 + 2 DMS 16) ÷ 4
= $2.058\dot{3}$ DMS = 2 h 3 min 30 s

b Convert 10 000 seconds to hours, minutes, seconds.

10 000 = 0 DMS 0 DMS 10 000
= $2.\dot{7}$ 2ndF DMS

∴ 10 000 seconds = 2 h 46 min 40 s

Checklist

Can you:

1 *Evaluate numerical expressions using the bracket keys on a calculator?* ☐
2 *Key directed numbers into a calculator using the +/– button?* ☐
3 *Evaluate numerical expressions using the exponent key on a calculator?* ☐
4 *Evaluate expressions involving fractions using a calculator?* ☐
5 *Perform operations involving time units using the calculator?* ☐

USING THE CALCULATOR

Number and Algebra

SKILLS CHECK

1 Evaluate:

a $75 \div 5(2 + 3)$ b $\dfrac{63 - 27}{4 \times 3}$ c $4[3 + 2(2 + 4)]$

d $\dfrac{12 + 8}{\sqrt{16}}$ e $\dfrac{\sqrt{40 + 3 \times 3}}{12 - 5}$ f $\sqrt{\dfrac{10 + 2 \times 3}{12 \div 3}}$

2 Calculate, correct to 3 decimal places:

a $\sqrt[3]{12.76}$ b $\dfrac{4}{(6.41)^2}$ c $\dfrac{3.54 - 2.6}{2.86 + 1.07}$

d $4.13^2 - 3.59^2$ e $\sqrt{\dfrac{3.51}{2.6}}$ f $\sqrt{15} - \sqrt{11}$

3 Evaluate:

a 1.5^4 b $(3.64 \times 25)^2$ c $\dfrac{1}{(2.5 \div 0.5)^3}$

4 If $a = 3$, $b = 4$ and $c = 2$, find:

a $2a - 3b$ b $b^2 - c^2$ c $\dfrac{ab - 3c}{c}$

d $3b^2 - 2a^2$ e $\sqrt{15 - ac}$ f $\dfrac{bc}{2c + ab}$

5 Simplify:

a $2 - \left(\dfrac{3}{5} + \dfrac{2}{3}\right)$ b $5\dfrac{3}{4} \times 1\dfrac{1}{3}$ c $\dfrac{3\frac{1}{3} - 1\frac{1}{4}}{3\frac{1}{3} + 1\frac{1}{4}}$

6 If $x = \dfrac{3}{4}$, $y = \dfrac{2}{3}$, evaluate:

a $(xy)^2$ b xy^2 c $3(x - y)$

7 Find:

a 3 h 4 min 16 s + 2 h 14 min 32 s

b 6 h 10 min 8 s − 2 h 14 min 9 s

c 2 h − 1 h 48 min 10 s

d 3 h 4 min 16 s − 28 min 19 s

8 As part of his morning fitness program, Kim ran for 12 min 15 s, 32 min 18 s and 27 min 48 s over three consecutive days. Find Kim's average running time.

PAGE 115

Answers **1 a** 3 **b** 3 **c** 60 **d** 5 **e** 1 **f** 2 **2 a** 2.337 **b** 0.097 **c** 0.239 **d** 4.169 **e** 1.162 **f** 0.556
3 a 5.0625 **b** 8281 **c** 0.008 **4 a** −6 **b** 12 **c** 3 **d** 30 **e** 3 **f** 0.5 **5 a** $\frac{11}{15}$ or $0.7\dot{3}$ **b** $7\frac{2}{3}$ or $7.\dot{6}$ **c** $\frac{5}{11}$ or $0.\dot{4}\dot{5}$
6 a $\frac{1}{4}$ or 0.25 **b** $\frac{1}{3}$ or $0.\dot{3}$ **c** $\frac{1}{4}$ or 0.25 **7 a** 5 h 18 min 48 s **b** 3 h 55 min 59 s **c** 11 min 50 s **d** 2 h 35 min 57 s
8 24 min 7 s

USING THE CALCULATOR

Number and Algebra

30 MINUTES

INTERMEDIATE TEST

Part A Multiple Choice

1 Evaluate $\frac{3.4 + 2.5}{4.6 - 1.8}$, correct to 2 decimal places. *Hint 1*

A 2.14 B 2.11 C 4.29 D 4.81 (1 mark)

2 On his 14th birthday, Bryce correctly calculates the number of seconds he has been alive. Which of the following is closest to Bryce's answer?

A 442 000 000 seconds B 18 396 000 seconds

C 248 600 000 seconds D 576 000 000 seconds (1 mark)

3 If $p = 2$ and $q = 4$, evaluate $\frac{pq}{(q-2)^2}$

A 4 B 8 C 16 D 2 (1 mark)

4 The reciprocal of $2 \div 2\frac{1}{4}$ is:

A $1\frac{1}{2}$ B $\frac{3}{8}$ C $1\frac{1}{8}$ D $\frac{9}{16}$ (1 mark)

Part B Short Answer

5 Find the value of:

a $\frac{20 - 4 \times 3}{6 - 4}$ b $\sqrt{\frac{30 + 6 \times 4}{9 - 3 \times 1}}$ c $\sqrt{3 + 4 \times 3 + 1}$ (6 marks)

6 Evaluate the following, correct to 2 decimal places:

a $\frac{3.057}{\sqrt{2.8 + 1.6}}$ b $\sqrt{\frac{8.402 - 3.47}{6.05}}$ c $\left(\frac{3.54}{2.9}\right)^3$

d $\sqrt[3]{4.07 - 2.96}$ e $\frac{1}{3.47} - \frac{3}{2.94}$ f $\frac{6.4 - 2.08}{3.92^2}$ (12 marks)

7 If $a = 5$, $b = 2$ and $c = 3$, evaluate:

a $(a - b + c)^3$ b $\sqrt{\frac{3a - 2b}{3c + 2}}$ c $\sqrt[3]{4ac + 2b}$ (6 marks)

8 Grant and Melissa both ran the Sydney Marathon and their finishing times were 2 h 28 min 16 s and 3 h 10 min 48 s respectively. If both started at the same time, how long did Grant wait for Melissa to finish the race? *Hint 2* (2 marks)

9 Complete:

a 6.4 hours = ______ h ______ min b 15.2 minutes = ______ min ______ s

c $8\frac{2}{3}$ minutes = ______ min ______ s d $\frac{4}{25}$ hour = ______ min ______ s (4 marks)

Hint 1: Use the brackets keys on the calculator.
Hint 2: Use the DMS key on the calculator (or similar).

Your Feedback

$\frac{\square}{34} \times 100\% = \square\%$

PAGE 116

PAGE 177

USING THE CALCULATOR

Number and Algebra

40 MINUTES

ADVANCED TEST

1 Evaluate:

a $70 \div (12 - 2 \times 1)$ (1 mark)

b $24 - [16 - (2 \times 4 + 3)]$ (1 mark)

c $(35 - 5 \times 2) \div (3 + 2)$ (1 mark)

d $27 \div [18 - (6 \times 2 + 3)]$ (1 mark)

e $3 \times [12 \div (9 + 3) + 4]$ (1 mark)

2 Evaluate:

a $\dfrac{\sqrt{22 - 2 \times 3}}{2 + 2}$ b $\sqrt{\dfrac{14 + 10}{15 - 9}}$

c $\sqrt{\dfrac{31 - 3 \times 2}{6 - 5 \times 1}}$ d $\dfrac{18 + 4 \times 3}{\sqrt{15 - 6}}$

e $\dfrac{12}{\sqrt{36}} + \dfrac{16}{\sqrt{64}}$ (1 mark each)

3 Evaluate:

a $(10 - 3 \times 2)^2$ b $1^2 + 2^3 + 3^4$

c $(16 - 3 \times 2)^5$ d $5.2^2 + 2.6^4$

e $10^2 - (12 - 4)^2$ (1 mark each)

4 Evaluate:

a $\sqrt[3]{5 \times 3 + 4 \times 3}$ b $\sqrt[3]{\dfrac{25 \times 5 + 3}{14 - 12}}$

c $\dfrac{14 + 2}{\sqrt[3]{14 - 3 \times 2}}$ d $\dfrac{\sqrt{25}}{\sqrt[3]{1000}}$

e $(\sqrt[3]{64})^2 + (\sqrt{64})^3$ (1 mark each)

5 Calculate, leaving your answer correct to 2 decimal places:

a $\sqrt{\dfrac{263.8}{11.45 \times 8.2}}$ b $\dfrac{8.3}{\sqrt{6.46 - 3.91}}$

c $\sqrt{\dfrac{4^2 + 11^2}{243 - 13^2}}$ (1 mark each)

6 Calculate:

a $\dfrac{2}{3} + \dfrac{3}{5} \times 1\dfrac{2}{3}$ b $2\dfrac{5}{8} - 1\dfrac{1}{4}$

(1 mark each)

7 Students were invited to submit photos for the school magazine. Only three-fifths of the submitted photos were used. There were 108 photos not used. How many photos were originally submitted? (2 marks)

8 Four friends competed in a triathlon and their finishing times were recorded in the table below.

Name	Time
Mike	2 h 18 min 32 s
Matt	2 h 29 min 16 s
Danielle	2 h 58 min 48 s
Kristen	3 h 11 min 7 s

Find the difference in finishing times between:

a Mike and Danielle (1 mark)

b Kristen and Matt (1 mark)

9 Two-fifths of 40 balloons at a party were red and the remainder blue. If 1 red and 4 blue balloons burst, what fraction of the remaining balloons were red? (2 marks)

10 In a bag there are red, blue and green balls. Three-eighths of the balls are blue and there are 13 green balls. If there are 9 more red balls than green balls, what was the total number of balls in the bag? (2 marks)

11 Thao has seen two solar eclipses. The first lasted for 6 minutes 28 seconds and the other for 5 minutes 52 seconds. What was the average length of the eclipses? (1 mark)

12 If $a = 4, b = 3$ and $c = 2$, find the value of M, to 1 decimal place, if:

a $M = \dfrac{ab}{\sqrt{c^2 + 7a}}$ (2 marks)

b $M = \sqrt{\dfrac{a - b}{a + bc}}$ (2 marks)

13 If $A = \dfrac{\sqrt{pq - r}}{t}$, find A, to the nearest tenth, if:

a $p = 3, q = 6, r = 2, t = 7$ (2 marks)

b $p = \dfrac{1}{2}, q = \dfrac{1}{4}, r = \dfrac{1}{10}, t = \dfrac{1}{5}$ (2 marks)

c $p = 3.6, q = 1.8, r = 2.1, t = 2.5$ (2 marks)

d $p = -2, q = -8, r = -12, t = 12$ (2 marks)

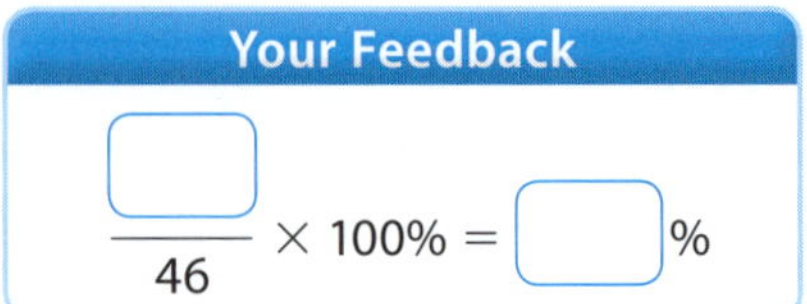

PAGE 117
PAGE 177

PATTERNS AND ALGEBRA

Number and Algebra

STUDY NOTES

1 Basic algebra concepts

a **Complete the table** for:
$y = 2x + 4$

x	0	1	2
y	4	6	8

b **Find the rule** used in this table:

x	0	1	2
y	-5	-2	1

$\therefore y = 3x - 5$

c If $a = 4$ and $b = 2$, **evaluate** $3a - 2b - 6$.

$\therefore 3 \times 4 - 2 \times 2 - 6$
$= 12 - 4 - 6$
$= 2$

d **Product** of $3a$ and $5ab$

$\therefore 3a \times 5ab = 15a^2b$

e **How many cents** in $\$p$?

$100 \times p = 100p$
$\therefore 100p$ cents

f **Sum** of $9m$ and the **quotient** of $6m$ and 2

$\therefore 9m + 6m \div 2 = 9m + 3m$
$= 12m$

2 Using algebra

a $3a - 2ab - a = 2a - 2ab$

b $4x \times 3x^2 = 12x^3$

c $12ab \div 6a = 2b$

d $\frac{5ab}{10a} = \frac{b}{2}$

e $5xy - yx = 4xy$
[as $xy = yx$]

f $12p - 2 \times 3p = 12p - 6p$
$= 6p$

3 Simple equations

a **i** Solve $a + 4 = 11$

$a + 4 - 4 = 11 - 4$
$a = 7$

ii Solve $x - 3 = 9$

$x - 3 + 3 = 9 + 3$
$x = 12$

iii Solve $5a = 14$

$\frac{5a}{5} = \frac{14}{5}$
$a = 2\frac{4}{5}$

iv Solve $\frac{b}{4} = 9$

$4 \times \frac{b}{4} = 4 \times 9$
$b = 36$

b The sum of a number and four equals twelve. Find the number.

Let the number be x.

$\therefore x + 4 = 12$
$x + 4 - 4 = 12 - 4$
$x = 8$

$\therefore$ the number is 8

c The product of 4 and a number is added to 7 to give a total of 19. What is the number?

Let the number be x.

$\therefore 4x + 7 = 19$
$4x + 7 - 7 = 19 - 7$
$4x = 12$
$\frac{4x}{4} = \frac{12}{4}$
$x = 3$

$\therefore$ the number is 3

Checklist

Can you:

1 *Recognise and use basic algebra concepts and rules from Year 7?* ☐
2 *Find the solution of basic equations?* ☐

PATTERNS AND ALGEBRA

Number and Algebra

SKILLS CHECK

1 Complete the table:

a $y = 2x - 1$

x	0	1	2	3
y				

b $q = 2p^2$

p	0	1	2	3
q				

2 Write the rule used in the following:

a

x	0	1	2	3
y	−2	−1	0	1

b

a	0	1	2	3
b	3	5	7	9

3 If $x = 4, y = 2$, find:

a $(xy)^2$ b $x^2 - y^2$ c $2x - 5y$

d $\sqrt{3x + 4y \div 2}$ e $\dfrac{5x + 4}{3y - 2}$ f $\dfrac{3x}{2} - \dfrac{8}{y}$

4 If $p = 0.2, q = 0.5$, find:

a $3p + 2q$ b $3p^2$ c $pq - (p - q)$

5 Simplify:

a $3 \times a \times a \times a \times b \times b$ b $4xy - 2yx$ c $3a - 2b + 4a - b$

d $14a \div 2$ e $5y \times 2x \times 8x$ f $\dfrac{12x^2y}{4x}$

6 Complete:

a $\$p =$ ______ cents b q km = ______ m c y mL = ______ L

7 Write an expression for the following:

a Find the total cost of p pens at q cents each and x pencils at y cents each.

b Jack bought a coil of rope t metres long. He cut m lengths of n metres each. What is the length of rope remaining?

c Find the average of a, b and c.

8 Solve the following equations:

a $x - 7 = 12$ b $y + 8 = 13$ c $a + 4 = 2$

d $3x = 39$ e $2a + 1 = 11$ f $\dfrac{y}{3} = 6$

PAGE 118

Answers **1 a** −1, 1, 3, 5 **b** 0, 2, 8, 18 **2 a** $y = x - 2$ **b** $b = 2a + 3$ **3 a** 64 **b** 12 **c** −2 **d** 4 **e** 6 **f** 2
4 a 1.6 **b** 0.12 **c** 0.4 **5 a** $3a^3b^2$ **b** $2xy$ **c** $7a - 3b$ **d** $7a$ **e** $80x^2y$ **f** $3xy$ **6 a** $100p$ **b** $1000q$ **c** $\dfrac{y}{1000}$
7 a $(pq + xy)$ cents **b** $(t - mn)$ metres **c** $(a + b + c) \div 3$ **8 a** 19 **b** 5 **c** −2 **d** 13 **e** 5 **f** 18

PATTERNS AND ALGEBRA

Number and Algebra

20 MINUTES

INTERMEDIATE TEST

Part A Multiple Choice

1 If $y = 3$, then $2y^2 =$

A 12 B 18 C 24 D 36 (1 mark)

2 The sum of 5 and the product of 4 and x is:

A $20x$ B $x + 9$ C $4x + 5$ D $9x$ (1 mark)

3 $5a + 3 - 2a - 5 =$

A $3a + 8$ B $3a - 2$ C $3a - 8$ D $8a - 2$ (1 mark)

4 $7 \times b - 3 \times b \times 4 =$

A $-5b$ B $3b - 2$ C $3b - 8$ D $8b - 2$ (1 mark)

5 $x = 2$ is the solution to the equation: *Hint 1*

A $x - 2 = 8$ B $2x = 6$ C $4 - x = 2$ D $x - 8 = 6$ (1 mark)

6 $b = -1$ is **not** the solution to the equation:

A $b - 3 = -4$ B $2 - b = 3$ C $b + 2 = 1$ D $3b = 3$ (1 mark)

Part B Short Answer

7 Solve the following equations:

a $2x - 1 = 9$ b $\frac{t - 1}{4} = 3$ c $2 + 3a = 8$ (6 marks)

8 For the rule $y = 3x - 1$, complete the table and then plot the points on a number plane.

x	0	1	2
y			

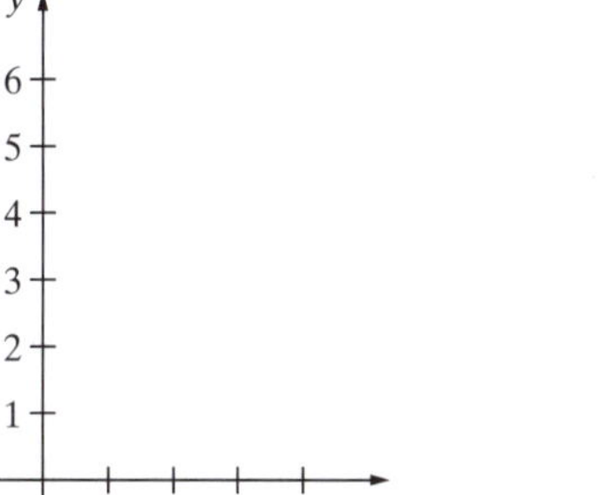

(3 marks)

9 Theo used a number rule to graph points on this number plane. What is his number rule? *Hint 2*

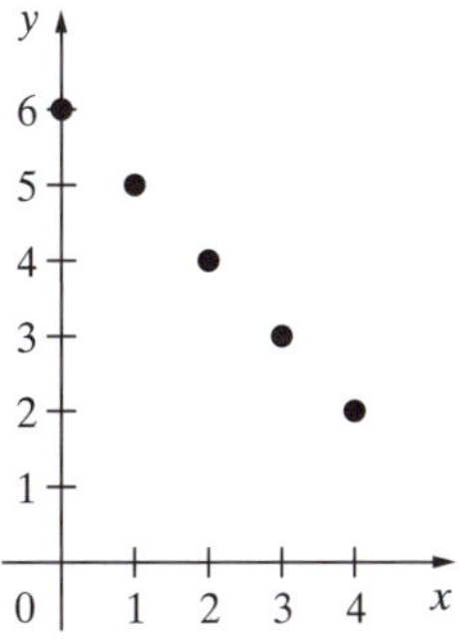

(2 marks)

Hint 1: Subs $x = 2$ into each of the alternatives.
Hint 2: Form a table and write the number rule as $y = \ldots$

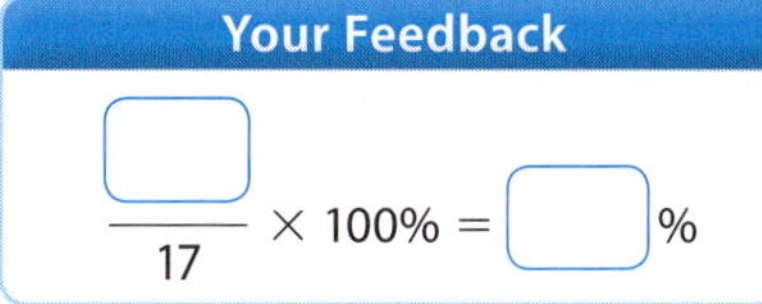

PATTERNS AND ALGEBRA

Number and Algebra

45 MINUTES

ADVANCED TEST

1 Find the number rule linking x and y:

a

x	0	1	2	3
y	−5	−2	1	4

(1 mark)

b

x	0	1	2	3
y	−11	−10	−3	16

(1 mark)

2 James fixes computers in clients' homes and uses a table to record the amount he charges for time of service.

n	1	2	3	4
c	75	120	165	210

a How much does he charge for 5 hours? (1 mark)

b In how many hours will he earn $345? (2 marks)

c Write the rule linking n and c:

$c =$ ____________ (1 mark)

d Use the rule in part **c** to find the amount he would receive for 12 hours of work. (1 mark)

3 If $a = 4, b = 5, c = 3$, find the value of:

a $\dfrac{ab-2}{c}$ b $(b-c)(a+c)$

c $\dfrac{\sqrt{a+b}}{c}$ d $\dfrac{3a-b+1}{(c+1)^2}$ (2 marks each)

4 Peta's pool pump needs to be fixed. The repairer charges $90 per hour plus $110 for parts. Write an expression for the cost (c) in dollars if the repairer takes n hours. (1 mark)

5 Evaluate A, where $A = p^2 - 2qr$, when

a $p = -3, q = 5$ and $r = -2$ (2 marks)

b $p = \dfrac{2}{3}, q = \dfrac{1}{4}$ and $r = \dfrac{3}{5}$ (2 marks)

c $p = 0.9, q = -1.6$ and $r = -0.5$ (2 marks)

6 Write an algebraic expression for the following by letting the number be x:

a The sum of half the number and two-thirds the number is less than twelve. (1 mark)

b The product of two consecutive odd numbers is sixty-three. (1 mark)

c The quotient of ten and three times the number is greater than or equal to the product of the number and six. (1 mark)

7 A square has an area of $64y^2$ cm^2. What is the perimeter of the square? (2 marks)

8

a Use the points to complete the table:

x				
y				

(1 mark)

b Write the rule that is used to plot the points. (1 mark)

9 Simplify:

a $5x - 3y - 2x + 7y$ (1 mark)

b $8a - 1 - 4 - 9a$ (1 mark)

c $3x^2 - 2xy - 5x^2 - yx$ (1 mark)

d $-3w - q - w + 2q$ (1 mark)

e $12ba + 3a - 2b - 13ab$ (1 mark)

10 Simplify:

a $4y \times (-7y)$ b $(-3a)^2$

c $18p^2 \div 6p$ d $\dfrac{36g}{9g^2}$

e $\dfrac{-52w^2}{13w}$ (1 mark each)

11 Simplify:

a $18c \div 3 - 4 \times 5c$ b $(8b - 6b \times 3)^2$

c $\dfrac{3a - 4a \times 2}{5a}$ d $\sqrt{16a^2} \div 4$

e $\dfrac{12y \div 3 + 2y \times 3}{14y - 6y \times 2}$ (2 marks each)

12 One number is five more than another number. The product of the two numbers is 300. By letting the smaller number be x, express the information in an equation. (2 marks)

13 Find the next term of the sequence:

a $2, 8c, 32c^2,$ ____ (1 mark)

b $9x - 6y, 6x - y, 3x + 4y,$ ____ (1 mark)

Your Feedback

$\dfrac{\square}{53} \times 100\% = \square\,\%$

PAGE 119

PAGE 177

AREA AND VOLUME

Measurement and Geometry

STUDY NOTES

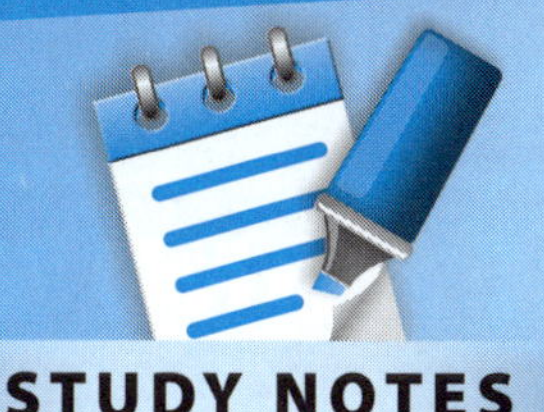

1 Units of measurement

Length: 1000 mm = 1 m
100 cm = 1 m
1000 m = 1 km

Area: 10 000 m^2 = 1 ha
100 mm^2 = 1 cm^2
10 000 cm^2 = 1 m^2
1 000 000 m^2 = 1 km^2

Capacity: 1000 mL = 1 L
1000 L = 1 kL
1000 kL = 1 ML

Volume and capacity: 1 cm^3 = 1 mL
1000 cm^3 = 1 L

2 The **area** is a measure of the space inside a plane shape.

Rectangle:

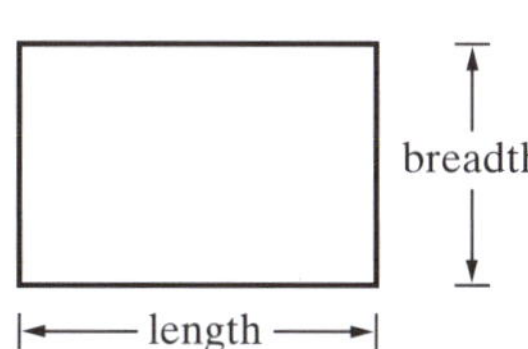

Area = length × breadth
$A = lb$

Parallelogram:

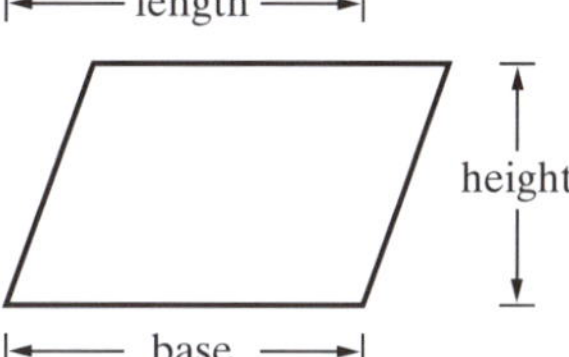

Area = base × perpendicular height
$A = bh$

Square:

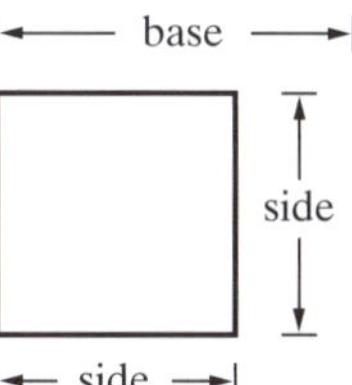

Area = side × side
$A = s^2$

Triangle:

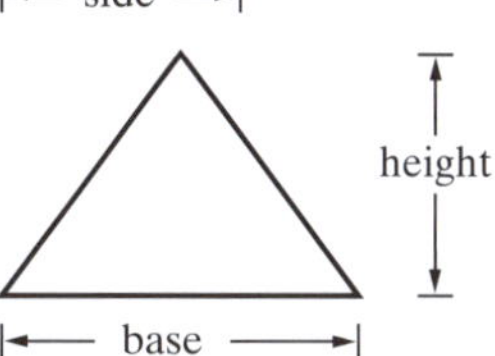

Area = $\frac{1}{2}$ × base × perpendicular height
$A = \frac{1}{2}bh$

3 A **composite shape** is formed by two or more familiar shapes.

Example: Find the area:

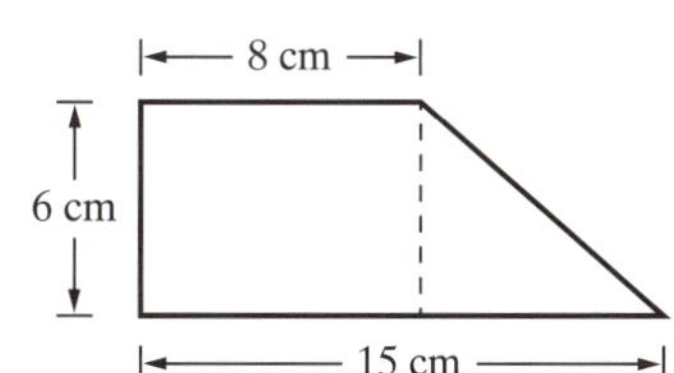

$$\begin{aligned}\text{Area} &= 8 \times 6 + \frac{1}{2} \times 7 \times 6 \\ &= 48 + 21 \\ &= 69 \quad \therefore 69 \text{ cm}^2\end{aligned}$$

4 The volume is a measure of space contained inside a solid shape.

Rectangular prism: **Volume = length × breadth × height**
$V = lbh$

Checklist

Can you:

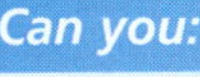

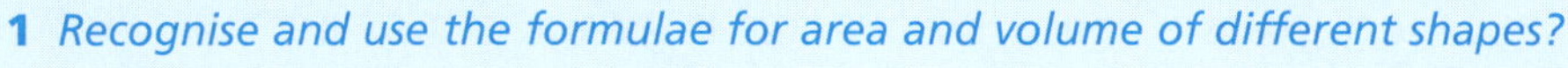

1 *Recognise and use the formulae for area and volume of different shapes?* ☐

AREA AND VOLUME

Measurement and Geometry

SKILLS CHECK

1 Convert:

a $342\text{ cm} = \_\_\_\_\_\_\_ \text{ m}$

b $1320\text{ mm} = \_\_\_\_\_\_\_ \text{ m}$

c $685\text{ m} = \_\_\_\_\_\_\_ \text{ km}$

d $3.2\text{ m} = \_\_\_\_\_\_\_ \text{ cm}$

e $12.9\text{ m} = \_\_\_\_\_\_\_ \text{ mm}$

f $9.04\text{ km} = \_\_\_\_\_\_\_ \text{ m}$

g $3\text{ ha} = \_\_\_\_\_\_\_ \text{ m}^2$

h $90\,000\text{ m}^2 = \_\_\_\_\_\_\_ \text{ ha}$

i $1200\text{ m}^2 = \_\_\_\_\_\_\_ \text{ ha}$

j $5\text{ L} = \_\_\_\_\_\_\_ \text{ mL}$

k $4600\text{ L} = \_\_\_\_\_\_\_ \text{ kL}$

l $65\text{ kL} = \_\_\_\_\_\_\_ \text{ ML}$

2 Find the perimeter:

a

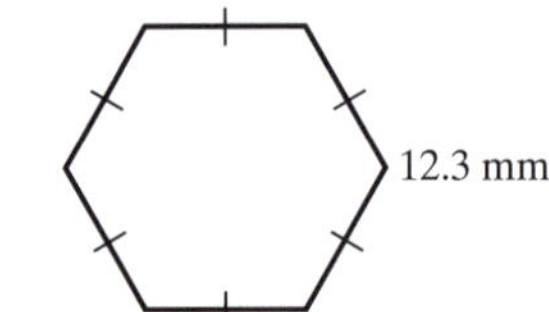

b

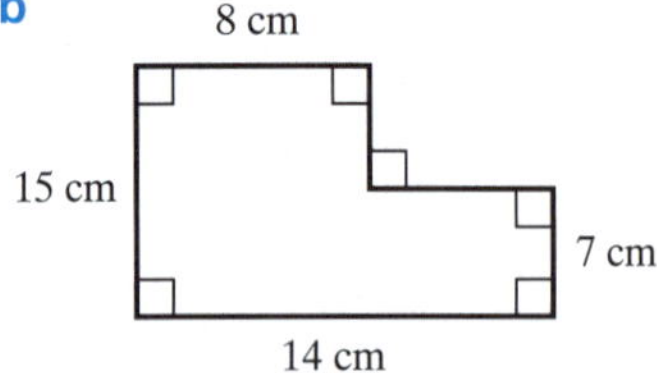

c

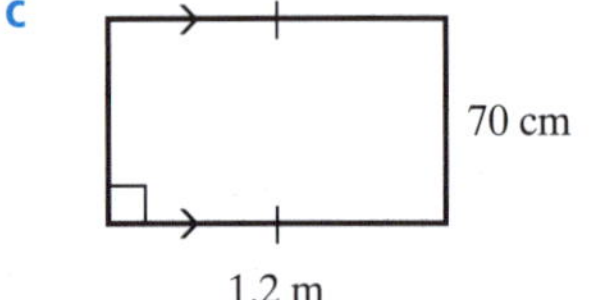

3 Find the area:

a

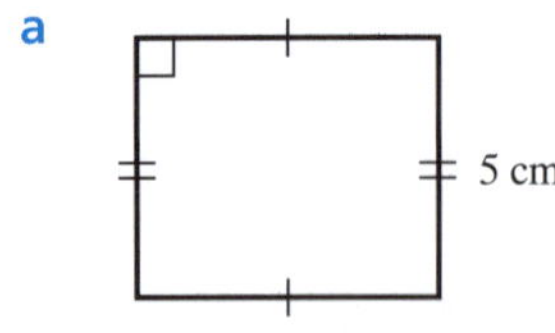

b

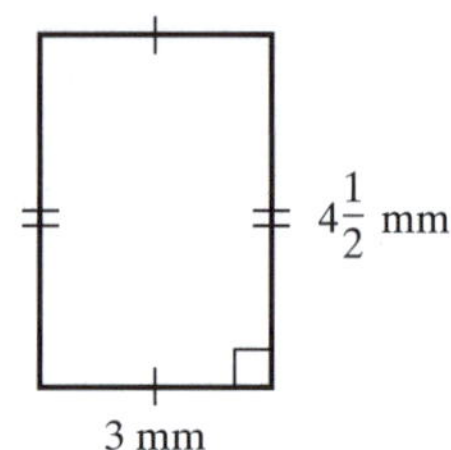

c

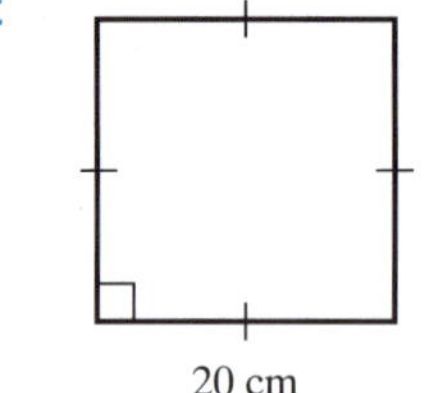

4 Find the area:

a

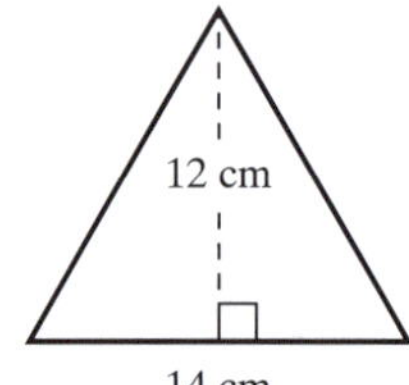

b

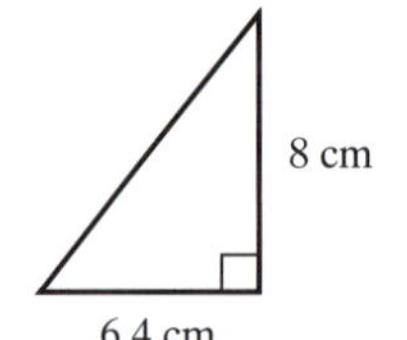

c

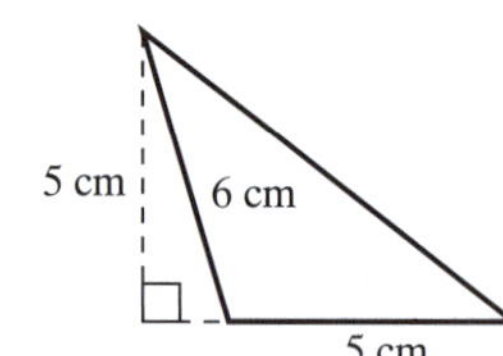

5 Find the area:

a

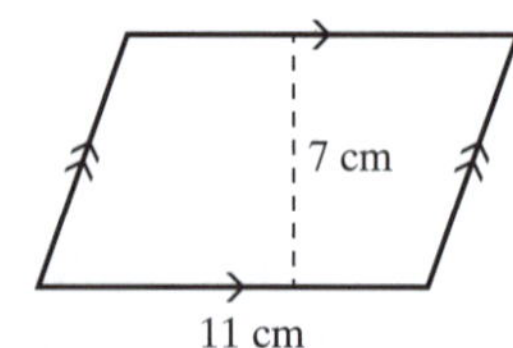

b

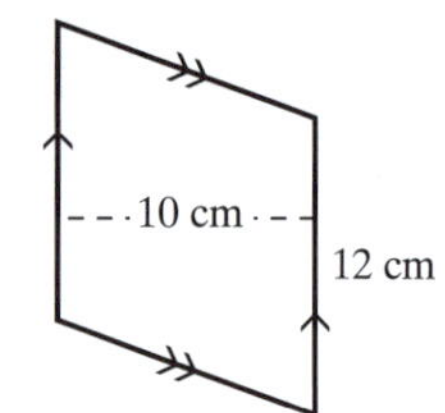

c

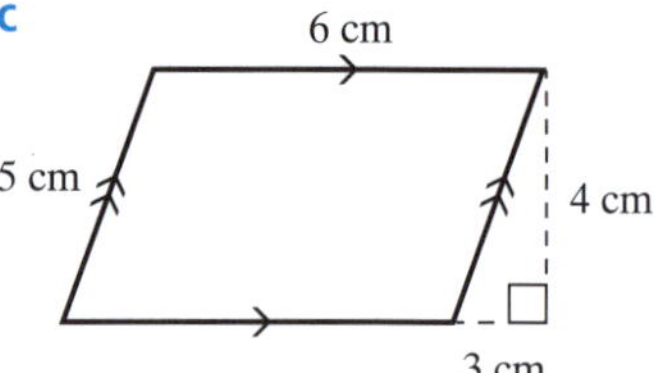

6 Find the area:

a

b

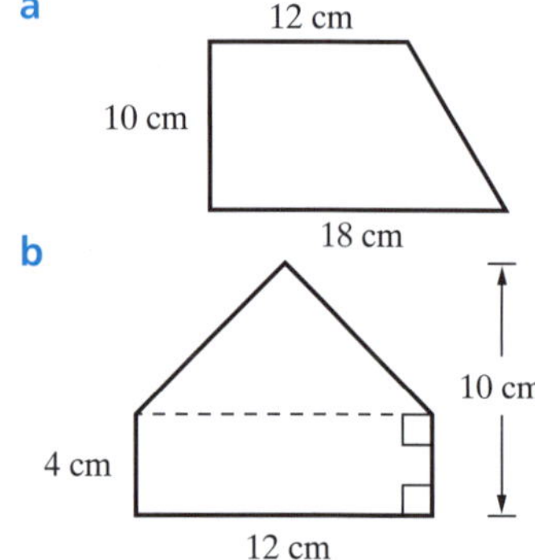

7 Find the cost of fertilising a rectangular paddock measuring 120 metres by 85 metres at a cost of \$1.80 per 10 m^2.

8 The perpendicular height of a parallelogram is 12.6 cm. If the area is 326.34 cm^2, what is the length of its base?

9 Find the volume of a rectangular prism with dimensions 12 cm, 8 cm and 7 cm.

PAGE 120

Answers **1 a** 3.42 **b** 1.32 **c** 0.685 **d** 320 **e** 12 900 **f** 9040 **g** 30 000 **h** 9 **i** 0.12 **j** 5000 **k** 4.6 **l** 0.065
2 a 73.8 mm **b** 58 cm **c** 3.8 m **3 a** 21 cm^2 **b** 13.5 mm^2 **c** 400 cm^2 **4 a** 84 cm^2 **b** 25.6 cm^2 **c** 12.5 cm^2
5 a 77 cm^2 **b** 120 cm^2 **c** 24 cm^2 **6 a** 150 cm^2 **b** 84 cm^2 **7** \$1836 **8** 25.9 cm **9** 672 cm^3

AREA AND VOLUME

Measurement and Geometry

25 MINUTES

INTERMEDIATE TEST

Part A Multiple Choice

1 Which of these is the same length as 0.04 m?

A 4 mm B 400 mm C 4 cm D 40 cm (1 mark)

2 What is the area in square millimetres of the rectangle shown?

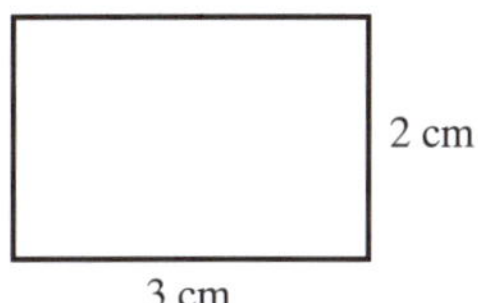

A 6 B 600 C 60 000 D 6 000 000 (1 mark)

3 Which of the following expressions could be used to find the area of the shape?

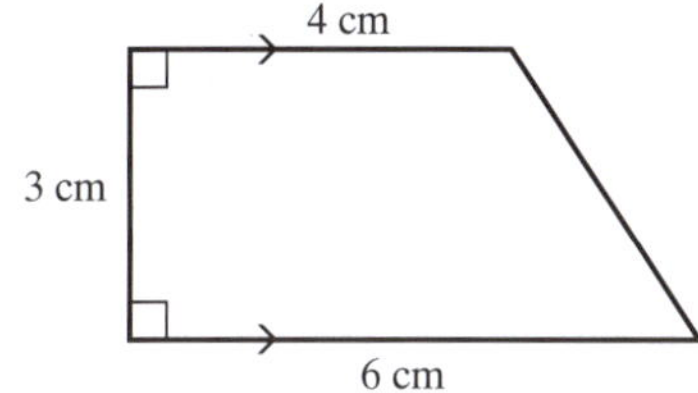

A $4 \times 3 \times 6$

B $\frac{1}{2} \times 6 \times 4 \times 3$

C $4 \times 3 + \frac{1}{2} \times 2 \times 3$

D $4 \times 3 + \frac{1}{2} \times 6 \times 3$ (1 mark)

4 The volume of the rectangular prism is 120 cm^3.

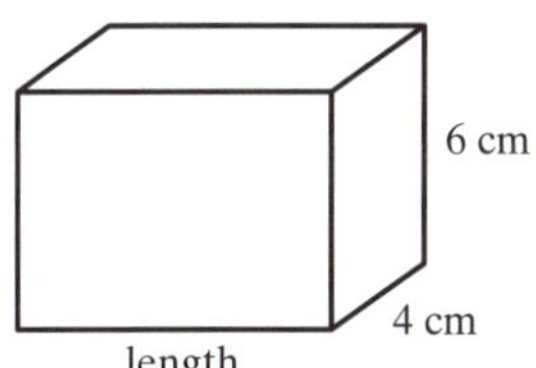

What is the length?

A 4 cm B 5 cm C 7 cm D 8 cm (1 mark)

5 The area of a rectangular paddock is 12 hectares.
How many square metres is this?

A 120 B 1200 C 120 000 D 1 200 000 (1 mark)

6 Rewrite 4.05 kilometres in centimetres.

A 405 B 4050 C 40 500 D 405 000 (1 mark)

(Cont.)

Part B Short Answer

7 Find the area:

a

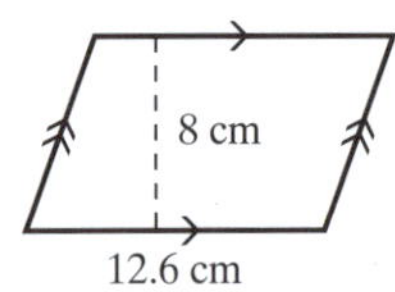

b

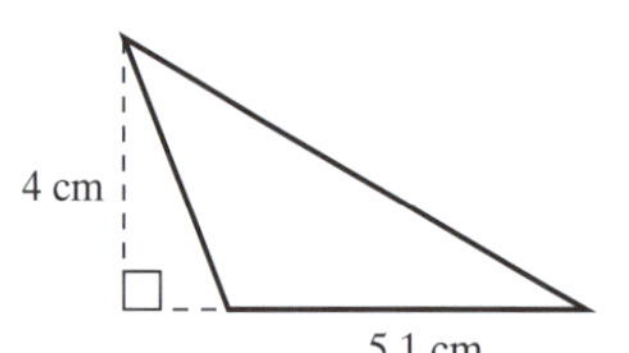

c

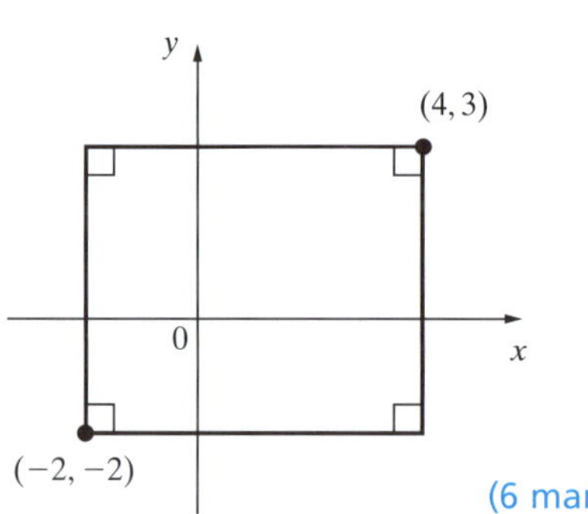

(6 marks)

8 Find the area of the shaded region:

a

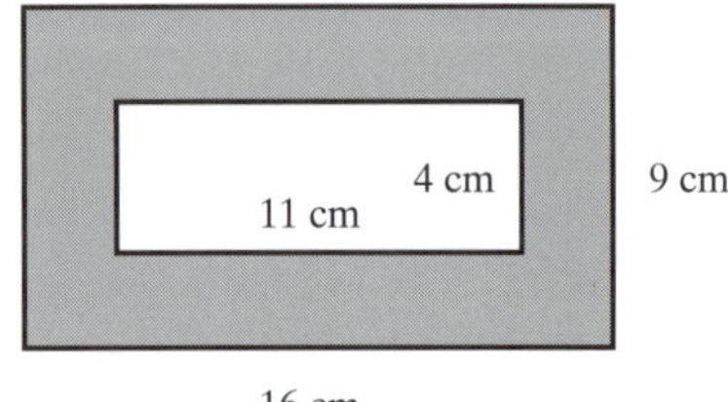

b

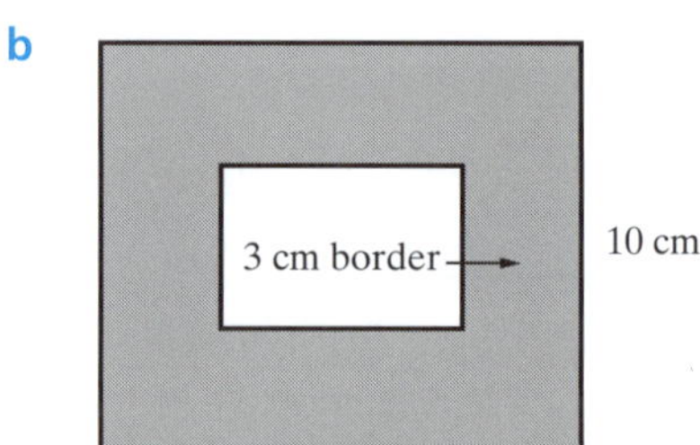

(6 marks)

9 A wall is rectangular in shape and measures 8.6 m by 3 m.

John paints the wall using 2 coats.

How much paint is needed if the paint covers 8 m^2 per litre? (3 marks)

10 A container is in the shape of a rectangular prism. It measures 20 cm by 25 cm by 10 cm.

Find the capacity of the container in litres, if 1 mL = 1 cm^3. (3 marks)

Your Feedback

$\frac{\square}{24} \times 100\% = \square\%$

PAGE 120

PAGE 177

AREA AND VOLUME

Measurement and Geometry

ADVANCED TEST

1 Find the area of a rectangle with:

- **a** length 53 cm and width 37 cm (1 mark)
- **b** length 3.7 cm and width 2.03 cm (1 mark)
- **c** length $1\frac{5}{8}$ cm and width $\frac{3}{4}$ cm (1 mark)

2 Find the area of a square with:

- **a** side 27 cm (1 mark)
- **b** side 0.15 cm (1 mark)
- **c** side $3\frac{1}{4}$ cm (1 mark)

3 Find the area of a parallelogram with:

- **a** base 23 cm and perpendicular height 18 cm (1 mark)
- **b** base 5.09 cm and perpendicular height 2.7 cm (1 mark)
- **c** base $3\frac{4}{5}$ cm and perpendicular height $2\frac{7}{10}$ cm (1 mark)

4 Find the area of a triangle with:

- **a** base of 17 cm and perpendicular height of 12 cm (2 marks)
- **b** base of 15.04 cm and perpendicular height of 11.7 cm (2 marks)
- **c** base of $3\frac{3}{5}$ cm and perpendicular height of $\frac{7}{8}$ cm (2 marks)

5 If the area of a:

- **a** rectangle is 560 cm^2, find the length if the width is 16 cm. (2 marks)
- **b** square is $33\frac{16}{25}$ cm^2, find the length of each side. (2 marks)
- **c** parallelogram is $23\frac{5}{6}$ cm^2, find the perpendicular height if the base is $6\frac{1}{2}$ cm. (2 marks)
- **d** triangle is 66.12 cm^2, find the length of the base if the perpendicular height is 5.8 cm. (2 marks)

6 A dentist's waiting room is rectangular, measuring 7 m by 6 m. The floor is to be covered with tiles costing $29.90/$m^2$. Find the cost of the tiles. (2 marks)

7 Ethan's lawn is in the shape of a parallelogram with base length of 24 metres and perpendicular height of 16 metres. Bottles of weedkiller cost $5.10 each and cover an area of 64 m^2. How many bottles are required and what will be the total cost of spraying the entire lawn? (2 marks)

8 Karensa has a pergola in the shape of a rectangle measuring 8 metres by 6 metres. She uses square tiles with side length of 40 cm to cover the floor area. If the tiles each cost $3.90, what will be the total cost of the tiles needed? (2 marks)

9 Rahul buys fencing material at a cost of $2.70/metre to fence a rectangular paddock. If he spends a total of $205.20, what is the largest area that he can fence? (3 marks)

10 A cereal box has a base measuring 24 cm by 7 cm and a height of 30 cm. The box is three-quarters filled with cereal. What is the volume of cereal inside the box? (2 marks)

11 GreenLawns supply rolls of turf 50 cm wide and 2.5 m long for $5.20 each. What will be the cost of the turf needed to cover a lawn measuring 20 m by 16 m? (2 marks)

12 A park has a rectangular garden 22 metres by 3 metres. How many kilograms of fertiliser is required to fertilise the garden at the rate of 85 grams per square metre? (2 marks)

13 A photograph is to be mounted on a rectangular sheet of cardboard leaving a 6.5 cm border around the outside. The photograph is 32 cm wide by 24 cm high. What is the area of the border? (2 marks)

14 One of the faces of a cube has an area of 1156 cm^2. As 1000 cm^3 = 1 L, find the capacity of the cube in litres. (2 marks)

15 The shape of an iceberg approximates a rectangular prism. The iceberg is 12 km long by 8 km wide. The height of the iceberg above water level is 60 m. If one-ninth of the iceberg is above water level, what is the total volume of ice in the iceberg? (2 marks)

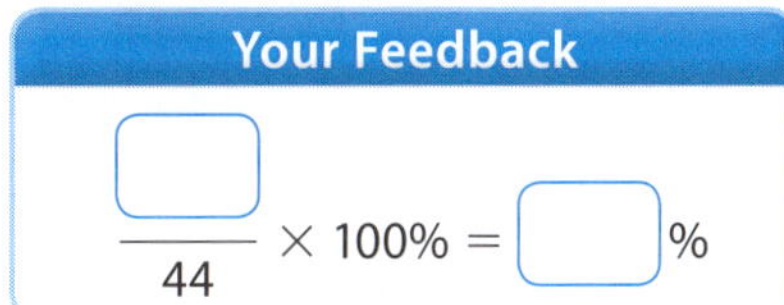

PAGE 121
PAGE 177

SHAPE AND GEOMETRIC REASONING

Measurement and Geometry

STUDY NOTES

1 **A three-dimensional shape can be viewed from different directions.**
Example: The solid below contains 13 small cubes. On separate diagrams draw a two-dimensional shape to represent the front view, the right view and the top view.

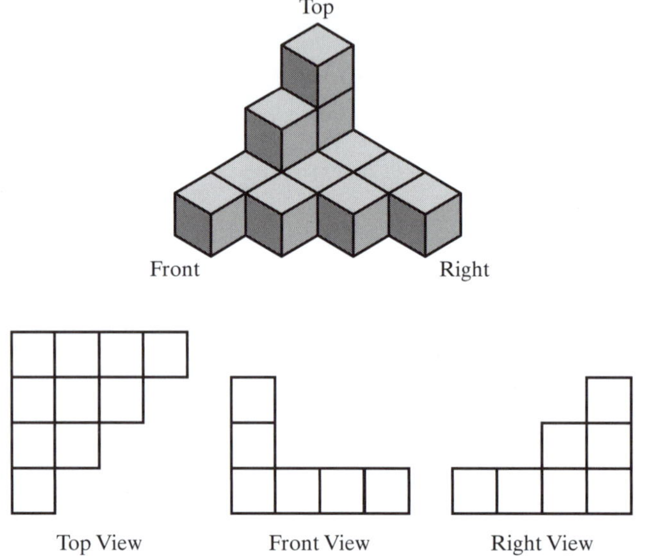

2 **The cross-section is the shape when an object is cut straight through.** In a prism the cross-section has a uniform shape.

Example: A solid is to be cut with a knife. Draw two diagrams (not to scale) to represent the cross-sections through a and b.

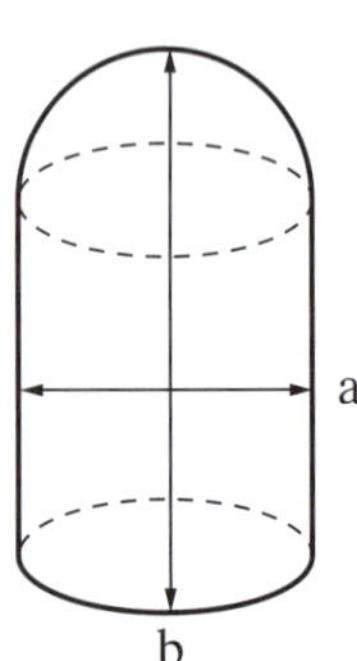

a

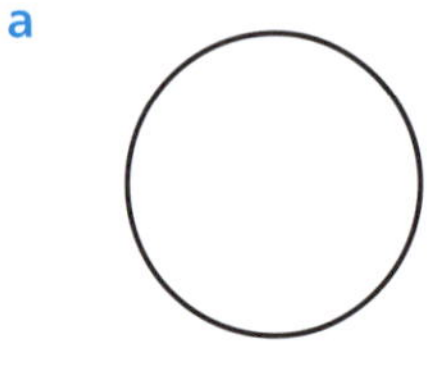

b

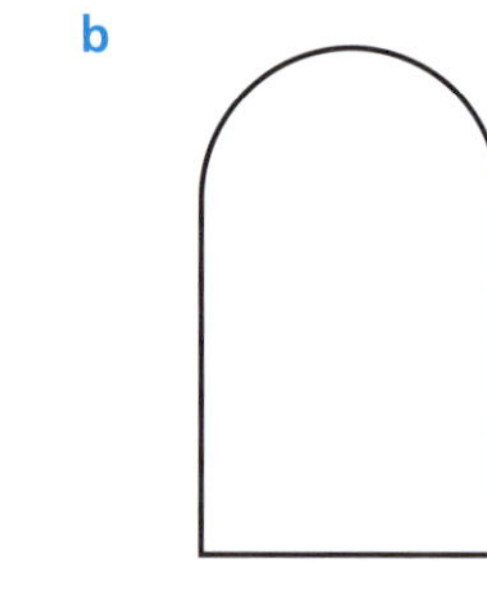

3 **A translation slides an object a certain distance in a given direction. The shape can also be reflected about an axis and can be rotated a fraction of a turn (or by degrees) in a clockwise or anti-clockwise direction.**
Example: Translate shape ABCD four units to the right, then reflect it about BC and then rotate it 90° in a clockwise direction about D.

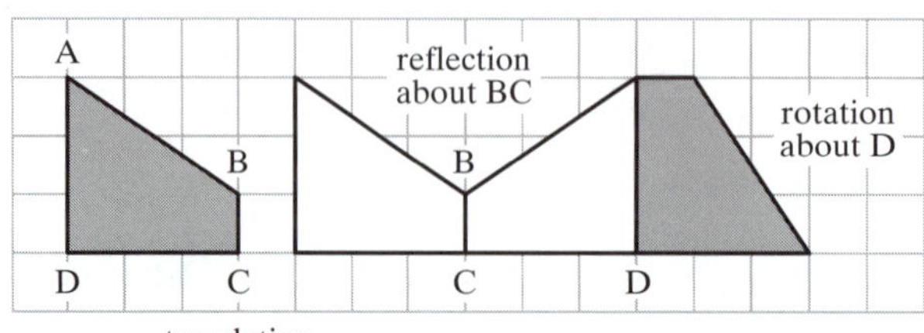

4
- **Complementary angles** add to 90°.
- **Supplementary angles** add to 180°.
- **Angles in a straight line** add to 180°.
- **Angles in a revolution** add to 360°.
- The **angle sum of a triangle** is 180°.
- The **angle sum of a quadrilateral** is 360°.
- The **rules for angles** formed between a **pair of parallel lines** and a **transversal** are:

  $\angle CDG = \angle FGH$ [**corresponding** $\angle$ s equal, $BC \parallel EF$]

  $\angle BDG = \angle DGF$ [**alternate** $\angle$ s equal, $BC \parallel EF$]

  $\angle CDG + \angle DGF = 180°$ [**co-interior** $\angle$ s supplementary, $BC \parallel EF$]

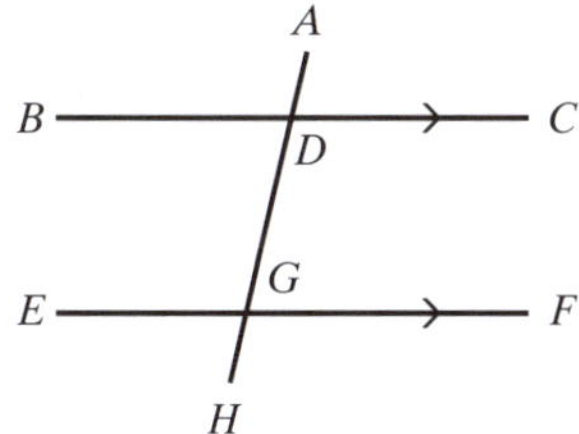

5

Special quadrilateral properties	Parallelogram	Rhombus	Rectangle	Square	Trapezium	Kite
Opposite sides equal	✓	✓	✓	✓		
Opposite sides parallel	✓	✓	✓	✓	one pair	
Adjacent sides equal		✓		✓		
Adjacent sides perpendicular			✓	✓		
Opposite angles equal	✓	✓	✓	✓		one pair
Diagonals equal in length			✓	✓		
Diagonals bisect each other	✓	✓	✓	✓		one is bisected
Diagonals cross each other at 90°		✓		✓		✓
Diagonals bisect angles of quadrilateral		✓		✓		two angles bisected

Checklist

Can you:

1 *Draw different views of solids?* ☐
2 *Describe translations, reflections and rotations?* ☐
3 *Use angle properties to solve problems involving triangles, quadrilaterals and parallel lines?* ☐
4 *Classify special quadrilaterals on the basis of their properties?* ☐

SHAPE AND GEOMETRIC REASONING

Measurement and Geometry

SKILLS CHECK

1 What is the view from the top of the solid?

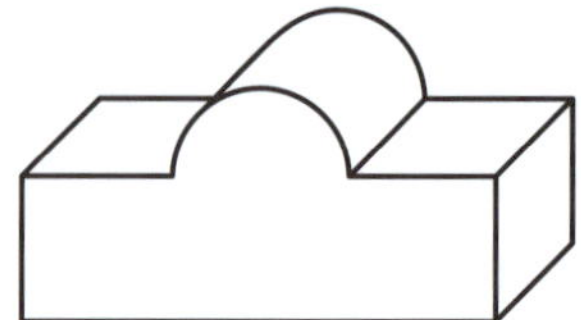

2 What is the order of rotational symmetry of:

a rectangle? b parallelogram? c kite?
d scalene triangle? e isosceles triangle? f equilateral triangle?

3 Find the complement of:

a 42° b $x°$

4 Find the value of the pronumeral, giving a reason:

a
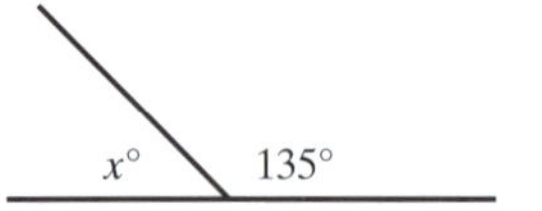

b
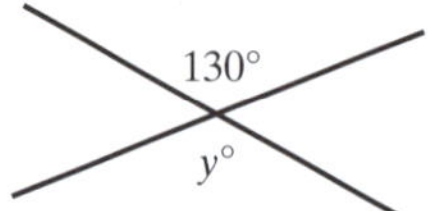

c
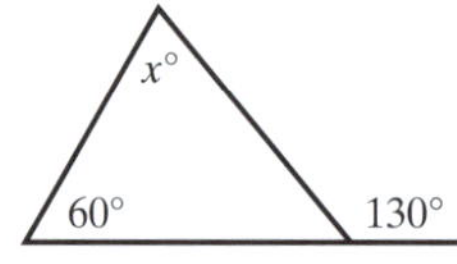

d
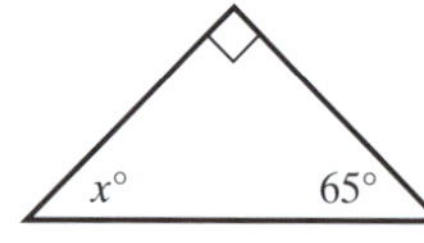

e
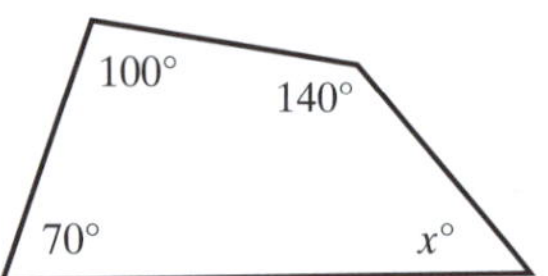

f
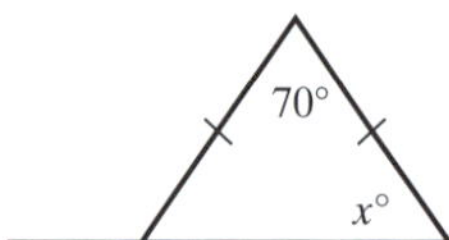

g
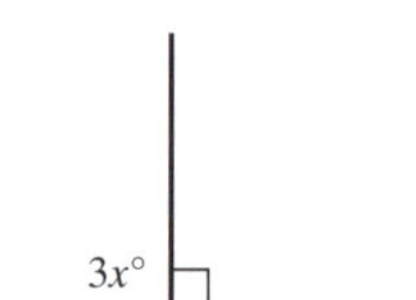

h
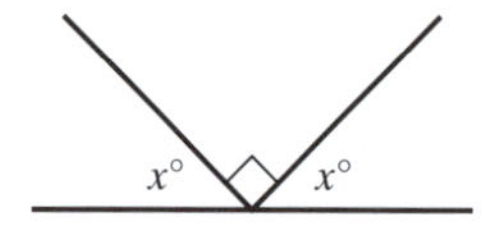

5 Find the value of the pronumerals:

a
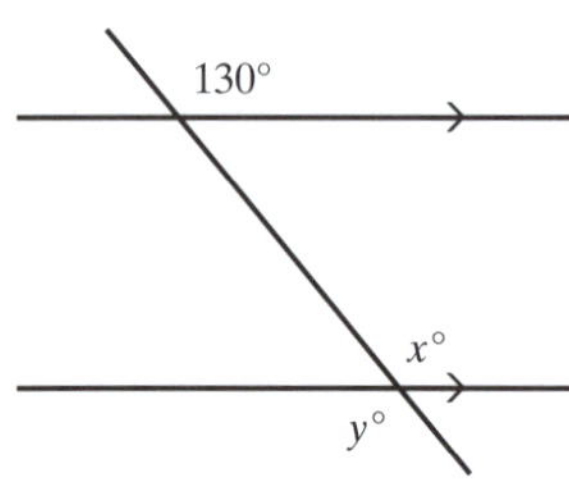

b
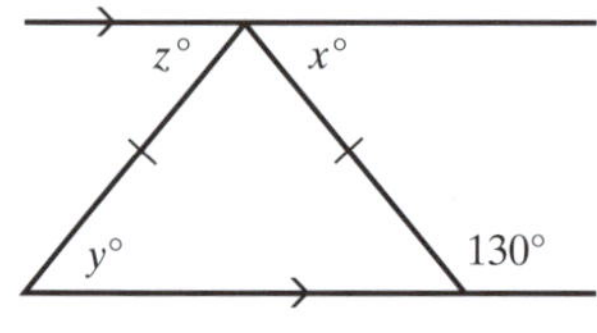

6 Determine whether the following pairs of lines are parallel:

a
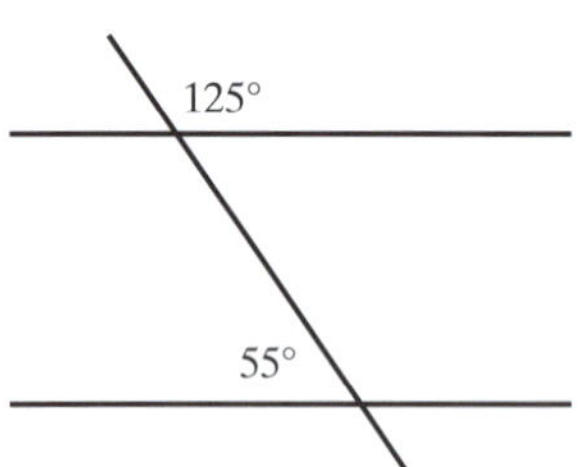

b
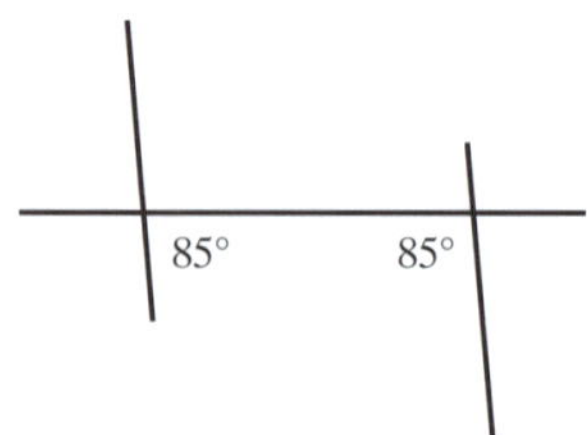

PAGE 122

Answers **1** see worked solutions **2 a** 2 **b** 2 **c** 1 **d** 1 **e** 1 **f** 3 **3 a** 48° **b** $(90 - x)°$ **4 a** 45 (straight angle) **b** 130 (vertically opposite angles) **c** 70 (exterior angle result) **d** 25 (angle sum of triangle) **e** 50 (angle sum of quadrilateral) **f** 55 (base angles of isosceles triangle) **g** 30 (straight angle) **h** 45 (straight angle) **5 a** $x = 130, y = 130$ **b** $x = 50, y = 50, z = 50$ **6 a** parallel **b** not parallel

SHAPE AND GEOMETRIC REASONING

Measurement and Geometry

INTERMEDIATE TEST

Part A Multiple Choice

1 What type of angle is the shaded angle?

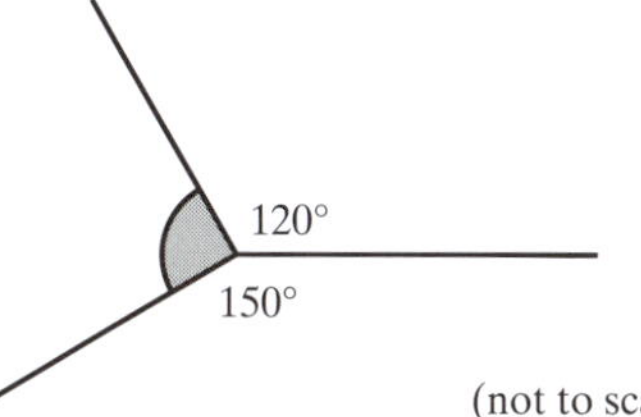

(not to scale)

- A acute
- B right
- C obtuse
- D reflex

(1 mark)

2 What is the value of x?

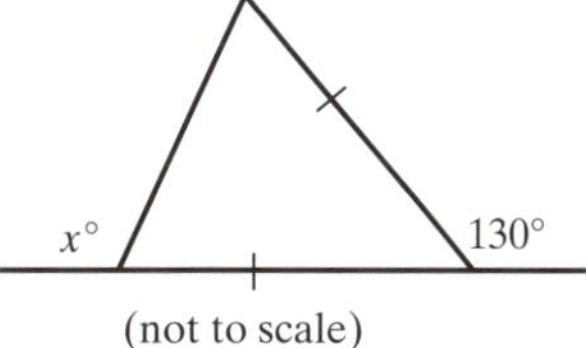

(not to scale)

- A 50
- B 130
- C 105
- D 115

(1 mark)

3 What is the value of x?

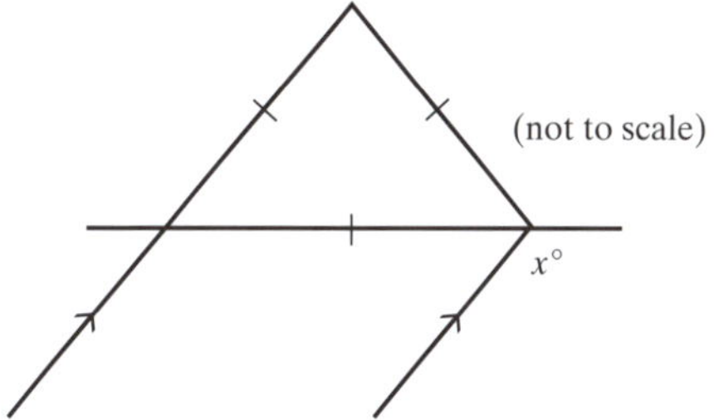

(not to scale)

- A 100°
- B 110°
- C 120°
- D 140°

(1 mark)

4 Which of the following is **not** true for a rhombus?

- A all sides equal
- B diagonals intersect at right angles
- C diagonals bisect each other
- D opposite angles complementary

(1 mark)

5 Which set of measurements **cannot** be the side lengths of a triangle?

- A 2 cm, 3 cm, 4 cm
- B 4 cm, 5 cm, 7 cm
- C 3 cm, 6 cm, 8 cm
- D 5 cm, 6 cm, 14 cm

(1 mark)

6 Which of the following is the top view of a square pyramid?

A 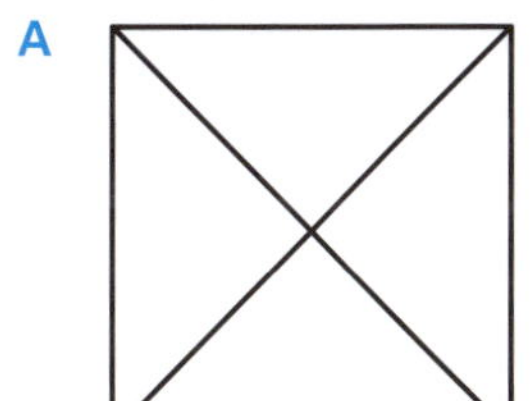

B 

C 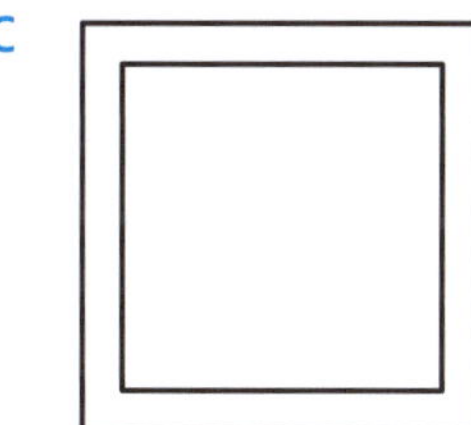

D 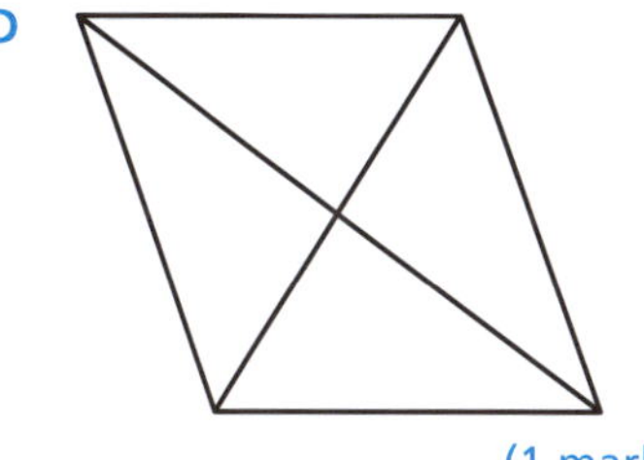

(1 mark)

(Cont.)

SHAPE AND GEOMETRIC REASONING

Measurement and Geometry (continued)

INTERMEDIATE TEST

Part B Short Answer

7 Translate the shape 3 units to the right, then rotate 90° clockwise around the image at X.

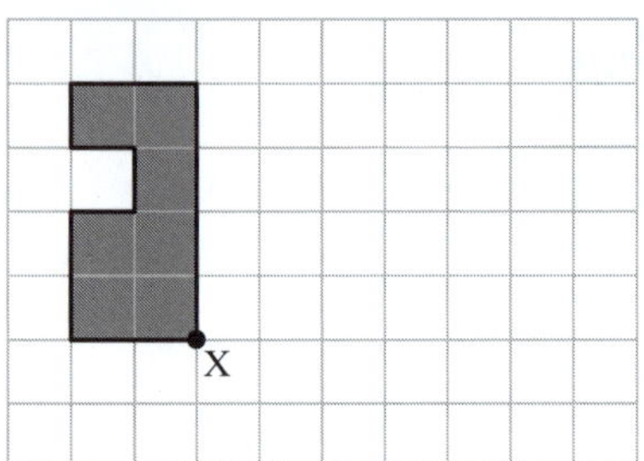

(3 marks)

8 Draw the front, right and top views of this object.

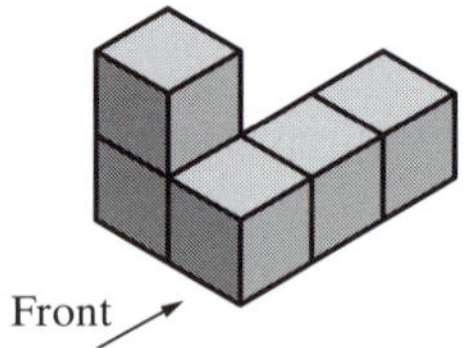

(3 marks)

9 In each of the diagrams a pair of angles is labelled with the letter P. What types of angles are these?

a

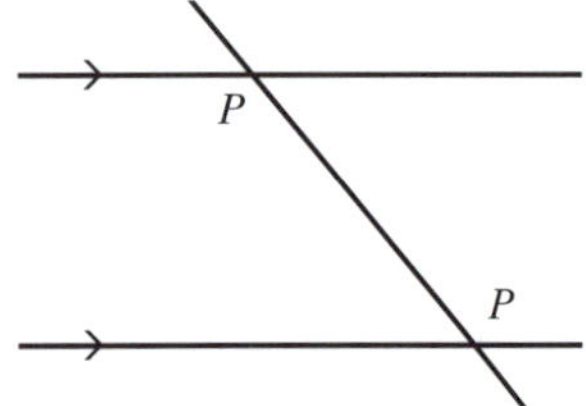

b

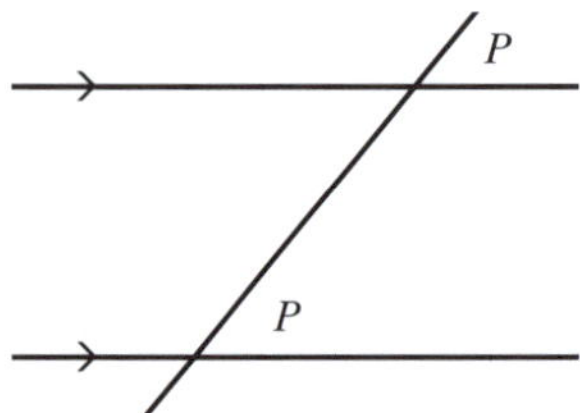

(1 mark each)

10 Find the value of the pronumerals.

a

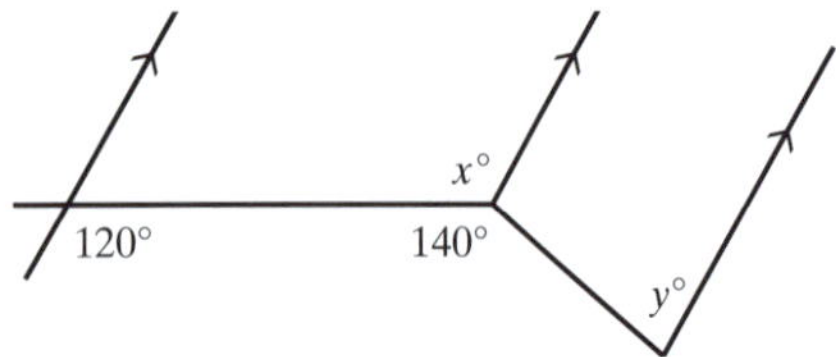

b

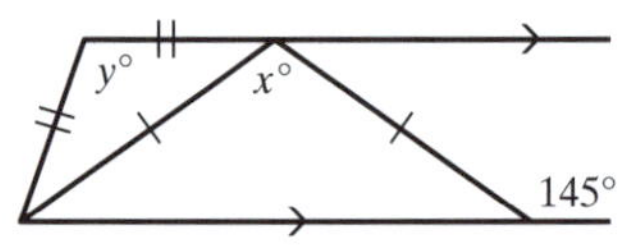

(2 marks each)

11 Find the value of the pronumeral.

a

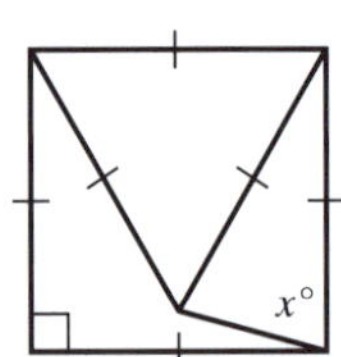

b

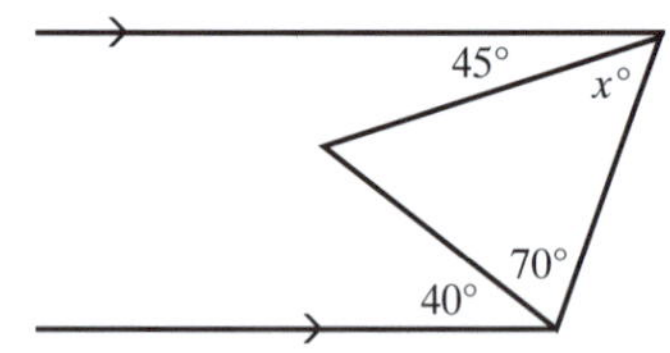

(2 marks each)

12 Find the value of the pronumerals.

a

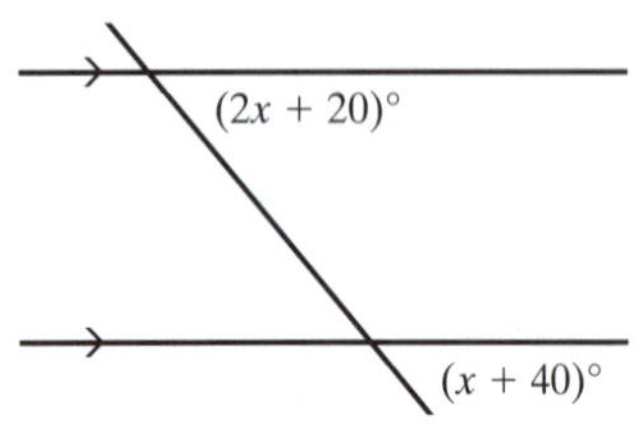

b

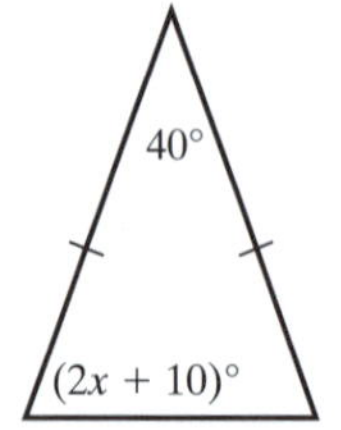

(3 marks each)

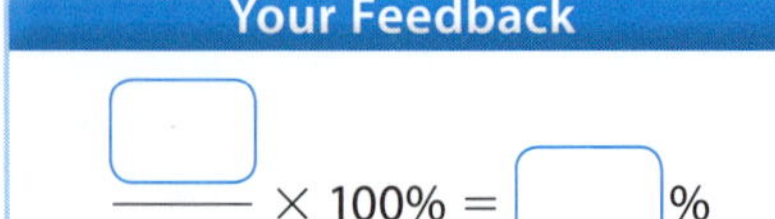

SHAPE AND GEOMETRIC REASONING

Measurement and Geometry

ADVANCED TEST

1 Draw the front, top and right views of the following: (18 marks)

a 

b 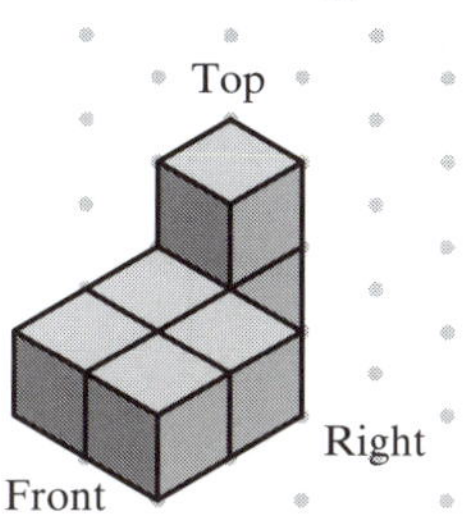

c 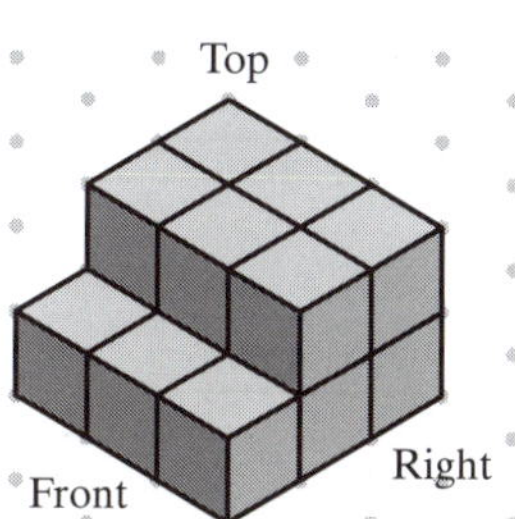

d 

e 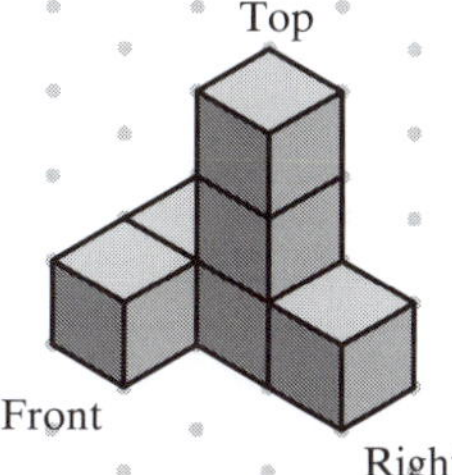

f 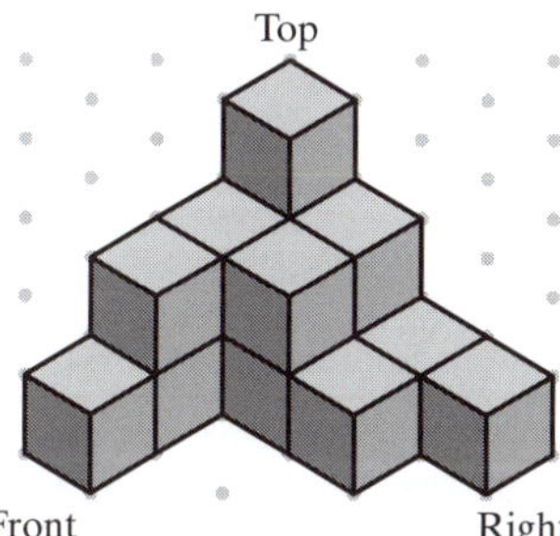

2 Find the complement of:

a $47°$ b $y°$ c $(90 - x)°$ (3 marks)

3 Find the supplement of:

a $47°$ b $y°$ c $(180 - x)°$ (3 marks)

4 Two complementary angles are $(2x - 20)°$ and $(x + 50)°$. Find the size of the two angles. (2 marks)

5 Supplementary angles are $(x + 30)°$, $(2x - 20)°$ and $(3x + 20°)$. Find the size of each angle. (2 marks)

6 Alternate angles on parallel lines are $(3x + 40)°$ and $(x + 80)°$. Find the size of the angles. (2 marks)

7 Find the value of the pronumerals: (18 marks)

a 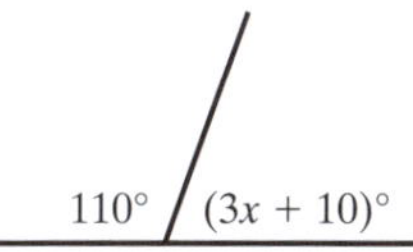

b 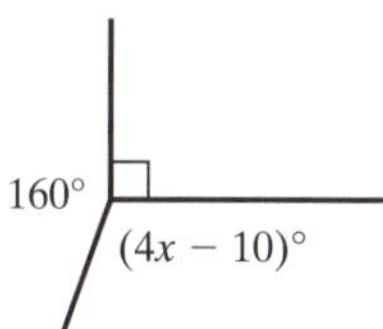

c 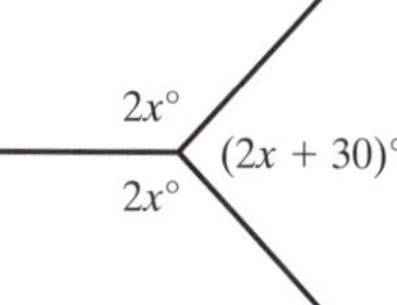

d 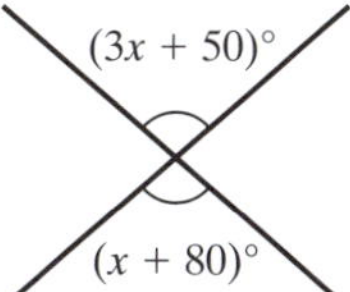

e 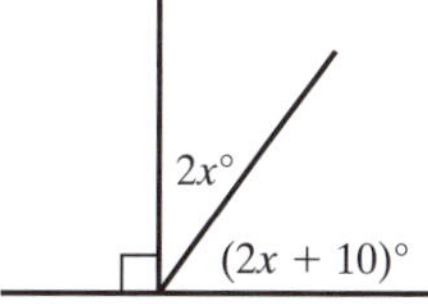

f 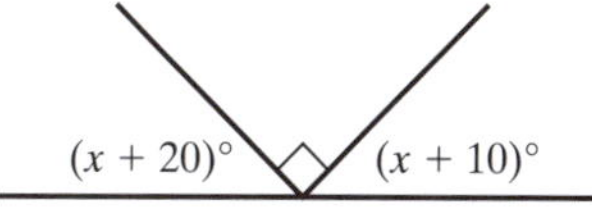

g 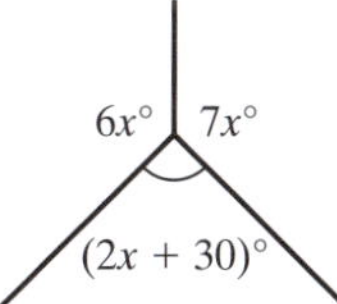

h 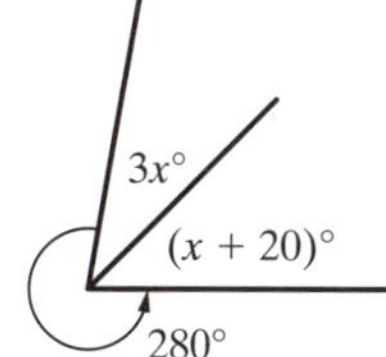

i 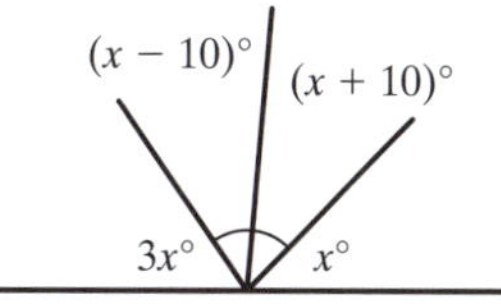

(Cont.)

8 Find the value of the pronumerals:

a
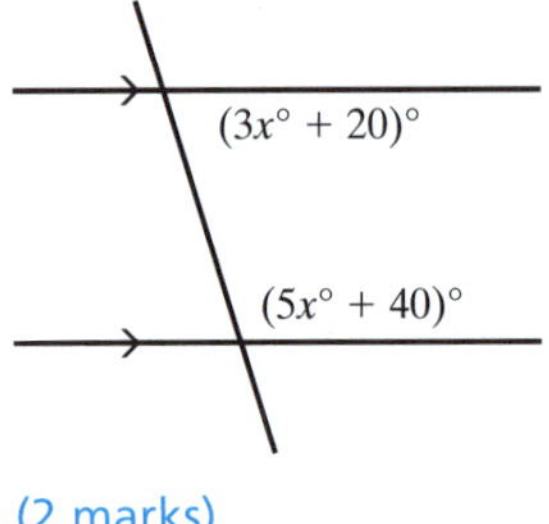

(2 marks)

b
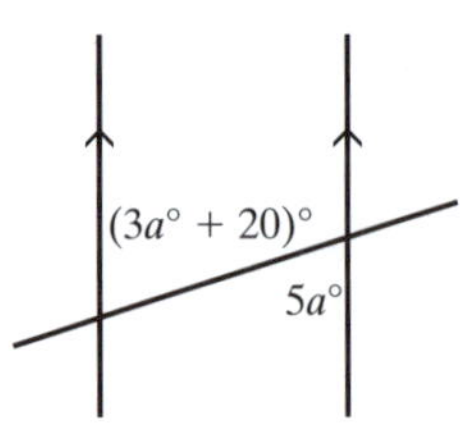

(2 marks)

c
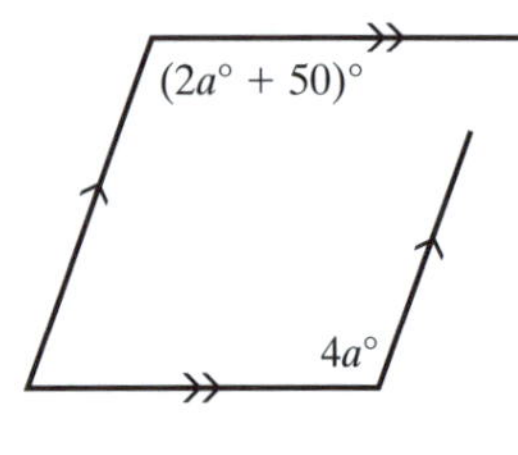

(2 marks)

9 Find the value of the pronumerals:

a
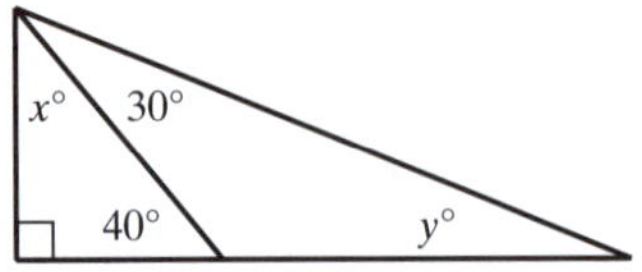

(2 marks)

b
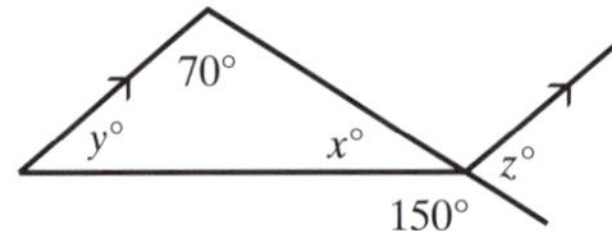

(3 marks)

c
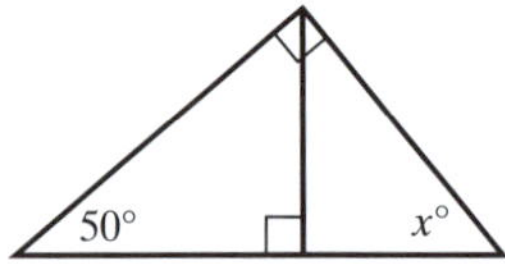

(1 mark)

d
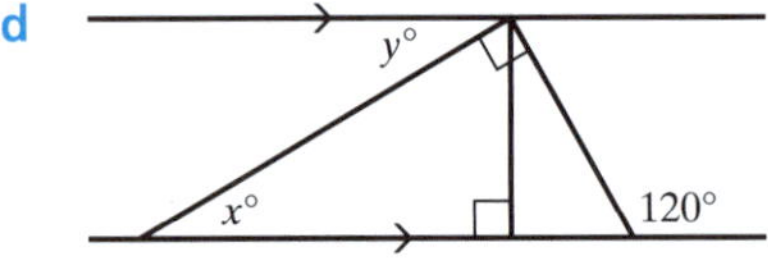

(2 marks)

e
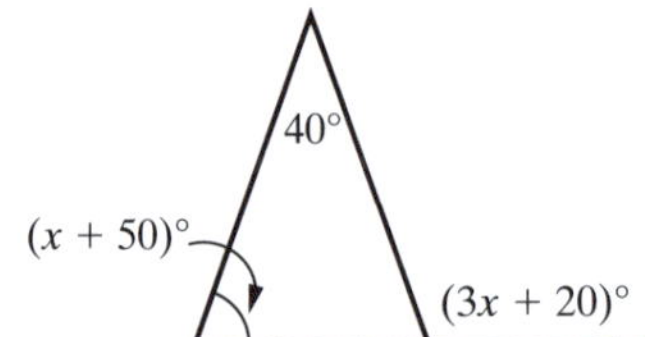

(2 marks)

f
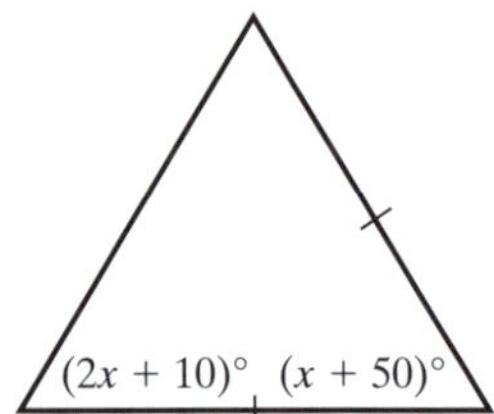

(2 marks)

10 Find the value of the pronumerals:

a
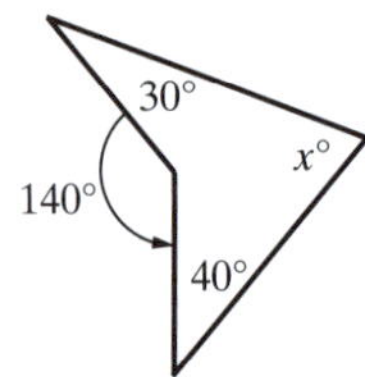

(1 mark)

b
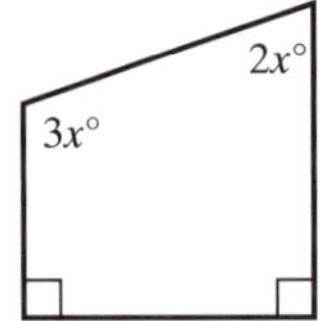

(2 marks)

c
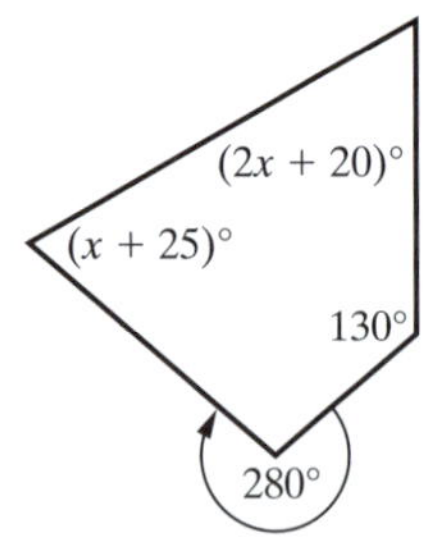

(2 marks)

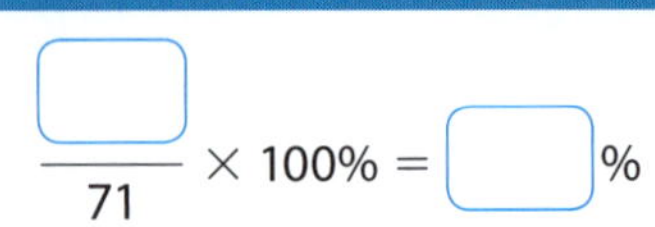

PAGE 124
PAGE 177

DATA REPRESENTATION AND CHANCE

Statistics and Probability

STUDY NOTES

1 Data can be represented in tabular form (e.g. **frequency distribution table**) or graphical form (e.g. **frequency histogram** or **frequency polygon**).

For example: use the frequency distribution table to draw a frequency histogram and polygon for the following **discrete** data.

Score	Tally	Frequency
41	𝍸	5
42	𝍸 II	7
43	𝍸 𝍸	10
44	𝍸 I	6
45	III	3

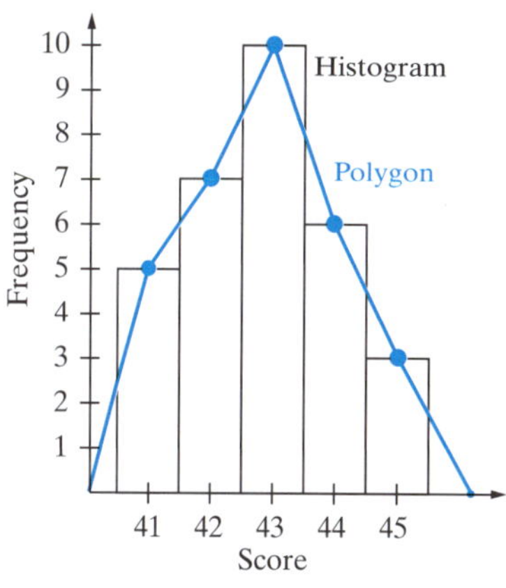

2 Another form of data representation is the **stem-and-leaf plot**.

For example: draw a stem-and-leaf plot for the heights of girls in class 8M1.

Girls (cm): 143, 148, 150, 153, 156, 151, 168, 139, 148, 151, 153, 150

- Many girls' heights are **clustered** in the low 150s.
- 168 cm is an **outlier** for the girls as it is a score which is much higher than the nearest score.

Stem	Leaf
13	9
14	3 8 8
15	0 0 1 1 3 3 6
16	8

3 We can use the following measures in statistics:

- **mean:** the average of the scores
- **median:** the middle score when arranged in order
- **mode:** the most common score
- **range:** the highest score minus the lowest score

4 **Probability** is the study of **chance**.

5 The **probability of an event** is expressed as a fraction, decimal or percentage.

6 An **event** will have a number of **outcomes**. For example, list the outcomes if a die is tossed. There are six outcomes: 1, 2, 3, 4, 5, 6.

7 A **simple event** is an event where each possible outcome is equally likely.

8 Probability ranges from **0** (impossible event) to **1** (certain event).

The **probability of an event Pr(E)** is written as: $\text{Pr(E)} = \dfrac{\text{number of favourable outcomes}}{\text{number of possible outcomes}}$

9 The **sum of all possible outcomes of an event is 1.**
For example, a coin is tossed. Write down the probability of throwing a:

a head

$\therefore \text{Pr(head)} = \dfrac{1}{2}$

b tail

$\therefore \text{Pr(tail)} = \dfrac{1}{2}$

As these are the only two possible outcomes, the sum of the probabilities is $\dfrac{1}{2} + \dfrac{1}{2} = 1$.

Checklist

Can you:

1. *Represent data in a number of forms?* ☐
2. *Define mean, median, mode and range?* ☐
3. *Recognise that the sum of probabilities is equal to 1?* ☐

DATA REPRESENTATION AND CHANCE

Statistics and Probability

SKILLS CHECK

1 For the scores 4, 7, 2, 6, 11, 5, 3, 6, 1 find:

a mean b median c mode d range

2 For the scores 12, 16, 12, 13, 20, 11 find:

a mean b median c mode d range

3 The number of mobile phones in households is recorded:

4	3	2	4	5	3
5	2	3	1	2	3
3	4	5	2	3	1
4	2	2	3	2	4

Complete the frequency table and draw a frequency histogram and polygon for the data.

Score	Tally	Frequency
1		
2		
3		
4		
5		

4 A group of swimmers represented the school at the state championships. The ages of the swimmers are recorded below:

12	17	14	15	14
15	12	13	15	12
13	16	14	13	14
14	15	16	14	16

Complete the frequency table and draw a dot plot for the data.

Score	Tally	Frequency
12		
13		
14		
15		
16		
17		

5 The number of bottles of soft drink sold from a vending machine each week is recorded below:

85	65	48	69	89
65	87	77	73	58
83	52	57	58	74
81	70	68	75	79

Complete a stem-and-leaf plot for the data.

Sales of bottles

Stem	Leaf
4	
5	
6	
7	
8	

6 A bag contains 6 red balls, 3 green balls and a blue ball. If a ball is removed from the bag what is the probability that the ball is:

a green? b blue? c red or green?

7 The numbers 1, 2, 3, … 8 are written on eight cards. The cards are shuffled and placed face down on a table. A card is chosen at random. What is the probability that the card is:

a even? b 6? c prime?

d composite? e less than 7? f greater than 8?

g a multiple of 3? h divisible by 2? i a factor of 12?

PAGE 125

Answers **1** a 5 b 5 c 6 d 10 **2** a 14 b 12.5 c 12 d 9 **3** see worked solutions **4** see worked solutions **5** see worked solutions **6** a $\frac{3}{10}$ b $\frac{1}{10}$ c $\frac{9}{10}$ **7** a $\frac{1}{2}$ b $\frac{1}{8}$ c $\frac{1}{2}$ d $\frac{3}{8}$ e $\frac{3}{4}$ f 0 g $\frac{1}{4}$ h $\frac{1}{2}$ i $\frac{5}{8}$

DATA REPRESENTATION AND CHANCE

Statistics and Probability

25 MINUTES

INTERMEDIATE TEST

Part A Multiple Choice

1 For the scores 3, 8, 4, 0, 5, the mean is:

A 4 B 15 C 5 D 3 (1 mark)

2 For the scores 4, −2, 6, 8, 12, −10, the range is:

A 6 B 12 C 22 D 6 (1 mark)

3 Which of these is **not** a mode of the scores 4, 3, 6, 8, 3, 7, 4, 8, 5?

A 5 B 4 C 8 D 3 (1 mark)

4 For the scores 6, 7, 3, 8, 8, 4, 1 Jay correctly found that 6 was the:

A mean B mode C range D median (1 mark)

5 A normal die is rolled.

What is the probability of rolling a number which is at least 4?

A $\frac{1}{4}$ B $\frac{3}{6}$ C $\frac{2}{6}$ D $\frac{6}{10}$ (1 mark)

6 From a normal deck of playing cards, a card is selected at random.

What is the probability that the card is a black 7? *Hint 1*

A $\frac{7}{52}$ B $\frac{7}{26}$ C $\frac{2}{52}$ D $\frac{2}{10}$ (1 mark)

Part B Short Answer

7

63	58	59	60	61	59	57	61	62	60
63	59	60	61	58	60	58	59	60	61

For the scores above, draw a:

a frequency table b frequency histogram and polygon (2 marks each)

8 For the scores 4, 0, 2, 7, 10, 5, 7, 4, 7, find the:

a median b mean c mode d range (4 marks)

9 For the scores below, draw a stem-and-leaf plot.

87	68	45	65	78	53	64	69	87	83
45	49	57	60	73	43	81	63	59	60

(3 marks)

10 The numbers 1 to 30 are written on thirty balls and placed in a bag. James is blindfolded and selects a ball at random from the bag. What is the probability that the ball is:

a divisible by 5? b at least 12? c a factor of 10?
d prime? e odd and divisible by 5? f even and less than 10? (6 marks)

11 Draw a stem-and-leaf plot for the heights listed below of the boys in a class.

Boys (cm): 165, 158, 167, 160, 153, 149 (2 marks)

Hint 1: 52 cards are in a normal deck.

Your Feedback

$\frac{\square}{25} \times 100\% = \square\,\%$

PAGE 126

PAGE 177

DATA REPRESENTATION AND CHANCE

Statistics and Probability

30 MINUTES

ADVANCED TEST

1 The graph shows the amount of time Beth spends on different activities at her gym.

treadmill	classes	weights	swim

a What percentage of the time does she spend swimming? (1 mark)

b If she spends 2 hours at the gym, how long does she spend:

i in a class? (1 mark)

ii using weights? (1 mark)

c If she uses the treadmill for 15 minutes, how long does she spend:

i swimming? (1 mark)

ii in a class? (1 mark)

2 A survey found the length of waiting time in a dentist's surgery.

Waiting Time at Surgery

Less than 5 min; More than 25 min; Between 5 and 15 min; Between 15 and 25 min

a Draw a divided bar graph for the data. (2 marks)

b If the survey involved 40 people, how many waited:

i less than 5 minutes? (1 mark)

ii more than 25 minutes? (1 mark)

c If 12 people waited between 15 and 25 minutes, how many waited between 5 and 15 minutes? (1 mark)

3 The table shows the age of the first child of a group of people.

Men	35, 31, 28, 19, 43, 37, 34, 29, 25
Women	18, 31, 28, 26, 25, 22, 33, 40, 35

Complete the ordered back-to-back stem-and-leaf plot. (2 marks)

Men		Women
	1	
	2	
	3	
	4	

4 The mean mass of Barry, Larry, Harry and Garry is 55 kg. If Barry's mass is 47 kg, and Harry and Larry each have a mass of 60 kg, what is Garry's mass? (2 marks)

5 A set of four different numbers has a range of 6 and a mean of 6. None of the numbers are 6. What is a possible set of numbers? (1 mark)

6 The median of four scores is 6.5. If the range is 3 and the mode is 7, find the four scores. (1 mark)

7 A score was added to the set of scores:

4 6 6 8 8 12

What is the new score, if the new:

a mode is 6? **b** mean is 7?

c median is 7? **d** range is 12?

(1 mark each)

8 The mean of five scores is 9. When one of the scores changes, the mean increases by 2. What is the change in that score? (2 marks)

9 Zhao has completed four tests and his mean mark is 70%. What mark (as a percentage) will he need to get in his next test to increase the mean to 75%? (2 marks)

10 This set of data is arranged in ascending order.

1, 3, 4, x, 8, 8

What will be the value of x, if the:

a mean is 5? (2 marks)

b median is 6? (1 mark)

11 A die has been renumbered with the number 4 replaced with the number 1. If the die is rolled, what is the probability that it is:

a a 1? **b** even?

c less than 3? (1 mark each)

12 A coloured ball is randomly chosen from a bag. The table shows the probabilities of the four colours.

	blue	green	red	yellow
probability	0.25	0.3		0.1

a What was the probability of selecting a red ball? (1 mark)

b If there were 40 balls in the bag, how many balls of each colour are there? (1 mark)

c Explain why there cannot be 10 balls in the bag. (1 mark)

d What is the smallest possible number of balls in the bag? (1 mark)

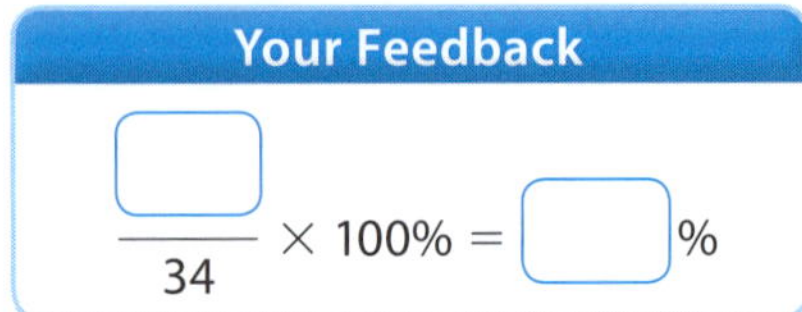

DIRECTED NUMBERS AND INDEX NOTATION

Number and Place Value

STUDY NOTES

1 **Summary of rules:**

$+ + = +$	$+ \times + = +$	$+ \div + = +$
$+ - = -$	$+ \times - = -$	$+ \div - = -$
$- + = -$	$- \times + = -$	$- \div + = -$
$- - = +$	$- \times - = +$	$- \div - = +$

For example:

a $4 + -2 = 4 - 2 = 2$ [as adding a negative is the same as subtracting]

b $-6 - (-2) = -6 + 2 = -4$ [as subtracting a negative is the same as adding]

c $-10 \times 3 = -30$ [as multiplying a negative by a positive gives a negative]

d $-12 \div -6 = 2$ [as dividing a negative by a negative gives a positive]

2 **Order of operations: BODMAS:** Brackets Orders Division and Multiplication then Addition and Subtraction.

For example: simplify

a $12 \div 2 - 4 \times 2 = 6 - 8 = -2$

b $(-25) \times 2 + (-64) \div (-8) = -50 + 8 = -42$

c $(3 - 4) \times (12 \div 6) = -1 \times 2 = -1$

d $2 \times [3 - 2 \times 4 \times (5 - 2)]$
$= 2 \times [3 - 2 \times 4 \times 3]$
$= 2 \times [3 - 24]$
$= 2 \times -21$
$= -42$

3 When a number is multiplied by itself several times it can be written in **index form.**

For example:

a Rewrite $3 \times 3 \times 3 \times 3$ in index form. $3 \times 3 \times 3 \times 3 = 3^4$

b Rewrite 5^3 in factor form. $5^3 = 5 \times 5 \times 5$

c Write the basic numeral of 10^7. $10^7 = 10 \times 10 \times 10 \times 10 \times 10 \times 10 \times 10 = 10\,000\,000$

4 Here are some **index laws**:

$\boldsymbol{a^m \times a^n = a^{m+n}}$ $\boldsymbol{a^m \div a^n = a^{m-n}}$ $\boldsymbol{(a^m)^n = a^{mn}}$ $\boldsymbol{a^0 = 1}$

For example:

a $5^3 \times 5^4 = 5^{3+4} = 5^7$

b $7^5 \div 7^3 = 7^{5-3} = 7^2$

c $(6^3)^4 = 6^{3 \times 4} = 6^{12}$

d $3^0 = 1$

Checklist

Can you:

1 *Perform operations involving directed numbers?* ☐

2 *Apply index laws to numerical expressions?* ☐

DIRECTED NUMBERS AND INDEX NOTATION

Number and Place Value

1 Simplify:

a $4 - 7$ b $-3 + 5$ c $2 - (+7)$

d $-4 - (-6)$ e $-6 - 8$ f $-2 + 5 - 3$

g $-5 + (-3)$ h $-1 - 1 - 1$ i $-5 - (-5) + 5$

2 Simplify:

a -3×-4 b 6×-7 c -12×-4

d $4 \times (-3)$ e $-1 \times -1 \times -1$ f $(-3)^2$

g $(-10)^3$ h $-5 \times -2 \times -3$ i $(-1)^{99}$

3 Evaluate:

a $-12 \div -4$ b $-16 \div -8$ c $(-81) \div 9$

d $-100 \div -5$ e $12 \div -2 \div -2$ f $(-24) \div (-3) \div (-4)$

g $\dfrac{-36}{4}$ h $\dfrac{-120}{-30}$ i $\dfrac{63}{-7}$

4 Evaluate:

a $12 - 4 \times 2$ b $16 \div (-4) + 3 \times -2$ c $(5 \times -2)^2$

d $\sqrt{-4 + 13}$ e $\dfrac{-6 \times 3}{15 \div -5}$ f $-8 \times -3 \div 12$

5 Write in index form:

a $5 \times 5 \times 5 \times 5$ b $8 \times 8 \times 8 \times 8 \times 8$ c $2 \times 2 \times 2$

d $7 \times 7 \times 4 \times 4 \times 4$ e $3 \times 3 \times 3 \times 2$ f $9 \times 9 \times 5 \times 5 \times 5 \times 5$

6 Write in factor form:

a 6^3 b $5^2 \times 3^4$ c $4^3 \times 2^5$

7 Simplify:

a $2^3 \times 2^4$ b $4^2 \times 4^4$ c $10^5 \times 10^4$

8 Simplify:

a $5^6 \div 5^2$ b $3^{11} \div 3^{10}$ c $7^4 \div 7$

9 Simplify:

a $(2^6)^2$ b $(3^4)^5$ c $(5^2)^{12}$

10 Simplify:

a 5^0 b $2^0 + 3^0$ c $(3^0 + 5^0)^0$

PAGE 128

Answers **1 a** -3 **b** 2 **c** -5 **d** 2 **e** -14 **f** 0 **g** -8 **h** -3 **i** 5 **2 a** 12 **b** -42 **c** 48 **d** -12 **e** -1 **f** 9 **g** -1000 **h** -30 **i** -1 **3 a** 3 **b** 2 **c** -9 **d** 20 **e** 3 **f** -2 **g** -9 **h** 4 **i** -9 **4 a** 4 **b** -10 **c** 100 **d** 3 **e** 6 **f** 2 **5 a** 5^4 **b** 8^5 **c** 2^3 **d** $7^2 \times 4^3$ **e** $3^3 \times 2$ **f** $9^2 \times 5^4$ **6 a** $6 \times 6 \times 6$ **b** $5 \times 5 \times 3 \times 3 \times 3 \times 3$ **c** $4 \times 4 \times 4 \times 2 \times 2 \times 2 \times 2 \times 2$ **7 a** 2^7 **b** 4^6 **c** 10^9 **8 a** 5^4 **b** 3 **c** 7^3 **9 a** 2^{12} **b** 3^{20} **c** 5^{24} **10 a** 1 **b** 2 **c** 1

DIRECTED NUMBERS AND INDEX NOTATION

Number and Place Value

25 MINUTES

INTERMEDIATE TEST

Part A Multiple Choice

1 Which of the following equals 12?

A $(-2)^2 \times (-3)^2$ B $-6 + 2 \times 3$ C $\dfrac{-48}{-6 + 2}$ D $3(12 - 5 \times 3)$ (1 mark)

2 The square of a number is equal to 16. The number could be:

A 2 B -4 C 8 D none of these (1 mark)

3 The average of three numbers is -4. If two of the numbers are 3 and -5, the third number is:

A -2 B -4 C -6 D -10 (1 mark)

4 What does $3^2 \times 2^3$ mean?

A $3 \times 2 \times 2 \times 3$ B 6×6 C 6×5 D $3 \times 3 \times 2 \times 2 \times 2$ (1 mark)

5 Sachin correctly rewrote 72 as a product of its prime factors in index form. Which is his answer? *Hint 1*

A $2^5 \times 3^5$ B 7×2 C 8×9 D $2^3 \times 3^2$ (1 mark)

6 Evaluate $3^0 \times 2^0$.

A 5 B 50 C 2 D 1 (1 mark)

Part B Short Answer

7 Simplify:

a $-3 + 4 + 3$ b $(-121) \div 11$ c $\sqrt{(-3)^2 + (-4)^2}$ (1 mark each)

8 Simplify: *Hint 2*

a $4 - 2 \times 3$ b $12 \div (6 \div 3)$ c $(-4 - 2) - 12 \times (3 - 4)$ (2 marks each)

9 Simplify, leaving the answer in index form:

a $2 \times 2^2 \times 2^3$ b $12^8 \div 12^4$ c $(3^5)^2$ (1 mark each)

10 Evaluate:

a $5^0 + 4$ b $(6 + 2)^0 - 6^0$ c $(3^4 \times 3^2 \div 3^5)^2$ (2 marks each)

11 The results of a golf tournament were as follows: Adam: -9, David: -6, Nick: -3 and Greg: $+2$. What was the average for the four golfers? *Hint 3* (2 marks)

12 Two numbers have a sum of -2 and a product of -24. What are the numbers? (2 marks)

Hint 1: Use a factor tree or start with two numbers that multiply to give 72.
Hint 2: Use order of operations rules and show working.
Hint 3: To find the average: add the scores and divide by the number of scores.

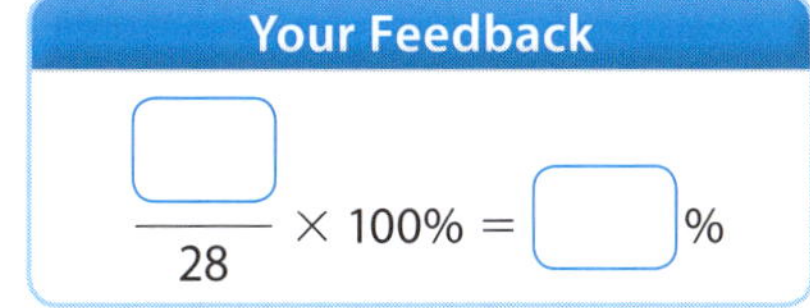

PAGE 128
PAGE 177

DIRECTED NUMBERS AND INDEX NOTATION

Number and Place Value

ADVANCED TEST

1 At 1300 hours, a submarine was at a depth of 120 metres underwater. In the next hour it descends a further 75 metres then ascends 56 metres. What is the new depth of the submarine? (1 mark)

2 The extreme temperatures of four places in the world are recorded in the table.

Place	Year	Temperature (°C)
Sydney	2013	46
Death Valley	1913	57
Charlotte Pass	1994	−23
Vostok Station	1983	−89

What is the difference in the temperatures between:

- **a** Sydney and Charlotte Pass? (1 mark)
- **b** Death Valley and Vostok Station? (1 mark)
- **c** Charlotte Pass and Vostok Station? (1 mark)

3 Without the use of calculators, evaluate:

- **a** $30 - [15 \div (3 - 6)]$ (2 marks)
- **b** $-5(2 - 8 \times 3)$ (2 marks)
- **c** $-18 \div (3 + 6) - (2 - 3)^3$ (2 marks)
- **d** $\sqrt{18 - 7 \times 2} \times \sqrt{5 \times 8 + 6 \times 4}$ (2 marks)
- **e** $\dfrac{-4 - 12}{2 - 6}$ (2 marks)
- **f** $\dfrac{5 - 20}{5} - \dfrac{20 - 5}{-5}$ (2 marks)
- **g** $\dfrac{(4 - 10)^2}{(3 - 6)^2}$ (2 marks)
- **h** $\dfrac{15 - 30 \div 6}{(6 + 24) \div (-6)}$ (2 marks)
- **i** $\dfrac{12 - 4 \times 8}{(12 - 4) \div 8}$ (2 marks)
- **j** $\dfrac{(-20) \div (5 \times 2) + 3 \times (6 - 2)}{(-20) \div 5 \times 2 + 3 \times 6 - 2}$ (2 marks)

4 For every increase of one kilometre of height, the temperature decreases at a rate of 6.5 °C.

- **a** If the temperature at ground level is 12 °C, what is the temperature at a height of:
  - **i** 2 kilometres? (1 mark)
  - **ii** 7 kilometres? (1 mark)
  - **iii** 9.5 kilometres? (1 mark)
- **b** If the temperature at a height of 6 kilometres is −24 °C, what is the temperature at a height of:
  - **i** 4 kilometres? (1 mark)
  - **ii** 10 kilometres? (1 mark)
  - **iii** ground level? (1 mark)

5 Evaluate, leaving in index form:

- **a** $(3^5 \div 3^3) \times (3^4 \div 3^3)$
- **b** $5^4 \times 5^2 \div 5^7$
- **c** $(2^{0.5})^4$
- **d** $(7^4)^{\frac{1}{2}}$
- **e** $\dfrac{5^5 \div 5}{5^0}$
- **f** $\dfrac{3^3 \times 3^4}{3^5}$
- **g** $\dfrac{2^8 \div 2^5}{2^7 \div 2^2}$

(1 mark each)

6 Evaluate, leaving in index form:

- **a** $9^2 \div 3^2$
- **b** $2^2 \times 4^3$
- **c** $\dfrac{(4^3)^4}{2^{10}}$

(1 mark each)

7 Caleb plots the points $A(-3, -4)$, $B(-1, 3)$, $C(4, 3)$ and the point D. When he joins the points a parallelogram $ABCD$ is formed.

- **a** What are the co-ordinates of D? (1 mark)
- **b** Find the area of $ABCD$. (1 mark)

8 The table shows the temperature (T) after t hours in a freezer.

t	0	1	2	3	4
T	3	1	−1		

- **a** Complete the table. (1 mark)
- **b** Write the rule linking t and T. (1 mark)
- **c** What was the initial temperature? (1 mark)
- **d** What will be the temperature after 6 hours? (1 mark)
- **e** How long will it take for the temperature to drop to −13°? (2 marks)

9 If $a = -3$, $b = -4$ and $c = -5$, find:

- **a** $ab^2 - c$
- **b** $2a - 9b + 4c$
- **c** $(ac + 7c)^2$
- **d** $2b^2 - 4a^2$
- **e** $c(3 - ab)$
- **f** $\dfrac{cb + 2a + 2}{b + 8}$
- **g** $\sqrt{\dfrac{-b^3}{(2a - b)^2}}$

(2 marks each)

Your Feedback

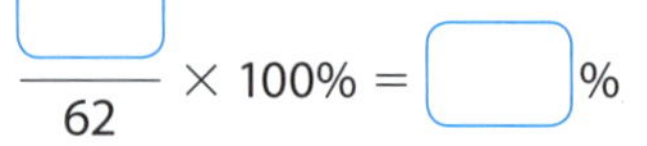

$\dfrac{\square}{62} \times 100\% = \square\%$

PAGE 129

PAGE 177

FINANCIAL MATHEMATICS

Real Numbers

STUDY NOTES

1 **Increasing or decreasing by a percentage.** When increasing a quantity by $R\%$ we multiply by $(100 + R)\%$. When decreasing a quantity by $R\%$ we multiply by $(100 - R)\%$.

For example:

a Increase \$80 by 16%.

$$\text{Amount} = 1.16 \times 80$$
$$= 92.8$$

$\therefore$ new amount is \$92.80

b Decrease \$250 by 15%.

$$\text{Amount} = 0.85 \times 250$$
$$= 212.5$$

$\therefore$ new amount is \$212.50

2 **Profit and loss.** For example, a stamp is purchased by a collector for \$16 and then sold for \$20. Express the profit as a percentage of the cost price.

$$\therefore \text{Profit} = \$20 - \$16$$
$$= \$4$$

$$\therefore \%\ \text{profit} = \frac{4}{16} \times 100\%$$
$$= 25\%$$

$\therefore$ percentage profit is 25%

3 **Discount.** For example, a video game originally marked at \$80 now sells for \$65. Find the percentage discount.

$$\therefore \text{Discount} = \$80 - \$65$$
$$= \$15$$

$$\therefore \%\ \text{discount} = \frac{15}{80} \times 100\%$$
$$= 18.75\%$$

$\therefore$ discount is 18.75%

4 If there is **more than one discount** we cannot simply add the discounts together—we have to treat them separately. For example, a television was discounted by 20% at a sale and Jack received a further 10% when he paid cash. If the original price was \$680, what amount was paid?

$$\text{Original price} = 680$$

$$\text{1st discounted price} = 0.8 \times 680$$
$$= 544$$

$$\text{2nd discounted price} = 0.9 \times 544$$
$$= 489.6$$

$\therefore$ amount paid was \$489.60

5 **GST (Goods and services tax).** This is a tax placed on many goods sold in Australia (except food) and services. This tax is currently set at 10%. To find the amount of GST charged by the government, we divide by 11.

For example:

a A drill costs \$85 plus GST. What is the amount of GST to be paid?

$$\text{Amount of GST} = 10\% \text{ of } 85$$
$$= 0.1 \times 85$$
$$= 8.5 \quad \therefore \text{GST of } \$8.50$$

b Heidi pays \$63.80 for a massage. What amount of GST has she been charged?

$$\text{Amount of GST} = 63.8 \div 11$$
$$= 5.8 \quad \therefore \text{GST of } \$5.80$$

6 **Unitary method.** Have a look at this example. Steve receives a pay rise of 4% which takes his salary to \$81 120. What was his original pay?

As original pay = 100%, then new pay is 104% of the original pay.

104% of pay is \$81 120

1% of pay is $\frac{81\,120}{104}$ so 100%

(original) pay is $\frac{81\,120}{104} \times 100 = 78\,000$

$\therefore$ Steve was originally paid \$78 000.

Checklist

Can you:

1 *Increase or decrease a quantity by a percentage?* ☐

2 *Use percentages to find profit or loss, discounts and GST?* ☐

2 *Apply the unitary method to problems involving percentages?* ☐

FINANCIAL MATHEMATICS

Real Numbers

SKILLS CHECK

1 Increase:

a 70 by 20% b $320 by 8% c $9400 by $7\frac{1}{2}$%

2 Decrease:

a $390 by 12% b $4.2 million by 9% c $4000 by $12\frac{1}{4}$%

3 Find the selling price of goods bought for:

a $420 and sold for a profit of 25%

b $6500 and sold for a profit of 40%

c $12 000 and sold for a loss of 22%

d $350 and sold for a loss of 15.5%

4 Willie bought his house four years ago for $360 000 and sold it this year for $576 000. Find the profit as a percentage of its cost price.

5 An electrical store had a '15% discount for cash' sale.

a How much is saved when buying a television for cash, originally marked at $320?

b If she paid cash, what would Sally pay for a dryer priced at $470?

6 A can of paint is priced at $62. If Pete buys five cans during a 10% off sale and then receives a further 5% trade discount, how much will he pay for the paint?

7 The GST in Australia is 10%. A mechanic charges $175 plus GST for a job. How much GST is to be paid?

8 Halley purchases a camera for $198. How much GST is paid?

9 Michael employs an electrician to install some power points in his unit. The electrician charges $320 plus GST. What will be the total cost of the power points?

10 Fletcher bought a litre of motor oil which cost him $4.95. What was the cost of the oil before the GST was included?

11 If 55% of an amount is $12 100, find:

a 1% of the amount

b the whole amount

12 a If 30% of an amount is 690 kg, what is the whole amount?

b Sarah is on an European holiday and has $2700 remaining in her account. This is 45% of the total she started her trip with. How much has she spent?

c A sale offers 25% off all paperbacks. If Robyn pays $36 for a novel, find the original price of the book.

13 A jeweller has a mark-up price of 40% on all her products. What was the cost price of a bracelet if she sells it for $560?

PAGE 131

Answers 1 a $84 b $345.60 c $10 105 2 a $343.20 b $3 822 000 c $3510 3 a $525 b $9100 c $9360 d $295.75 4 60% 5 a $48 b $399.50 6 $265.05 7 $17.50 8 $18 9 $352 10 $4.50 11 a $220 b $22 000 12 a $2300 b $3300 c $48 13 $400

FINANCIAL MATHEMATICS

Real Numbers

INTERMEDIATE TEST

Part A Multiple Choice

1 When a \$780 television is discounted by $12\frac{1}{2}\%$ the new price is:
A \$95.55 B \$682.50 C \$767.50 D \$712.25 (1 mark)

2 A diamond ring valued at \$1470 increases in price by 8% each year. The value of the ring after one year is:
A \$117.60 B \$1176 C \$2646 D \$1587.60 (1 mark)

3 An item is sold for \$22.00 including 10% GST. What is the cost before the GST is added?
A \$18 B \$19.80 C \$20 D \$24.20 (1 mark)

4 A dress valued at \$80 is discounted by \$4. The percentage discount was:
A 4% B 5% C 20% D 76% (1 mark)

5 Increase \$400 by 10% and then decrease this amount by 10%. The new amount is: *Hint 1*
A \$400 B \$395 C \$405 D \$396 (1 mark)

6 Jay has saved 70% of the cost of a car. If he has saved \$16 800, what is the price of the car?
A \$11 760 B \$22 300 C \$24 000 D \$28 560 (1 mark)

Part B Short Answer

7 Harry buys a house for \$315 000 and sells it at a profit of 22%.
a What was his selling price? b How much profit did Harry make? (2 marks)

8 A shop holds a 15% discount sale on all televisions. If Jack's television was discounted by \$102, what was the original price? (2 marks)

9 The table lists a variety of items bought and sold by a second-hand goods business.

a Find the loss as a percentage of the cost price of the lounge. (2 marks)
b The table is sold at a loss of 5%. Find its sale price. (2 marks)
c If the television was sold for a profit of 15% find its cost price. (2 marks)

Product	Cost price	Selling price	Profit	Loss
Lounge	\$1200			\$360
Table	\$360			5%
Television		\$230	15%	

10 Chen purchases a wheelbarrow with a price of \$120. He is given a discount of 20% and then receives a further 10% discount for being a loyal customer. What is:
a the price he pays for the wheelbarrow? (2 marks)
b the overall discount percentage he receives? (2 marks)

11 Kim sold a Blu-ray recorder for \$150. This was 60% less than she originally paid for it. What did Kim originally pay for the player? (2 marks)

12 The existing GST rate of 10% is increased by 5%
a What is the new price of a dress currently priced at \$72? (2 marks)
b Find the existing price of a pair of shoes, if it is to be sold at \$84. (2 marks)

Hint 1: Increasing then decreasing by 10% means multiplying by 110% then multiplying by 90%.

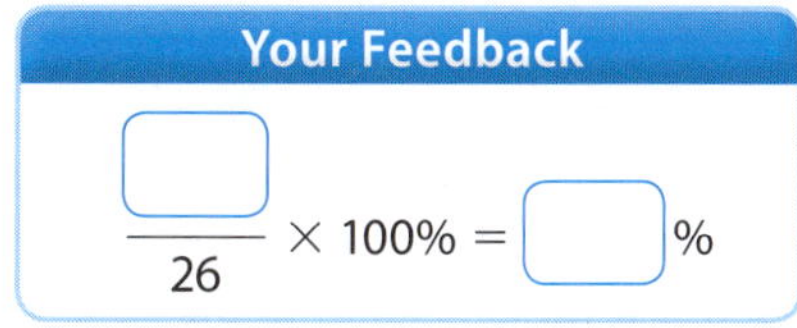

PAGE 131
PAGE 177

ADVANCED TEST

1 a Increase \$5000 by 20% and then decrease the result by 15%. What is the new amount? (1 mark)

b Decrease \$5000 by 15% and then increase the result by 20%. What is the new amount? (1 mark)

2 The normal price for a tray of mangoes is \$18. On Friday the price was reduced by 25%, but then on Saturday it was increased back to its original price. What was the percentage increase? (2 marks)

3 The price of a pair of shoes drops by 35% to \$71.50. What was the original price? (2 marks)

4 The difference between a discount of 25% and 40% on a pair of headphones is \$24. What was the original price? (2 marks)

5 The 'DailyDiscount' app is offering a 6 week fitness program at a 60% discount. If the new price is \$48,

a what was the original price? (2 marks)

b how much is the savings? (1 mark)

6 Ethan and Asha have a meal at a cafe. They use a voucher which offers '2nd meal half price'. The discount applies to their cheaper meal. If their meals cost \$22 and \$18, what percentage of the total cost has been saved? (2 marks)

7 Complete the table: (10 marks)

Cost P	Selling P	Profit % of Cost	Profit % of Selling
\$36	\$45		
\$20		15%	
	\$90		50%
\$150		20%	
	\$80		25%

8 The table shows the prices of items with 0% GST, a 10% GST and a 15% GST. Complete the table: (6 marks)

Item	0%	10%	15%
A	\$32		
B		\$77	
C			\$27.60

9 When Liam sold his bike for \$630, he made a loss of 30% on the amount he had paid when he purchased it. At what price did he buy the bike? (2 marks)

10 An antique dealer recorded his purchases, his markup (or profit) and selling prices in the following table. Complete the table: (3 marks)

Object	Cost P	Markup	Selling P
table	\$120	160%	
vase	\$290		\$478.50
lamp		120%	\$83.60

11 The recommended retail price of a novel is \$28. Shop A has a '35% discount on all books', while Shop B has a '\$10 off normal prices' sale. Which shop is selling the book for the lowest price and by how much? (2 marks)

12 On Monday a hardware store discounts its wheelbarrows by 20%, and then on Wednesday takes a further 10% off. What is the total percentage discount off the original price? (2 marks)

13 A house increases in value each year by 2.5%. If it was valued at \$820 000 in 2013,

a what is the value in 2015? (1 mark)

b what was the value in 2012? (1 mark)

14 Bella and Travis live together overseas and they pay income tax at the following rate:

- 15% on the first \$20 000 earned
- 22% on the remainder earned.

How much tax will be paid by:

a Bella who earns \$17 500? (1 mark)

b Travis who earns \$45 750? (2 marks)

15 The Medicare levy is increased from 1.5% to 1.75% of taxable income. This means that Conrad will pay an extra \$156. What is Conrad's taxable income? (2 marks)

16 A jewellery store is having a discount on a certain line of watches. On Day 1 they are having a 1% discount. On Day 2, a 2% discount on the previous day's price. If the original price was \$200, on what day will the price be first under \$100? (3 marks)

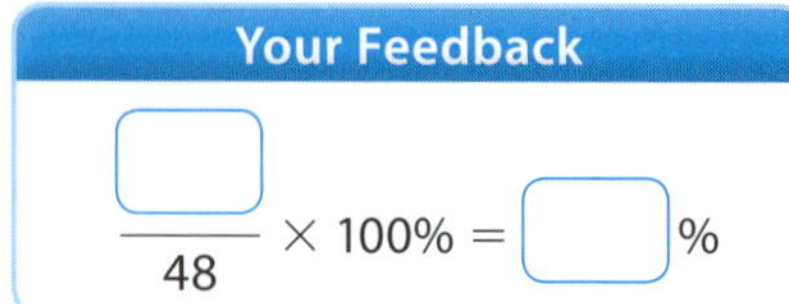

RATIO AND RATES

Real Numbers

STUDY NOTES

1 **Ratio** is a comparison between quantities of the same units. The ratio of 'a to b' is written as $\boldsymbol{a : b}$, but can also be written as a fraction, i.e. $\frac{a}{b}$.

2 A **proportion** is a statement that two ratios are equal. For example, find the value of x if $x : 3 = 20 : 12$.

If we match 3 and 12, then we have multiplied 3 by 4 to get 12. This means that the missing number is multiplied by 4 to give 20. The missing number is 5.
$\therefore x = 5$

3 **Ratios** can be **simplified** in a similar manner to fractions. For example, simplify:

a $12 : 16 : 20$

As each has a highest common factor of 4, we divide through by 4:

$12 : 16 : 20 = 3 : 4 : 5$

b \$3.50 : \$5

Change both to cents, ignore common units and then divide by 50:

\$3.50 : \$5 = 350c : 500c = 7 : 10

c $1\frac{1}{2} : \frac{3}{4}$

Rewrite with the same denominator, ignore the denominators and simplify:

$1\frac{1}{2} : \frac{3}{4} = \frac{3}{2} : \frac{3}{4} = \frac{6}{4} : \frac{3}{4} = 6 : 3 = 2 : 1$

d $4000 \text{ cm}^2 : 2 \text{ m}^2$

Using $10\,000 \text{ cm}^2 = 1 \text{ m}^2$, rewrite each in the same units and simplify:
$4000 : 20\,000 = 1 : 5$

4 The **unitary method** can be used to solve some ratio problems. For example, the ratio of cordial to water in a drink is 2 : 5. If 160 mL of cordial is poured into a container, how much water should be added?

['Cordial' and '2' are mentioned first.]

2 parts = 160
1 part = 80
5 parts = $5 \times 80 = 400$
$\therefore$ 400 mL of water is required.

5 Quantities can be **divided in a given ratio.** For example, share \$700 in the ratio of 3 : 5.

As $3 + 5 = 8$, there are 8 parts in total.

$\frac{3}{8} \times 700 = 262.5$ and $\frac{5}{8} \times 700 = 437.5$

$\therefore$ \$262.50 and \$437.50

6 A **rate** is a comparison of quantities of different units. A commonly used rate is speed (s) which relates distance (d) and time (t):

$s = \frac{d}{t} \quad d = s \times t \quad t = \frac{d}{s}$

For example, Grace left home at 7:00 am and travelled 240 kilometres, arriving at her destination at 9:40 am. Find her average speed.

Time taken = 2 h 40 min = $2\frac{2}{3}$ h,

distance travelled = 240 km

Average speed $= 240 \div 2\frac{2}{3}$
$= 90$

$\therefore$ 90 km/h

7 The **scale** on a map is often written as a ratio. For example, rewrite 5 cm = 20 km as a ratio.

5 cm : 20 km = 5 : 2 000 000
= 1 : 400 000

Checklist

Can you:

1 *Simplify ratios?* ☐
2 *Apply the unitary method to problems involving ratio and rates?* ☐
3 *Divide a quantity in a given ratio?* ☐
4 *Calculate speed given distance and time?* ☐
5 *Calculate rates for given information?* ☐

RATIO AND RATES

Real Numbers

SKILLS CHECK

1 Simplify:

a $12:16$ b $4:40:400$ c $\$2:\$12$

d $\frac{2}{3}:\frac{3}{5}$ e $\frac{3}{4}:1$ f $1\frac{1}{2}:2\frac{1}{4}$

2 Simplify:

a $0.6:1$ b $0.3:0.25$ c 20 seconds : 3 minutes

d 4.5 L : 200 mL e $3x^2:15x$ f 350 g : 2 kg : 0.6 t

3 A piece of timber is cut in the ratio of $4:5:6$. If the largest piece is 180 cm, how long is:

a the smallest piece? b the original piece of timber?

4 In the town of Blue Ridge, the ratio of adults to children is $4:3$. If the population of the town is 3829, how many children live in Blue Ridge?

5 A scale model of a ship is built. A scale of 1 cm = 10 metres is used and the ship is 275 metres long.

a Write the scale as a simplified ratio. b How long is the model?

6 Angles of a scalene triangle are in the ratio of $3:2:4$. Find the size of the largest angle.

7 Find the value of x in the following proportions:

a $x:5 = 18:15$ b $\frac{1}{2}:4 = x:16$ c $\frac{x}{3} = \frac{8}{12}$

8 Complete the table:

Distance	Speed	Time
200 km	25 km/h	
	150 km/h	4 h
150 m	20 m/min	
396 km		5 h 30 min
	64 km/h	3 h 45 min
352 km	66 km/h	

9 If light travels at 300 000 km/s, how far will it travel in one minute?

10 Sandy left home at 7:20 am and arrived at her destination at 10:40 am, averaging 90 km/h for the trip. How far did Sandy travel?

11 A petrol tanker discharges 600 litres per minute. If the service station requires 4800 L:

a how long will it take the tanker to discharge the quantity?

b find the cost of the petrol if it costs \$1350 per kL.

12 A pipe is leaking at the rate of 8 mL every four seconds. How much water is wasted in one day?

PAGE 133

Answers **1 a** 3 : 4 **b** 1 : 10 : 100 **c** 1 : 6 **d** 10 : 9 **e** 3 : 4 **f** 2 : 3 **2 a** 3 : 5 **b** 6 : 5 **c** 1 : 9 **d** 45 : 2 **e** x : 5 **f** 7 : 40 : 12 000 **3 a** 120 cm **b** 450 cm **4** 1641 **5 a** 1 : 1000 **b** 27.5 cm **6** 80° **7 a** 6 **b** 2 **c** 2 **8** 8 h, 600 km, 7 min 30 s, 72 km/h, 240 km, 5 h 20 min **9** 18 000 000 km **10** 300 km **11 a** 8 min **b** \$6480 **12** 172.8 L

RATIO AND RATES

Real Numbers

INTERMEDIATE TEST

Part A Multiple Choice

1 Simplify $3 : \frac{2}{3}$ *Hint 1*

A 3 : 2 B 3 : 1 C 9 : 2 D 6 : 1 (1 mark)

2 The ratio of 4 km to 200 metres is:

A 1 : 50 B 50 : 1 C 20 : 1 D 2 : 1 (1 mark)

3 The ratio of male passengers to female passengers on a bus is 4 : 7. This means that the bus could be carrying:

A 18 males B 2 males C 35 females D 28 passengers (1 mark)

4 The angles of a triangle are in the ratio of 2 : 3 : 4. One of the angles could be: *Hint 2*

A 20° B 80° C 90° D 100° (1 mark)

5 A cyclist leaves Gresford at 7:40 am and averages 24 km/h, arriving at Elderslie at 9:20 later that morning. How far is it from Gresford to Elderslie?

A 30 km B 40 km C 50 km D 60 km (1 mark)

6 This week Marcus is paid \$360 for working 25 hours. If last week he was paid at the same rate and received \$259.20, how many hours did he work? *Hint 3*

A 12 hours B 16 hours C 17 hours D 18 hours (1 mark)

Part B Short Answer

7 Simplify:

a \$2.40 : \$6 b 1 hectare : 1000 m^2 c 100 mL : 0.2 kL (3 marks)

8 At Matt's Movies, the ratio of DVDs to Blu-ray disks is 5 : 2. If there are 340 Blu-ray disks, how many DVDs are there? (2 marks)

9 In a newspaper the ratio of advertisements for job, cars and property is noted. The ratio of job ads to car ads is 3 : 2, while the ratio of car ads to property ads is 4 : 3.

a If there are 600 job ads, how many ads are there for cars? (2 marks)

b If there are a total of 959 car and property ads, how many of these are car ads? (2 marks)

c Find the ratio of job ads to car ads to property ads. *Hint 4* (2 marks)

d If there are 930 property ads, how many job ads are there in the newspaper? (2 marks)

10 Ross travels 372 kilometres averaging 72 km/h. If he commenced his trip at 11:40 am, at what time did he arrive at his destination? (2 marks)

11 Riya leaves her home at 20:10 and arrives at Launceston at 23:30.

a How long did the journey take? (1 mark)

b Find the distance from Launceston to Peta's home, if she averaged 78 km/h. (2 marks)

c Peta used 32 L of petrol. What was the fuel consumption rate of her car in L/100 km? Give your answer correct to 2 decimal places. (2 marks)

d If the petrol cost Peta 162.9 cents/L, find the cost of the petrol used. (2 marks)

Hint 1: Express both with the same denominator.
Hint 2: Angle sum of a triangle is 180°.
Hint 3: Use the unitary method.
Hint 4: Use the lowest common multiple of 2 and 4.

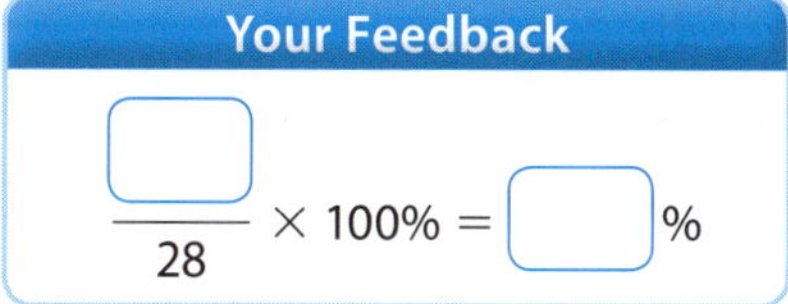

RATIO AND RATES

Real Numbers

40 MINUTES

ADVANCED TEST

1 Simplify:

a $12:16:20$

b $0.7:0.35:0.05$

c $2:2\frac{3}{4}:3$

d 20 mm : 3 cm : 0.6 m

e 350 s : 10 min : 1 h

f 120 mL : 2 L : 0.006 kL (1 mark each)

2 a Increase \$400 in the ratio of 5 : 7. (1 mark)

b Decrease \$162 in the ratio of 9 : 2. (1 mark)

c Increase \$600 in the ratio of 5 : 8 and then decrease the result in the ratio of 3 : 2. (2 marks)

3 Find the value of x in the following proportions:

a $\frac{x}{3} = \frac{12}{18}$

b $\frac{5}{6} = \frac{x}{30}$

c $\frac{14}{x} = \frac{24}{36}$ (1 mark each)

4 A camera was purchased for \$600 and later sold for \$450. What is the ratio of:

a selling price : cost price? (1 mark)

b selling price : loss? (1 mark)

c loss : cost price : selling price? (1 mark)

5 Three-quarters of the males at a boxing match are males. What is the ratio of:

a females : total? (1 mark)

b males : females? (1 mark)

6 The ratio of the length and width of a rectangle is 4 : 3. If the perimeter is 56 cm, what is the area? (2 marks)

7 Thea wrote down two supplementary angles. If one of the angles is 40°, what is the ratio of the larger angle to the smaller angle? (2 marks)

8 A two-metre length of timber is cut into two lengths so that the difference in their lengths is 40 cm. Write the ratio of:

a the short length to the long length (1 mark)

b the long length to the original length (1 mark)

9 In the PE storeroom the ratio of footballs to basketballs is 6 : 5 and the ratio of basketballs to netballs is 4 : 3. If there are 48 footballs, how many basketballs and netballs? (2 marks)

10 Complete the following:

a 54c/10 mL = \$____________/L (1 mark)

b 48 m/s = ____________ km/h (1 mark)

c 9.2 L/100 km = ____________ km/L (1 mark)

11 On a 30 kilometre trip, a cyclist rode the first half of the distance at an average speed of 20 km/h and the remainder at 15 km/h. What was the average speed for the entire trip, to 2 decimal places? (2 marks)

12 Brisbane and Charleville are 760 km apart. A car leaves Brisbane travelling toward Charleville at an average speed of 90 km/h. At the same time, a second car leaves Charleville and heads toward Brisbane at an average speed of 100 km/h. How long will it take for the two cars to meet, and where will they meet? (2 marks)

13 At 12:15 pm Helen leaves Norseman to drive to Eucla, a distance of 700 km. If she arrives at her destination at 9:00 pm that night, what was her average speed? (2 marks)

14 A scale on a map is expressed as 1 : 200 000. If the distance between two places on the map is 8.5 cm, how far apart are they in kilometres? (2 marks)

15 Jack pays \$11.40 per kg for 750 grams of chocolate sultanas and \$8.60 per kg for 500 grams of chocolate bullets. If Jack mixes both together, what is his cost per kg? (2 marks)

16 How much longer does it take to drive a kilometre at 60 km/h compared to 100 km/h? (2 marks)

17 Cody drove from his home to work at an average speed of 50 km/h. On the way home the traffic was heavier and he averaged 10 km/h slower. If the homeward trip took half an hour,

a how far is it from home to work? (1 mark)

b how long did it take to drive to work? (1 mark)

18 Mim ran at an average speed of 5 metres per second for 10 minutes. How far did she run? (1 mark)

19 A paint mixture contains blue paint to white paint in the ratio 2 : 3. How many litres of blue paint must be added to 10 litres of the mixture to obtain a new mixture which has 60% blue paint? (2 marks)

Your Feedback

$\frac{\square}{46} \times 100\% = \square\%$

PAGE 135

PAGE 177

ALGEBRA

Patterns and Algebra

STUDY NOTES

1 We can only **add or subtract like terms**. If terms are not like terms, we cannot add or subtract. For example, simplify:

a $4a + 7a = 11a$

b $6x - 2y = 6x - 2y$

c $-3a^2b + 3a^2b = 0$

d $-7m - 3m = -10m$

2 We can **multiply or divide like and unlike terms**. For example:

a $3a \times 2b \times 4c = 24abc$

b $12p^2q \div (-6p^2) = -2q$

c $(-3a)^2 = 9a^2$

d $\dfrac{-10k}{-5k} = 2$

3 The expression before (or after) a grouping symbol **multiples** its contents. For example, $3(2a - 5)$ means $3 \times (2a - 5)$.

4 The most common grouping symbols are **parentheses** ( ) and **brackets** [ ].

5 To remove the grouping symbols we **expand** the expression.

For example, expand:

a $3(2a + 5) = 3 \times (+2a) + 3 \times (+5) = 6a + 15$

b $a(a - 7) = a \times (+a) + a \times (-7) = a^2 - 7a$

c $-4(3x + 2) = -4 \times (+3x) - 4 \times (+2) = -12x - 8$

d $-3(-7a - 5) = -3 \times (-7a) - 3 \times (-5) = 21a + 15$

6 Expressions of the form $-1(x + 3)$ we **rewrite** as $-(x + 3)$.

For example, expand:

a $-(-7y + 8) = -1 \times (-7y) - 1 \times (+8) = 7y - 8$

7 Some questions require **expanding** and then **simplifying** of the expression.

For example, expand:

a $2(y - 4) + 5(3y + 2) = 2y - 8 + 15y + 10 = 17y + 2$

b $5(2c + 6) - 4(3c - 2) = 10c + 30 - 12c + 8 = -2c + 38$

c $2(3 - y) - (2 + y) = 6 - 2y - 2 - y = 4 - 3y$

8 To **factorise** an algebraic expression, first find the **highest common factor** of the terms and then use grouping symbols. Factorising is the **opposite** of **expanding**.

For example, factorise:

a $3x - 15$
$= 3(x - 5)$

b $8a^2 - 12a$
$= 4a(2a - 3)$

c $3a - 6b - 9$
$= 3(a - 2b - 3)$

d $-12cd + 15c$
$= -3c(4d - 5)$

e $x^3 + x^2$
$= x^2(x + 1)$

f $x(x + y) - 2(x + y)$
$= (x + y)(x - 2)$

Checklist

Can you:

1 *Simplify algebraic expressions involving the four operations?* ☐

2 *Expand algebraic expressions?* ☐

3 *Factorise algebraic expressions?* ☐

ALGEBRA

Patterns and Algebra

SKILLS CHECK

1 Simplify:

a $5x - 3y - 2x + 7y$ b $8ab - 10ba$ c $5a^2 - 6a^2$
d $7 - a - 10 + 2a$ e $3x - 9y - x + 2y$ f $9y^3 - 10y^3$
g $6a \times (-3a)$ h $(-2c) \times (-3d)$ i $(-3y)^2$
j $10m \div (-5m)$ k $\dfrac{-4x}{2}$ l $(-24x^2) \div (-4x)$

2 If $p = -3$ and $q = -4$, evaluate:

a $p^2 - q^2$ b $(p + q)^2$ c $q(p - 1)$

3 If $a = -2$, $b = -4$, and $c = 6$, evaluate:

a $\dfrac{c - b}{a}$ b $\sqrt{1 - bc}$ c $(3a)^0$

4 Expand:

a $4(x + 7)$ b $(4y - 2)6$ c $5(3a - 6)$
d $6(3a - 9)$ e $2(9 - a)$ f $7(2a - 3b + 1)$

5 Expand:

a $-7(2z + 1)$ b $-2(a + 4b)$ c $-4(3c - 4d)$
d $-(3x - y)$ e $-(3x - y + z)$ f $-(-a + b)$

6 Expand:

a $x(x - 3)$ b $3a(4a - 5)$ c $-6y(2y + 5)$
d $g(3 - g)$ e $y(-3 - 4x)$ f $-3w(w - 2)$

7 Expand and simplify:

a $6(2a + 5) + 3(3a - 1)$ b $5(y - 3) + 7(2y + 1)$
c $4(2y + 5) - 2(5y + 1)$ d $2(3a - 1) - (5 - a)$

8 Expand and simplify:

a $2 + 3(2x - 3)$ b $9 - 2(3a + 4)$
c $1 - (a - 7)$ d $y - (4 - y)$

9 Factorise:

a $3x - 6$ b $10y - 12$ c $60x - 40xy$
d $12ab + 9a$ e $\pi r^2 - 2\pi r$ f $36p - 30pq$

10 Factorise:

a $x(x + y) - 7(x + y)$ b $a(a - b) - b(a - b)$ c $c(c - 4) - (c - 4)$

Answers 1 a $3x + 4y$ b $-2ab$ c $-a^2$ d $-3 + a$ e $2x - 7y$ f $-y^3$ g $-18a^2$ h $6cd$ i $9y^2$ j -2 k $-2x$ l $6x$ 2 a -7 b 49 c 16 3 a -5 b 5 c 1 4 a $4x+28$ b $24y-12$ c $15a-30$ d $18a-54$ e $18-2a$ f $14a-21b+7$ 5 a $-14z-7$ b $-2a-8b$ c $-12c+16d$ d $-3x+y$ e $-3x+y-z$ f $a-b$ 6 a x^2-3x b $12a^2-15a$ c $-12y^2-30y$ d $3g-g^2$ e $-3y-4xy$ f $-3w^2+6w$ 7 a $21a+27$ b $19y-8$ c $-2y+18$ d $7a-7$ 8 a $6x-7$ b $1-6a$ c $8-a$ d $2y-4$ 9 a $3(x-2)$ b $2(5y-6)$ c $20x(3-2y)$ d $3a(4b+3)$ e $\pi r(r-2)$ f $6p(6-5q)$ 10 a $(x+y)(x-7)$ b $(a-b)^2$ c $(c-4)(c-1)$

ALGEBRA

INTERMEDIATE TEST

Part A Multiple Choice

1 Simplify $5m - 12 - 3m + 2$:

A $2m - 10$ B $2m - 14$ C $8m - 10$ D $8m - 14$ (1 mark)

2 Evaluate ab^2 given $a = 2$ and $b = -3$: *Hint 1*

A -36 B -18 C 18 D 36 (1 mark)

3 Expand $(3x - 1)5$:

A $3x - 5$ B $15x - 1$ C $15x - 5$ D $3x - 4$ (1 mark)

4 Expand $-4(5c - 4)$:

A $-20c - 16$ B $-20c + 16$ C $-c - 8$ D $-20c - 8$ (1 mark)

5 Factorise $4a^2 - 12a$:

A $4(a^2 - 6)$ B $2a(a - 6)$ C $4a(a - 3)$ D $4a(a + 1)$ (1 mark)

6 If $ax - ay + bx - by = a(x - y) + b(x - y)$, then $ax - ay + bx - by$ equals:

A $(x - y) + (a + b)$ B $(x - y)(a + b)$ C $(x + y)(a - b)$ D $(x - y)(a - b)$ (1 mark)

Part B Short Answer

7 Simplify:

a $4y - 2 \times 7y$ b $3a - 2 + a^2 - 3$ c $20r \div -5r$ (1 mark each)

8 Expand:

a $2(5x - 2y + z)$ b $-3(4 - 2xy)$ c $xy(2x - 3y)$

d $-(4 - a + 2b)$ e $-y(2y - 1)$ f $-(a - b - 2c)$ (1 mark each)

9 Expand and simplify:

a $2(3a + 5) + 3(a - 1)$ b $2 + 3(a - 1)$ c $3k + 2(k - 3)$

d $8 - 3(2g - 5)$ e $2(a - b) - (b - a)$ f $4a - 3a(1 - 2a)$ (2 marks each)

10 Factorise:

a $18xy - 6x$ b $m^4 - 3m^3$ c $12a^2b + 8ab^2$ (1 mark each)

Hint 1: Take care with substitution—only the value of b is squared.

Your Feedback

$\frac{\square}{30} \times 100\% = \square\%$

PAGE 137

PAGE 177

ALGEBRA
Patterns and Algebra

ADVANCED TEST

1 Expand and simplify:
- a $3(2 - 7y) + 2(y - 8)$ (2 marks)
- b $6(5a - 2) - 3(a + 1)$ (2 marks)
- c $-(a - 2b + 3c) - a + b$ (2 marks)
- d $5(a - b) - 5(b - a)$ (2 marks)
- e $a(a - 1) - 2a(2 - 5a)$ (2 marks)
- f $a^2(a - 1) + 2a(a^2 - 1)$ (2 marks)
- g $6x(3x - 3) - (2x^2 - 5x - 1)$ (2 marks)

2 Find the product of:
- a $3x - 6$ and -3
- b -5 and $2x - 7$
- c $-7t - 3$ and -2
- d $2a - 7$ and $3a$

(1 mark each)

3 Find the sum of:
- a $3a - 6$ and $2 - 8a$ (1 mark)
- b $2x^2 + 3x - 1$ and $4x - 3x^2 - 1$ (1 mark)
- c $1 - 3x - x^2$ and $5 + 2x + 2x^2$ (1 mark)

4 Find the difference between:
- a $7x - 1$ and $5x - 2$ (2 marks)
- b $2a + 8$ and $2 - 6a$ (2 marks)
- c $-4a - 9$ and $-2a + 3$ (2 marks)
- d $2x^2 - x + 5$ and $x^2 + 6x + 9$ (2 marks)
- e $4 - 2m - m^2$ and $9 + 4m - 5m^2$ (2 marks)

5 Find the perimeter of a:
- a square with side length $(3a - 2)$ cm (1 mark)
- b equilateral triangle with side length $(15 - 2x)$ cm (1 mark)
- c rectangle with length $(3b + 2)$ cm and width $(2b - 5)$ cm (1 mark)
- d regular hexagon with side length $(4x - 2)$ cm (1 mark)

6 Find the area of a:
- a triangle with base length 12 cm and perpendicular height $(3g - 2)$ cm (1 mark)
- b rectangle with length $(5y - 2)$ cm and width 7 cm (1 mark)
- c parallelogram with base 10 cm and perpendicular height of $(2 - 3w)$ cm (1 mark)
- d rectangle with dimensions $4x$ cm and $(2x - 1)$ cm (1 mark)

7 Write an expression for the area of a:
- a square with side length $(2x - 5)$ cm (1 mark)
- b rectangle with dimensions $(3x - 1)$ and $(x + 2)$ cm (1 mark)
- c triangle with base length $(3p - 1)$ cm and perpendicular height $(2p + 1)$ cm (1 mark)

8 From the product of $3x$ and $(2x - 1)$ subtract $(4 - 2x)$. (2 marks)

9 Expand and simplify:
- a $2 - 3(p - 3)$
- b $5a + 4(a - 1)$
- c $2y - (8 - 3y)$
- d $2a^2 - 3a(a + 2)$
- e $3y^2 - (4y^2 + y - 2)$

(2 marks each)

10 Factorise:
- a $5ab - 30b$
- b $12xy - 18x$
- c $x^2 + 5xy$
- d $-2a - 8a^2$
- e $-5ab + 30b$
- f $-x^3 - x^2 - x$

(1 mark each)

11 Factorise:
- a $a(a - b) + 3(a - b)$ (1 mark)
- b $2y(x + y) - x(x + y)$ (1 mark)
- c $5w(a - b) - 2(b - a)$ (1 mark)

12 Factorise:
- a $a^2 + 3a + ab + 3b$ (2 marks)
- b $pq - 5q - 2p + 10$ (2 marks)
- c $2x + 8y - 3xz - 12yz$ (2 marks)
- d $3a + 2b + ab + 6$ (2 marks)

13 The product of two expressions is $6a^2 + 21a$. If one of the expressions is $3a$, what is the other expression? (1 mark)

14 A rectangle has an area of $(6ab + 10a)$ cm^2. If the width is $2a$ cm, find the length. (1 mark)

15 The base of a parallelogram is $(3x - 2)$ cm. If the area is $(6x^2 - 4x)$ cm^2, what is the perpendicular height? (1 mark)

16 By factorising first, simplify:
- a $\dfrac{4x^2 - 12x}{2x - 6}$ (2 marks)
- b $\dfrac{xy - x^2 - x + y}{2x - 2y}$ (3 marks)
- c $\dfrac{4x}{4x - 8} \times \dfrac{3x^2 - 6x}{x^2 - x}$ (2 marks)
- d $\dfrac{3a + 6b}{x - 4y} \times \dfrac{2x - 8y}{2a + 4b}$ (2 marks)

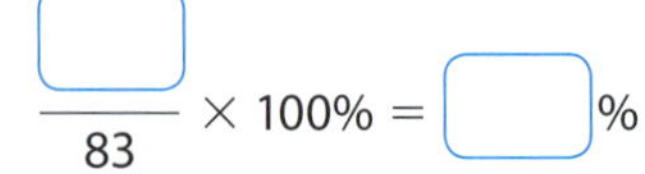

PAGE 137

PAGE 177

BASIC EQUATIONS

Patterns and Algebra

STUDY NOTES

1 An **equation** is a mathematical sentence which includes an **equals** sign.

2 Equations are **solved** and the answer is called the **solution**.

3 There are **four basic types of equations**:

$x + 7 = 9$	$x - 3 = 5$	$3x = 12$	$\frac{x}{2} = 6$
$x + 7 - 7 = 9 - 7$	$x - 3 + 3 = 5 + 3$	$\frac{3x}{3} = \frac{12}{3}$	$\cancel{2} \times \frac{x}{\cancel{2}} = 2 \times 6$
$x = 2$	$x = 8$	$x = 4$	$x = 12$

4 We save time by using the rule: when we **change sides we change signs**.
For example, solve:

a
$$3x - 2 = x + 6$$
$$3x - x = 6 + 2$$
$$2x = 8$$
$$\frac{2x}{2} = \frac{8}{2}$$
$$\therefore x = 4$$

b
$$6 - 2y = 12$$
$$-2y = 12 - 6$$
$$-2y = 6$$
$$\frac{-2y}{-2} = \frac{6}{-2}$$
$$\therefore y = -3$$

c
$$3(a - 7) = 2(2 - a)$$
$$3a - 21 = 4 - 2a$$
$$3a + 2a = 4 + 21$$
$$\frac{5a}{5} = \frac{25}{5}$$
$$\therefore a = 5$$

5 To solve an equation involving a **fraction,** multiply both sides of the equation by the same number.

a
$$\frac{3x + 4}{2} = 5$$
$$2 \times \frac{3x + 4}{2} = 2 \times 5$$
$$3x + 4 = 10$$
$$3x = 10 - 4$$
$$\frac{3x}{3} = \frac{6}{3}$$
$$\therefore x = 2$$

b
$$\frac{2 - 5b}{4} = 3$$
$$4 \times \frac{2 - 5b}{4} = 4 \times 3$$
$$2 - 5b = 12$$
$$-5b = 12 - 2$$
$$\frac{-5b}{-5} = \frac{10}{-5}$$
$$\therefore b = -2$$

6 We can **check the solution** of an equation by using substitution.

For example, determine whether $x = 5$ is the solution of $5x - 1 = 4x + 4$:

Substitute $x = 5$ in $5x - 1 = 4x + 4$
$$\therefore 5(5) - 1 = 4(5) + 4$$
$$25 - 1 = 20 + 4$$
$$24 = 24$$

This means $x = 5$ is the solution of $5x - 1 = 4x + 4$.

Checklist

Can you:

1 *Solve equations using algebraic methods?* ☐

2 *Check the solution to an equation by substitution?* ☐

BASIC EQUATIONS

Patterns and Algebra

1 Solve:

a $a - 7 = 3$ b $4 + a = 9$ c $12 = p - 6$

2 Solve:

a $4y = 16$ b $-3y = 9$ c $8p = -12$

3 Solve:

a $\frac{a}{2} = 7$ b $\frac{x}{-5} = 3$ c $\frac{y}{3} = -4$

4 Solve:

a $\frac{3g}{4} = 6$ b $\frac{-a}{3} = 4$ c $\frac{2p}{5} = 12$

5 Solve:

a $3a - 4 = 8$ b $3 = 4y - 2$ c $2a = a - 1$

6 Solve:

a $4y - 2 = y + 4$ b $3(a - 1) = 9$ c $2(3t + 5) = 2t$

7 Solve:

a $5(2a - 1) = 3(3a + 4)$ b $6y - 2(y + 1) = 0$ c $5 - (a + 1) = a + 3$

8 Solve:

a $4(b - 2) - 3(b + 1) = -7$ b $3(r - 2) - 4(3 - r) = 4(2r + 5)$

9 Solve:

a $\frac{3y - 4}{2} = 7$ b $\frac{5 - 2y}{3} = 8$ c $\frac{2a + 5}{2} = -4$

10 Solve $\frac{5(2a - 1) - (a + 3)}{2} = 5$

PAGE 138

Answers 1 a $a=10$ b $a=5$ c $p=18$ 2 a $y=4$ b $y=-3$ c $p=-1.5$ 3 a $a=14$ b $x=-15$ c $y=-12$
4 a $g=8$ b $a=-12$ c $p=30$ 5 a $a=4$ b $y=1.25$ c $a=-1$ 6 a $y=2$ b $a=4$ c $t=-2.5$
7 a $a=17$ b $y=0.5$ c $a=0.5$ 8 a $b=4$ b $r=-38$ 9 a $y=6$ b $y=-9.5$ c $a=-6.5$ 10 $a=2$

BASIC EQUATIONS

Patterns and Algebra

25 MINUTES

INTERMEDIATE TEST

Part A Multiple Choice

1 The solution to $3a - 4 = a + 8$ is: *Hint 1*

A $a = 2$ B $a = 4$ C $a = 6$ D $a = 8$ (1 mark)

2 In attempting to solve the equation $3 - 2x = 5$, Lindy wrote the following:

$3 - 2x = 5$

$-2x = 5 - 3$ Line 1

$-2x = 2$ Line 2

$\frac{-2x}{-2} = \frac{2}{-2}$ Line 3

$x = 1$ Line 4

Lindy made a mistake in:

A Line 1 B Line 2 C Line 3 D Line 4 (1 mark)

3 $b = -1$ is the solution of:

A $3b + 1 = b - 1$ B $2b = b - 3$ C $2(b + 1) = 3$ D $4 = 3b + 1$ (1 mark)

4 $x = 2$ is a solution of:

A $2x - 1 = 4$ B $3x = -12$ C $4 - x = 6$ D $3x = 2x + 2$ (1 mark)

5 Which of these equations does **not** have $a = 1$ as the solution?

A $2a + 1 = 3$ B $2 + a = 1$ C $3a - 2 = 1$ D $a + 1 = 2a$ (1 mark)

6 Jordie solved the equation $3(x - 1) - 2(x + 1) = 2$ but made a mistake.

$3(x - 1) - 2(x + 1) = 2$

$3x - 3 - 2x + 2 = 2$ Line 1

$x - 1 = 2$ Line 2

$x = 2 + 1$ Line 3

$x = 3$ Line 4

In what line is his mistake?

A Line 1 B Line 2 C Line 3 D Line 4 (1 mark)

Part B Short Answer

7 Solve:

a $3p - 7 = 2p + 11$ b $5(a - 2) = 3a + 4$ c $\frac{2x - 7}{3} = 5$ d $\frac{x}{2} - \frac{x}{3} = 4$ (2 marks each)

8 Solve: *Hint 2*

a $5 - 2(x + 1) = 3$ b $\frac{2(3a - 1) - (2a + 1)}{4} = 1$

c $\frac{3p - 2}{5} - 2 = 6$ d $\frac{4a - 1}{3} - \frac{2a - 1}{2} = 4$ (3 marks each)

Hint 1: Substitute alternatives into the equation to see whether LHS = RHS.

Hint 2: Take care when expanding grouping symbols.

Your Feedback

$\frac{\square}{26} \times 100\% = \square\%$

PAGE 139

PAGE 177

BASIC EQUATIONS
Patterns and Algebra

ADVANCED TEST

1 Solve:

a $3x - 2 = 2x + 5$ (2 marks)

b $5m + 3 = 4m - 6$ (2 marks)

c $5 + 2a = 8 - a$ (2 marks)

d $14 + 5x = 7 - 2x$ (2 marks)

e $11 - 2c = c + 5$ (2 marks)

f $7 - 3k = k + 3$ (2 marks)

g $3b = 8 - b$ (2 marks)

h $6q = 16 - 2q$ (2 marks)

i $12 = 4x - 8$ (2 marks)

j $-10 = 3p + 2$ (2 marks)

2 Solve:

a $3(2x - 1) = 5x - 6$ (2 marks)

b $5(2a - 2) = 9a - 6$ (2 marks)

c $2(4y + 2) = 2(3y - 1)$ (2 marks)

d $3(5x - 1) = 4(x + 7)$ (2 marks)

e $3 - 2(x + 1) = 2(1 - 3x)$ (2 marks)

f $6 - 5(2n + 3) = 4(2 - 5n)$ (2 marks)

g $10 - (w - 4) = 3w - (2 - w)$ (2 marks)

h $2 - (3t + 1) = 4t - (6 - 4t)$ (2 marks)

i $4a - 3(a + 5) = 2 - (a - 1)$ (2 marks)

j $8p - 2(3p + 1) = 7p - (2 - 5p)$ (2 marks)

3 Solve:

a $\dfrac{3y - 4}{2} = y$ (2 marks)

b $\dfrac{5a - 2}{3} = 2a$ (2 marks)

c $\dfrac{5x - 2}{3} = x - 1$ (2 marks)

d $\dfrac{4c + 1}{5} = 2c - 3$ (2 marks)

e $\dfrac{3 - a}{2} = 4a + 3$ (2 marks)

f $\dfrac{7 - 3y}{4} = 2 - 4y$ (2 marks)

g $\dfrac{3a + 7}{-2} = 6a - 3$ (2 marks)

4 Solve:

a $\dfrac{3y - 2}{y} = 2$ (2 marks)

b $\dfrac{3 - 5m}{m} = 4$ (2 marks)

c $\dfrac{5 - 2p}{3p} = 2$ (2 marks)

d $\dfrac{3a + 2}{-5a} = -3$ (2 marks)

5 Solve:

a $\dfrac{m + 4}{2} - 3m = 5$ (2 marks)

b $2w - \dfrac{3 - w}{3} = 4$ (2 marks)

c $3p - \dfrac{p + 2}{5} = 2$ (2 marks)

6 Solve:

a $\dfrac{2a + 1}{4} - \dfrac{3a - 2}{3} = 1$ (3 marks)

b $\dfrac{3x + 2}{2} - \dfrac{2 - x}{5} = 2$ (3 marks)

7 Solve:

a $x^2 + 3 = 12$ (2 marks)

b $y^2 - 11 = 25$ (2 marks)

c $4a^2 = 100$ (2 marks)

d $\dfrac{4}{x} = x$ (2 marks)

8 By substituting the given value of the pronumeral into both sides of the equation, determine whether it is a solution: (12 marks)

a $3m + 2 = m - 6$ $[m = -4]$

b $2(3y - 1) = 1 + 3(y + 5)$ $[y = 6]$

c $2g - 3(2g + 5) = 7 - 2g$ $[g = -11]$

d $\dfrac{2a - 5}{3} = a + 4$ $[a = -17]$

e $\dfrac{7 - 4p}{3p} = p$ $[p = 1]$

f $\dfrac{2a - 3}{3} - \dfrac{a + 1}{4} = a - 1$ $[a = 3]$

Your Feedback

$\dfrac{\square}{94} \times 100\% = \square\%$

FORMULAE AND USING EQUATIONS

Patterns and Algebra

STUDY NOTES

1 A **formula** consists of two or more **variables** (pronumerals). The **subject** of the formula is the variable on the left-hand side of the equals sign.

For example, s is the subject of the formula $s = \frac{d}{t}$.

2 The **value of an unknown pronumeral** is found after **substituting** given values for the other pronumerals. For example:

a If $P = 2(l + b)$, find P when $l = 8$ and $b = 6.5$.

$P = 2(8 + 6.5)$
$= 2 \times 14.5 = 29$

$\therefore P = 29$

b If $A = \frac{1}{2}h(a + b)$ find b when $A = 20, h = 4, a = 8$.

$20 = \frac{1}{2} \times 4 \times (8 + b)$ [substitute the known, or given, pronumerals]

$20 = 2(b + 8)$ [simplify]

$2b + 16 = 20$ [swap sides to have unknown on LHS and expand]

$2b = 20 - 16$

$= 4$

$\therefore b = 2$

3 Sometimes the **formula may first have to be developed**. For example:

a Write a formula linking c and T.

b If $T = 60$, find the value of c.

c	2	3	4	5	6
T	0	2	4	6	8

$\therefore T = 2c - 4$

$60 = 2c - 4$

$2c = 60 + 4$

$\therefore c = 32$

4 **Equations can be used to solve problems**. For example:

a The sum of three consecutive whole numbers is 45. Find the numbers.

Let the numbers be $x, x + 1, x + 2$.

$\therefore x + (x + 1) + (x + 2) = 45$

$3x + 3 = 45$

$3x = 42$

$x = 14$

$\therefore$ the numbers are 14, 15, 16

b Find the value of x:

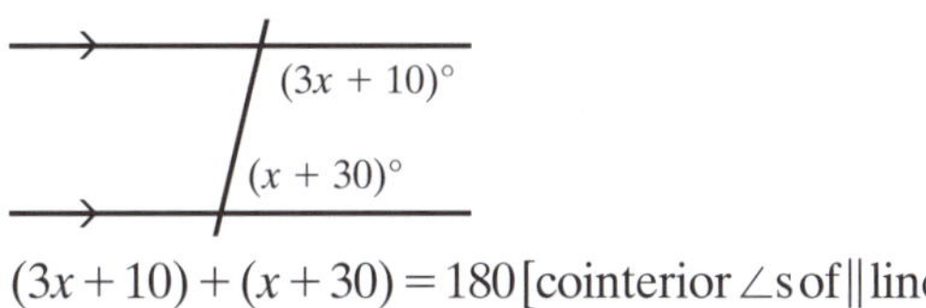

$(3x + 10) + (x + 30) = 180$ [cointerior ∠s of || lines = 180°]

$4x + 40 = 180$

$4x = 140$

$\therefore x = 35$

Checklist

Can you:

1 *Recognise the subject of a formula?* ☐

2 *Solve equations by substitution?* ☐

3 *Establish a formula or rule from a table of values?* ☐

4 *Develop and solve an equation based on a problem, and express the answer in terms of the problem?* ☐

FORMULAE AND USING EQUATIONS

Patterns and Algebra

SKILLS CHECK

1 If $y = mx + b$, find y when:

a $m = 3, x = 2, b = 5$

b $m = -2, x = 3, b = -4$

2 If $A = \dfrac{x + y + z}{3}$, find the value of A when:

a $x = 4, y = 7, z = 10$

b $x = -4, y = 0, z = 7$

3 If $C = \dfrac{5(F - 32)}{9}$, find:

a C, if $F = 68$

b F, if $C = 100$

4 If $A = \dfrac{bh}{2}$, find:

a A, if $b = 20$ and $h = 5$

b h, if $A = 16$ and $b = 4$

5 If $S = \dfrac{a}{1 - r}$, find:

a S, if $a = 15$ and $r = 0.8$

b a, if $S = 36$ and $r = 0.5$

6 The table illustrated displays the results of a function.

b	2	3	4	5	6
p	0	1	2	3	4

a Write a formula linking b and p.

b If $b = 20$, find the value of p.

c If $p = 48$, what is the value of b?

7 Solve each of the following by expressing the problem as an equation:

a The sum of a number and 4 is multiplied by 2. The result is 12. What is the number?

b Three consecutive whole numbers add to 36. Find the numbers.

c Find the two consecutive even numbers such that four times the first number equals three times the second.

d The average of a number, twice that number and 3 is equal to 5. Find the number.

8 Find the value of x:

a

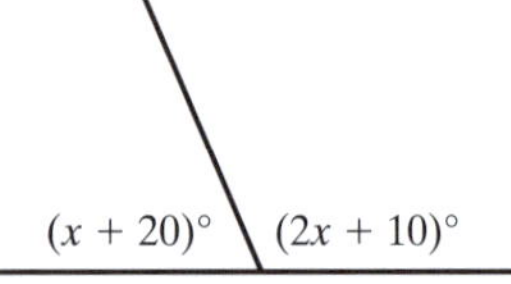

b

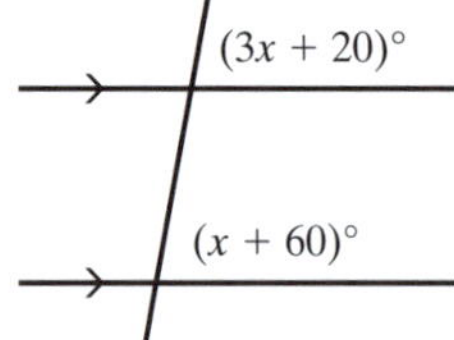

c

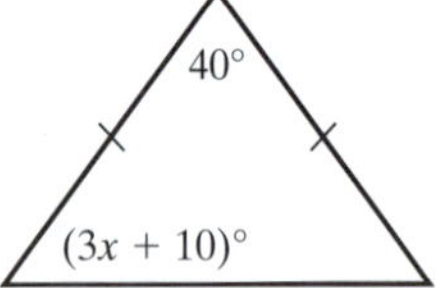

d

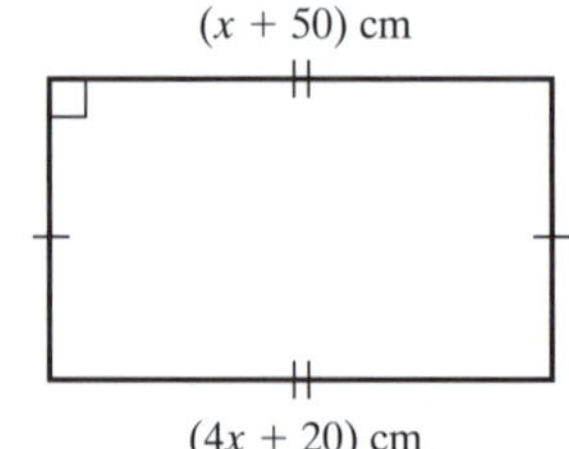

Answers 1 a $y = 11$ b $y = -10$ 2 a $A = 7$ b $A = 1$ 3 a $C = 20$ b $F = 212$ 4 a $A = 50$ b $h = 8$
5 a $S = 75$ b $a = 18$ 6 a $p = b - 2$ b $p = 18$ c $b = 50$ 7 a 2 b 11, 12, 13 c 6 and 8 d 4
8 a $x = 50$ b $x = 20$ c $x = 20$ d $x = 10$

FORMULAE AND USING EQUATIONS

Patterns and Algebra

INTERMEDIATE TEST

Part A Multiple Choice

1 If $X = \dfrac{a + b + c}{3}$ and $a = 4, b = 2, c = 6$, find the value of X.

A 8 B 4 C 3 D 6 (1 mark)

2 If $V = \pi r^2 h$, find V if $\pi = 3.1, r = 4, h = 5$.

A 248 B 768.8 C 3844 D 384.4 (1 mark)

3 If $S = \dfrac{n}{2}(a + l)$, find a when $S = 120, n = 16, l = 10$.

A 5 B 6 C 10 D 12 (1 mark)

4 If $T = a + (n - 1)d$, and $T = 64, n = 6, a = 14$, find the value of d.

A 7 B 8 C 9 D 10 (1 mark)

5 The diagram shows an isosceles triangle.
Which of the following is **not** a correct equation?

A $2x + 20 + x + 45 = 140$ B $2x + 20 = 70$

C $x + 45 + 40 = 2x + 20$ D $2x + 20 = x + 45$ (1 mark)

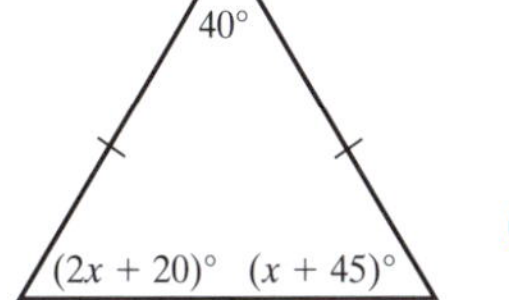

Part B Short Answer

6 The sum of four consecutive odd numbers is 64.

a Write an equation to represent the sum of the numbers using x as the pronumeral. *Hint 1* (1 mark)

b Solve the equation to find the four numbers. (2 marks)

7 The area of this triangle is 136 cm².
Find the value of x. (3 marks)

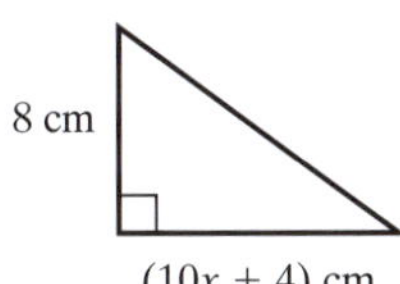

8 Twice a number plus three is the same as four times the number minus seven.

a Write an equation, in terms of x, that represents this statement. (1 mark)

b Find the number. (2 marks)

9 Find the value of x: (6 marks)

a 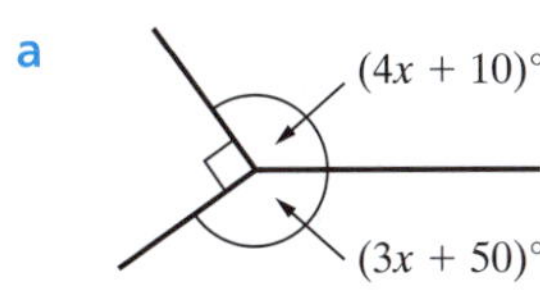

b 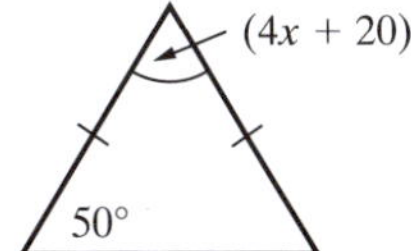

c 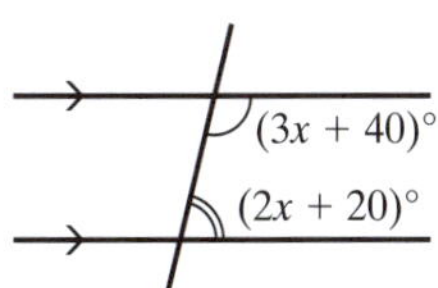

10 Using this diagram:

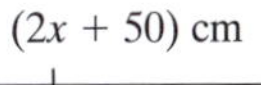

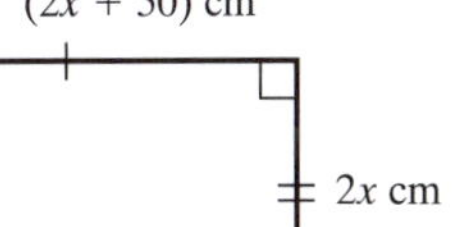

a Write an equation in terms of x. *Hint 2* (1 mark)

b Find the value of x. (1 mark)

c Find the numerical value of the area and perimeter. (4 marks)

Hint 1: Let the numbers be x, $x + 2$, $x + 4$, $x + 6$.
Hint 2: Opposite sides of a rectangle are equal.

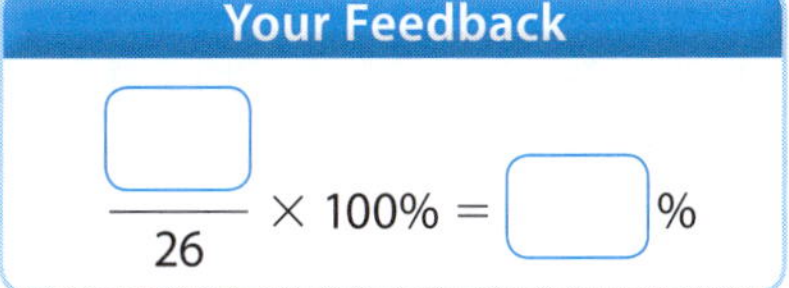

FORMULAE AND USING EQUATIONS

Patterns and Algebra

40 MINUTES

ADVANCED TEST

1 a Find C, if $C = \frac{5}{9}(F - 32)$ and $F = 68$. (2 marks)

b Find V, if $V - E + F = 2$, using $E = 30$ and $F = 20$. (2 marks)

c Find the positive value of c, if $c^2 = a^2 + b^2$, using $a = 1.05$ and $b = 2.08$ (2 marks)

2 Using $x_1 = 2, x_2 = 4, y_1 = 3, y_2 = -5$, find the value of:

a d, if $d = \sqrt{(x_2 - x_1)^2 + (y_2 - y_1)^2}$. (2 marks)

b m, if $m = \frac{y_2 - y_1}{x_2 - x_1}$. (2 marks)

3 The sum of three consecutive odd numbers is 45. By letting the smallest number be x, and solving an equation, find the three numbers. (2 marks)

4 The ages of three cousins are added together and the total is 47. Aiden is three years older than Lucas and two years younger than Jayden. Solve an equation to find the age of each boy. (2 marks)

5 The sum of Mia's age and Stella's age is 34. Mia is now 4 times as old as Stella was 4 years ago. How old are they now? (2 marks)

6 Dylan sold a Don Bradman signed mini cricket bat online for \$1620. This was \$40 more than twice the amount that he paid for the bat six years ago. Write an equation and solve it to find the cost price. (2 marks)

7 A survey was held to find the gender of people at a concert. The number of females at the concert was 8 more than three times the number of males. If there were 1772 people at the concert, solve an equation to find the number of males at the concert. (2 marks)

8 In a maths test the highest mark was 22 marks more than twice the lowest mark. The sum of the two marks was 118. Solve an equation to find the highest mark. (2 marks)

9 Claire earned \$60 more than three times the amount that Zoe earned. If the total amount earned by the two people was \$2420, solve an equation to find the amount of money earned by both people. (3 marks)

10 Layla spent a total of \$135 on a skirt and a pair of shoes. The price of the pair of shoes was \$18 less than twice what she paid for the skirt. Solve an equation to find the cost of the pair of shoes. (2 marks)

11 \$2600 is shared among three people so that the first will have \$60 more than the second and \$20 less than the third. Use an equation to find the amount each received. (2 marks)

12 Find the size of each angle in a triangle if the second is three times the size of the first and the third is twice the size of the second. (2 marks)

13 The price of a science textbook is \$12 more than twice the price of a maths study guide. If the total cost of both books is \$84, what is the price of each book? (2 marks)

14 The supplement of an angle is 40° more than twice its complement. Find the angle. (2 marks)

15 One side of a triangle is three times the length of another. The third side is 14 cm long. If the perimeter is 42 cm, what is the length of the shortest side? (2 marks)

16 The sum of two numbers is 40. Six times the smaller number is equal to four times the larger number. What are the two numbers? (2 marks)

17 Dino is 5 years older than Maryanne. Billy is 3 times as old as Maryanne. Rick is 4 years younger than Maryanne. The combined age of the four is 49. How old is each person? (2 marks)

18 Ticket prices for a drama group's play are \$8 for a student ticket and \$12 for an adult ticket. There were 600 tickets sold and the gate takings totalled \$5640. By letting the number of student tickets sold $= x$, find the number of each ticket sold. (2 marks)

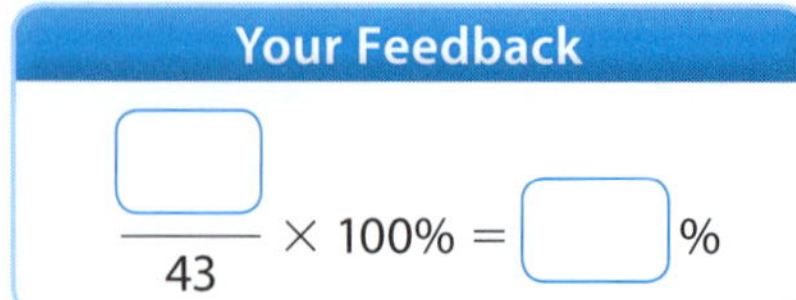

COORDINATE GEOMETRY

Linear and Non-linear Relationships

STUDY NOTES

1 The **number plane** is used to locate points which link two variables. A **line** can be drawn through these points **if the data is continuous.**

For example, a cyclist starts 20 kilometres from home and travels further away at 40 km/h.

time (t) (hours)	0	1	2	3	4
distance (d) (km)	**20**	**60**	**100**	**140**	**180**

a Complete the table (see top right).

b Write an equation linking d and t.

$d = 40t + 20$

c Sketch a graph showing the relationship between time (t) and distance (d).

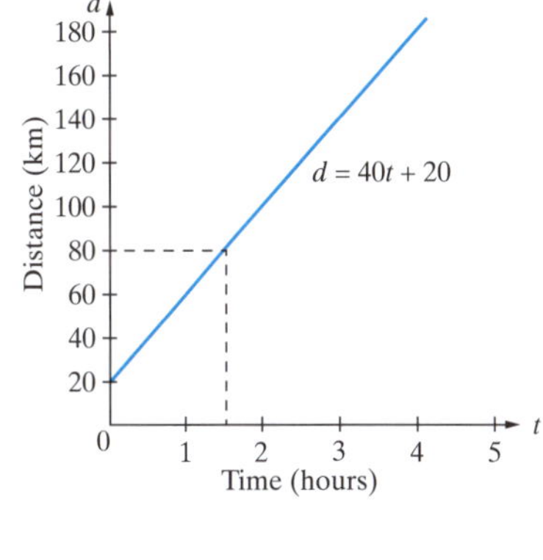

d Use the graph to find the distance from home after the cyclist travelled for 90 minutes. ∴ distance is 80 km.

2 To **graph a line** on a number plane, first complete a **table of values.**

For example, graph $y = 2x - 3$.

x	0	1	2
y	−3	−1	1

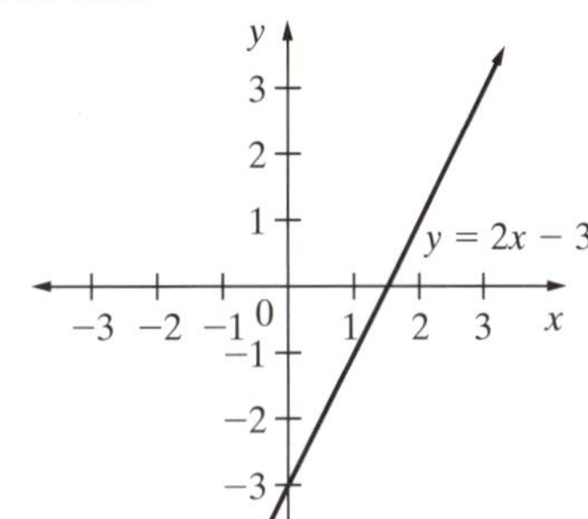

3 **Horizontal** and **vertical lines** can be drawn without the need for a table of values. For example, graph the lines $x = 4$ and $y = -2$.

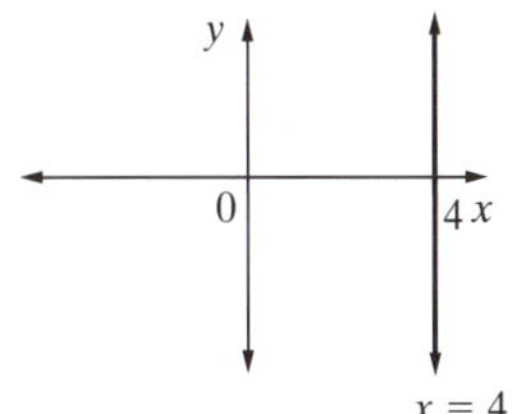

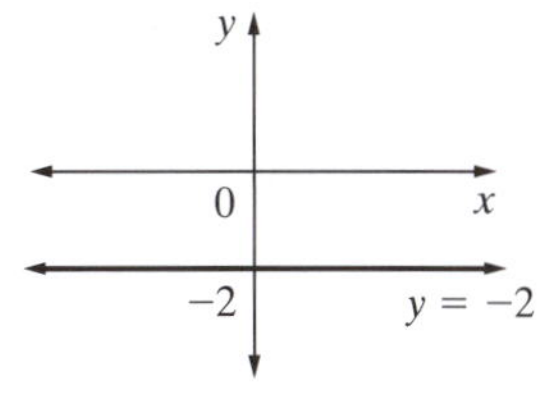

4 **Straight lines** can be written in the form $\boldsymbol{y = mx + b}$. The **coefficient** of x (**m**) represents the **slope (gradient)** of the line. The **constant term** (**b**) represents the place the line cuts the y-axis (**y-intercept**). For example,

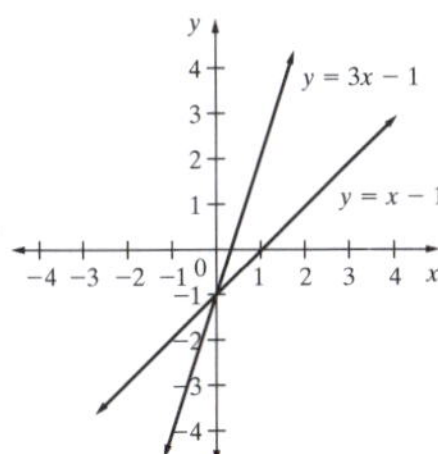

The line $y = 3x - 1$ with gradient $m = 3$ is steeper than $y = x - 1$ with gradient $m = 1$ (as $3 > 1$).

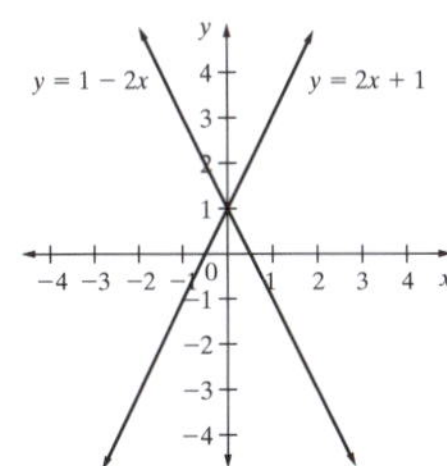

The line $y = 2x + 1$ has a positive slope ($m = 2$) while $y = 1 - 2x$ has a negative slope ($m = -2$).

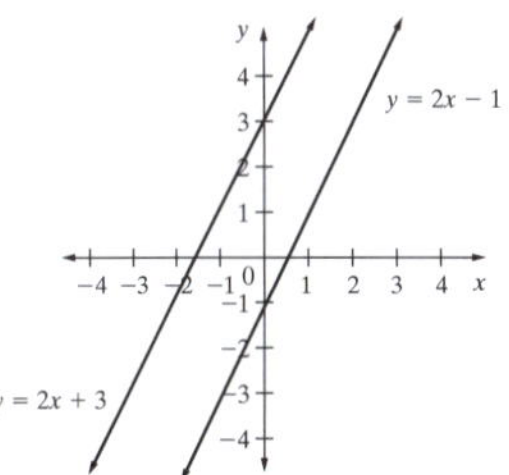

The lines have the same slope ($m = 2$). We say the lines are parallel.

Checklist

Can you:

1 *Graph a line on a number plane by first plotting points?* ☐
2 *Recognise lines with different slopes (gradients)?* ☐
3 *Compare lines that are parallel or intersect?* ☐

COORDINATE GEOMETRY

Linear and Non-linear Relationships

SKILLS CHECK

1 Complete the table for:

a $y = 2x + 1$

x	0	1	2
y			

b $y = 4 - x$

x	0	1	2
y			

c $x + y = 2$

x	0	1	2
y			

2 Answer true or false:

a $(1, 3)$ lies on the line $y = 2x - 3$.

b $(3, -1)$ lies on the line $y = 2x - 7$.

c The line $y = 4x - 3$ passes through $(1, 1)$.

d The line $y = 4 - x$ passes through $(2, -1)$.

3 Sam's Home Repairs charge a $50 call-out fee plus $40 per hour worked.

a Complete the table.

Hours (h)	0	2	4	6
Cost (c)				

b Write a formula linking h (hours) and c (cost in $).

c Draw a graph using the data in a.

d Find:

i the cost of three hours' work

ii the hours worked for a charge of $330

4 Use a number plane to graph:

a $y = 3x - 4$

b $y = 3 - x$

5 A line is graphed on the number plane. Complete the table and find the equation of the line.

x	−1	0	1	2	3
y					

$\therefore y =$ ______

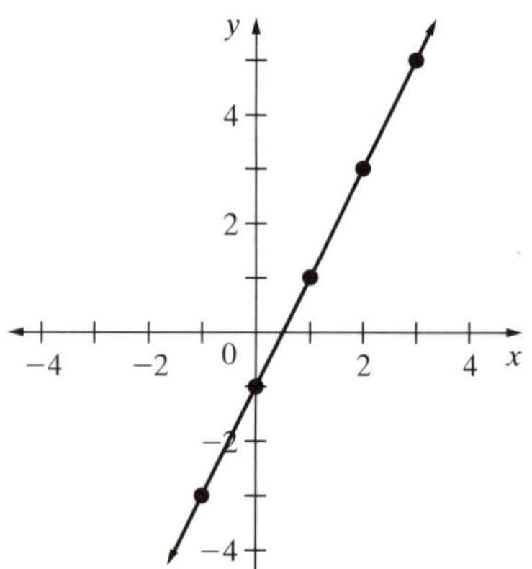

6 a Match the lines to the equations:

i $y = 2x + 3$

ii $y = -x + 3$

iii $y = 2x - 2$

b Find the point of intersection of lines l and n.

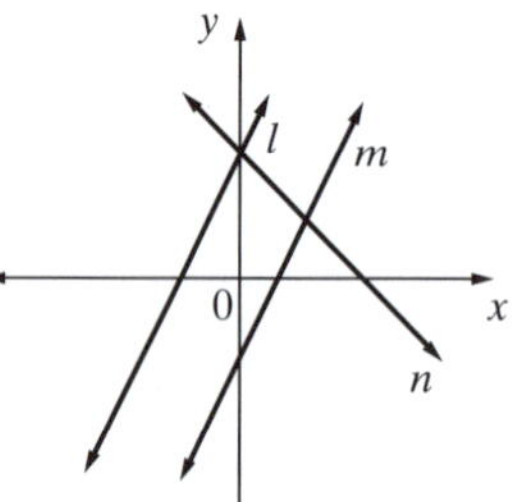

7 On the same number plane, graph $y = 3$ and $x = -2$.

Answers **1 a** 1, 3, 5 **b** 4, 3, 2 **c** 2, 1, 0 **2 a** F **b** T **c** T **d** F **3 a** 50, 130, 210, 290 **b** $c = 50 + 40h$ **c** see worked solutions **d i** $170 **ii** 7 **4** see worked solutions **5** −3, −1, 1, 3, 5; $y = 2x - 1$ **6 a i** l **ii** n **iii** m **b** $(0, 3)$ **7** see worked solutions

COORDINATE GEOMETRY

Linear and Non-linear Relationships

25 MINUTES

INTERMEDIATE TEST

Part A Multiple Choice

1 The line $y = 2 - 3x$ passes through the point X. The coordinates of X could be: *Hint 1*

A $(1, 4)$ B $(-1, 2)$
C $(-2, 1)$ D $(2, -4)$ (1 mark)

2 The point $(-1, 3)$ lies on the line:

A $y = 2x - 1$ B $y = x + 4$
C $y = 4x$ D $y = 3 - x$ (1 mark)

3 The equation of the line l could be: *Hint 2*

A $y = x + 3$ B $y = 3x$
C $y = 1 - 3x$ D $y = -3 - x$

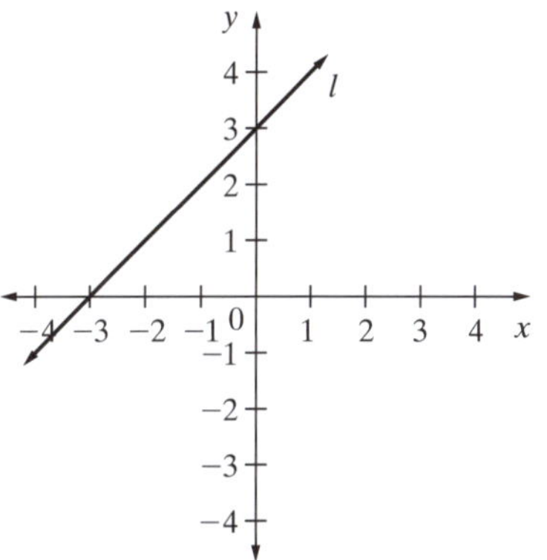

(1 mark)

4 The line $y = 3 - 2x$ passes through the point $(a, 5)$. The value of a is:

A -1 B -2
C 1 D 2 (1 mark)

5 The number plane shows the intersection of two lines. The point of intersection is:

A $(-1, 3)$ B $(1, -3)$
C $(3, -1)$ D $(-3, 1)$

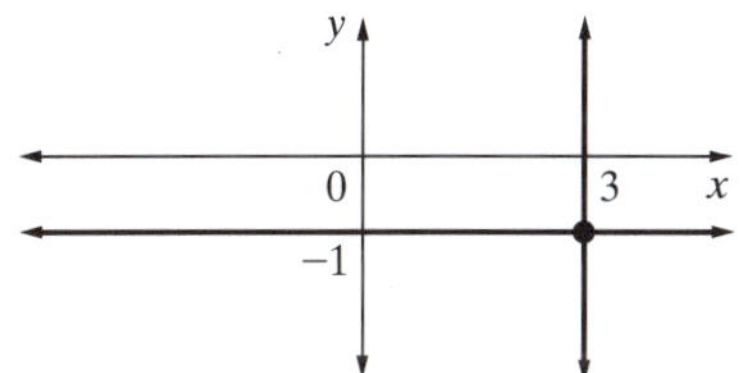

(1 mark)

Hint 1: Substitute the point into the equation.
Hint 2: Substitute $(0, 3)$ into the equation of the line.

Part B Short Answer

6 a Complete this table for $y = 2x - 4$. (1 mark)

x	0	1	2
y			

b Graph the line $y = 2x - 4$. (2 marks)

c Show that $(3, 2)$ lies on the line $y = 2x - 4$. (1 mark)

d If the line cuts the x axis at $(a, 0)$, find the value of a. (1 mark)

7 a On the same number plane, graph $y = x + 2$ and $y = 3x - 4$. (4 marks)

b Find the point of intersection of the two lines. (1 mark)

8 Working as a clown, Krustie charges $40 to appear at a party, plus $20 per hour worked.

a Complete the table linking hours (h) and cost (c). (1 mark)

Hours (h)	0	2	4	6
Cost (c), $				

b Complete the formula:

$c =$ ____________ (1 mark)

c Using a number plane, graph the relationship between cost and hours. (2 marks)

d Mrs Jamieson hired Krustie for her daughter's party and was charged $140. How many hours did Krustie work? (1 mark)

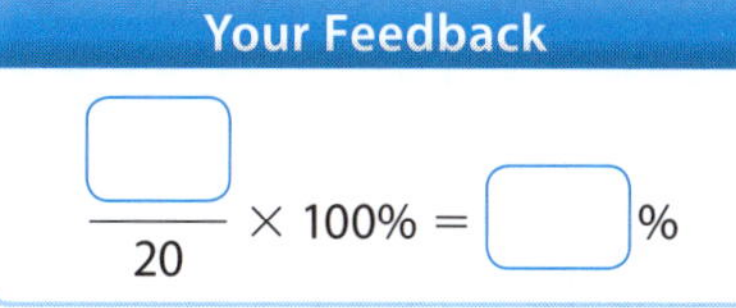

Your Feedback

$\frac{\square}{20} \times 100\% = \square\%$

PAGE 148

PAGE 177

COORDINATE GEOMETRY

Linear and Non-linear Relationships

ADVANCED TEST

1 The position of a table is expressed using the coordinates of its legs. The four legs are at $(-5, -2)$, $(-5, -5)$, $(-2, -5)$ and $(-2, -2)$. If the table is moved 7 units to the right and 6 units up, what are the new coordinates of the legs? (2 marks)

2 Liana is drawing a design with chalk on the footpath. The corners of her design are at $(4, 2)$, $(-1, 5)$ and $(-4, 3)$. If she wants to reflect the design over the x-axis, what are the new coordinates of the corners? (2 marks)

3 Four lines are graphed on the number plane below.

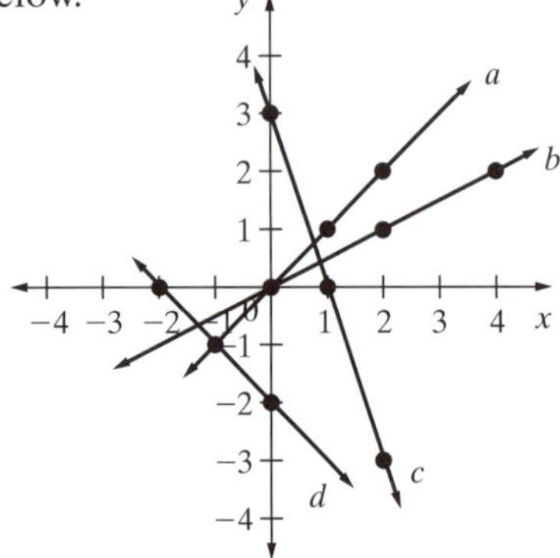

For each line, complete the table and write the equation.

a

x	0	1	2
y			

(2 marks)

b

x	0	2	4
y			

(2 marks)

c

x	0	1	2
y			

(2 marks)

d

x	−2	−1	0
y			

(2 marks)

4 Graph the lines $y = 2x - 1$ and $y = 2 - x$ on the same number plane and use the lines to solve the equation $2x - 1 = 2 - x$. (3 marks)

5 Yang graphs two lines to find the solution of $3x + 2 = x - 5$. If one line has the equation $y = 3x + 2$, write down the equation of the other line. (1 mark)

6 Write down the number of points of intersection of the following pairs of lines with equations:

a $y = 4x - 7$ and $y = 2x + 1$ (1 mark)

b $y = 3$ and $y = 2x - 1$ (1 mark)

c $y = 2x + 3$ and $y = 2x - 5$ (1 mark)

7 A tank contains 1200 litres. A tap is turned on and 40 litres of water escape each minute.

a Complete a table using n = number of minutes and V = volume of water remaining in the tank. (2 marks)

n	0	5	10	15
V	1200			

b Write the formula linking n and V. (1 mark)

c Using the number plane below draw the graph representing the relationship between n and V. (1 mark)

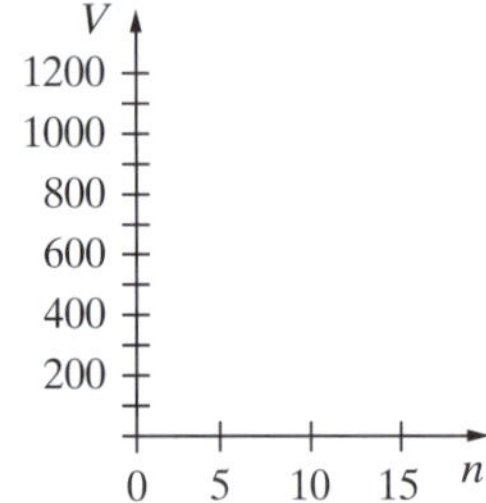

d According to the formula, how much water has escaped in twelve minutes? (1 mark)

8 A new tollway is built. For the first month there is no toll to use the road and each day 4800 vehicles use it. After the first month it is estimated that for each dollar increase in the toll, 800 fewer vehicles will use the tollway.

a Complete the table using c = cost of the toll and v = number of vehicles.

c	0	1	2	3
v	4800			

(2 marks)

b Write a formula linking c and v. (1 mark)

c What is the lowest toll for which no vehicles will use the tollway? (2 marks)

d Draw a graph for the formula. (2 marks)

e The company needs to set the toll at a level that maximises its income. What will be the toll? (2 marks)

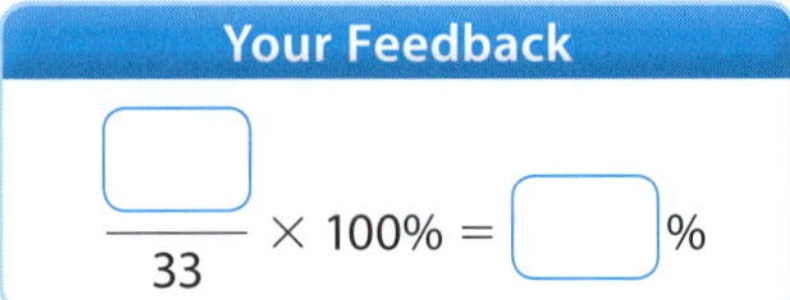

PAGE 149
PAGE 177

LENGTH, AREA AND VOLUME

Using Units of Measurement

STUDY NOTES

1 Units of measurement

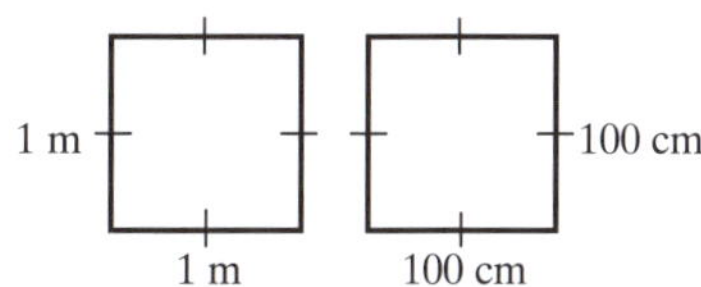

These two squares are identical—the areas of the squares will be the same.

$\therefore$ 1 m^2 = 10 000 cm^2

This approach can be used to find other area and volume relationships.

- 1 m^2 = 1 000 000 mm^2
  1 cm^2 = 100 mm^2 (Also, 1 ha = 10 000 m^2)
- 1 m^3 = 1 000 000 000 mm^3
  1 cm^3 = 1000 mm^3

For example, convert:

a 6 cm^2 = ______ mm^2
$\therefore$ 6 cm^2 = 600 mm^2

b 4.3 ha = ______ m^2
$\therefore$ 4.3 ha = 43 000 m^2

c 5400 mm^3 = ______ cm^3
$\therefore$ 5400 mm^3 = 5.4 cm^3

2 The perimeter is a measure of the distance around a plane shape.

For example, a paddock measures 86 m by 42 m. What is the cost of fencing the paddock at \$3.40/m?

$\therefore$ Perimeter = 2(length + breadth)
= $2(l + b)$
= 2(86 + 42)
= 256

$\therefore$ perimeter is 256 m

Cost = 3.40 × 256
= 870.40

$\therefore$ the fencing costs \$870.40

3 The area is a measure of space inside a plane shape.

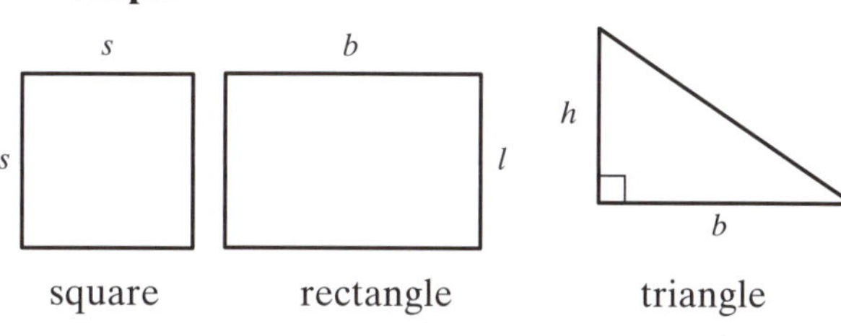

square $A = s^2$ — rectangle $A = lb$ — triangle $A = \frac{1}{2}bh$

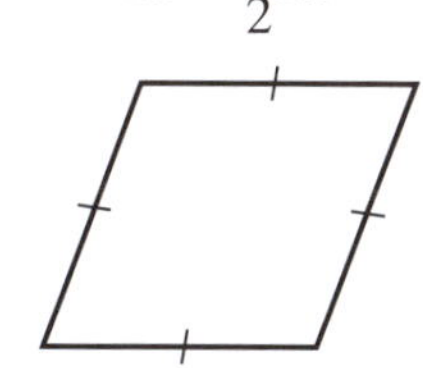

parallelogram $A = bh$ — trapezium $A = \frac{1}{2}h(a + b)$ — rhombus/kite $A = \frac{1}{2} \times$ product of diagonals

For example, find the area of a kite with diagonals 8 cm and 5 cm.

Area $= \frac{1}{2} \times$ product of diagonals
$= \frac{1}{2} \times 8 \times 5$
= 20 $\therefore$ area is 20 cm^2

4 The volume of a solid shape is a measure of space inside the solid. The volume of a prism is found by multiplying the area of its base by its height, i.e. $V = Ah$

Rectangular prism

$V = Ah$

$\therefore V = lbh$

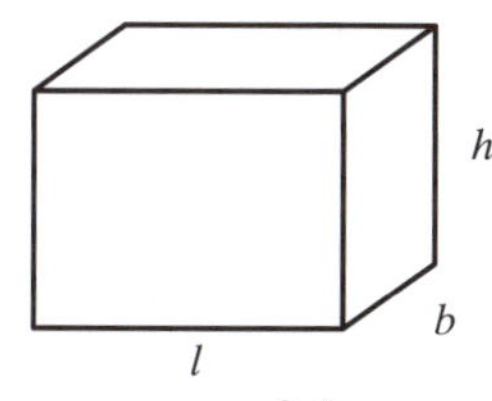

5 The capacity of a solid is a measure of the volume it will hold. The litre (L) is the basic unit of capacity, where 1 cm^3 = 1 mL (and 1 m^3 = 1 kL)

Checklist

Can you:

1 *Convert between different units used in area and volume?* ☐
2 *Use formulae to find area of quadrilaterals?* ☐
3 *Solve problems involving area, volume and capacity?* ☐

LENGTH, AREA AND VOLUME

Using Units of Measurement

SKILLS CHECK

1 Convert:

a 4.72 m = _______ mm

b 3.86 cm = _______ mm

c 264 cm = _______ m

2 Convert:

a 300 mm^2 = _______ cm^2

b 90 000 cm^2 = _______ m^2

c 5.3 m^2 = _______ cm^2

d 900 cm^2 = _______ m^2

e 2 000 000 m^2 = _____ km^2

f 0.5 m^2 = _______ mm^2

3 Convert:

a 3 ha = _______ m^2

b 65 000 m^2 = _______ ha

c 0.078 ha = _______ m^2

4 Convert:

a 7000 mm^3 = _______ cm^3

b 60 000 000 cm^3 = _____ m^3

5 The perimeter of a rectangle is 48 cm. If the length is 18 cm, what is the width?

6 Find the area:

a

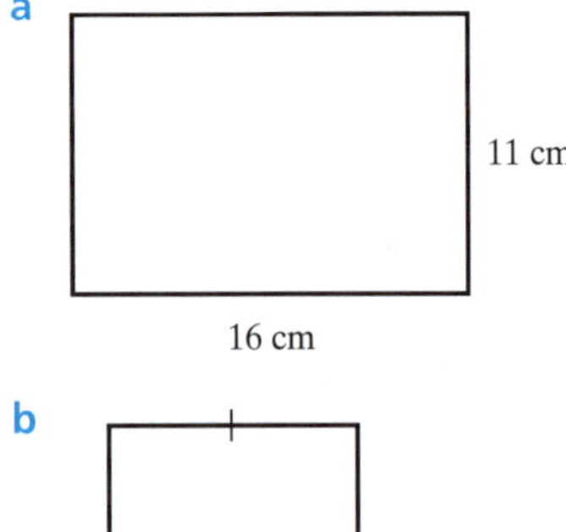

b

12.2 cm

c

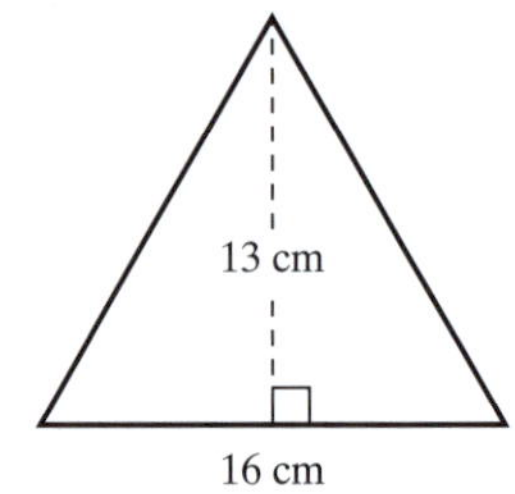

d

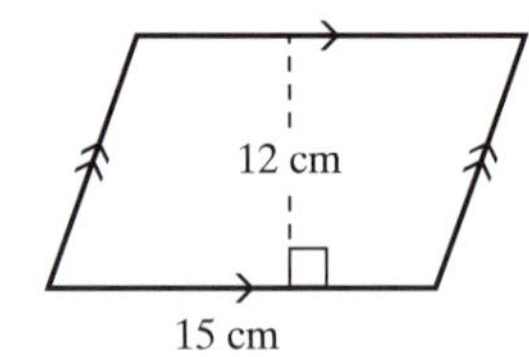

e

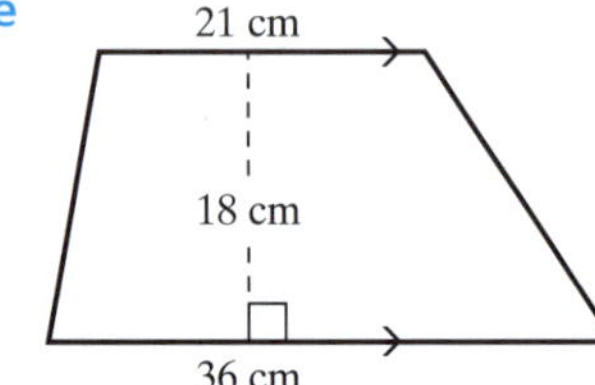

f

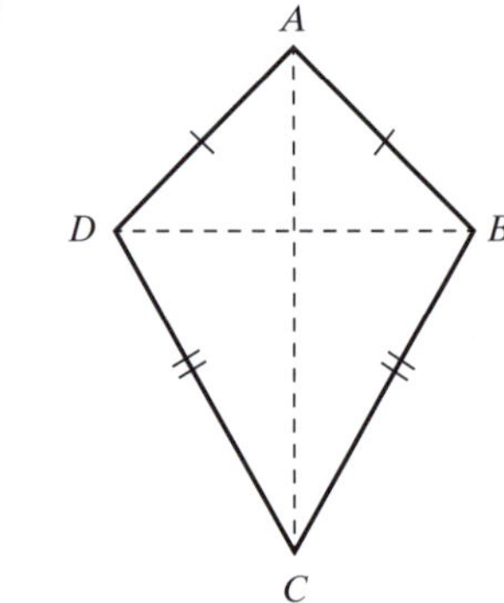

AC = 18 cm
BD = 14 cm

g

P Q S R

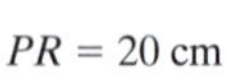

PR = 20 cm
QS = 24 cm

7 Find the volume:

a

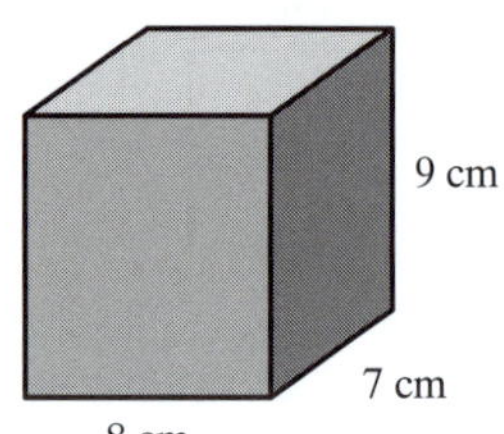

b

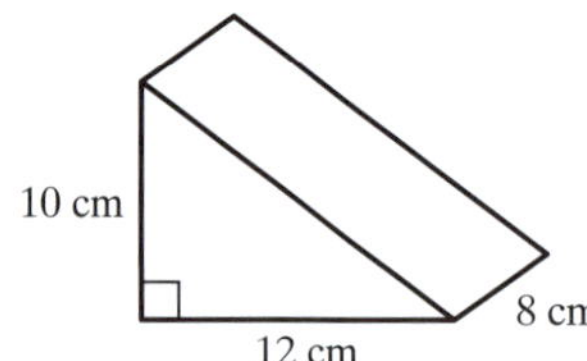

c

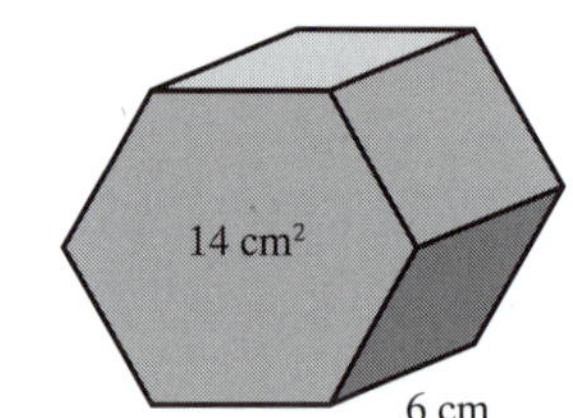

d

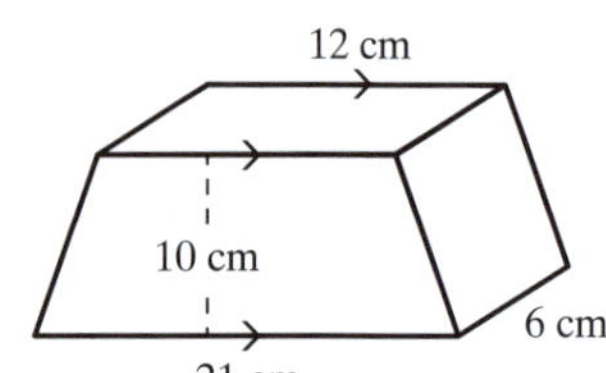

8 Find the capacity of a rectangular prism with dimensions 65 cm by 45 cm by 40 cm.

Give your answer in litres, using 1000 cm^3 = 1000 mL.

PAGE 151

Answers **1 a** 4720 **b** 38.6 **c** 2.64 **2 a** 3 **b** 9 **c** 53 000 **d** 0.09 **e** 2 **f** 500 000 **3 a** 30 000 **b** 6.5 **c** 780
4 a 7 **b** 60 **5** 6 cm **6 a** 176 cm^2 **b** 148.84 cm^2 **c** 104 cm^2 **d** 180 cm^2 **e** 513 cm^2 **f** 126 cm^2 **g** 240 cm^2
7 a 504 cm^3 **b** 480 cm^3 **c** 84 cm^3 **d** 990 cm^3 **8** 117 L

LENGTH, AREA AND VOLUME

Using Units of Measurement

25 MINUTES

INTERMEDIATE TEST

Part A Multiple Choice

1 What is the area in square centimetres of the rectangle? *Hint 1*

A 12 **B** 1200

C 12 000 **D** 120 000

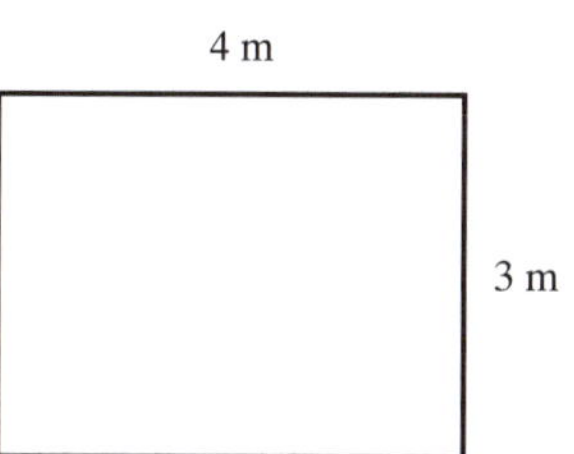

(1 mark)

2 Which of these expressions could be used to find the area of the trapezium?

A $\frac{1}{2} \times 6(5 + 4)$ **B** $\frac{1}{2} \times 4(6 + 3)$

C $\frac{1}{2} \times 5(6 + 3)$ **D** $\frac{1}{2} \times 3(5 + 4)$

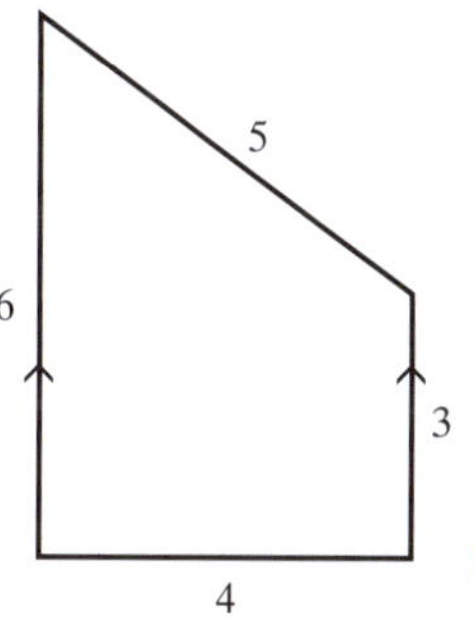

(1 mark)

3 What is the perimeter of this shape?

A 18 cm **B** 20 cm

C 22 cm **D** 30 cm

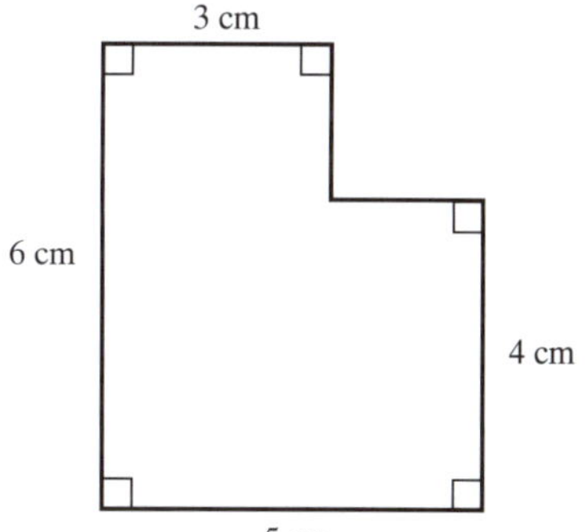

(1 mark)

4 The area of a block of land is 6 hectares. What is this area in square metres?

A 60 000 m^2 **B** 6 000 m^2 **C** 600 m^2 **D** 60 m^2 (1 mark)

5 What is the area of this shape?

A 28 cm^2 **B** 48 cm^2

C 96 cm^2 **D** 120 cm^2

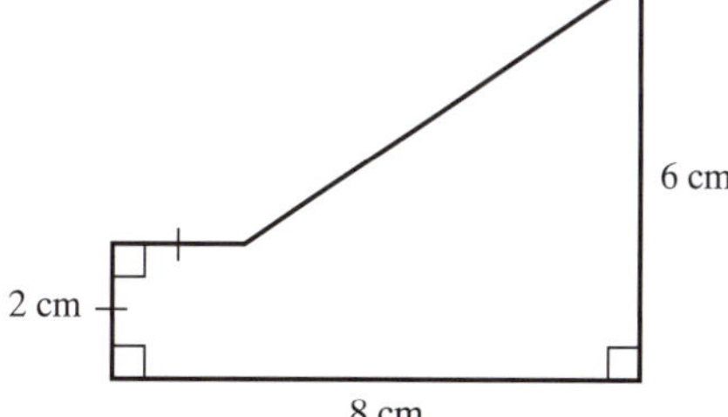

(1 mark)

6 The capacity of the rectangular prism is 24 L. What is the value of h? *Hint 2*

A 10 cm **B** 30 cm

C 40 cm **D** 60 cm

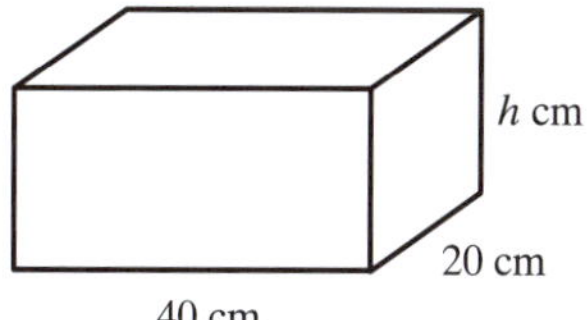

(1 mark)

(Cont.)

Part B Short Answer

7 Find the area of these shapes:

a
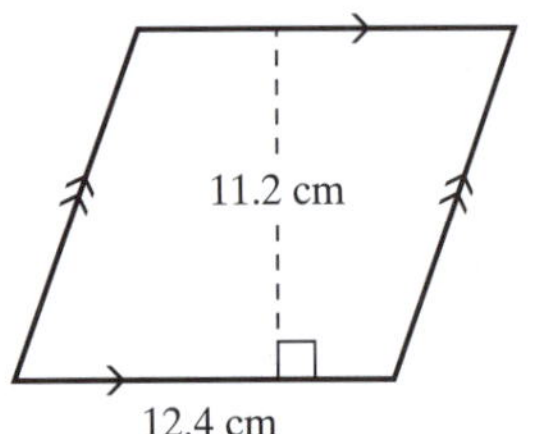

b
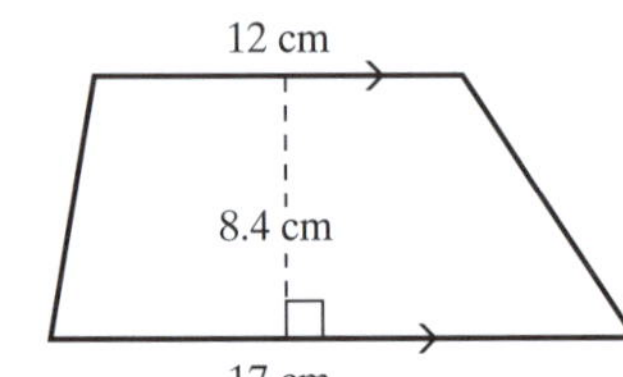

c
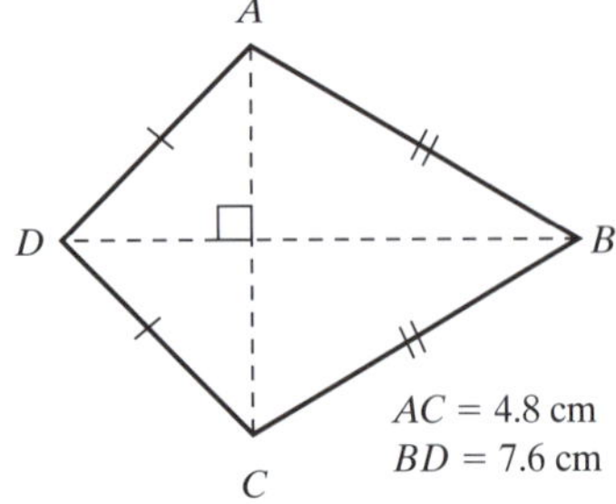

d
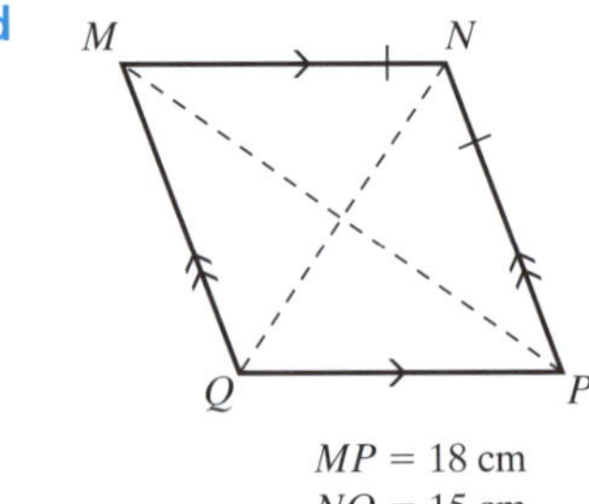

(2 marks each)

8 Jo is digging a garden which measures 6.8 m by 4.5 m.

a How much will edging cost at \$2.60/m?

b Find the cost of fertilising at 70 c/m^2.

c If the garden is dug to a depth of 20 cm, find the volume of the garden. (2 marks each)

9 A rectangle has a perimeter of 28 cm and an area of 48 cm^2. Another shape is formed by joining the midpoints of each side.

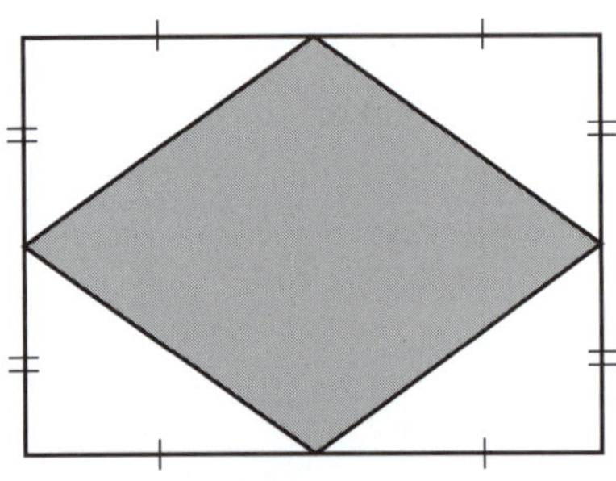

a Find the dimensions of the rectangle. (1 mark)

b Find the area of each of the triangles. (1 mark)

c What is the area of the shaded region? (1 mark)

Hint 1: Use 1 m^2 = 10 000 cm^2
Hint 2: Use 1 cm^3 = 1 mL

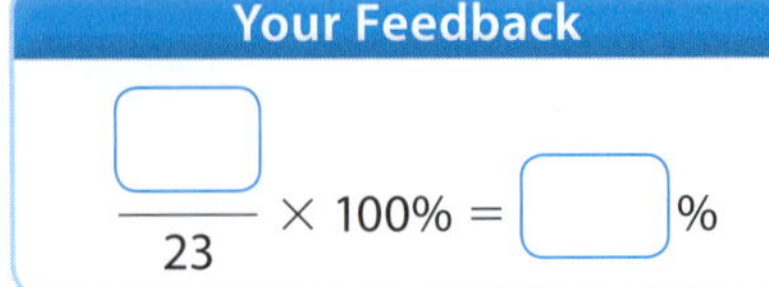

LENGTH, AREA AND VOLUME

Using Units of Measurement

ADVANCED TEST

1 A rectangular paddock is twice as long as it is wide. It is to be fenced using four lengths of wire. A 400-metre roll of wire costs $105. If the length of the paddock is 120 metres, find the:

a perimeter of the paddock (2 marks)

b cost of the wire to complete the fence (2 marks)

2 A 60 cm by 40 cm photograph is to be mounted on a piece of cardboard and framed. When completed, there will be a 4 cm border around the photograph. What length of framing timber is required? (2 marks)

3 Find the area of a:

a rhombus with diagonals 45 cm and 0.1 m (2 marks)

b trapezium with parallel sides 12 cm and 18 cm and perpendicular height of 9.2 cm (2 marks)

c kite with diagonals $\frac{4}{5}$ cm and $1\frac{1}{2}$ cm (2 marks)

d rectangle with base length 1.5 m and perpendicular height of 97 mm (2 marks)

e parallelogram with both diagonals 16 cm (2 marks)

4 Find the perpendicular height of a trapezium with an area of 68 cm^2 and parallel sides of 9 cm and 11 cm. (2 marks)

5 Convert:

a 3.6 cm^2 to mm^2 (1 mark)

b 430 cm^2 to m^2 (1 mark)

c 183 mm^3 to cm^3 (1 mark)

d 5300 cm^3 to m^3 (1 mark)

6 A triangular prism has a base length of 50 cm and a perpendicular height of 40 cm. The prism is 1.2 metres in length. Find the capacity of the prism in litres. (2 marks)

7 The area of one face of a rectangular prism is 60 cm^2 and the area of another is 80 cm^2. If one edge of the prism is 10 cm, find the:

a area of the other faces (2 marks)

b capacity of the prism (1 mark)

8 The length of the diagonals in a square is $\sqrt{18}$ cm. What is the perimeter of the square? (3 marks)

9 A glass vase is in the shape of a square-based prism. When 180 mL of water is poured into the vase, the depth of water is 5 cm.

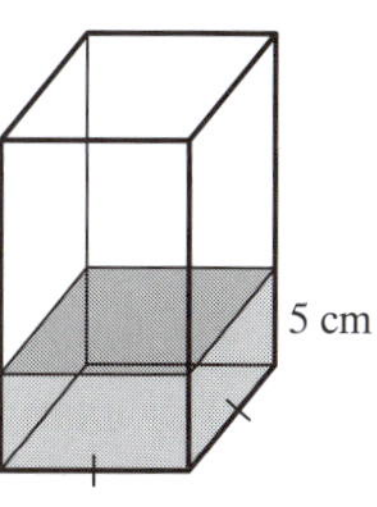

It takes another 900 mL to completely fill the vase, what are the dimensions of the vase? (3 marks)

10 During a flood, 3.5 hectares of land was covered by 25 cm of water. Find the volume of water, in kilolitres. (2 marks)

11 A rectangular-shaped swimming pool has a length of 8 metres and a width of 4 metres. The depth of the pool at one end is 1.4 metres and at the other end 2.2 metres. What is the capacity of the pool in kilolitres? (2 marks)

12 Find the area of the shape: (2 marks)

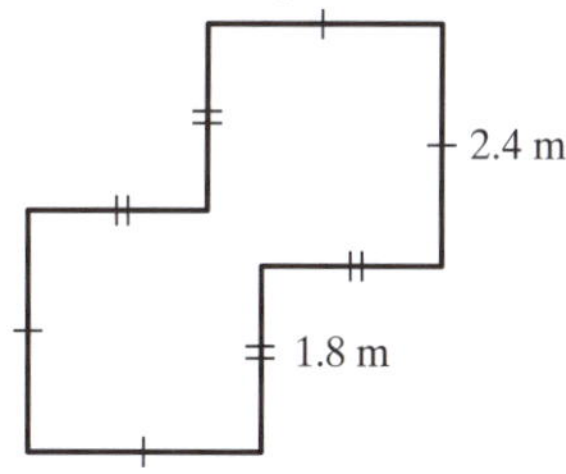

13 Two solids have the same volume. Solid A is a cube with side length 24 cm. Solid B is a square-based prism with a length of 54 cm and width and height are the same size. How high is Solid B? (2 marks)

14 The diagram shows a shape comprised of a trapezium on top of a rectangle. The area of the rectangle is 96 cm^2.

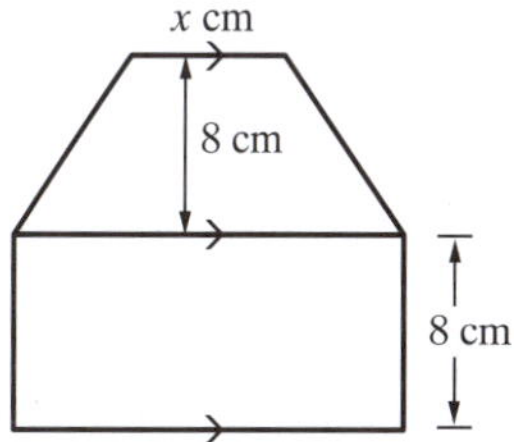

If the area of the trapezium is 40% of the entire shape, find the value of x. (3 marks)

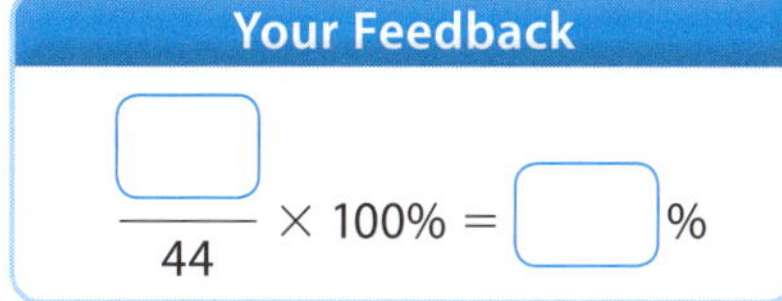

PAGE 152
PAGE 177

CIRCLES AND CYLINDERS

Using Units of Measurement

STUDY NOTES

1 The perimeter of a circle is called the **circumference**.

2 In any circle, the **ratio of the circumference to the diameter is equal to pi (π)**, or $\pi = \dfrac{\text{circumference}}{\text{diameter}}$

3 Pi (π) is an **irrational number,** and is **approximately equal** to 3.142.

4 To find the **circumference**, we use $C = 2\pi r$, or $C = \pi d$ (use the exact value of π in the calculator).
For example, find the circumference, correct to 2 decimal places:

a

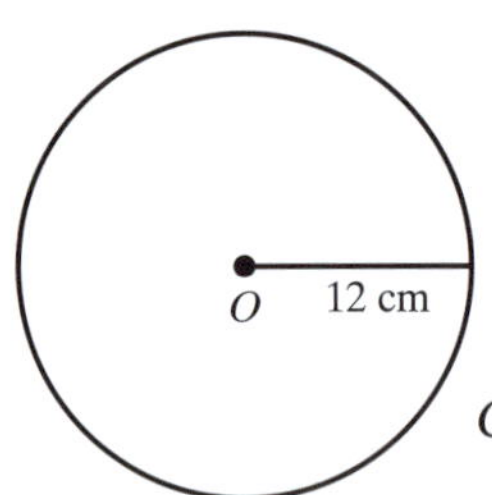

$C = 2 \times \pi \times 12$
$= 75.40$ [2 decimal places]
$\therefore$ circumference is 75.40 cm

b

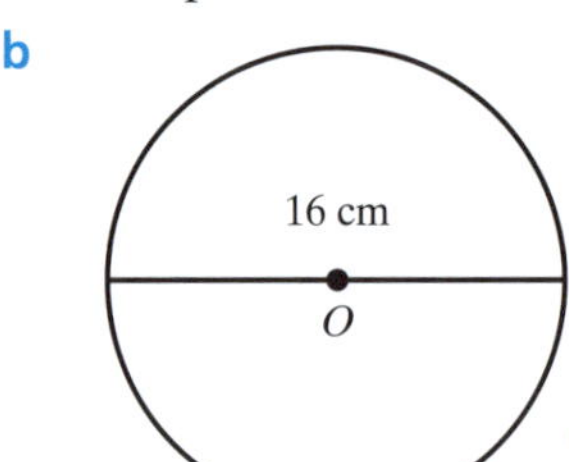

$C = 2 \times \pi \times 8$
$= 50.27$ [2 decimal places]
$\therefore$ circumference is 50.27 cm

5 The **area of a circle** is found using $A = \pi r^2$.
For example, find the area, leaving your answer in terms of π:

a

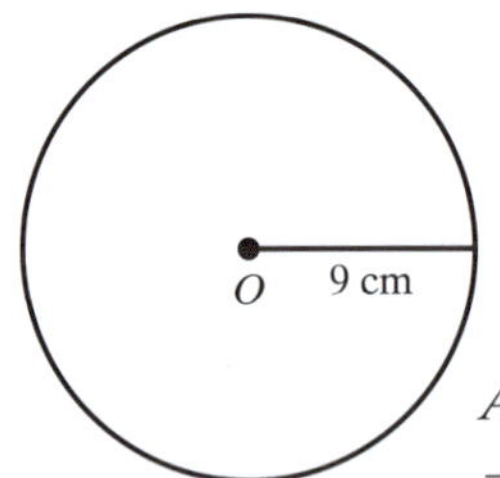

$A = \pi \times 9^2$
$= 81\pi$ $\quad\therefore$ area is 81π cm^2

b

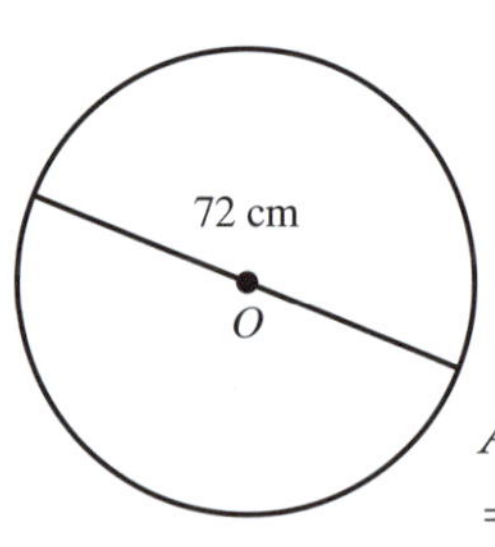

$A = \pi \times 36^2$
$= 1296\pi$ $\quad\therefore$ area is 1296π cm^2

6 The **radius of a circle** can be found if we know the circle's circumference or area.
For example, find the length of the radius, correct to 1 decimal place, if the area is 30 cm^2.

Area = 30 cm^2

$\therefore A = \pi r^2$
$\therefore 30 = \pi r^2$
$r = \sqrt{\dfrac{30}{\pi}}$
$= 3.1$ [1 decimal place] i.e. radius of 3.1 cm

7 The **volume of a cylinder** is found using $V = \pi r^2 h$
For example, find the volume of the cylinder in terms of π.
radius = 6 cm
i.e. $V = \pi \times 6^2 \times 8$
$= 288\pi$ $\quad\therefore$ volume is 288π cm^3

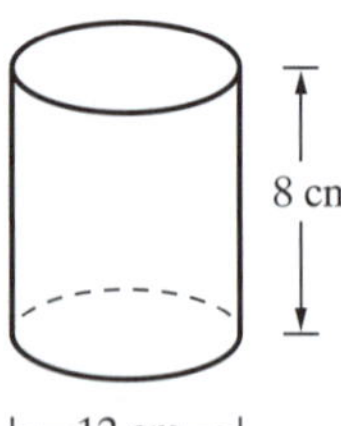
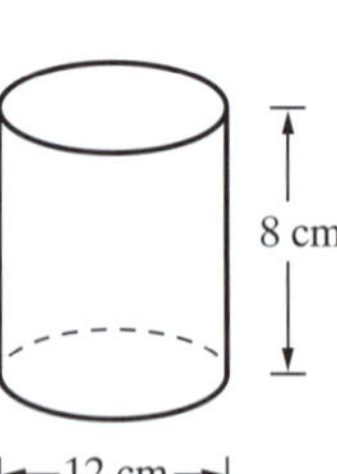

Checklist

Can you:

1 *Calculate the circumference and area of a circle?* ☐
2 *Find the radius of a circle if the area or circumference is known?* ☐
3 *Find the volume of a cylinder?* ☐

CIRCLES AND CYLINDERS

Using Units of Measurement

SKILLS CHECK

1 Find the circumference, correct to 2 decimal places, of the circle with:

a radius of 4 cm　　b diameter = 10 cm　　c radius 3.7 mm

d diameter of 2.5 cm　　e radius = $3\frac{1}{2}$ mm　　f diameter of 320 cm

2 Find the area, in terms of π, of a circle with:

a diameter 12 cm　　b radius 5 m　　c diameter 7 cm

d radius = 1 m　　e diameter = $\frac{4}{5}$ mm　　f radius = $1\frac{1}{8}$ cm

3 Find the volume, correct to 3 decimal places, of the cylinder with:

a radius 4 cm and height 8 cm　　b diameter 4 cm and height 8 cm

c radius = 8 cm, height = 5 cm　　d diameter = 18 cm, height = 4.5 cm

4 Find the area, to the nearest whole number:

a

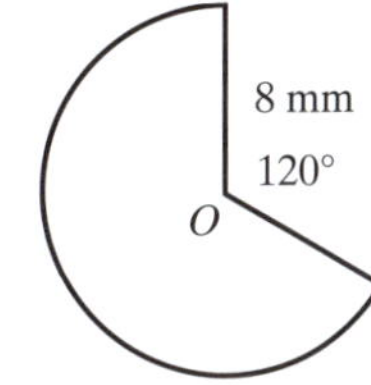

b

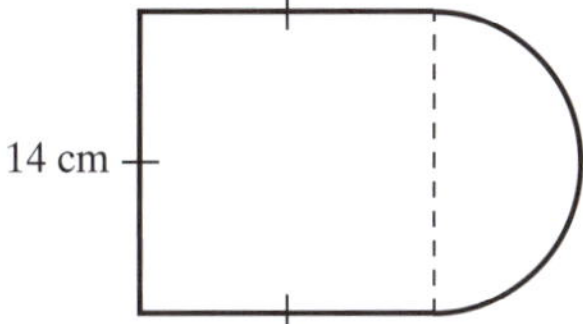

5 Find the volume, correct to 2 decimal places:

a

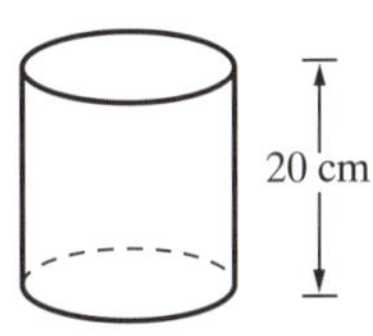

b

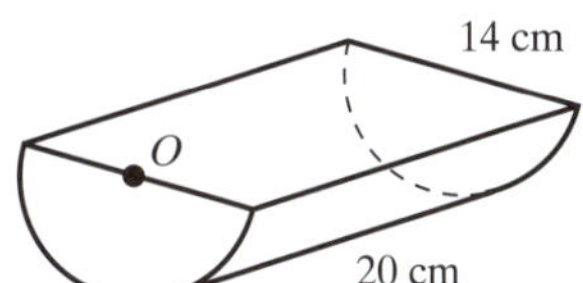

6 Find the capacity of a cylinder with diameter 12 cm and height 18 cm to the nearest millilitre.

7 Find the radius, correct to 1 decimal place, if a circle has:

a a circumference of 16 cm　　b an area of 14 cm^2

8 Find the perimeter in terms of π:

a

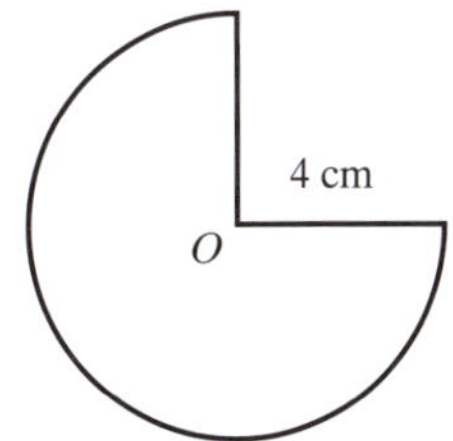

b

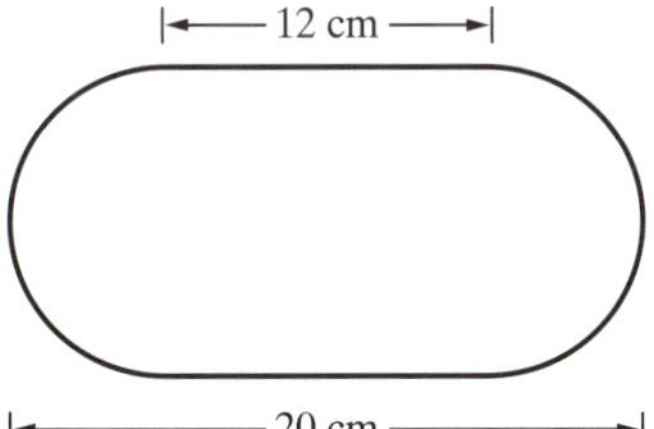

Answers 1 a 25.13 cm b 31.42 cm c 23.25 mm d 7.85 cm e 21.99 mm f 1005.31 cm 2 a 36π cm^2 b 25π m^2 c $\frac{49\pi}{4}$ cm^2 d π m^2 e $\frac{4\pi}{25}$ mm^2 f $\frac{81\pi}{64}$ cm^2 3 a 402.124 cm^3 b 100.531 cm^3 c 1005.310 cm^3 d 1145.111 cm^3 4 a 134 mm^2 b 273 cm^2 5 a 3534.29 cm^3 b 1539.38 cm^3 6 2036 mL 7 a 2.5 cm b 2.1 cm 8 a $(8 + 6\pi)$ cm b $(24 + 8\pi)$ cm

CIRCLES AND CYLINDERS

Using Units of Measurement

25 MINUTES

INTERMEDIATE TEST

Part A Multiple Choice

1 A wheel has a radius of 10 cm. How far will it travel after 50 revolutions, to the nearest metre?

A 31 m B 157 m C 314 m D 16 m (1 mark)

2 $OA = 4$ cm and $OB = 8$ cm. O is centre of circle.
The area of the shaded region is:

A 2π cm^2 B 4π cm^2
C 8π cm^2 D 48π cm^2

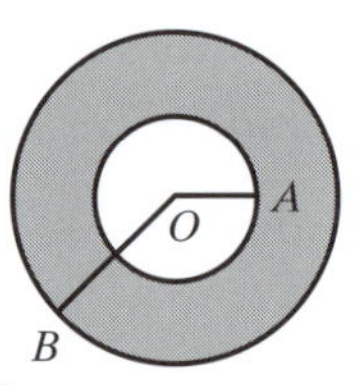

(1 mark)

3 The circumference of a circle with an area of π cm^2 is:

A π cm B π^2 cm C 2π cm D $2\pi^2$ cm (1 mark)

4 The perimeter of the semi-circle is closest to:

A 15.7 mm B 31.4 mm
C 25.7 mm D 41.4 mm

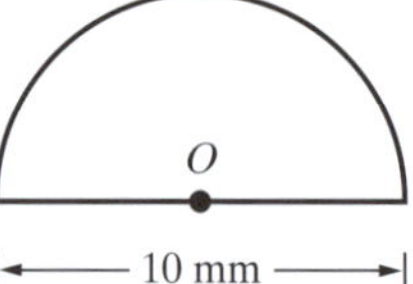

(1 mark)

Part B Short Answer

5 Tess cycles around the track shown.

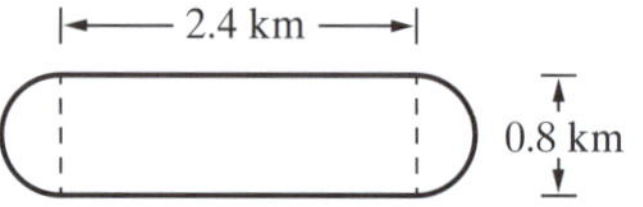

a Find the distance travelled in one lap, to the nearest metre. (2 marks)

b How many complete laps would be required for the cyclist to travel 100 km? (1 mark)

6 Find the area, correct to 2 decimal places:

a *Hint 1*

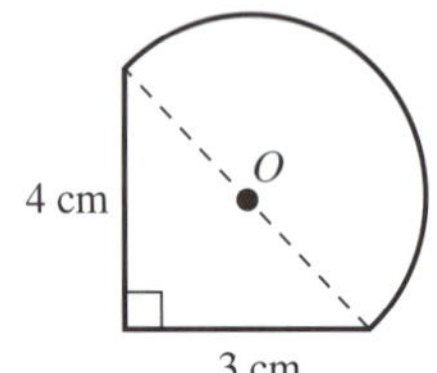

b

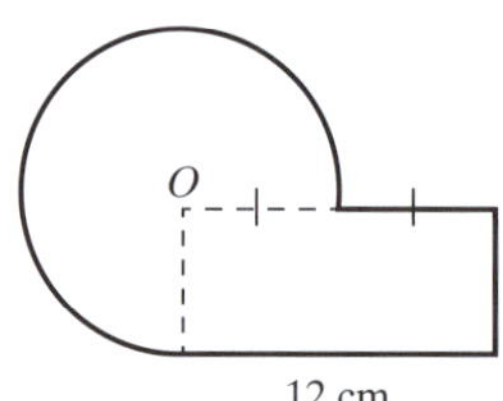

(6 marks)

7 Find the volume, to the nearest cubic centimetre:

a

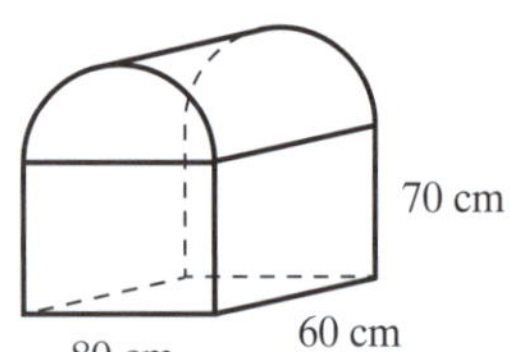

b

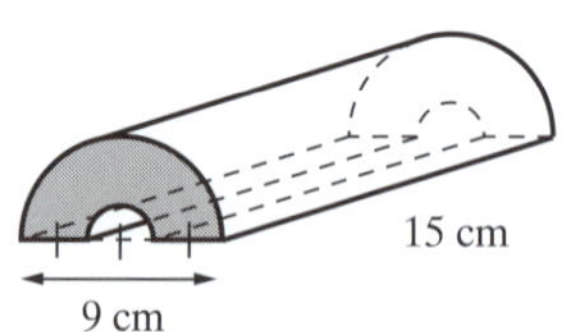

(4 marks)

8 Find the capacity, in litres, of a cylindrical water tank, with radius 1.2 m and height 2 m. *Hint 2* (2 marks)

Hint 1: Use Pythagoras' theorem to find the diameter. (see page 70)
Hint 2: Use 1 m^3 = 1000 L.

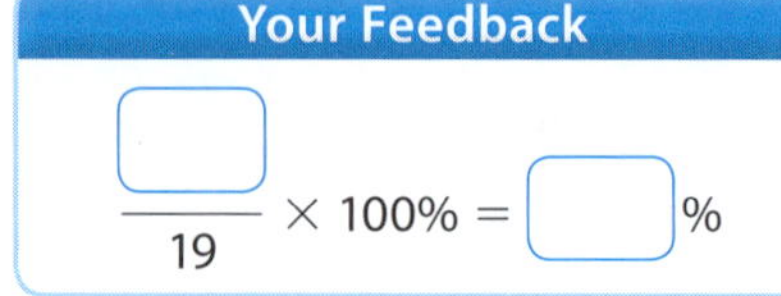

PAGE 154
PAGE 177

CIRCLES AND CYLINDERS

Using Units of Measurement

ADVANCED TEST

1 Liam runs the inside lane of a circular track with a diameter of 82 metres. Ciaran runs in the outside lane which is 6 metres further from the centre of the track. In one lap, how much further does Ciaran run than Liam, to the nearest metre? (3 marks)

2 A penny-farthing bike is built with a front wheel radius of 0.75 m and a rear wheel diameter of 0.35 m. If the bike travels one kilometre, how many more revolutions of the rear wheel than the front wheel occur, to the nearest hundred? (3 marks)

3 Find the area of a circle with circumference:

a 28 cm, to two decimal places. (2 marks)

b 16π cm, in terms of π. (2 marks)

4 The diagram shows a circle inside a square of side 12 cm. What percentage of the area of the square is covered by the circle, to 2 decimal places? (3 marks)

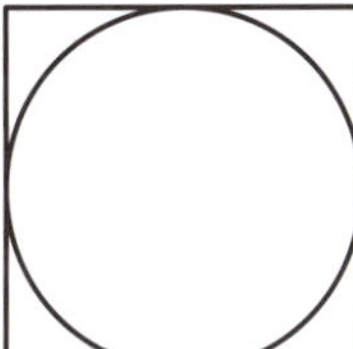

5 The circumferences of the two circles are 8π cm and 12π cm.

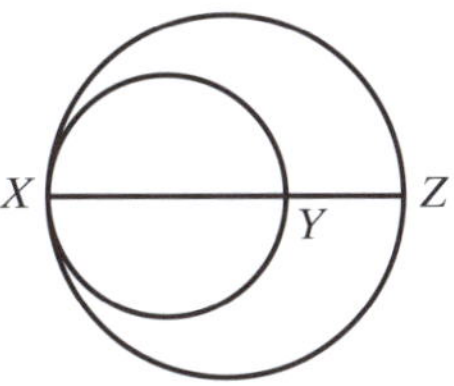

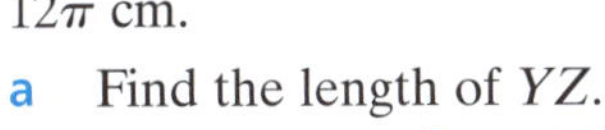

a Find the length of YZ. (2 marks)

b Find the area of the larger circle not covered by the smaller circle in terms of π. (2 marks)

6 Find the perimeter and area, leaving your answer to 2 decimal places:

a

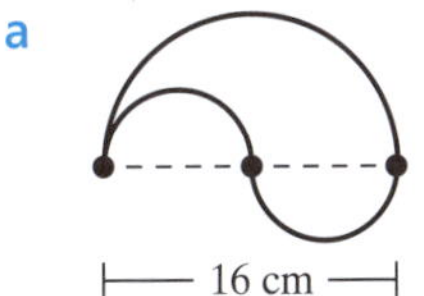

b

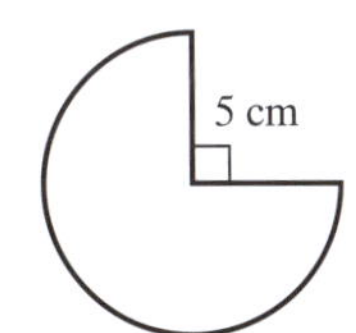

(2 marks each)

7 Four semi-circles are cut from a square. Another semi-circle is joined to the shape. Find the area of the figure.

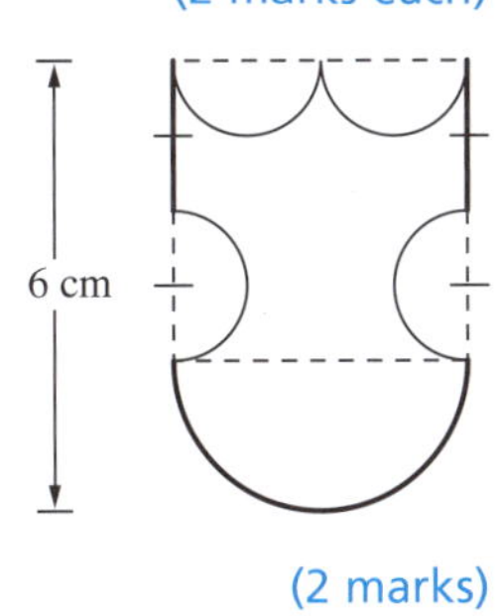

(2 marks)

8 A cylinder has a capacity of 5 litres. If the diameter is 20 cm, what is the height, to the nearest centimetre? (2 marks)

9 A cube with side 12 cm is filled with water. If all the water is then tipped into a cylinder with diameter 12 cm, what is the depth of water? Give your answer to the nearest centimetre. (2 marks)

10 The kite $ABCD$ lies on the circle with centre O. If $DB = 8$ cm and the area of the kite is 48 cm^2, find the area of the shaded region, to the nearest square centimetre.

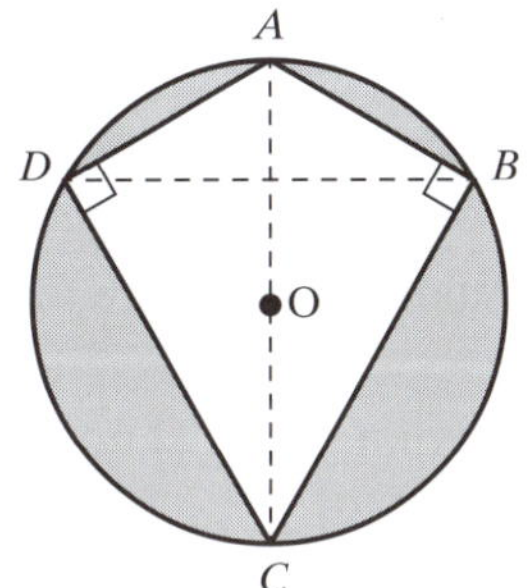

(3 marks)

11 Find the volume, correct to two decimal places.

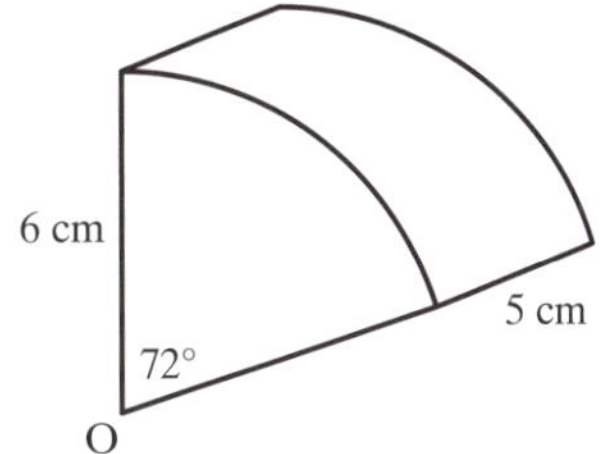

(2 marks)

12 A circular swimming pool has a diameter of 6.4 metres. It is filled with water to a depth of 1.4 metres. The pool has a deck surrounding the pool of width 1.8 m. Find, to 2 decimal places:

a the volume of water in the pool (2 marks)

b the area of the deck (2 marks)

13 Six identical ice cubes of side length 4 cm are placed in a cylindrical glass of diameter 8 cm. What will be the depth of water in the glass after the cubes melt, to the nearest centimetre? (3 marks)

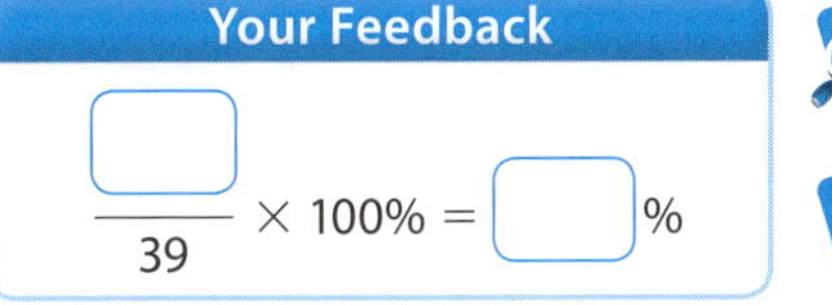

PAGE 155
PAGE 177

TIME AND PYTHAGORAS' THEOREM

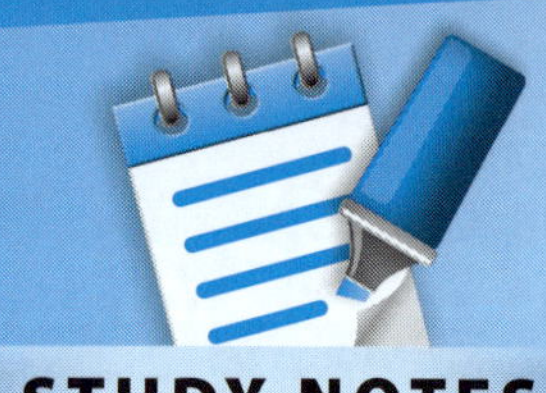

Using Units of Measurement

STUDY NOTES

1 **12-hour and 24-hour time**

Times expressed as 'am' and 'pm' are in **12-hour time**. For 24-hour time, four digits are used, with midnight being 0000.

For example:

a Change to 24-hour time

- **i** 7:42 am ∴ 0742
- **ii** 4:37 pm ∴ 1637

b Change to 12-hour time

- **i** 1347 ∴ 1:47 pm
- **ii** 0200 ∴ 2:00 am

2 **Calculations involving time**

Care needs to be taken—remember 60 s in one minute, and 60 min in one hour.

For example, find the sum of 3 h 24 min and 2 h 48 min.

i.e. 3 h 24 min + 2 h 48 min = 5 h 72 min
[but 72 min = 1 h 12 min]
= 6 h 12 min

∴ the sum is 6 h 12 min

[Calculators with a (DMS) button can be used when calculating h, min and s. Although designed for degrees, minutes and seconds, the example above:
3 (DMS) 24 + 2 (DMS) 48 = 6°12′]

3 **Time zones**

The earth is divided into time zones. These are either ahead, or behind, **GMT (Greenwich Mean Time)**.

For example, Sydney is 7 hours ahead of Baghdad. If it is 4 am Wednesday in Sydney, what time is it in Baghdad?

i.e. 4 am minus 7 hours = 9 pm previous day
∴ local time in Baghdad is 9 pm Tuesday

4 In a right-angled triangle (**right triangle**), the side opposite the right angle (which is always the longest side) is called the **hypotenuse**.

5 **Pythagoras' theorem** states: in any right triangle, the square of the hypotenuse equals the sum of the squares of the other two sides.

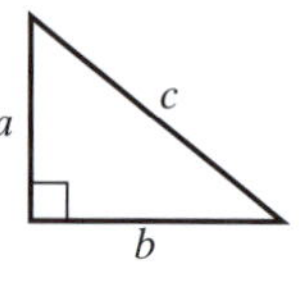

This can be summarised as $c^2 = a^2 + b^2$ (see diagram above).

6 Have a look at this example. Decide whether a triangle with sides of 6 cm, 8 cm and 10 cm is a right triangle. Justify your answer.

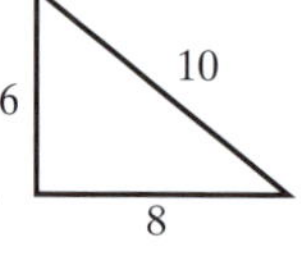

If it is a right triangle then

$10^2 = 6^2 + 8^2$

$100 = 36 + 64$

∴ The triangle is a right triangle as Pythagoras' theorem holds.

7 A **Pythagorean triad** is a set of numbers that would represent the sides of a right triangle.

For example: is {3, 4, 5} a Pythagorean triad? Justify your answer.

If Pythagorean then $5^2 = 3^2 + 4^2$

$25 = 9 + 16$

∴ {3, 4, 5} is a Pythagorean triad as Pythagoras' theorem is satisfied.

8 Pythagoras' theorem can be used to find the **length of the hypotenuse.**

For example: find the value of x in the diagram below, leaving your answer as a surd.

$x^2 = 7^2 + 10^2$
$= 49 + 100$
$= 149$
∴

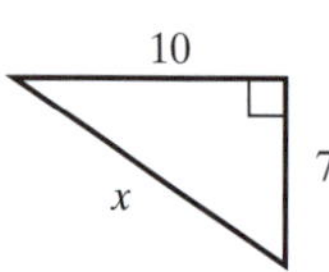

9 To find the **length of one of the shorter sides,** Pythagoras' theorem is used in a different form.

For example: find the value of x in the diagram below, leaving your answer as a surd.

$9^2 = x^2 + 5^2$, so

$x^2 = 9^2 - 5^2$
$= 81 - 25$
$= 56$

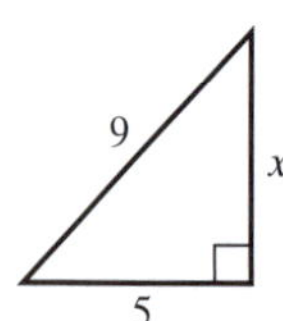

Checklist

Can you:

1. *Solve problems using 12- and 24-hour times and involving international time zones?* ☐
2. *Apply Pythagoras' theorem to solve problems?* ☐

TIME AND PYTHAGORAS' THEOREM

Using Units of Measurement

SKILLS CHECK

1 Convert to 12-hour time:

a 0920 b 2120 c 2355

2 Convert to 24-hour time:

a 6:40 am b 12:50 pm c 12:50 am

3 The table shows the present local times in four cities.
This afternoon, when it is 2:15 pm in Adelaide, find the local time in:

a Perth b Auckland

City	Local time
Auckland	12:40 pm
Sydney	10:40 am
Adelaide	10:10 am
Perth	8:40 am

4 New York is 15 hours behind Newcastle.
If it is 4:30 pm Monday in New York, what is the local time in Newcastle?

5 Decide whether the following are Pythagorean triads:

a {2, 3, 4} b {5, 12, 13} c {9, 12, 15}

6 For $\triangle ABC$, $AB = 8$ cm, $BC = 15$ cm, $AC = 17$ cm, is $\triangle ABC$ right-angled? Justify your answer.

7 Find the value of x, leaving your answer as a surd.

a
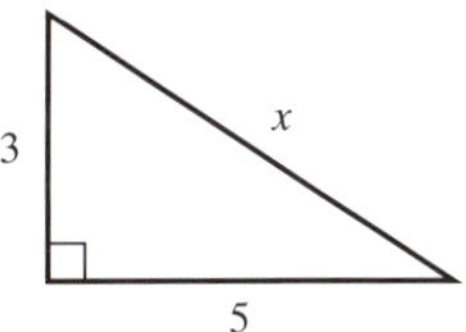

b
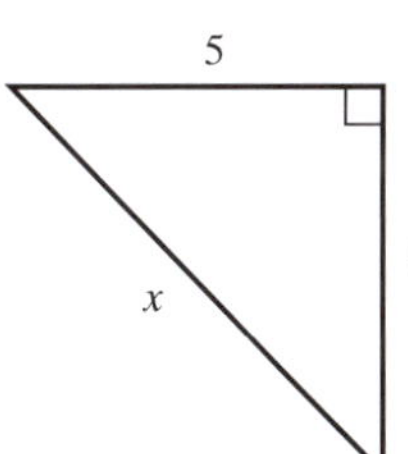

c
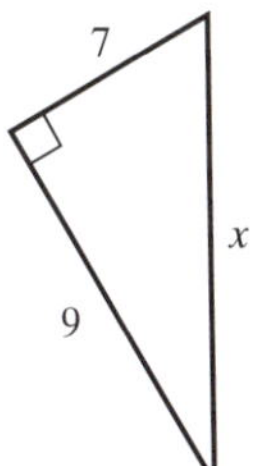

8 Find the value of the pronumeral, correct to 2 decimal places.

a
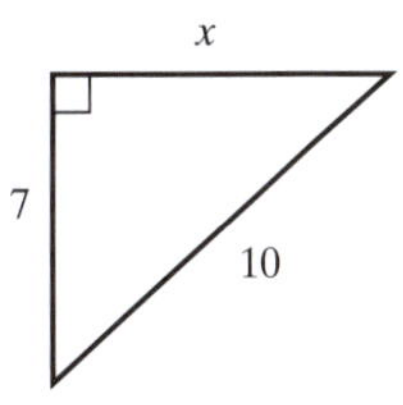

b
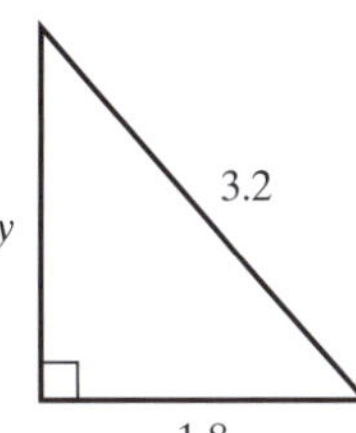

c
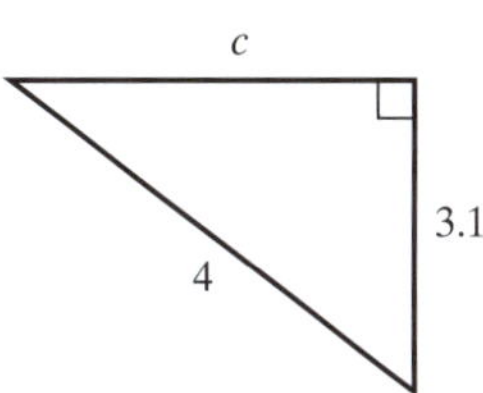

9 Find the length of the diagonal of a rectangle measuring 12 cm by 16 cm.

10 Find the perimeter of the following, correct to 3 decimal places.

a
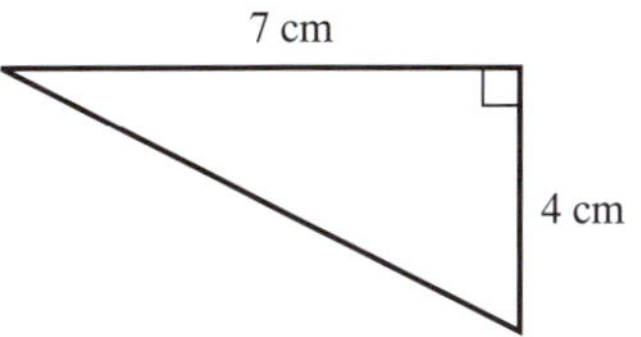

b
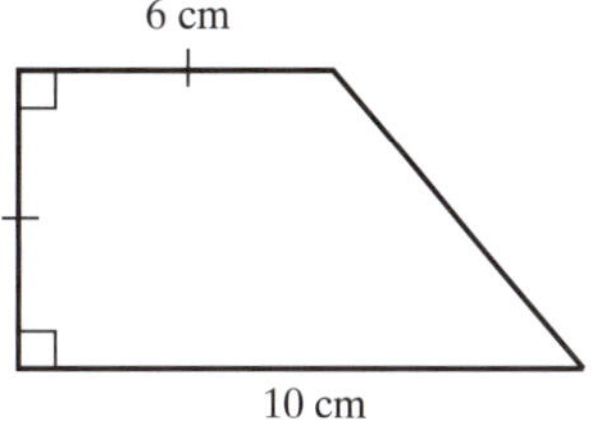

PAGE 156

Answers 1 a 9:20 am b 9:20 pm c 11:55 pm 2 a 0640 b 1250 c 0050 3 a 12:45 pm b 4:45 pm
4 7:30 am Tuesday 5 a no b yes c yes 6 yes 7 a b c 8 a 7.14 b 2.65 c 2.53
9 20 cm 10 a 19.062 cm b 29.211 cm

TIME AND PYTHAGORAS' THEOREM

Using Units of Measurement

INTERMEDIATE TEST

Part A Multiple Choice

1 The clock on the right is 15 minutes slow.

The correct time, expressed in 24-hour time, is:

A 0632 **B** 2032

C 1802 **D** 0602 (1 mark)

2 When it is 7:45 pm in Melbourne it is 2:15 pm in New Delhi. If it is 2:10 am in Melbourne, what is the time in New Delhi?

A 9:40 pm **B** 8:40 pm

C 10:40 pm **D** 9:50 pm (1 mark)

3 On Thursday the sun will rise at 0548 and set at 1742. How long is it between sunrise and sunset?

A 11 h 54 min **B** 11 h 56 min

C 12 h 6 min **D** 12 h 54 min (1 mark)

4 Find the time difference between 3 h 14 min and 2 h 42 min:

A 32 min **B** 42 min

C 1 h 12 min **D** 1 h 28 min (1 mark)

5 Which of the following is a Pythagorean triad?

A {2, 3, 4} **B** {8, 10, 13}

C {7, 24, 25} **D** {5, 7, 9} (1 mark)

6 If $\triangle XYZ$ is right-angled, which of the following is not possible? *Hint 1* (1 mark)

A $XY = 9$ cm, $YZ = 40$ cm, $XZ = 41$ cm

B $XY = 10$ cm, $YZ = 26$ cm, $XZ = 24$ cm

C $XY = 8$ cm, $YZ = 15$ cm, $XZ = 17$ cm

D $XY = 11$ cm, $YZ = 60$ cm, $XZ = 62$ cm

Part B Short Answer

7 The tide table shows the times for low and high tides.

Day	Time	Tide (m)
Monday	0133	0.54
	0751	1.62
	1420	0.57
	2025	1.42
Tuesday	0215	0.49
	0729	1.61
	1352	0.36
	1958	1.48

a At what time is the lowest tide? (1 mark)

b Sam arrives at 6:20 am to fish on Monday's high tide. (1 mark)

How long does he have to wait?

c What is the longest time between consecutive low tides? *Hint 2* (2 marks)

8 Find the value of x, correct to 2 decimal places:

a

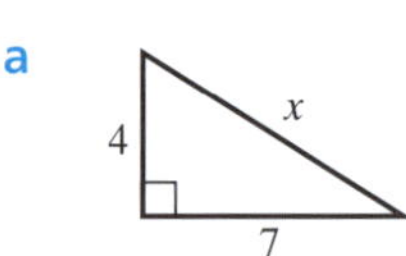

b

c

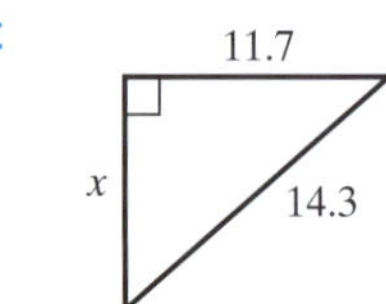

(6 marks)

9 **a** Jen holds a kite string 1.5 metres above the ground. How high is the kite above the ground? (2 marks)

b

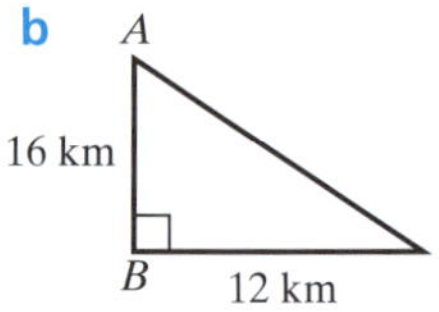

A boat leaves A and sails south for 16 km before turning east at B and sailing for 12 km to C. Find the distance from A to C. (2 marks)

c

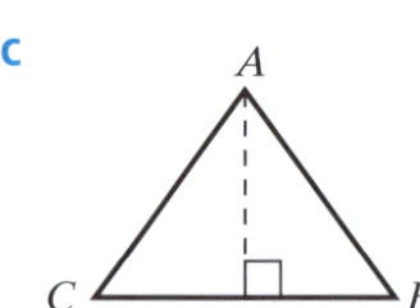

$\triangle ABC$ is equilateral and $AB = 10$ cm. Find the height of the triangle, correct to 2 decimal places. (2 marks)

Hint 1: Use Pythagoras' theorem.
Hint 2: Consecutive means 'one after another'.

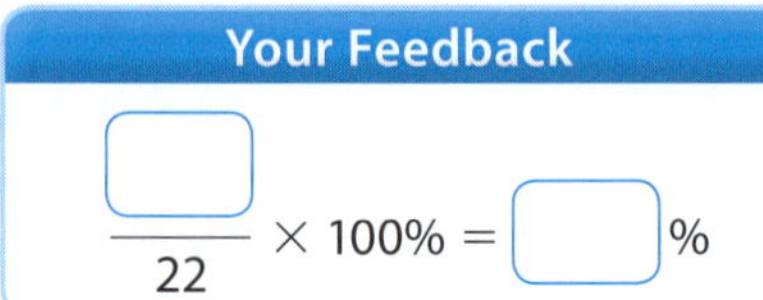

TIME AND PYTHAGORAS' THEOREM

Using Units of Measurement

ADVANCED TEST

1 Bethany takes 5 minutes 35 seconds to walk one lap of her local park. How long would it take to walk nine laps, if she maintains the same pace? (2 marks)

2 Erin left on a journey at 11:45 am and travelled 316 km. If she averaged a speed of 60 km/h, what time did she arrive at her destination? (2 marks)

3 Perth is 8 hours ahead of Johannesburg. A plane leaves Perth at 7 am and flies to Johannesburg. The flight takes 10 hours 50 minutes. What time is it in Johannesburg when the plane lands? (2 marks)

4 Two cars are travelling towards each other at 80 km/h and 100 km/h. How far apart are they 20 minutes before they pass each other? (2 marks)

5 In December, Hobart is 11 hours ahead of London and Dallas is 6 hours behind London. Brae lives in Hobart and on Christmas Day at 13:00 he calls his grandmother in Dallas. What time and date is it in Dallas? (2 marks)

6 On a certain day the sun rises at 0548 and sets at 1915.

- **a** How many hours and minutes are there between sunrise and sunset? (2 marks)
- **b** If the next sunrise is two minutes earlier than the previous morning, how many hours and minutes are there from the sunset to the next sunrise? (2 marks)

7 Lily had a 10:30 am appointment 20 km from her home. Due to the heavy traffic she could only average 40 km/h for the trip. If she arrived 10 minutes late for the trip, what time did she leave home? (2 marks)

8 Determine whether a triangle with the sides 2.6 cm, 16.8 cm and 17 cm is right angled? (2 marks)

9 The hypotenuse of a right-angled triangle is 65 cm. If one of the sides is 33 cm, find the perimeter and area of the triangle. (3 marks)

10 A right-angled isosceles triangle has a hypotenuse of 16 cm. What is the perimeter of the triangle, to the nearest centimetre? (3 marks)

11 Simone is at the movies and sees two ex-boyfriends. One is 7 metres directly ahead of her and the other is 5 metres to her right. How far apart are the two ex-boyfriends, to the nearest metre? (2 marks)

12 A ladder, 8 metres long, leans against a building and reaches a window ledge. If the foot of the ladder is 2 metres from the building, how high is the ledge from the ground, to the nearest centimetre? (2 marks)

13 The diagram shows a tangram made from square $ABCD$ with side 4 cm.

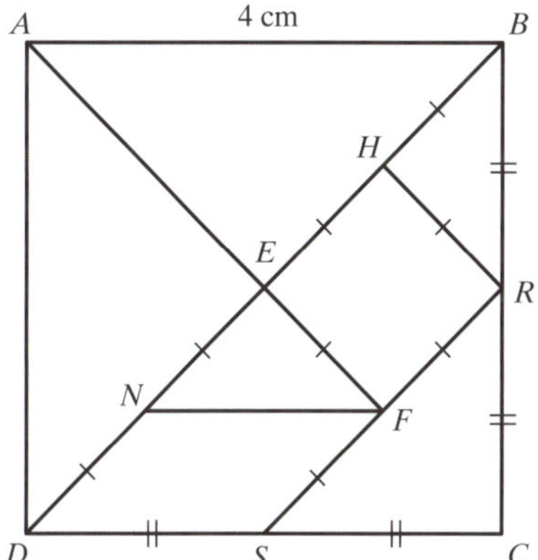

Find the

- **a** exact length of BD (2 marks)
- **b** area of square $EHRF$ (2 marks)
- **c** area of trapezium $DSFE$ (2 marks)
- **d** area of trapezium $DSRB$ (1 mark)

14 The points $(3, -2)$ and $(-1, 1)$ are plotted on a number plane. Find the distance between the two points. (2 marks)

15 The cube has a side length of 8 cm. What is the length of AH (the diagonal of the cube). Give your answer to the nearest millimetre.

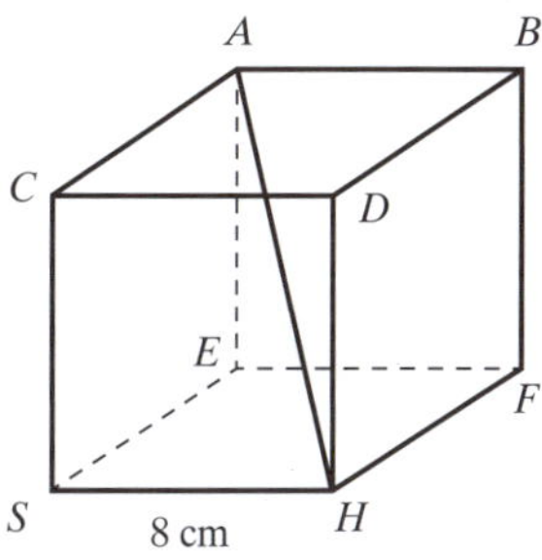

(3 marks)

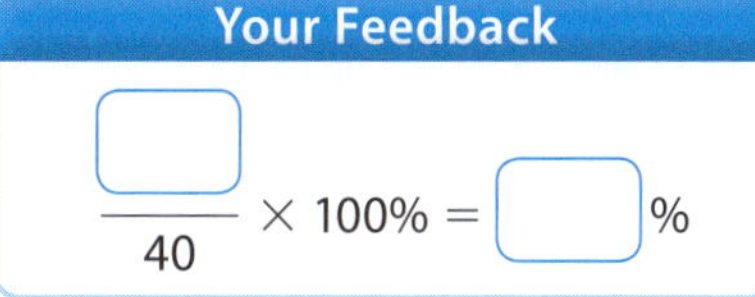

CONGRUENT TRIANGLES AND TRANSFORMATIONS

Geometric Reasoning

STUDY NOTES

1 A **transformation** is a process which changes the size, orientation or position of a shape. When the original figure is transformed, the new shape is called the **image.**

2 The size of the shape remains the same when we translate, reflect or rotate. The image and the original are **congruent shapes**. For example:

a Translate ABC to the right 4 units, then reflect about the line XY

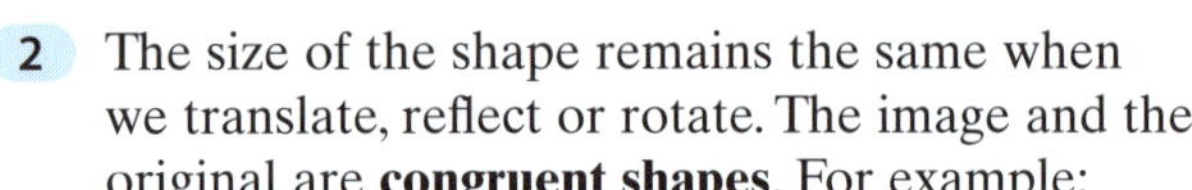

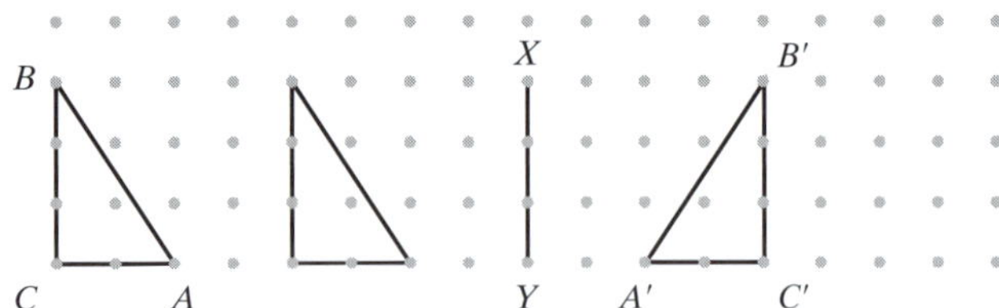

b Rotate $PQRS$ anti-clockwise 90° about P and then translate to the left 5 units

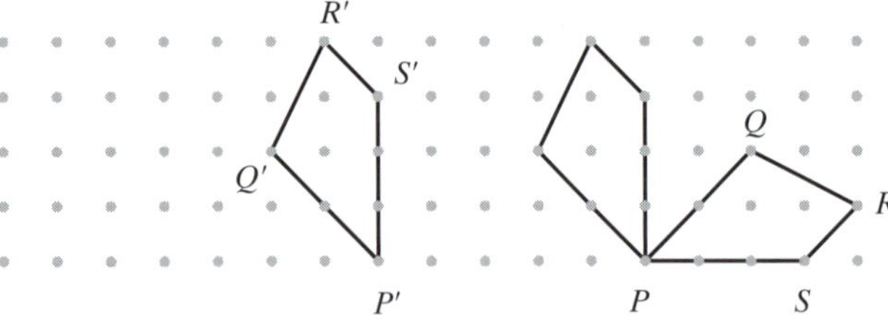

3 Two shapes are congruent if they have the same shape and size—the figures are identical. There are **four tests** that can be used to prove **congruent triangles**:

- **SSS—Side Side Side**—all corresponding sides are equal lengths
- **SAS—Side Angle Side**—two sides and the included angle are equal
- **AAS—Angle Angle Side**—two angles and matching side are equal
- **RHS—Right-angle Hypotenuse Side**—for right-angled triangles, the hypotenuse and a matching side are equal.

For example, what test is used to show that these triangles are congruent?

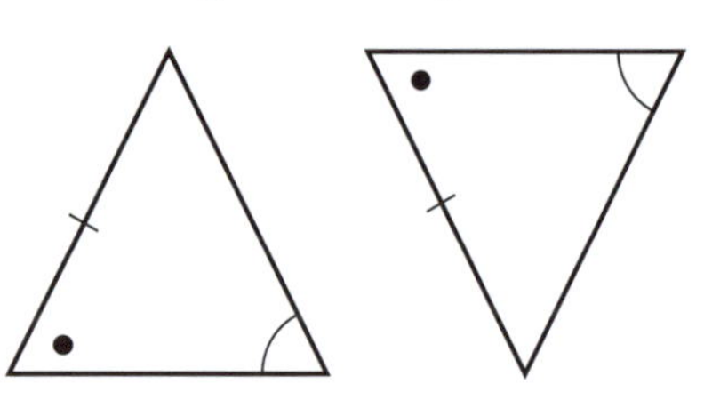

AAS Test

4 If $\triangle ABC$ and $\triangle DEF$ are congruent, we write $\triangle \boldsymbol{ABC} \equiv \triangle \boldsymbol{DEF}$. This means the **matching** (corresponding) **sides and angles are equal**.

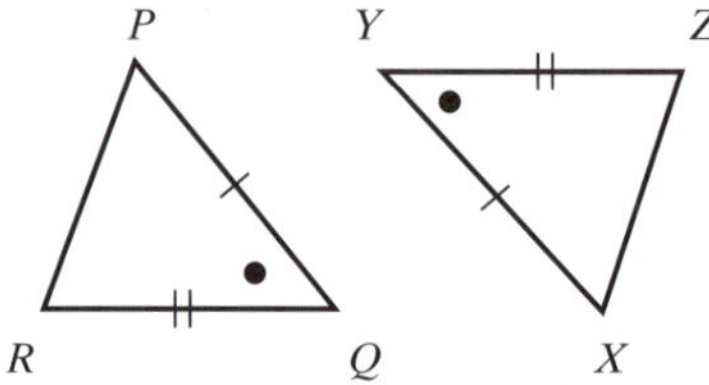

For example, if $\triangle PQR \equiv \triangle XYZ$, write the matching pairs of sides and angles.

$\therefore PQ = XY, PR = XZ, QR = YZ,$

$\angle PQR = \angle XYZ$

$\angle PRQ = \angle XZY, \angle RPQ = \angle ZXY$

5 If two figures are known to be congruent, then **unknown sides and angles** can be found. For example, if $PQRS \equiv BADC$, find the value of the pronumerals.

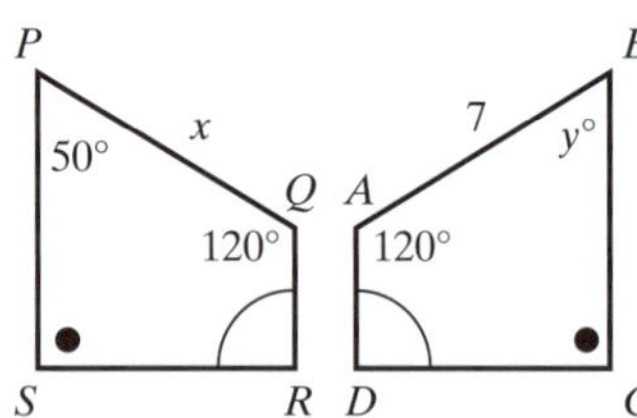

$\therefore$ As $PQ = BA$, then $x = 7$

Also, if $\angle PQR = \angle BAD$,

then $\angle SPQ = \angle CBA, y = 50$

Checklist

Can you:

1 *Use and identify transformations to form congruent shapes?* ☐
2 *Identify congruent triangles using the four tests?* ☐
3 *Match sides and angles of congruent triangles?* ☐

CONGRUENT TRIANGLES AND TRANSFORMATIONS

Geometric Reasoning

SKILLS CHECK

1 Translate these figures in the direction given:

a

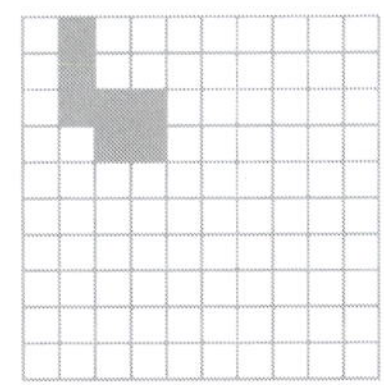

3 units down, 4 units right

b

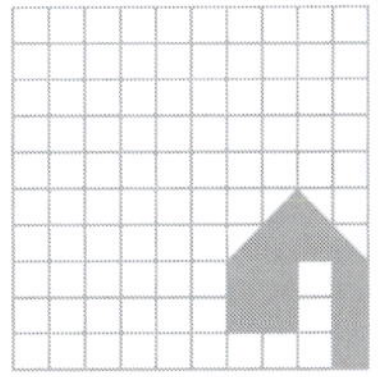

4 units left, 3 units up

c

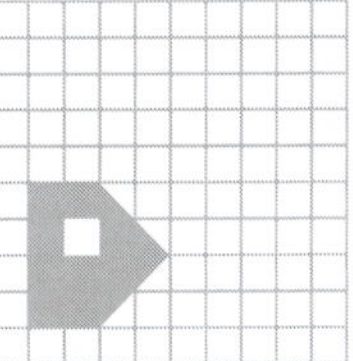

2 units up, 5 units right

2 Reflect these figures about the line AB:

a

b

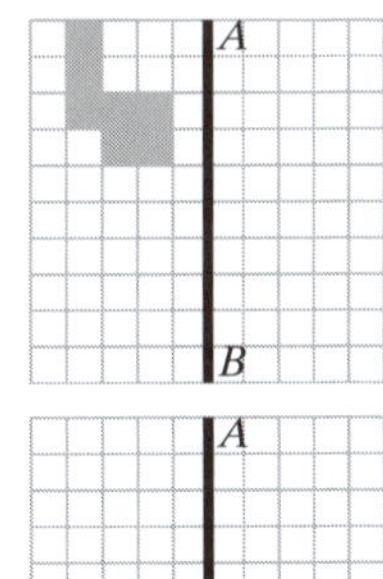

c

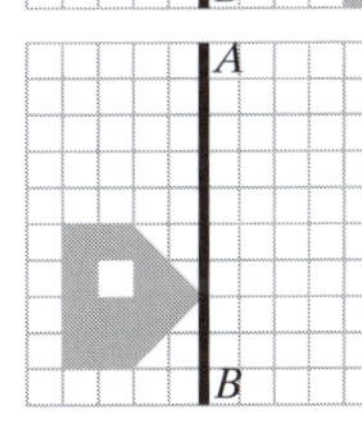

3 Rotate these figures through O, using the angle indicated:

a

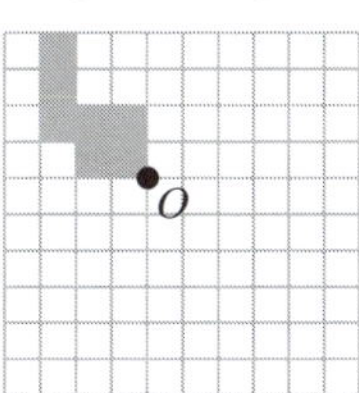

clockwise 90°

b

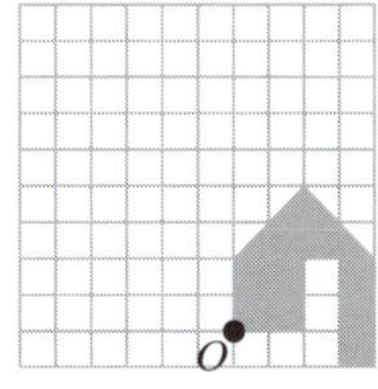

anti-clockwise 90°

c

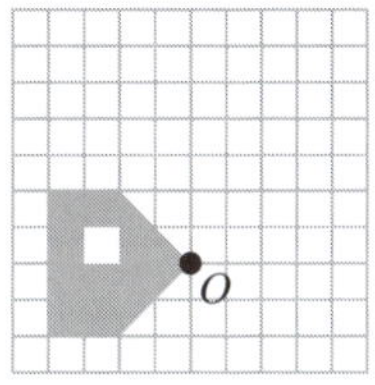

clockwise 90°

4 Determine whether the following pairs of triangles are congruent. If so, write the congruency test used.

a

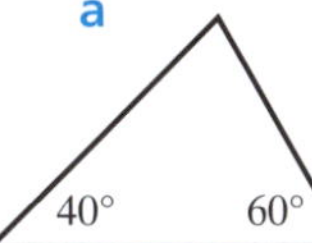

60°
6 cm
40°

b

c

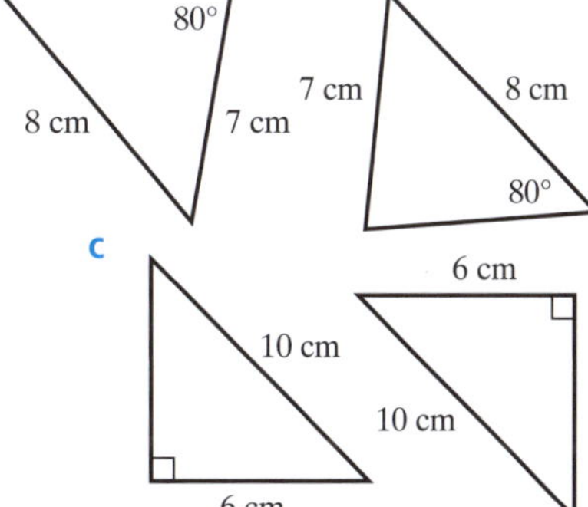

d

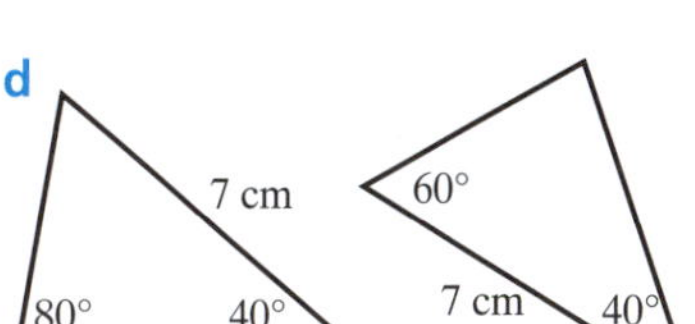

5 If $\triangle ABC \equiv \triangle LMN$, complete:

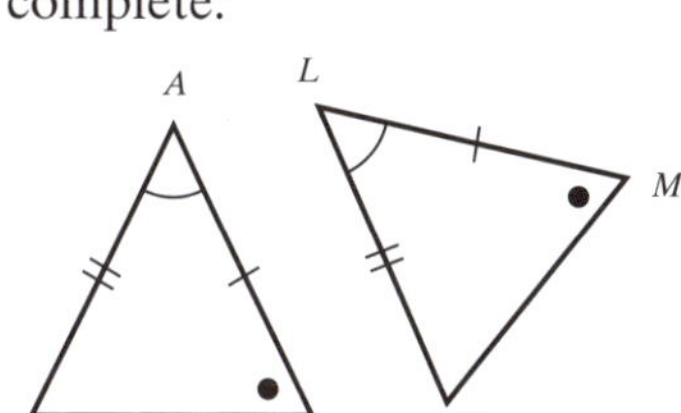

a $AB =$ _______

b $AC =$ _______

c $MN =$ _______

d $\angle ABC =$ _______

e $\angle MLN =$ _______

f $\angle LNM =$ _______

6 Find the value of the pronumerals, if $\triangle PQR \equiv \triangle XYZ$:

a

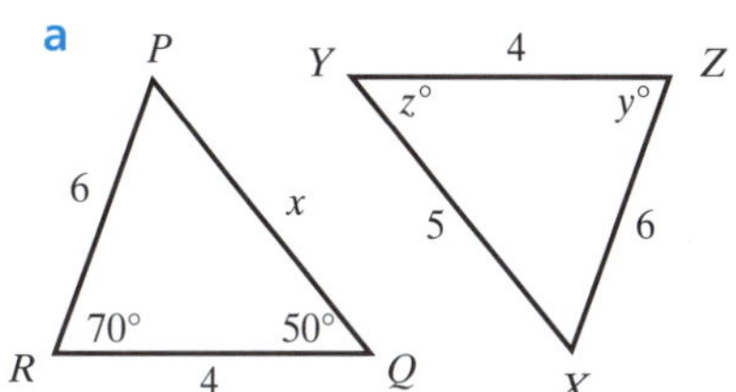

b

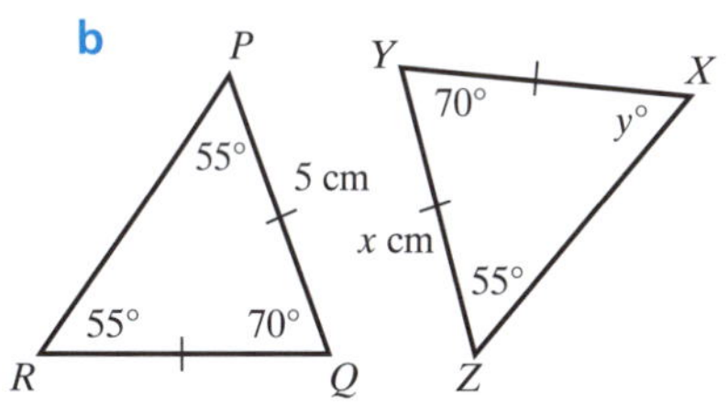

PAGE 158

Answers **1** see worked solutions **2** see worked solutions **3** see worked solutions
4 **a** congruent (AAS test) **b** not congruent **c** congruent (RHS test) **d** congruent (AAS test)
5 **a** LM **b** LN **c** BC **d** $\angle LMN$ **e** $\angle BAC$ **f** $\angle ACB$ **6** **a** $x = 5$ $y = 70$ $z = 50$ **b** $x = 5$ $y = 55$

CONGRUENT TRIANGLES AND TRANSFORMATIONS

Geometric Reasoning

INTERMEDIATE TEST

Part A Multiple Choice

1 Laura knows that the triangles are congruent. By matching, Laura correctly wrote: *Hint 1*

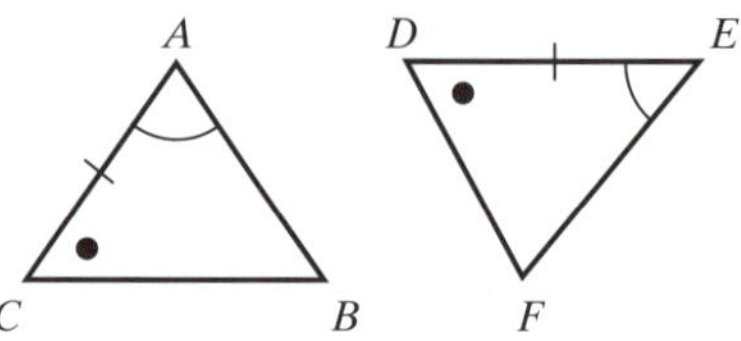

A $AB = DE$ **B** $\angle ACB = \angle FED$ **C** $DF = CB$ **D** $\angle DFE = \angle ACB$ (1 mark)

2 If these two triangles are congruent, what additional information is required?

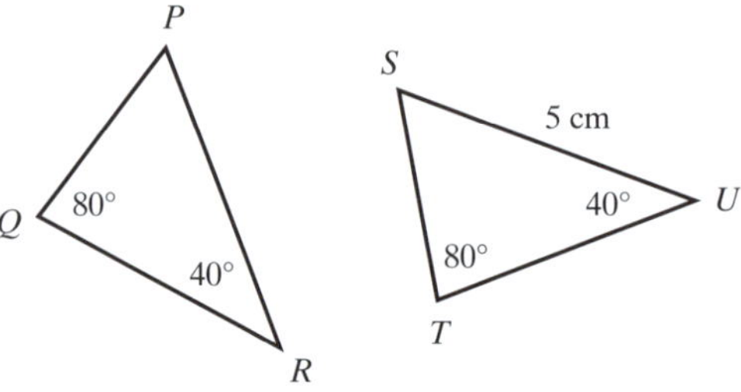

A $\angle RPQ = 60°$ **B** $PR = 5$ cm **C** $PQ = 5$ cm **D** $QR = 5$ cm (1 mark)

3 Which of these triangles is congruent to $\triangle ABC$?

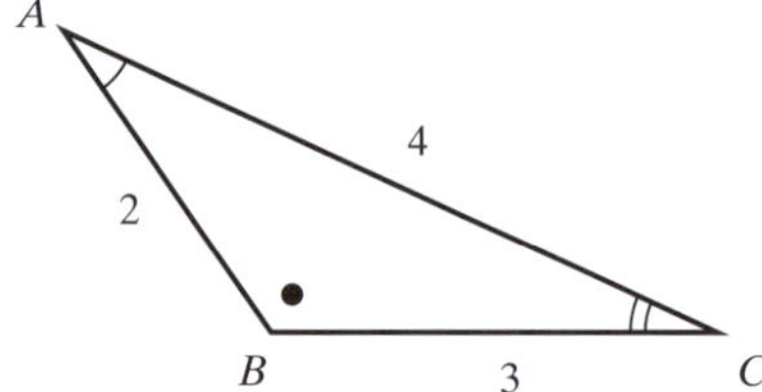

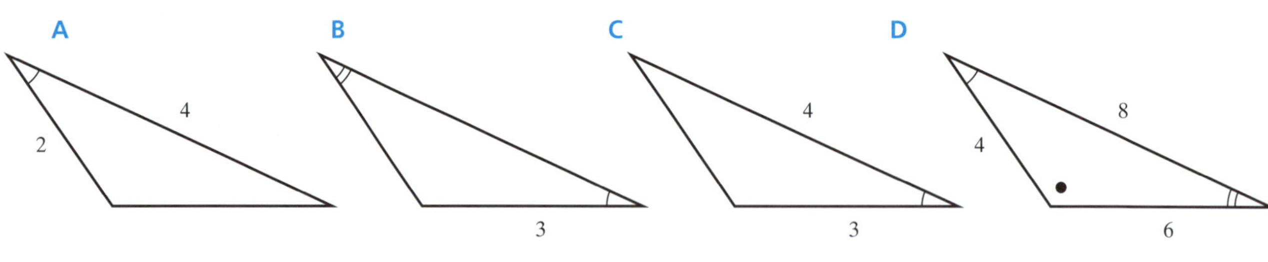

(1 mark)

4 A transformation has been used to move triangle ABC to the new position DBE.

The transformation used was a:

A reflection **B** enlargement
C translation **D** rotation

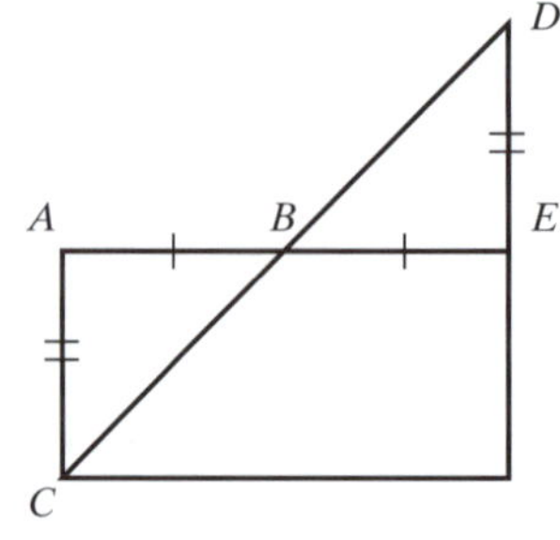

(1 mark)

Hint 1: Match equal sides and equal angles.

Part B Short Answer

5 Find the value of the pronumerals if:

a $\triangle ADC \equiv \triangle ABC$

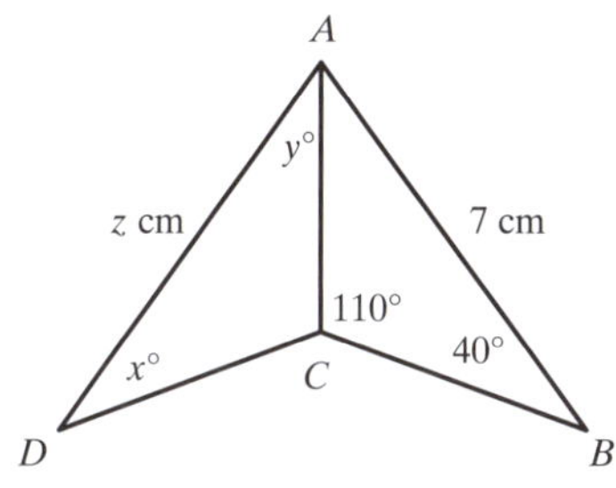

b $\triangle PQR \equiv \triangle TSR$

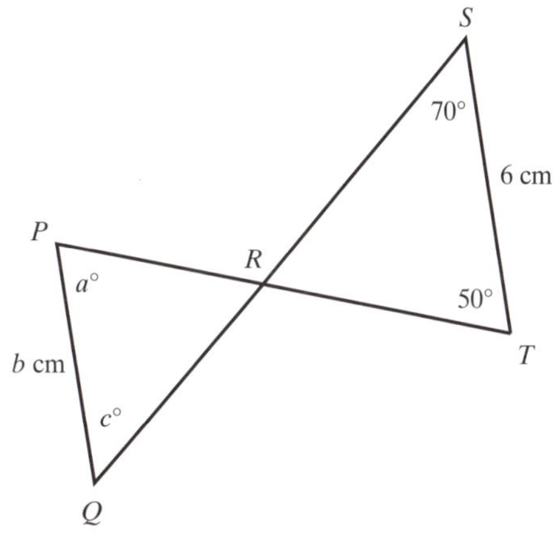

(6 marks)

6 The quadrilateral $ABCD$ has opposite sides equal.

a What test should be used to prove $\triangle ADC \equiv \triangle CBA$? (1 mark)

b Complete:

i $\angle ADC =$

ii $\angle BAC =$ (2 marks)

c Name two pairs of alternate angles. (2 marks)

d What type of quadrilateral is $ABCD$? (1 mark)

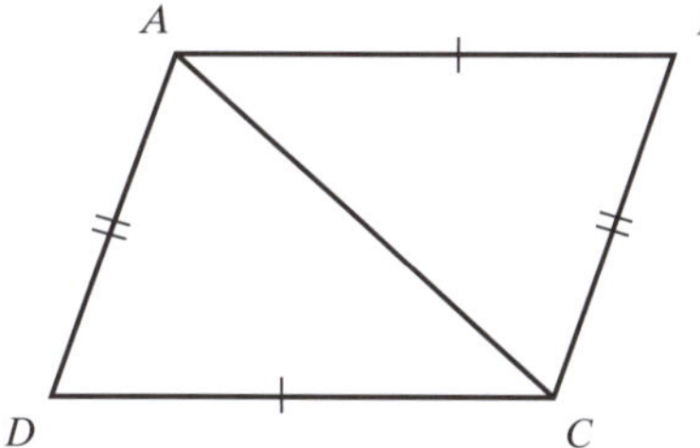

7 $PQRS$ is a kite.

a What test is used to prove $\triangle SPQ \equiv \triangle SRQ$?

b Complete $\angle PST =$

c What test is used to prove $\triangle PST \equiv \triangle RST$?

d Find the size of $\angle PTS$.

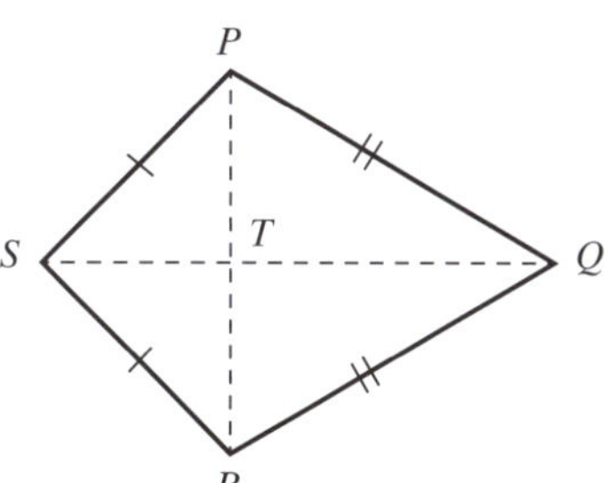

(4 marks)

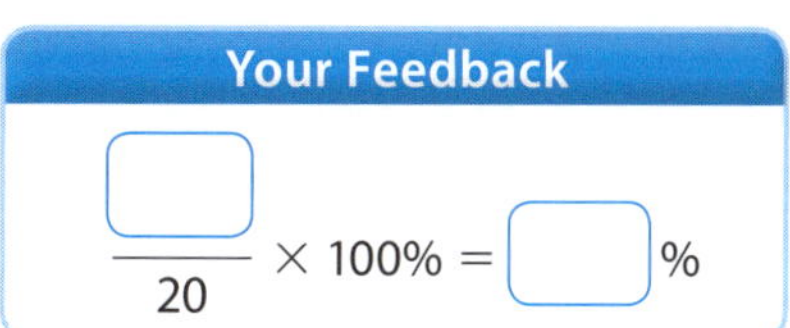

PAGE 159
PAGE 177

CONGRUENT TRIANGLES AND TRANSFORMATIONS

Geometric Reasoning

25 MINUTES

ADVANCED TEST

1 Each of the following diagrams shows two congruent triangles. Describe the transformation used. (3 marks)

a 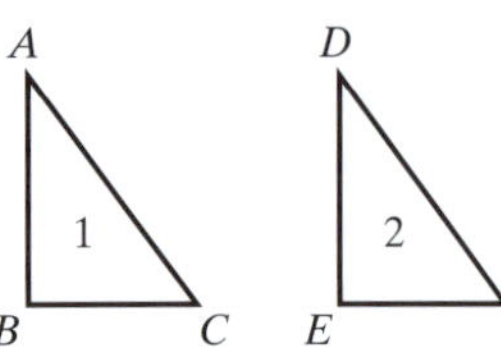

b 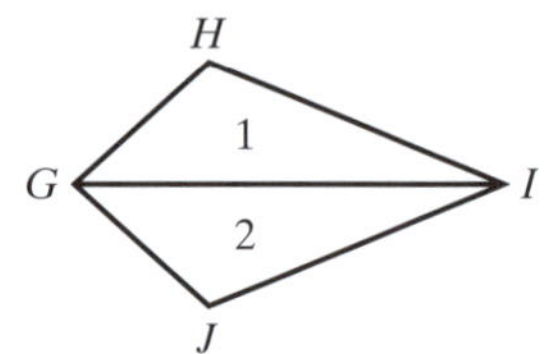

c 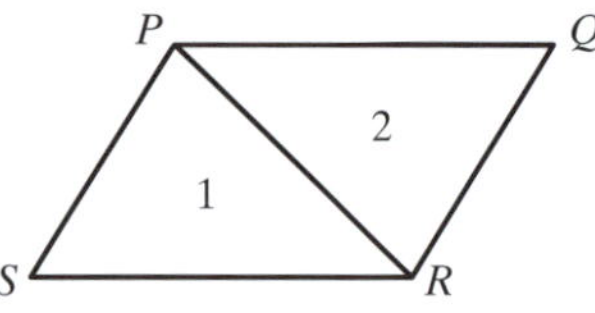

2 By matching equal sides, write a congruence statement for each pair of triangles in question 1. (3 marks)

3 Complete the table showing abbreviations and explanations used in geometric proofs. (9 marks)

Abbreviations	Explanation
$\triangle ABC \equiv \triangle PQR$	
corr. $\angle$s equal, $BC \parallel ST$	
alt. $\angle$s equal, $\parallel$ lines	
co-int. $\angle$s supp., $XY \parallel MN$	
vert. opp. $\angle$s equal	
$\angle$ sum of $\triangle$	
matching $\angle$s of cong. $\triangle$s	
base $\angle$s of isos. $\triangle$s equal	
opp. $\angle$s of parallelogram	

4 Complete the following proofs:

a 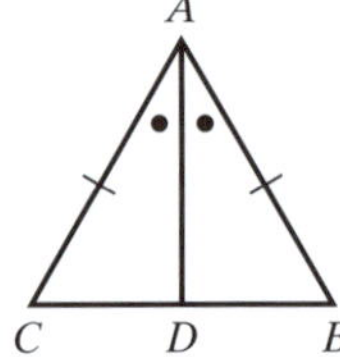

Prove $\triangle ADC \equiv \triangle ADB$
______ is common
$\angle CAD$ = ______ (given)
AC = ______ (given)
$\therefore \triangle ADC \equiv \triangle ADB$
(________ test) (4 marks)

b 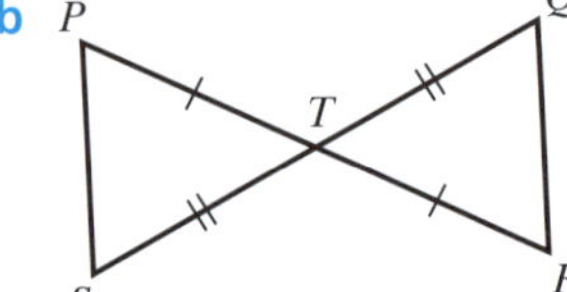

Prove $\triangle PTS \equiv \triangle RTQ$
PT = ______ (given)
$\angle PTS$ = ______ (________)
ST = ______ (________)
$\therefore \triangle PTS \equiv \triangle RTQ$
(________ test) (4 marks)

c 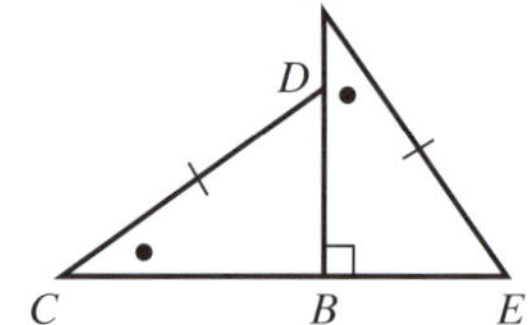

Prove $\triangle DBC \equiv \triangle EBA$
DC = ______ (________)
$\angle DBC$ = ______ (________)
$\angle DCB$ = ______ (________)
$\therefore \triangle DBC \equiv \triangle EBA$
(________ test) (4 marks)

5 Prove the following congruent triangles, giving reasons:

a 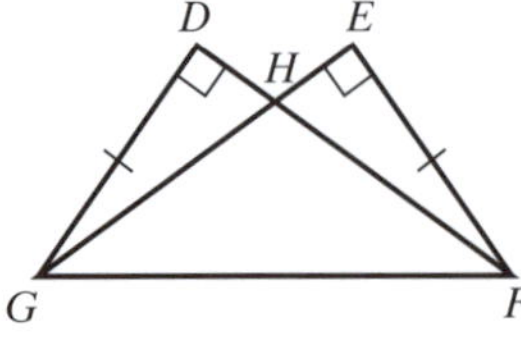

Prove $\triangle GDF \equiv \triangle FEG$
(4 marks)

b 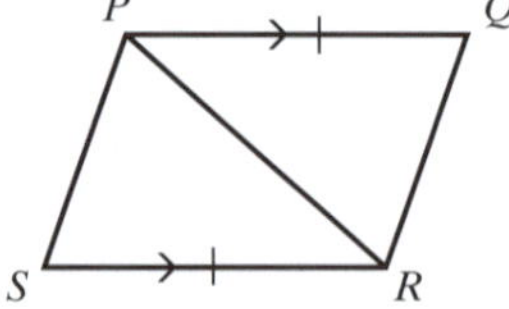

Prove $\triangle SPR \equiv \triangle RQP$
(4 marks)

c 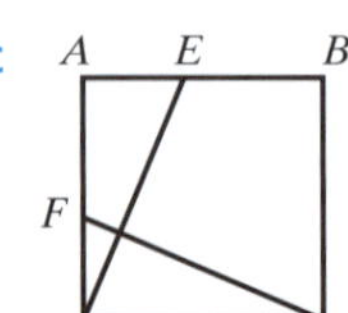

$ABCD$ is square
$AE = DF$

Prove $\triangle DAE \equiv \triangle CDF$
(4 marks)

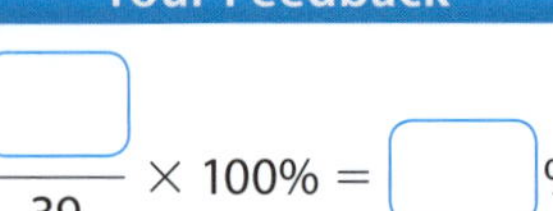

PROBABILITY

Chance

STUDY NOTES

1 **Probability** is the study of **chance**.

2 **Probability ranges** from **0** (impossible event) to **1** (certain event).

3 The **probability of an event Pr(E)**, or P(E), is written as:

$$\text{Pr(E)} = \frac{\text{number of favourable outcomes}}{\text{number of possible outcomes}}$$

For example, a bag contains 3 red balls and 2 blue balls. If a ball is chosen at random, what is the probability that the ball is red?

$$\text{Pr(red)} = \frac{3}{5}$$

4 When we identify **complementary events**, we can quickly determine probabilities. For example, a die is tossed. Find the probability of not tossing a four.

$$\text{Pr(not tossing a 4)} = 1 - \text{Pr(tossing a 4)}$$
$$= 1 - \frac{1}{6} = \frac{5}{6}$$

5 Experiments or trials are conducted to provide data which is used to forecast outcomes. **Experimental probability** refers to the probability of an event occurring when an experiment is conducted. The **relative frequency** is the frequency of an event divided by the number of trials and is used to estimate the probability of an event. For example, 3 coins were tossed 40 times and the number of tails thrown each time recorded in the table. What was the relative frequency of throwing at least 2 tails?

Tails	0	1	2	3
Number of times	4	15	16	5

$\therefore$ Relative frequency $= \frac{21}{40}$

6 Sometimes data is expressed in two variables and is displayed in a **two-way table**. For example, a class of music students is surveyed to find the number of students who play the guitar and the results displayed. If a student is chosen at random, what is the probability that the student is a guitar-playing female?

		Gender	
		Male	Female
Plays guitar	Yes	7	5
	No	4	6

$\therefore$ Probability $= \frac{5}{22}$

7 A **Venn diagram** is comprised of a rectangle and circles that show the relationship between different groups. For example, a survey of customers in a sports store found the number of people who had played cricket and tennis in the previous year. Of the 21 customers surveyed, 11 had played cricket and 9 had played tennis. Four customers had played neither sport. Record the data in a Venn diagram. If a customer is chosen at random, what is the probability that he or she played tennis but not cricket?

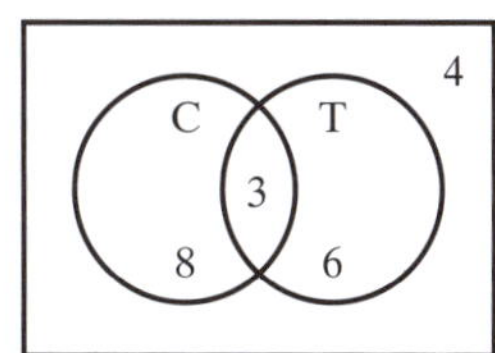

$\therefore$ Record the 4 outside the circles. Now, 21 − 4 gives 17. But as 11 + 9 = 20 then there must be 3 who had played both sports. Then complete the diagram. This means Pr(tennis but not cricket) $= \frac{6}{21} = \frac{2}{7}$

Checklist

Can you:

1 *Recognise that the sum of probabilities is equal to 1?* ☐

2 *Identify and find the probability of the complement of an event?* ☐

3 *Use two-way tables and Venn diagrams to solve problems involving probability?* ☐

PROBABILITY

Chance

SKILLS CHECK

1 A person is chosen at random. What is the probability that the person was:

a born on a Tuesday? **b** born on a weekend? **c** not born on a Monday?

2 A bag contains 3 blue marbles, 5 yellow marbles and 2 green marbles. One marble is selected at random. What is the probability of:

a choosing a yellow marble? **b** choosing a white marble?

c not choosing a blue marble? **d** not choosing a yellow or green marble?

3 The possible three-child families are GGG, GGB, GBG, GBB, BGG, BGB, BBG, BBB where G = girl, B = boy. What is the probability that in a three-child family there will be:

a 3 boys? **b** exactly 2 girls? **c** at least one boy? **d** at most one boy?

4 A standard deck of cards contains 52 cards. Lee selects a card at random from the deck. What is the probability that the card is:

a queen of diamonds? **b** red? **c** five?

d spade? **e** not a spade? **f** not a nine?

5 Write a complementary event for:

a rolling a die and getting a three

b selecting a prime number from the numbers less than 10

6 A survey was conducted to find the number of students who have a dog or a cat as a pet at home and the results are displayed in the table. One of the students was chosen at random. What is the probability that the student:

	Has a dog	Not have a dog
Has a cat	7	8
Not have a cat	4	3

a has a dog but not a cat? **b** has a cat and a dog?

7 The grades of 20 students were recorded in a table. Complete the table. If a student is chosen at random, what is the probability that the student:

a scored A in both courses?

b scored at least one A?

c did not score an A?

		English			
		A	B	C	Total
Maths	A			3	9
	B	1	2	2	
	C	3			
	Total	9		6	

8 A gelato shop introduced two new flavours. Sixty people were given free samples and 32 said they liked Avocado while 38 voted for Tiramisu. Twenty liked both flavours. Use a Venn diagram to find the probability that a person chosen at random:

a liked Avocado but not Tiramisu **b** did not like either flavour

9 A survey of 20 teachers was conducted to find whether they could surf and play the piano. Eight of the teachers could surf and 9 played the piano. Five teachers could do neither. Summarise this information in a Venn diagram and a table.

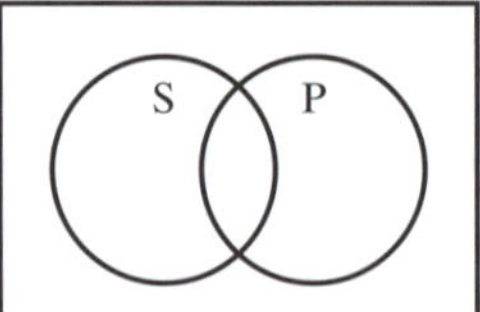

	Surf	Not surf
Piano		
Not piano		

PAGE 160

Answers 1 a $\frac{1}{7}$ b $\frac{2}{7}$ c $\frac{6}{7}$ 2 a $\frac{1}{2}$ b 0 c $\frac{7}{10}$ d $\frac{3}{10}$ 3 a $\frac{1}{8}$ b $\frac{3}{8}$ c $\frac{7}{8}$ d $\frac{1}{2}$ 4 a $\frac{1}{52}$ b $\frac{1}{2}$ c $\frac{1}{13}$ d $\frac{1}{4}$ e $\frac{3}{4}$ f $\frac{12}{13}$ 5 a not getting a three b not a prime 6 a $\frac{2}{11}$ b $\frac{7}{22}$ 7 a $\frac{1}{4}$ b $\frac{13}{20}$ c $\frac{7}{20}$ 8 a $\frac{1}{5}$ b $\frac{1}{6}$
9 see worked solutions

PROBABILITY
Chance

25 MINUTES

INTERMEDIATE TEST

Part A Multiple Choice

1 A spinner is numbered as shown opposite. What is the probability of spinning a 4?

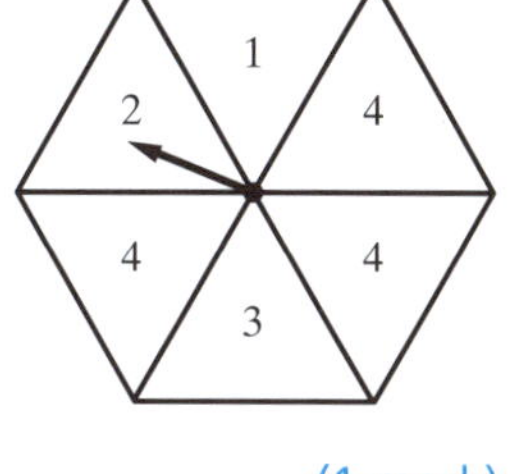

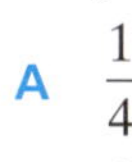
A $\frac{1}{4}$ B $\frac{1}{3}$

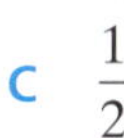
C $\frac{1}{2}$ D $\frac{1}{6}$ (1 mark)

2 The faces on a 10-sided die are numbered 1 to 10. What is the probability of **not** rolling a 2?

A $\frac{5}{6}$ B $\frac{1}{2}$ C $\frac{1}{10}$ D $\frac{9}{10}$ (1 mark)

3 Leyton has a bag of 24 balls. The probability of selecting a yellow marble from the bag is $\frac{2}{3}$. How many yellow marbles are in the bag?

A 16 B 18 C 15 D 20 (1 mark)

4 Four teams remain in a knockout competition. The Tigers have a 50% chance of winning the competition while the other teams, the Magpies, Lions and Cats, are equally likely to win. What is the probability that the Cats will win the competition? *Hint 1*

A $\frac{1}{4}$ B $\frac{1}{3}$ C $\frac{1}{2}$ D $\frac{1}{6}$ (1 mark)

5 Jess and Jay are playing a game where a standard six-sided die is rolled.

Jess wins if a prime number is rolled. Jay wins if an even number is rolled.

What is the probability that Jess wins but Jay loses? *Hint 2*

A $\frac{1}{6}$ B $\frac{1}{3}$ C $\frac{2}{3}$ D $\frac{1}{2}$ (1 mark)

6 Rafael and Novak are playing each other in a game of tennis. Novak is three times more likely to win than Rafael. What is the probability that Novak will win?

A $\frac{1}{3}$ B $\frac{2}{3}$ C $\frac{3}{4}$ D $\frac{1}{2}$ (1 mark)

Part B Short Answer

7 A survey of students was conducted to find the method of transport to school.

Mode of transport

	Car	Bus	Walk	Train	Total
Boys	8	12	6	10	
Girls	6	14	2	12	
Total					

a Complete the table. (2 marks)

b If a student is selected at random, what is the probability that the student is:

i a girl?

ii a train traveller?

iii a girl who caught a bus?

iv a boy who walked?

v a girl who did not catch a bus? (5 marks)

8 Thirty people at a suburban park were interviewed. Each of them had driven a car or ridden a bike in the past month. Twenty-six had driven a car while 10 had ridden a bike. Draw a Venn diagram with this information and find the probability that a person chosen at random rode a bike but did not drive a car in the past month. (3 marks)

9 A group of 65 year-12 students were surveyed to find the number of students studying biology, chemistry or physics. Thirty-five studied biology, 30 chemistry and 25 physics. Sixteen students studied both biology and chemistry, 13 both biology and physics and 10 both chemistry and physics. Six students studied all three subjects.

a Record the information in a Venn diagram. *Hint 3* (2 marks)

b How many students in the survey did not study one of the science courses? (1 mark)

c If a student is chosen at random, what is the probability that they studied chemistry only? (1 mark)

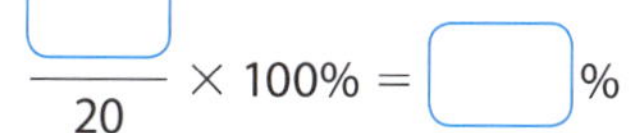

Hint 1: Change 50% to a fraction.
Hint 2: Both students can win at the same time.
Hint 3: The Venn diagram needs three circles.

35 MINUTES

ADVANCED TEST

1 The diagram shows two spinners used to play a game. When the two spinners are played, the results are added to give a score.

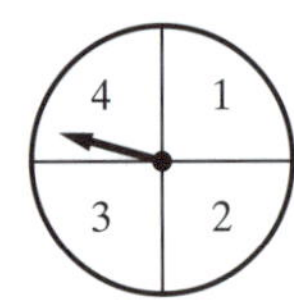

a Complete the table to find the possible scores: (2 marks)

	1	**2**	**3**	**4**
1	2	3	4	5
2	4			
4				

b What is the most likely score? (1 mark)

c What is the probability that the score will be:

i odd? ii less than 7?
iii a square number? iv prime?
v divisible by 3? vi a multiple of 4?
vii a factor of 12? (1 mark each)

2 A new game is played with the spinners used in question 1. This time the score is the difference between the two results.

a Complete the table to find the possible scores: (2 marks)

	1	**2**	**3**	**4**
1	0	1	2	3
2	1			
4				

b Which is the most likely score? (1 mark)

c What is the probability that the score will be:

i odd? ii prime?
iii not prime? (1 mark each)

3 A bag contains numbered balls. The probability of selecting a 2 was $\frac{1}{2}$, a 3 was $\frac{1}{3}$. The remainder of the balls were numbered 1.

a What is the probability of selecting:

i a 1? (1 mark)
ii less than 3? (1 mark)

b What is the smallest possible number of balls in the bag with the digit 2? (2 marks)

4 A survey of forty customers at a service station on a Saturday morning found 16 customers bought a newspaper and petrol, 12 only bought petrol, 5 bought neither petrol nor a newspaper.

a Draw a Venn Diagram. (1 mark)

b Complete a two-way table. (1 mark)

c If a customer was selected at random, what was the probability that the person:

i bought both petrol and a newspaper?
ii bought a newspaper and no petrol? (1 mark each)

d What percentage of people bought a newspaper? (1 mark)

5 The diagram shows a spinner. What is the probability of recording:

a 1? b an even?
c a composite? d 4 or 5?
e a factor of 6? f not a 7?
g not a prime? h more than 3? (1 mark each)

6 A bag contains balls which are of four different colours. It is twice as likely to choose an orange ball than it is to choose a pink ball. It is three times as likely to choose a pink ball than a green ball, and twice as likely to choose a red ball than a green ball.

a Find the probability of choosing each colour. (2 marks)

b What is the smallest possible number of balls in the bag? (1 mark)

c If there are 60 balls in the bag, how many are red? (1 mark)

d If the red balls were removed from the bag, what is the probability of choosing a green or an orange ball? (1 mark)

7 There are three athletes in a race. Lee is twice as likely to win as Bree, and Bree is three times more likely to win than Dee. Write down the probabilities of each athlete winning. (2 marks)

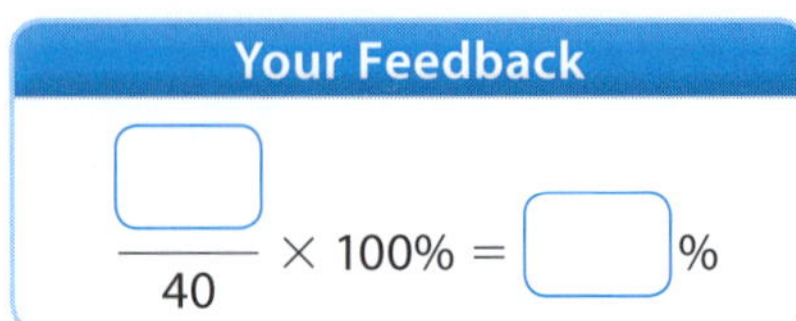

INTERPRETING DATA

Data Representation and Interpretation

STUDY NOTES

1 Data is collected using a census or a sample. A **census** involves collecting data about every individual in the whole population. For example, the Australian Bureau of Statistics (ABS) conducts a census of the Australian population every five years. A **sample** involves collecting data from part of the population. If a large enough sample is taken, we can get some idea about the whole population. For example, to ascertain the popularity of the prime minister, phone calls to 1000 adults might be conducted.

2 **Data** can be **categorical** (e.g. car colours) or **numerical** (e.g. marks scored in a test).

3 A sample is **biased** if it does not represent fairly the whole population. For example, a sample of 1000 adults to ascertain the popularity of the prime minister would be biased if all of the adults sampled lived in the same suburb. In order to be fair the sample would have to include adults from different parts of Australia and from different age groups.

4 **Scores** may be **clustered** together or an outlier might exist. An **outlier** is a score much lower or higher than other scores. For example, in the scores 3, 8, 5, 7, 6, 6, 31, 6 the scores are clustered about 6 and there is an outlier of 31.

5 A **frequency table** can be used to find:
mean (average)—by inserting an additional column, frequency × score (***fx***), the mean is found by dividing the sum of the '*fx*' column by the sum of the '*f*' column;
median (middle)—by using the frequency column to find the middle score;
mode (most common)—the score with the highest frequency;
range—the highest score minus the lowest score.

For example: complete the table (right) and then find the mean, median and mode.

Scores (x)	Frequency (f)	fx
4	4	**16**
5	6	**30**
6	7	**42**
7	2	**14**
	$\Sigma f = $ **19**	$\Sigma fx = $ **102**

$$\text{Mean} = \frac{\Sigma fx}{\Sigma f} \quad [\Sigma \text{ means 'sum of'}]$$
$$= \frac{102}{19}$$
$$= 5.37 \text{ [correct to 2 decimal places]}$$

Median: the scores have been arranged in ascending order. There are 19 scores so the middle score will be the 10th score. Working down the frequency column from the top row, we can see that the 10th score was a 5 (there were four scores of 4 and six scores of 5). ∴ Median = 5

Mode: the score with the highest frequency was 6. ∴ Mode = 6

Range: 7 − 4 = 3 ∴ Range = 3.

6 A **dot plot**, **frequency histogram**, or **frequency polygon** can also be used to find measures of location: **mean**—by using the formula, sum of scores ÷ number of scores; **median**—by crossing off the low and high scores in pairs to find the middle score; **mode**—the score with the tallest 'column'.

For example: find the mean, median and mode of the data represented by the dot plot below.

$$\text{Mean} = \frac{(16 \times 3) + (17 \times 4) + (18 \times 6) + (19 \times 4) + (20 \times 2)}{3 + 4 + 6 + 4 + 2}$$
$$= \frac{340}{19}$$
$$= 17.89 \text{ [correct to 2 decimal places]}$$

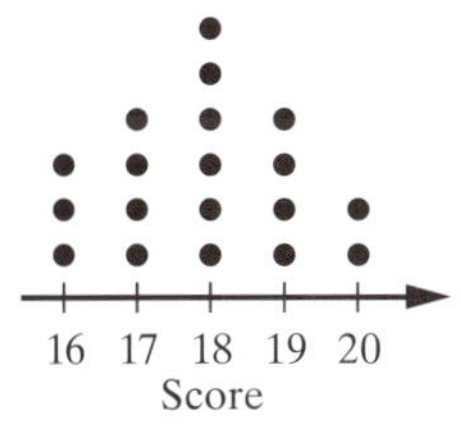

Median: cross off low and high scores in pairs.

We end in the middle column ∴ median = 18

Mode = 18

7 When data is **continuous**, it can be grouped in **classes**, or **class intervals**, to make it easier to tabulate and graph. The middle of the class is called the **class centre** and is often used when graphing. For example, complete a frequency table for the following data, and graph a frequency histogram and polygon.

21 39 28 36 33 32 27 24 32 34 29

25 33 40 28 31 27 26 26 34 34 38

21 23 35 39 32 22 35 24

Class interval	Class centre	Tally	Frequency
21–25	23	卌 II	7
26–30	28	卌 II	7
31–35	33	卌 卌 I	11
36–40	38	卌	5

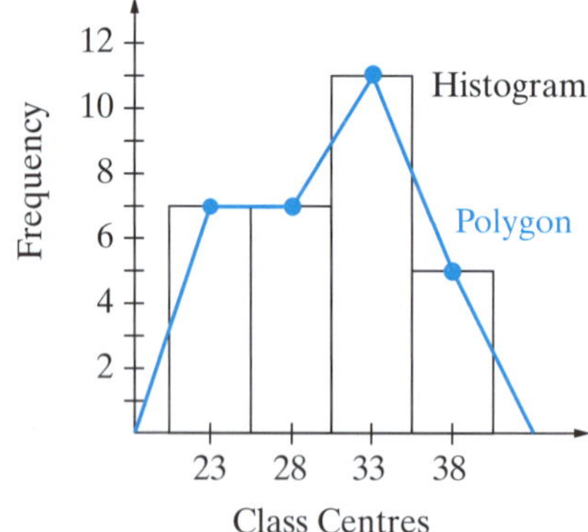

Checklist
Can you:

1 *Recognise the difference between a census and a sample?* ☐
2 *Recognise and understand the effect of outliers on the mean and median?* ☐
3 *Calculate mean, mode, median and range from a frequency table, histogram, polygon and a stem-and-leaf plot?* ☐
4 *Construct tables and graphs for grouped data?* ☐

INTERPRETING DATA

Data Representation and Interpretation

SKILLS CHECK

1 A cafe recorded the number of smoothies it sold over a three-week period.

Number of smoothies sold

12	16	15	26	23	19
31	28	26	19	4	17
30	25	22	19	29	33
32	27	22			

- **a** Draw a stem-and-leaf plot.
- **b** Find the median, mode, range.
- **c** What is the outlier?

2 **a** For the scores 21, 19, 17, 1, 27 find the mean and the median.

- **b** If the outlier is ignored, what change is there to the mean and the median?

3 A fitness test was conducted on a group of year 8 students and the results were recorded.

Fitness test results

5	6	8	11	9	8
8	9	10	10	8	7
7	8	9	9	6	8

- **a** Draw a frequency table.
- **b** Use the table to find the median, mode, range and mean.
- **c** Draw a frequency histogram and polygon

4 An internet site invited people to rate a movie using the scale 1 to 5. The results are listed.

Movie ratings

2	3	5	4	3	3
2	4	4	3	5	3
3	5	4	3	4	3

- **a** Draw a dot plot.
- **b** Find the median, mode and range.

5 The number of goals scored by a soccer team in six matches is 0, 4, 2, 1, 3, 2. In the seventh match the team scores 2 goals. Determine whether the mean, mode, median and range changes and by how much.

6

Type of food	Number sold
Pies	32
Sausage rolls	18
Hot dogs	22
Sausage sandwiches	28

To find out the eating habits of young people, the food sold at a netball canteen was recorded one Saturday morning and the results listed in the table.

- **a** Is the data categorical or numerical?
- **b** What is the mode?
- **c** Is this a good sample? Give reasons.

7 The heights (in cm) of 16 students are recorded below. By first finding class centres, complete the frequency table and then draw a frequency histogram.

138 137 161 154 148 155 158 162
152 150 148 142 149 153 160 163

Class	Class centre	Frequency
132–138		
139–145		
146–152		
153–159		
160–166		

8 The results of a test were recorded in the stem-and-leaf plot below.

Test results

5	0 2 9
6	0 4 7 8
7	2 4 8 8 9
8	1 5 9

- **a** Find:
  - **i** the mean of the scores
  - **ii** the median
  - **iii** the mode
  - **iv** the range
- **b** What percentage of scores are less than the mean? Give your answer to one decimal place.

PAGE 163

Answers **1 a** see worked solutions **b** 23, 19, 25 **c** 4 **2 a** 17, 19 **b** mean increase by 4, median increase by 1 **3 a** see worked solutions **b** 8, 8, 6, 8.11 **c** see worked solutions **4 a** see worked solutions **b** 3, 3, 3 **5** all unchanged **6 a** categorical **b** pies **c** no—see worked solutions **7** see worked solutions **8 a i** 70.4 **ii** 72 **iii** 78 **iv** 39 **b** 46.7%

Part A Multiple Choice

1 The Osborne family has 6 children. The mean age of the 4 boys is 8, and the mean age of the 2 girls is 14. What is the mean age of the 6 children altogether? *Hint 1*

A 10 B 11 C 12 D 14 (1 mark)

2 What is the range and mode of the data in this dot plot?

A range = 5, mode = 6
B range = 5, mode = 8
C range = 3, mode = 6
D range = 3, mode = 8

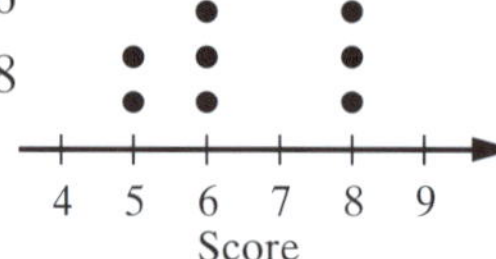

(1 mark)

3 A survey of car colours was conducted.
Which measure could be used to analyse the data? *Hint 2*

A mode B range
C mean D median

(1 mark)

4 Janson drew a frequency table. What is the missing value in his relative frequency column?

Score	Frequency	Relative frequency
6	10	0.5
7	3	
8	7	0.35

A 0.3 B 0.6
C 0.15 D 1 (1 mark)

5 Shane drew a histogram to show the number of children in 20 families. What percentage of the families have 2 or more children?

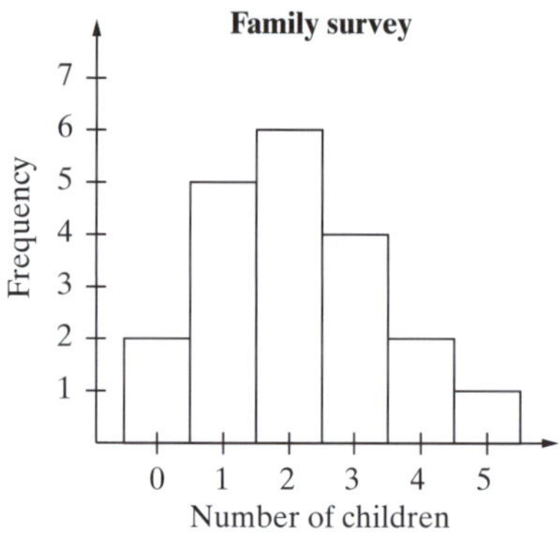

A 40% B 55% C 65% D 80% (1 mark)

Hint 1: Find the total of the ages of the boys and girls first.
Hint 2: The data is categorical.

Part B Short Answer

6 Using the histogram in question 5, find:

a the total number of children (2 marks)

b i range
ii mode
iii median (3 marks)

c the mean (2 marks)

7 A score is added to these scores: 4, 2, 8, 0, 6.
If the mean increases by 2, find the new score. (3 marks)

8 Alison listed these marks for a test out of 15:
14 10 8 13 11 8 8
If she included another mark, her mode is equal to her range. What is the new mark? (2 marks)

9 For the following scores 12 9 6 x 11 5:

a if the range is 8, write down possible values for x. (2 marks)

b if the mean is 8, find the value of x. (2 marks)

c if the median is 8, find the value of x. (1 mark)

10 The median of these ascending scores is the same as its range. 37 48 50 y 81 92
What is the value of y? (2 marks)

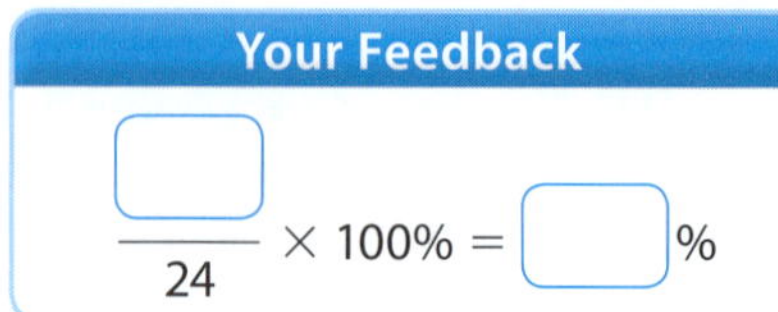

INTERPRETING DATA

Data Representation and Interpretation

ADVANCED TEST

1 A stem-and-leaf plot is shown below.

Stem	Leaf
3	*a* 3 4
4	0 0 5 7 *b*
5	2 3 4 4 4
6	5 8 9

What is the value of:

a a, if the range is 37? (1 mark)

b b, if the median is 50.5? (1 mark)

2 The boys and girls in a year eight class are surveyed to find the number of mobile phones in their homes.

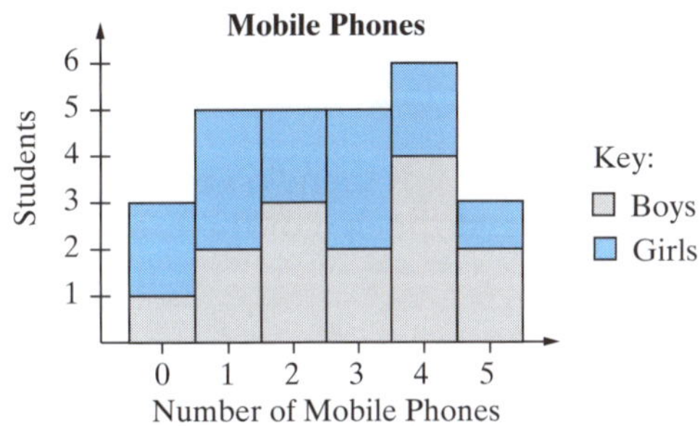

a How many students were surveyed? (1 mark)

b How many girls were surveyed? (1 mark)

c How many girls had 3 mobiles in their homes? (1 mark)

d What was the total number of mobile phones? (2 marks)

e What was the mode, median and mean number of phones for the:

  i group? ii girls? (3 marks each)

3 A survey of coffee drinkers was held to find the number of cups already consumed that particular day and the results were displayed on a side-by-side column graph.

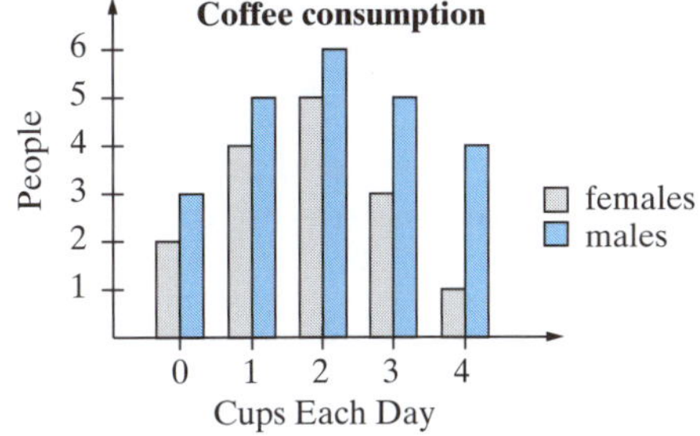

Compare and contrast the mean, mode and median for each gender. (6 marks)

4 The dot plots below show the results of a maths quiz for 8M1.

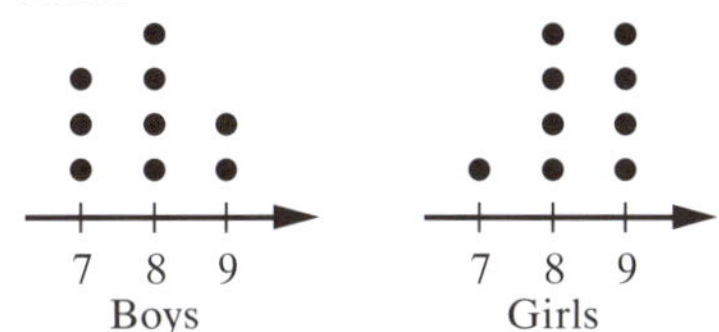

Compare the mean, mode and median for each gender. (6 marks)

5 Mia conducted a survey of 40 people to find the number of people who owned a laptop and/or a tablet. She started to record her results below. Complete the Venn diagram and two-way table.

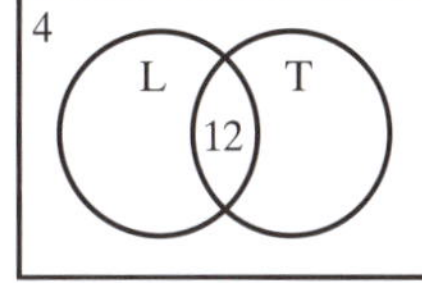

		Tablet		
		Yes	No	Total
Lap-top	Yes			
	No			
	Total	26		40

(2 marks)

6 A set of 12 scores has a range of 7, a median of 4.5, a mean of 5 and a mode of 6. Draw a frequency histogram to represent the scores. (2 marks)

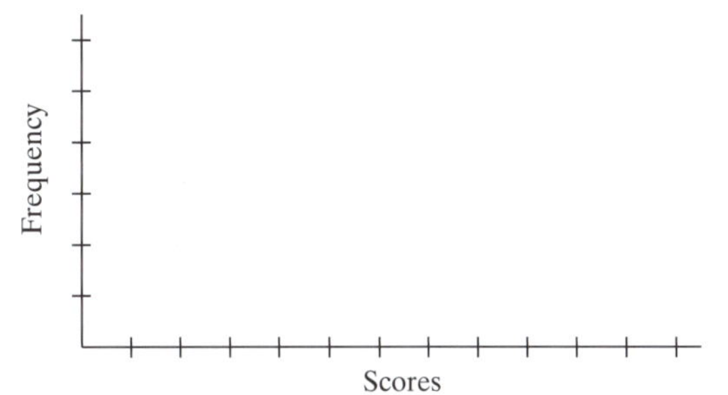

7 After four hockey games the average scored per game was three goals. In the fifth game the team won by five goals, and the overall game average increased by one goal. What was the score in the fifth game? (2 marks)

8 Here are three scores: x, 4, y. The median and the range are both 3. What are the missing scores? (1 mark)

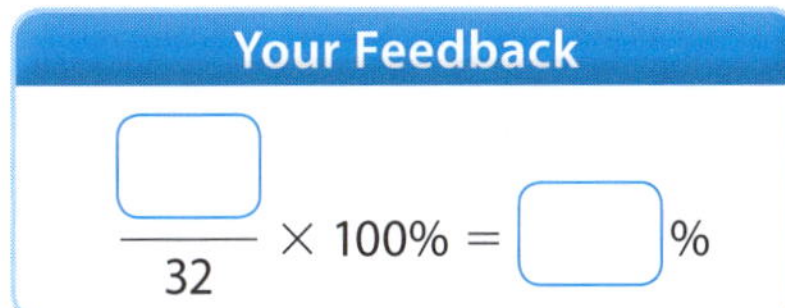

TIPS FOR THE SAMPLE EXAM PAPERS

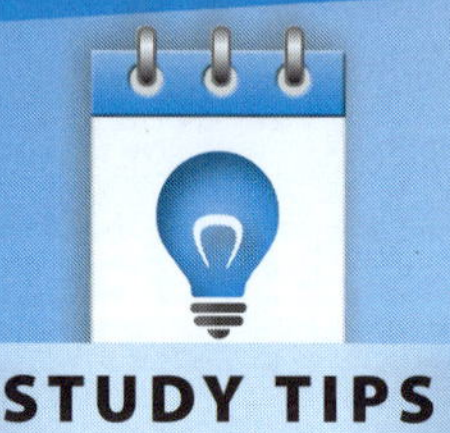

STUDY TIPS

Know what to expect

- **Find out** from your teacher exactly what topics will be assessed in the exam.
- Yearly exams normally test **all work covered** throughout the year.
- **Determine what format** is being used for the exam. Are there multiple-choice questions? Will calculators be allowed in any part of the exam?

Show all working

- **Read the instructions** on the exam paper—marks may be allocated for working.
- Even when **marks are not allocated**, working is important and it is rewarded, even though your answer may be incorrect.
- **Never use correction fluid**—just put a line through any incorrect working. Let your teacher see all your work.

Allocate your time

- Ensure you are **working through the paper efficiently** and not spending too much time on each question, only to find you run out of time at the end of the exam.

Understand mark allocations

- **Questions worth more marks** are often more complex and difficult. Working is crucial in these types of questions.

Reread and check

- Once you have **completed a question**, rather than moving on to the next, reread that question to make sure you have in fact answered the correct question. This will only take a second or two.
- If you **finish the exam** with time still remaining, check your answers—often mistakes are found and can be corrected.

Use quality diagrams

- Diagrams should be of **good quality, large and drawn with a lead pencil**. Use an eraser, not correction fluid, to delete mistakes.

Be ready

- Finally, you need to be **prepared for the exam**.
- Always **study Mathematics actively**. Active study means using pen and paper to make notes, writing down difficult questions and their solutions, and recording rules to learn.

SAMPLE EXAM PAPERS

Level of difficulty—Average

PAPER 1

Part A Multiple Choice

(10 marks)

1 Express $\frac{7}{8}$ as a percentage.

A 78% B 87% C 88% D 87.5% (1 mark)

2 Which of the following lies between $\frac{1}{3}$ and $\frac{1}{2}$?

A 20% B 30% C 40% D 60% (1 mark)

3 A die is rolled. Find the probability of tossing a 2.

A $\frac{1}{2}$ B $\frac{1}{6}$ C $\frac{1}{3}$ D $\frac{5}{6}$ (1 mark)

4 Which of the following is not a factor of $6x^2$?

A $3x$ B $2x^2$ C 6 D 4 (1 mark)

5 The solution of $3x - 2 = x + 6$ is:

A $x = 2$ B $x = 3$ C $x = 8$ D $x = 4$ (1 mark)

6 If $a = 3$ and $b = 4$, the value of $2a - b$ is:

A 19 B 2 C 1 D 6 (1 mark)

7 The line $y = 2x + 1$ passes through the point:

A (1, 1) B (1, 2) C (1, 3) D (1, 4) (1 mark)

8 Each letter of the word PROBABILITY is written on a card and placed in a bag. One card is chosen at random. The chance of choosing the letter B is:

A double the chance of choosing an I
B half the chance of choosing a P
C less than the chance of choosing an R
D the same chance as choosing an I (1 mark)

9 20% of a number is 40. What is the number?

A 8 B 16 C 80 D 200 (1 mark)

10 Which of the following is not equal to 8?

A the mean
B the median
C the mode
D the range

Score	Frequency
6	3
7	4
8	6
9	4
10	3

(1 mark)

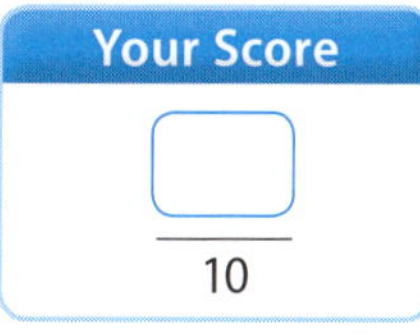

Part B Short Answer **(30 marks)**

11 Express 140% as a mixed numeral. (1 mark)

12 Write $8\frac{1}{2}\%$ as a decimal. (1 mark)

13 Find 35% of $3000. (1 mark)

14 Find 5% of 8 litres. (1 mark)

15 Simplify $12:16$ (1 mark)

16 Simplify 50c : $2 (1 mark)

17 I travel 480 km at an average speed of 80 km/h. How long will it take me to reach my destination? (1 mark)

18 Expand $3(2x + 1)$ (1 mark)

19 Simplify $12x^2 \times 3xy$ (1 mark)

20 Simplify $\frac{3ab}{12a}$ (1 mark)

21 If $y = 4$, then $2y - 3 =$ (1 mark)

22 If $p = 6$ and $q = 3$, find $2p + q$ (1 mark)

23 Factorise $3ab - 6a$ (1 mark)

24 Rewrite 2150 in 12-hour time. (1 mark)

25 If $2a - 1 = 9$, find the value of a. (1 mark)

26 Expand $-4(2 - 3y)$ (1 mark)

27 Rewrite $a \times a \times a \times a \times a \times b \times b \times b \times b$ (1 mark)

28 The line $y = 3x - 2$ is graphed on the number plane. Find the point where the line crosses the y-axis. (1 mark)

29 Does the point (3, 1) lie on the line $y = 2x - 5$? (1 mark)

30 Find the range of the scores 4, 6, 2, 8, −1, 30, 4. (1 mark)

31 Calculate $4.2^2 + 2.3^2$ (1 mark)

32 Evaluate $\sqrt{3.74}$ correct to two decimal places. (1 mark)

33 Evaluate $3^0 + (2 \times y)^0$ (1 mark)

34 Find the circumference of a circle with radius 9 cm.

Give your answer correct to 2 decimal places. (1 mark)

35 Find the area of the circle, in terms of π:

O

6 cm

(1 mark)

36 Find the value of the pronumeral:

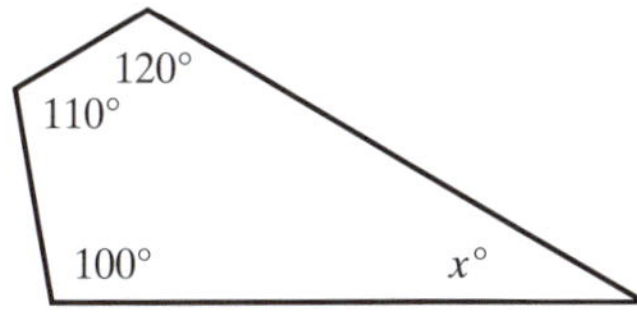

(1 mark)

37 Find the value of x:

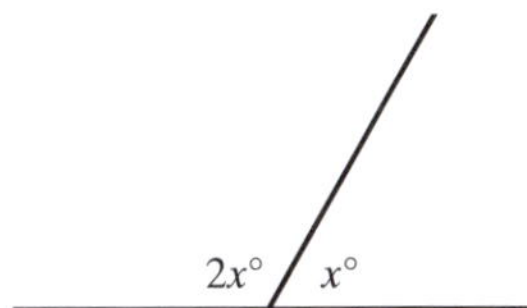

(1 mark)

38 Write the equation of the line graphed on the number plane.

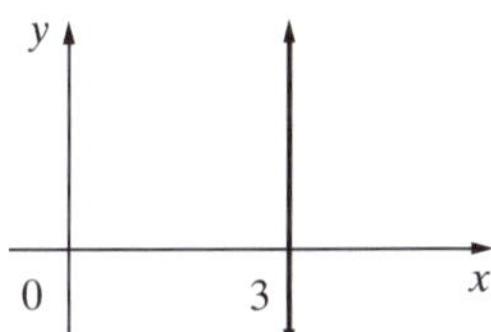

(1 mark)

39 Which two of the following triangles are congruent?

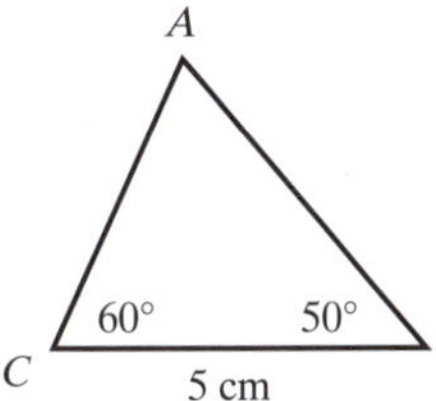

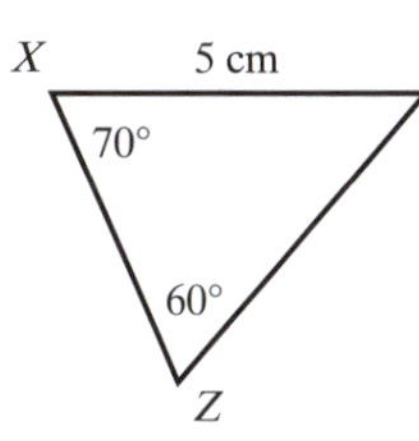

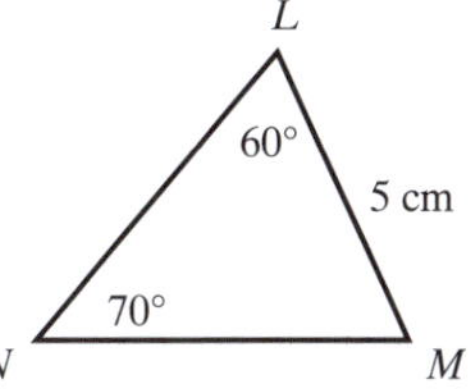

(1 mark)

40 Give a reason why $\triangle ABC \equiv \triangle PQR$.

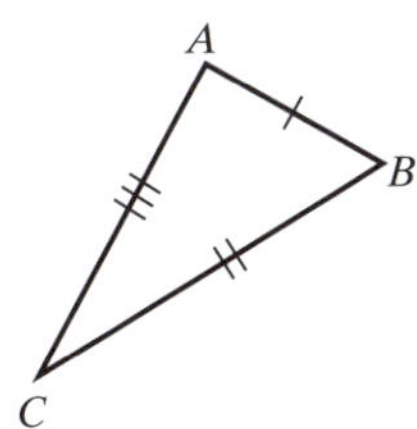

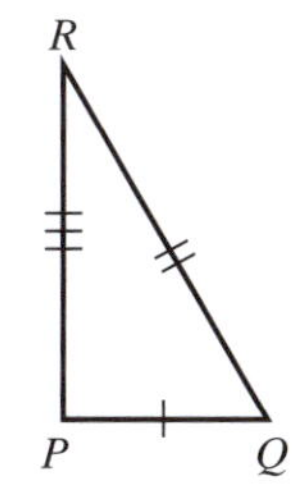

(1 mark)

Your Score

/30

PAGE 166

Part C Show All Working (60 marks)

41 Find 12.5% of \$640. (2 marks)

42 A stamp is bought for \$45 and sold later for \$60. Express the profit as a percentage of the cost price. (2 marks)

43 A car is discounted by 15% from \$18 990. Find the new price. (2 marks)

44 The area of a square is 64 cm^2. What is its perimeter? (2 marks)

45 If 25% of the price of a DVD recorder is \$120, find the whole price. (2 marks)

46 Divide \$56 in the ratio 3 : 5. (2 marks)

47 It takes Maria 6 hours to travel 510 kilometres. Find her average speed. (2 marks)

48 From a flock of 2400 sheep a farmer sold 80 bales of wool, each averaging 120 kilograms of wool. What is the average yield of wool per sheep? (2 marks)

49 A bag contains 2 black balls, 5 white balls and 3 green balls. A ball is chosen at random. What is the probability that the ball is:

a white? b not black? (2 marks)

50 Expand and simplify $3(a + 2) + 4(2a + 6)$ (2 marks)

51 Solve $3a - 2 = 2a + 5$ (2 marks)

52 Solve $2(3x - 1) = 5x + 8$ (2 marks)

53 Find the area, in hectares, of a rectangular paddock with dimensions 600 m by 400 m. (2 marks)

54

x	0	1	2	3
y	4	7	10	13

a Write a rule linking y and x.
b If $x = 5$, find the value of y. (2 marks)

55 If $A = xy$, find A when $x = 12.8$ and $y = 0.04$. (2 marks)

56 a Find an expression for the perimeter in terms of x. (1 mark)
b If the perimeter is 48 cm, find the value of x. (1 mark)

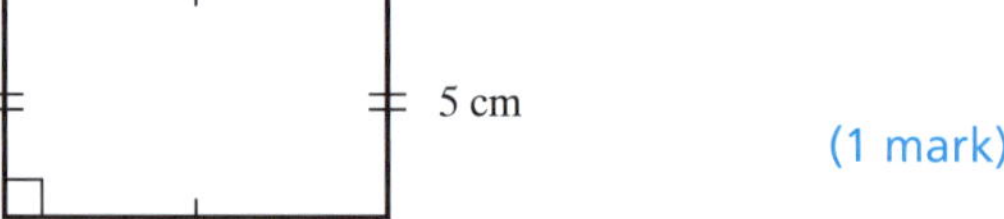

57 Find the value of x.

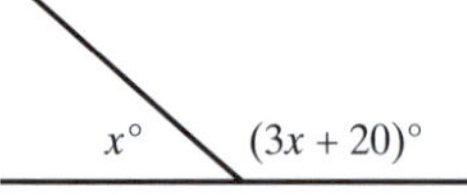

(2 marks)

58 Complete the table for $y = 2x - 1$ and graph the line on the number plane. (2 marks)

x	0	1	2
y			

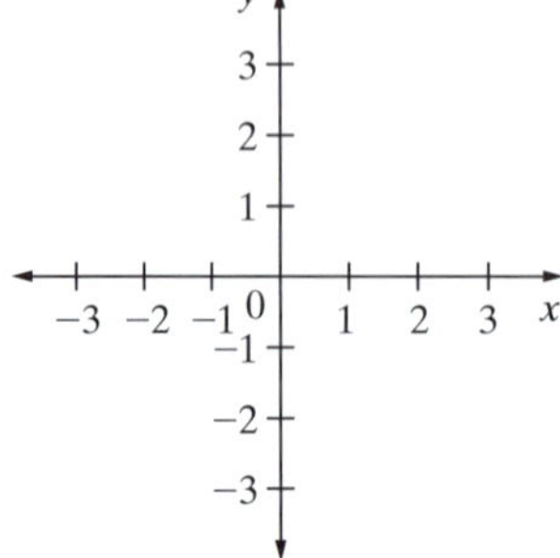

59 The cost (C) of a hire car in dollars is found using $C = 50 + 4d$ where d = distance, in kilometres.

a Complete the table. (1 mark)

d	0	5	10	20	40
C					

b Draw a graph for $C = 50 + 4d$

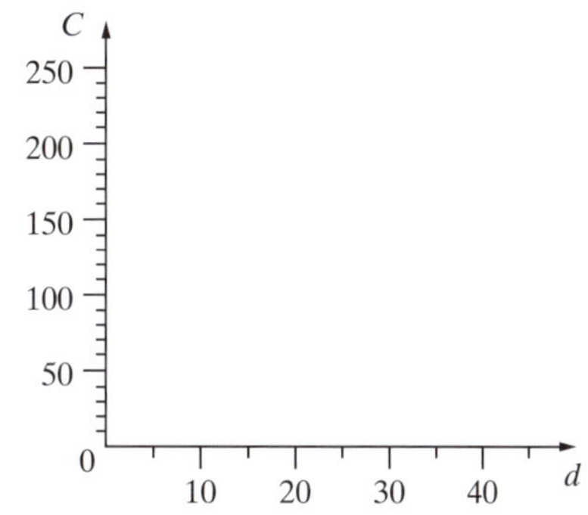

(1 mark)

60 Draw a dot plot for the data recorded in the frequency table below:

Score	Frequency
12	2
13	4
14	5
15	3

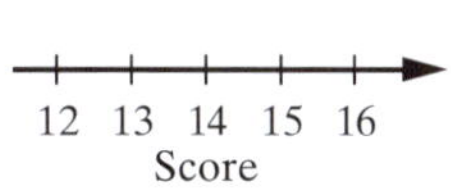

(2 marks)

61 For the scores 3, 5, 2, −1, 6, 8, 9, 2, find the:

a mode b median (2 marks)

62 Find the mean of 5, 2, 3, 10, 6, 8, 2, 4, 8, 11. (2 marks)

63 Find the value of x if the median of the following scores is the same as the range.

Stem	Leaf
2	3 7
3	2 8 9
4	2 2 4 5 7
5	3 8
6	x

(2 marks)

64 a Complete the frequency table. (1 mark)

b Find the mean.

Score (x)	Frequency (f)	fx
6	2	12
7	4	28
8	7	56
9	6	
10	3	
Total		

(1 mark)

65 Find the value of the pronumeral:

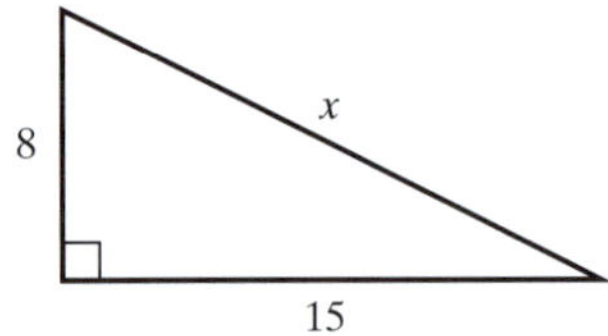

(2 marks)

66 Find the area:

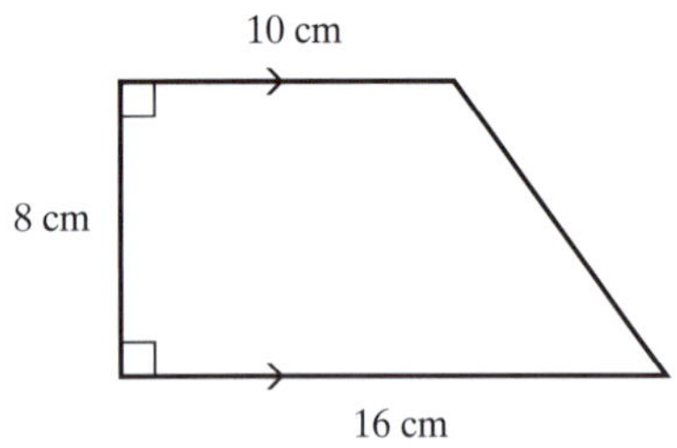

(2 marks)

67 Bronwyn bought a bracelet for \$360 and later sold it for \$240.
What was her loss as a percentage of her cost price? (2 marks)

68 Find the volume of the cylinder, correct to 2 decimal places.

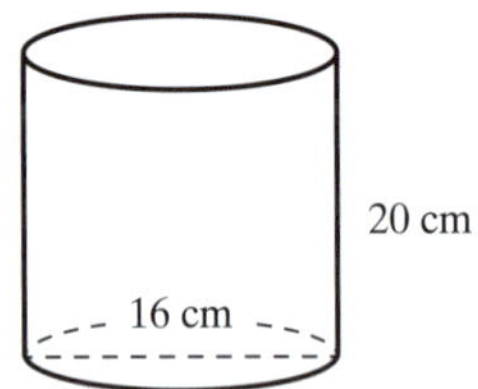

(2 marks)

69 Find the value of the pronumerals:

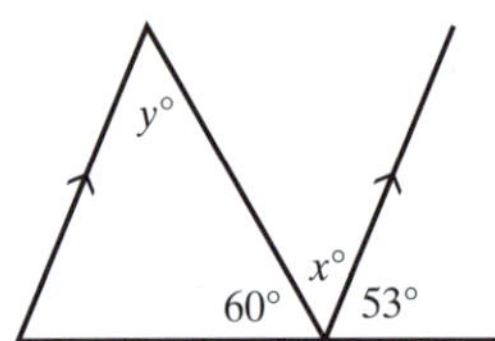

(2 marks)

70 Expand and simplify: $3 - (2 - x) - 4(x + 1)$ (2 marks)

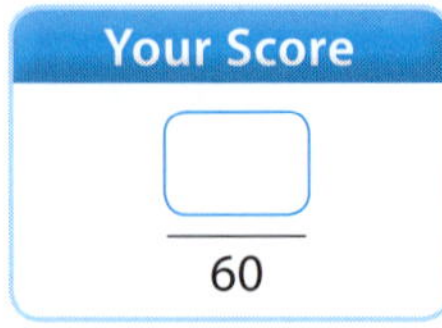

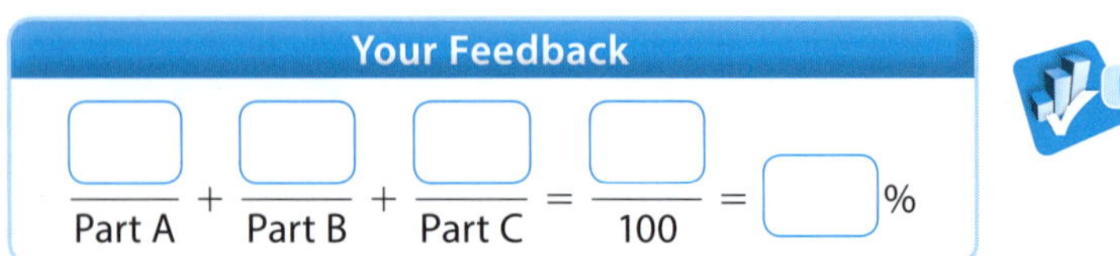

SAMPLE EXAM PAPERS

Level of difficulty—Above average

PAPER 2

Part A Multiple Choice (10 marks)

1 Find 18% of \$600.

A \$0.11 B \$1.08 C \$10.80 D \$108 (1 mark)

2 What percentage is 50c of \$4?

A 8% B 80% C 12.5% D 1.25% (1 mark)

3 The area of a square with perimeter 32 mm is:

A 16 cm^2 B 64 cm^2 C 6.4 cm^2 D 0.64 cm^2 (1 mark)

4 Which is the best pay rate?

A \$845 per week B \$1695 per fortnight
C \$3655 per month D \$43 946 per year (1 mark)

5 Kayla solved the equation $3(x + 4) = 18$

Her solution is detailed below.

$3(x + 4) = 18$
$3x + 12 = 18$ Line 1
$3x = 18 + 12$ Line 2
$\frac{3x}{3} = \frac{30}{3}$ Line 3
$x = 10$ Line 4

Kayla has made one mistake. She made the mistake in:

A Line 1 B Line 2 C Line 3 D Line 4 (1 mark)

6 Rahul travelled from his home and arrived at his friend's house two-and-a-quarter hours later. If he arrived at 1340, he left home at:

A 11:15 am B 11:25 am C 10:15 am D 10:25 am (1 mark)

7 If $x = -4$, $y = 2$, $z = 3$, the value of $xy - z$ is:

A -45 B -11 C -5 D -9 (1 mark)

8 The point of intersection of the lines $y = 3$ and $x = -2$ is:

A $(-2, 3)$ B $(-3, 2)$ C $(2, -3)$ D $(3, -2)$ (1 mark)

9 The median of the scores 40, 24, 38, 26, x, 16 is 29. The value of x is:

A 24 B 29 C 31 D 32 (1 mark)

10 Which of the following could represent the three sides of a right-angled triangle?

A 5 cm, 6 cm, 10 cm
B 7 cm, 24 cm, 25 cm
C 10 cm, 12 cm, 24 cm
D 21 cm, 27 cm, 28 cm (1 mark)

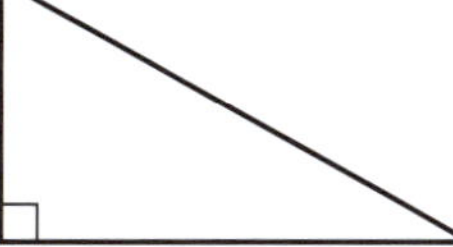

Your Score

/10

PAGE 168

Part B Short Answer (30 marks)

11 Find $3\frac{1}{2}\%$ of \$940. (1 mark)

12 In one day Dominic slept for 9 hours.
What percentage of the day was Dominic awake? (1 mark)

13 Increase \$110 by $12\frac{3}{4}\%$ (1 mark)

14 At a hardware store all power tools are reduced in price by 15%.
The original price of a cordless drill is \$48. Find the new price. (1 mark)

15 If 12 oranges cost \$10.20, find the cost of 7 oranges. (1 mark)

16 Simplify \$3.75 : \$4 (1 mark)

17 Simplify $\frac{3}{4} : \frac{2}{3}$ (1 mark)

18 A car travels 475 km in 6 hours 20 minutes.
What is the average speed? (1 mark)

19 A raffle consists of 100 tickets and John buys one ticket.
A ticket is drawn for first prize but John's name is not called out.
A second ticket is then drawn.
What is the probability that John wins this prize? (1 mark)

20 A circle is split into 12 equal parts.
The sectors are numbered using the digits 1, 2 and 3.
Find the probability of spinning an odd number.

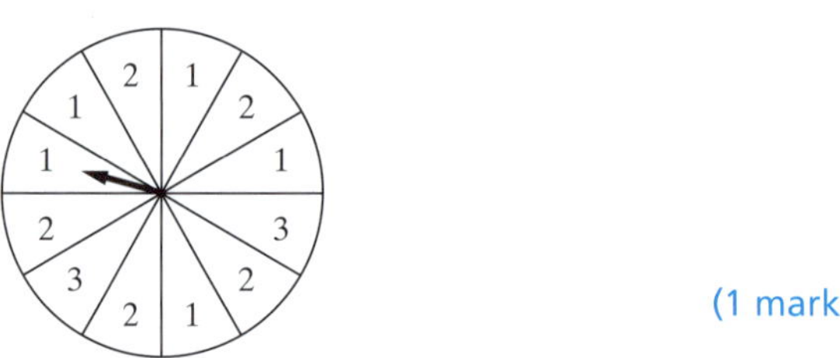

(1 mark)

21 Expand and simplify $3(2a - 1) - 2(a + 6)$ (1 mark)

22 Factorise $\pi r^2 - 2\pi r$ (1 mark)

23 A plant grows at a rate of 12 m in 80 days. Express this rate in cm per hour. (1 mark)

24 Find the value of x if $3x - 2 = x + 6$ (1 mark)

25 Find the solution of $4(g + 1) = 16$ (1 mark)

26 Simplify $3pq - p^2 - qp + 2p^2$ (1 mark)

27 If $x = 5$, find the value of $(2x)^2 - 2x^2$ (1 mark)

28 If $p = -2$ and $q = -3$, evaluate $p^2 - q^2$ (1 mark)

29 The number plane shows the graph of $y = x + 4$ and $x = -2$.
Find the point of intersection of the two lines.

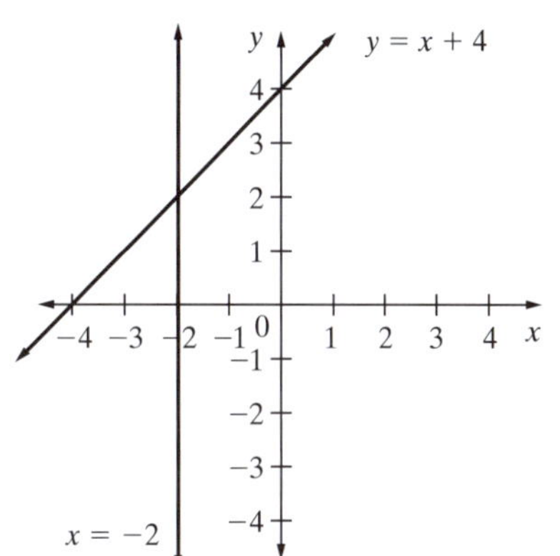

(1 mark)

30 After 6 games of soccer, Jenny's team has a mean of 3 goals per game.
After another game the mean has increased to 4.
How many goals were scored in the seventh game? (1 mark)

31 Write another score to make the range equal to the mode:
10, 8, 12, 10, 14, 10 (1 mark)

32 Find the mean of $2x$, $5x$, $2x$ and $3x$. (1 mark)

33 Find the length of AB.

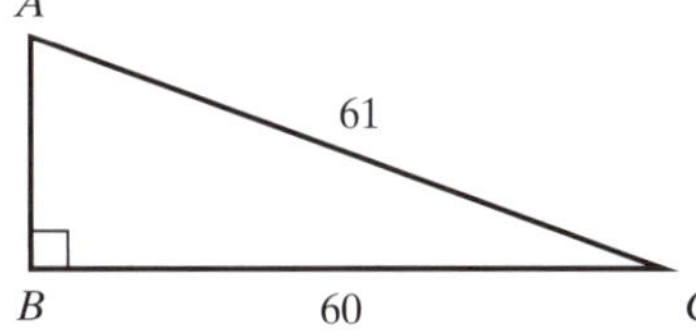

(1 mark)

34 Find the area of the shaded region.

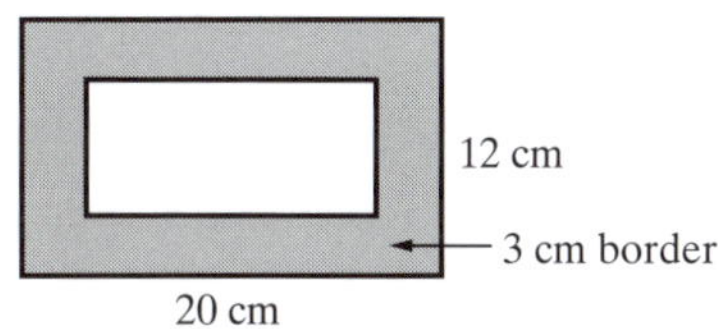

(1 mark)

35 A solid metal cube has a side length of 4 cm. Every cm^3 of the metal has a mass of 50 grams.
What is the total mass of the cube in kilograms? (1 mark)

36 Find the circumference, correct to 2 decimal places.

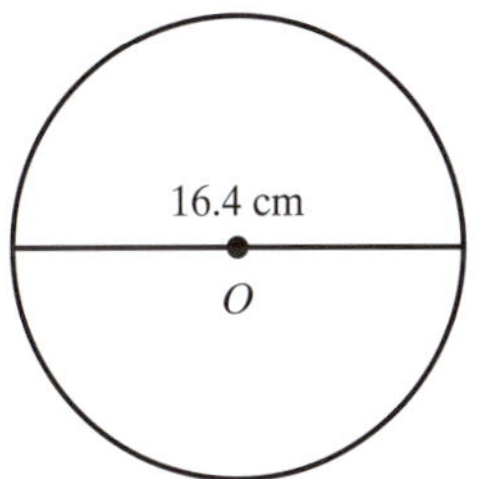

(1 mark)

37 Find the radius of a circle with an area of 36π cm^2. (1 mark)

38 Find the value of the pronumeral:

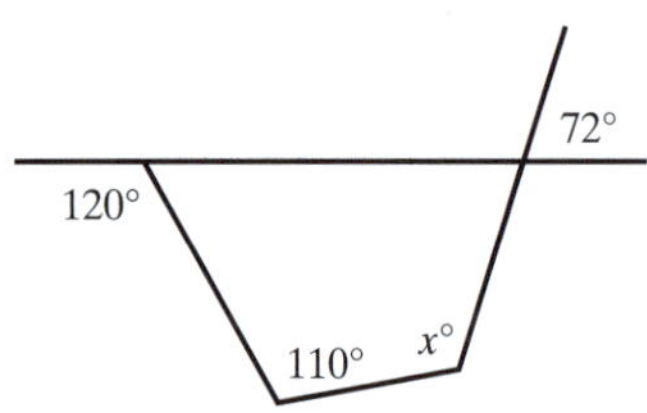

(1 mark)

39 Find the area of *ACBD*.

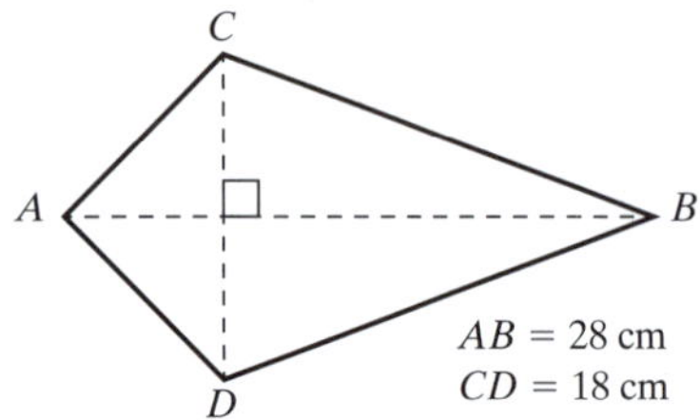

(1 mark)

40 In the diagram $\triangle ACD \equiv \triangle ABD$

Complete the following:

CD = ______ [____________________]

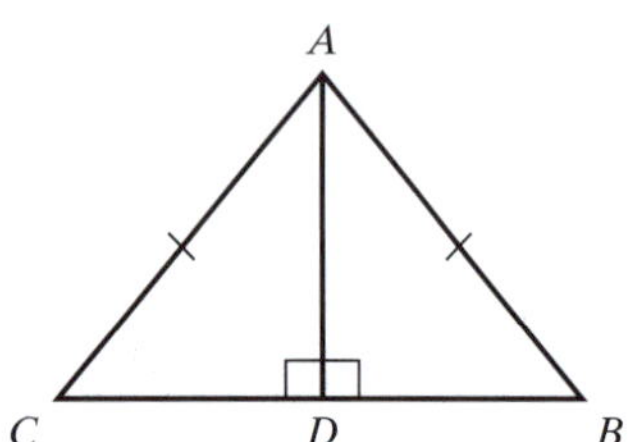

(1 mark)

Your Score

/30

Part C Show All Working (60 marks)

41 Calculate, correct to 2 decimal places: $\dfrac{\sqrt{3.6 \times 2.05}}{1.4 - 0.07}$ (2 marks)

42 The angles in a right-angled triangle are in the ratio 5 : 3 : 2.
Find the size of the smallest angle. (2 marks)

43 In our year 8 visual arts class the ratio of boys to girls is 5 : 4. If there are 8 girls in the class how many more boys are in the class than girls? (2 marks)

44 Dean leaves Nambucca Heads at 4:20 am and travels 660 km at an average speed of 75 km/h. What time does Dean arrive at his destination? (2 marks)

45 A bag contains 9 identical balls numbered from 1 to 9. If a ball is chosen at random, what is the probability that the number on the ball is:

a even? **b** not divisible by 3? (2 marks)

46 If $a = -1, b = -2$ and $c = 3$, find T if $T = b^2 - ac$. (2 marks)

47 The height of a shrub increases by 5% each month. At the end of April the shrub was 84 cm tall. How high was the shrub at the beginning of April? (2 marks)

48 Solve $3(2x - 1) = 2(2x + 8)$ (2 marks)

49 If $A = \frac{1}{2}h(a + b)$, find b, if $A = 75, h = 10$ and $a = 6$. (2 marks)

50 Find the value of the pronumeral.

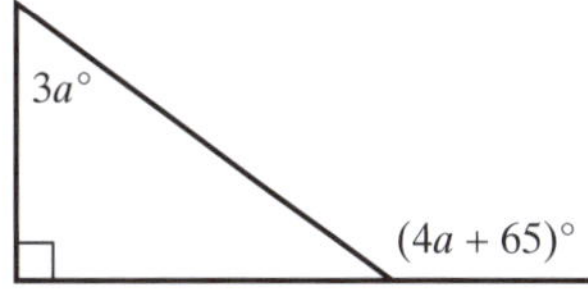

(2 marks)

51 The sum of three consecutive odd numbers is 9. By solving an equation, find the numbers. (2 marks)

52 **a** Using the table, write an equation linking C and n. (1 mark)

n	2	3	5	7	10
C	11	15	23	31	43

b Use your answer in part **a** to find the value of n, given $C = 195$. (1 mark)

53 Graph the line $y = 3 - 2x$ on the number plane provided. (2 marks)

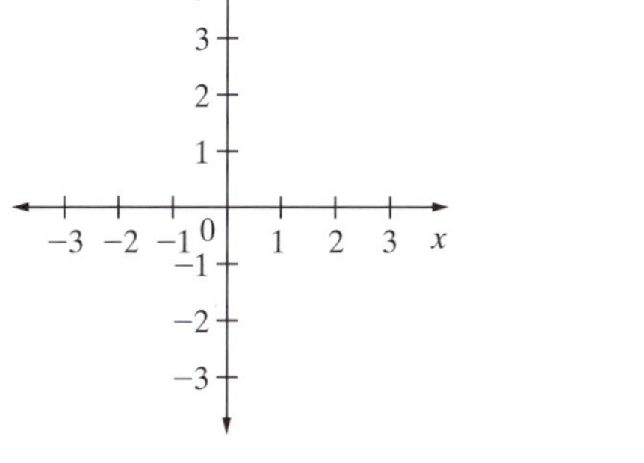

54 Complete the table to find the values of a and b. (2 marks)

Score (x)	Frequency (f)	fx
16	4	
17		119
18	10	180
19	a	b
20	6	
Total	35	635

55 The shoe sizes of a group of students were recorded in the histogram.

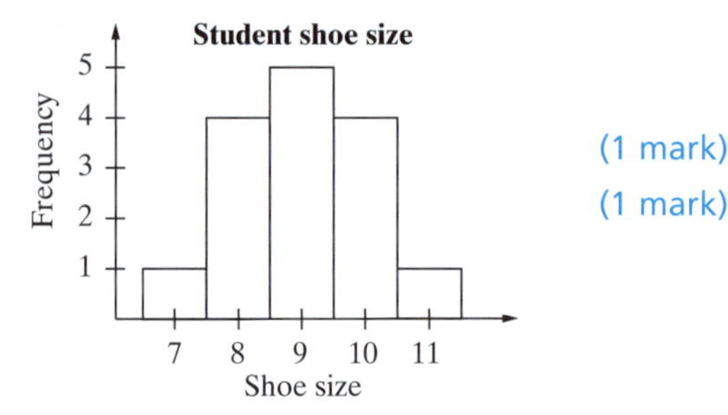

a How many students participated in the survey? (1 mark)

b Find the mean shoe size. (1 mark)

56 Find the:

a mode b median

Score	10	11	12	13	14	15
Frequency	2	4	7	6	3	3

(2 marks)

57 Find the:

a median b mean

Stem	Leaf
0	2 4 7
1	0 0 4 7 9
2	3 8 9
3	4 4 5 5 5 8
4	0 9

(2 marks)

58 In the frequency table, the median is identical to the range.

a Find a possible value of a. (1 mark)

b Find the mode. (1 mark)

Score	Frequency
4	a
8	10

59 Draw a frequency histogram and frequency polygon for the following frequency distribution table:

Score	Frequency
21	4
22	6
23	8
24	10
25	6

(2 marks)

60 Find the value of x, correct to 2 decimal places.

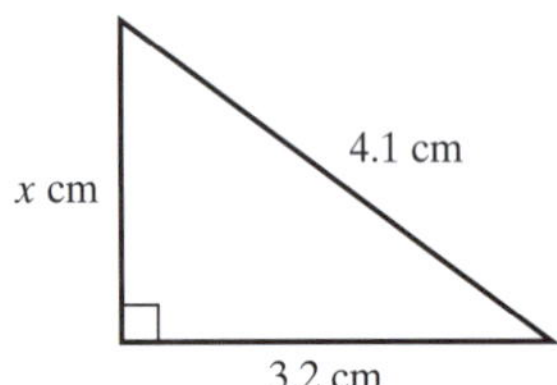

(2 marks)

61 Find the length of PQ.

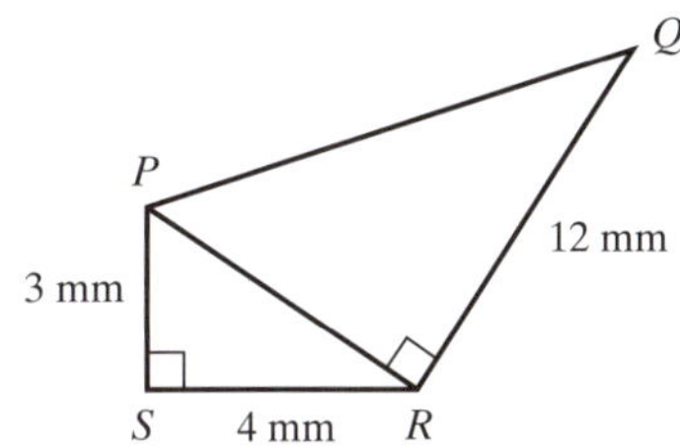

(2 marks)

62 Find the perimeter.

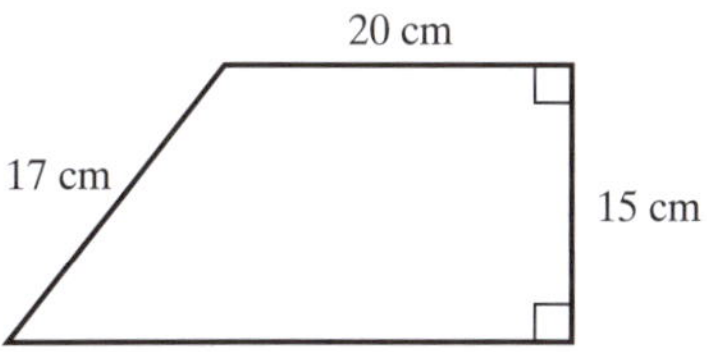

(2 marks)

63

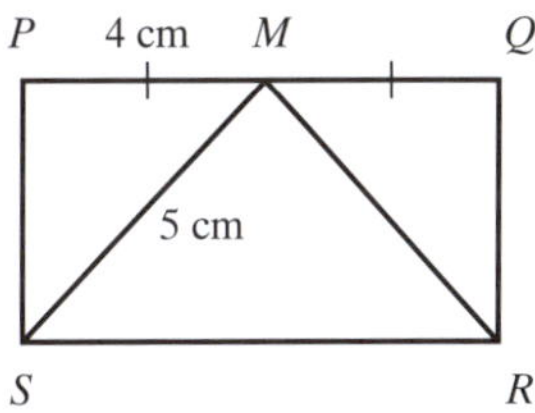

$PQRS$ is a rectangle.
M is the midpoint of PQ, where $PM = 4$ cm.
MS is 5 cm.
Find the perimeter of $\triangle PMS$.

(2 marks)

64 A mechanic charged $167.20 to service a car. The price includes 10% GST.
Find the cost of the service without GST. (2 marks)

65 Find the perimeter of the semi-circle. Leave the answer in terms of π.

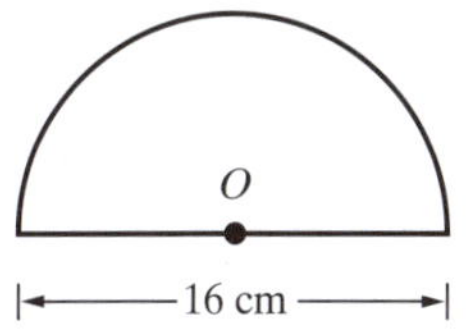

(2 marks)

66 A garden has been designed using two identical semi-circles of radius 5 metres, as shown in the diagram.

What is the area of the garden, correct to 2 decimal places?

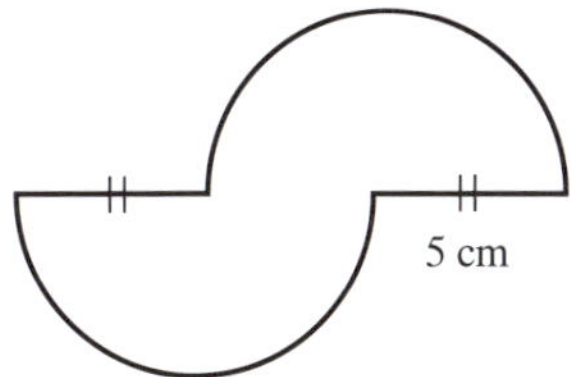

(2 marks)

67 A bag contains red, blue and green balls. The ratio of red balls to blue balls is 3 : 4 and the ratio of blue balls to green balls is 2 : 5. If there are 340 balls, how many are red? (2 marks)

68 Find the volume of the solid. Give your answer to 2 decimal places.

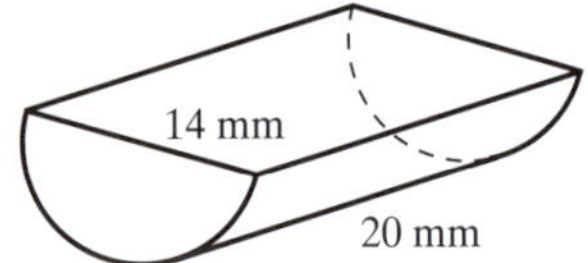

(2 marks)

69 Find the value of the pronumerals.

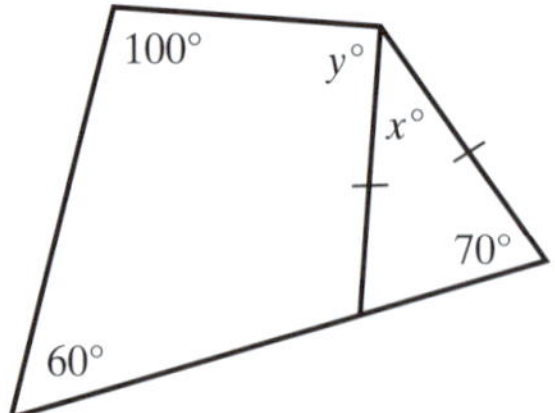

(2 marks)

70 A group of 75 students visited three Gold Coast theme parks for their end-of-year activity. When they arrived home they completed a survey. Thirty-four students enjoyed Movie World, 32 students Wet-and-Wild and 40 students enjoyed SeaWorld. Sixteen students liked Movie World and Wet-and-Wild, 13 liked Movie World and SeaWorld while 11 liked Sea World and Wet-and-Wild. Five liked Movie World, Sea-World and Wet-and-Wild. Draw a Venn diagram to find the number of students who did not like any of the theme parks. (2 marks)

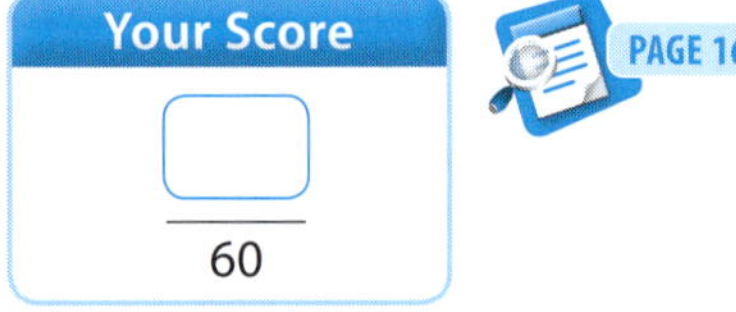

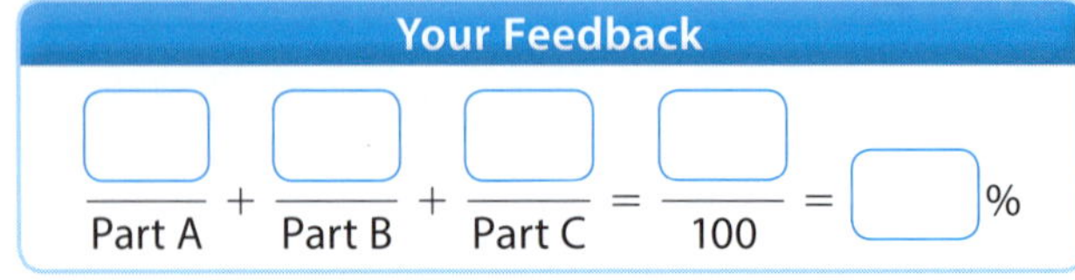

SAMPLE EXAM PAPERS

Level of difficulty—Difficult

60 MINUTES

PAPER 3

Part A Multiple Choice (10 marks)

1 Which is the greatest?

A 2% of \$20 B 4% of \$40 C 6% of \$60 D 8% of \$80 (1 mark)

2 What percentage of $\angle ABC$ is $\angle DBA$?

A $66\frac{2}{3}\%$ B 40%

C 75% D 80%

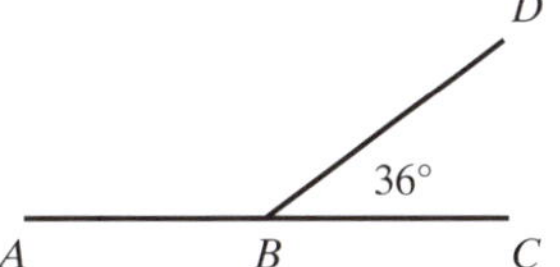

(1 mark)

3 The price of a dress was \$160. This price was increased by 15%. A fortnight later Laura bought the dress at a 15% discount sale. How much did she pay for the dress?

A \$160 B \$158.40 C \$156.40 D \$162.50 (1 mark)

4 To make cordial, Josh pours 375 mL of concentrate into an empty two-litre container. He then fills the remainder of the container with water. Find the ratio of concentrate to water in the container.

A 375 : 2 B 3 : 16 C 3 : 13 D 1 : 3 (1 mark)

5 Melissa plays this game: Think of a number. Add 3. Double your answer. Take away 1. The probability that the result is even is:

A 0 B $\frac{1}{2}$ C 1 D 2 (1 mark)

6 The mean of four numbers is 10. Two more numbers are included and the mean increases by 1. If one of these new numbers is 8, the other number is:

A 12 B 14 C 16 D 18 (1 mark)

7 The point of intersection of the lines $y = 2$ and $y = x + 3$ is:

A $(-1, 2)$ B $(0, 2)$ C $(1, 2)$ D $(-2, 2)$ (1 mark)

8 The number plane shows the graph of $y = 2x - 3$

The line k could be:

A $y = 2x + 4$ B $y = x - 3$

C $y = 3x - 2$ D $y = 2x$

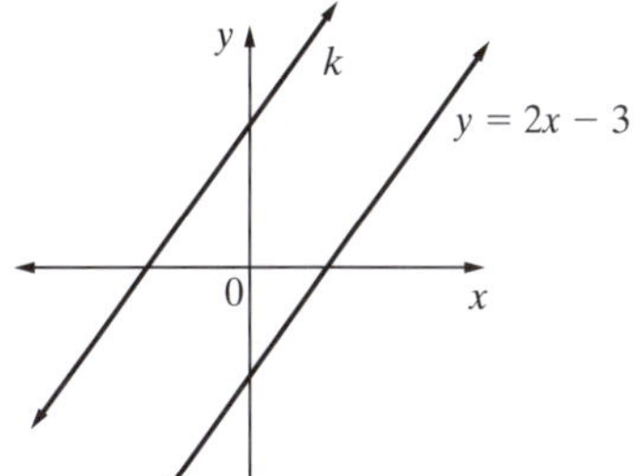

(1 mark)

9 The mean of a set of scores is the same as the median. The scores could not be:

A 3, 5, 8, 10 B 4, 7, 8, 11 C 2, 6, 7, 9 D 4, 6, 8, 10 (1 mark)

10 Divide \$440 between Liam, Jackson and Shae, so that Shae has \$40 more than Liam but \$60 less than Jackson. What is Jackson's share?

A \$200 B \$180 C \$220 D \$240 (1 mark)

Your Score

/10

PAGE 171

Part B Short Answer (30 marks)

11 Express $\frac{7}{9}$ as a percentage. (1 mark)

12 Find $12\frac{3}{4}\%$ of \$680. (1 mark)

13

Shopping centre	Number of students
Smith Plaza	23
Town Square	
Garden Mall	18
Jones Centre	7

A survey was conducted involving 60 students to find their favourite shopping centre. The results are detailed in the table to the left:

What percentage of the students preferred shopping at Town Square? (1 mark)

14 Next month, Helen will receive a 12% pay rise to increase her pay to \$2072 per fortnight.
Find Helen's existing pay. (1 mark)

15 Darcy owns a five-hectare property and decides to sell a 750 m^2 portion to his son.
What percentage of his original area will remain? (1 mark)

16 On the same number plane, Tess graphed the lines $x = 3$ and $2x - y = 5$
What is the point of intersection of the two lines? (1 mark)

17 Sandy sought sponsorship for '100 000 seconds of silence'.
Express this time in hours minutes seconds. (1 mark)

18 Simplify 25 m^2 : 50 cm^2 (1 mark)

19 Mark, Kim and Simon form a syndicate to purchase lottery tickets.
Each week Mark contributes \$2, Kim \$2.50 and Simon \$1.50.
If they win a prize of \$7200, how much will Kim receive if their winnings are shared in the ratio of their contributions? (1 mark)

20 Jason left his home at 9:20 am and travelled to Albany, a distance of 360 km, averaging 75 km/h.
What time did Jason arrive in Albany? (1 mark)

21 A game of 'memory' is played using 16 identical cards.
The cards have pictures of animals such that there are 2 matching cards with dogs, 2 matching cards with cats and so on.
The cards are placed randomly face down on a table and Adam turns one card to reveal a dog.
Adam now turns a second card.
What is the probability that this card also has a picture of a dog? (1 mark)

22 Expand and simplify $3 - (3 - 3y) - 3y$ (1 mark)

23 Factorise $a(a + b) - 2(a + b)$ (1 mark)

24 If $M = \frac{3}{4}(N - 24)$ find N when $M = 84$. (1 mark)

25 Find the area of the triangle.

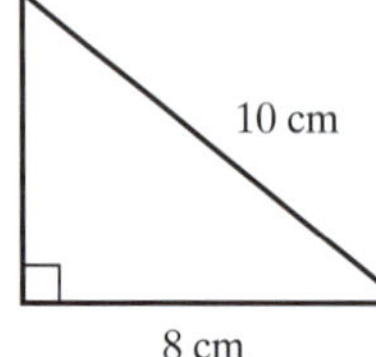

(1 mark)

26 $A(-2, -1)$, $B(4, -1)$ and $C(4, 7)$ are plotted on a number plane.
Find the perimeter of $\triangle ABC$.

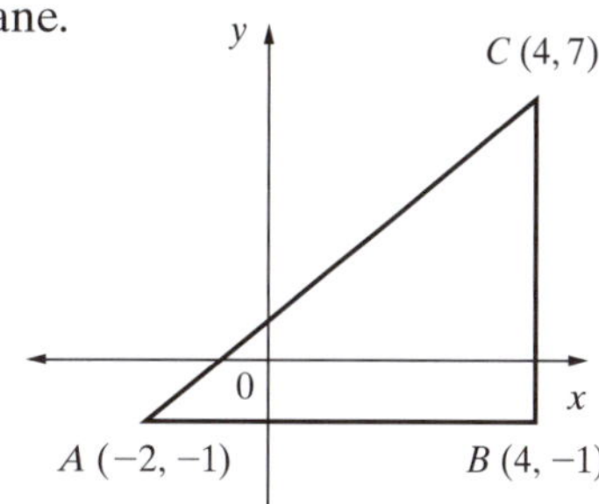

(1 mark)

27 The area of $\triangle PQR$ is 36 cm^2 and the base QR is 12 cm.
Find the perimeter, correct to 2 decimal places.

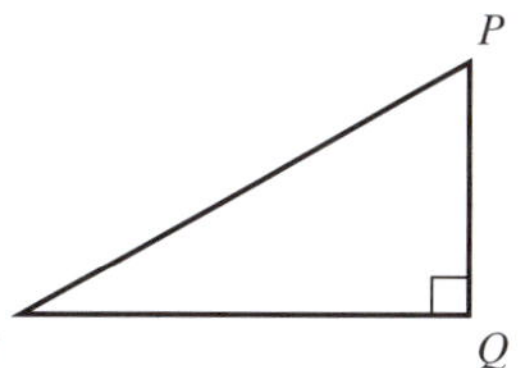

(1 mark)

28 $ABCD$ is a kite. $AC = 10$ cm, $AB = 5$ cm, $DB = 6$ cm.
Find the length of EC.

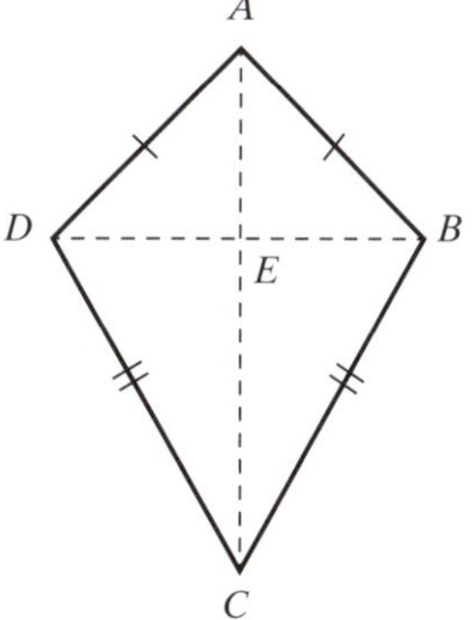

(1 mark)

29 The sum of three times a number and 18 is decreased by 12 and the result is 30.
Use an equation to find the number. (1 mark)

30 One hundred thousand litres of water is used to fill an ice skating rink.
If the area of the rink is quarter of an hectare, find the depth of the water before it is frozen. (1 mark)

31 Eighty students at a school had their eyes tested and the results were recorded in the table.
If a student was chosen at random, what is the probability the student is a male who does not require glasses? (1 mark)

Results of eye tests

	Females	Males	**Total**
Requires glasses	7		
Does not require glasses			68
Total	46		

32 Find the circumference of a circle with diameter $4\frac{1}{2}$ cm. Leave your answer in terms of π. (1 mark)

SAMPLE EXAM PAPERS

Level of difficulty—Difficult (continued) PAPER 3

33 By measurement and calculation, find the area of the circle, correct to 2 decimal places.

(1 mark)

34 A piece of cotton 50 metres long has been wound tightly around a cotton reel.
The cotton reel has a diameter of 3 cm.
Approximately how many times has the cotton been wound around the reel?
Leave your answer to the nearest hundred. (1 mark)

35 Find the value of the pronumeral.

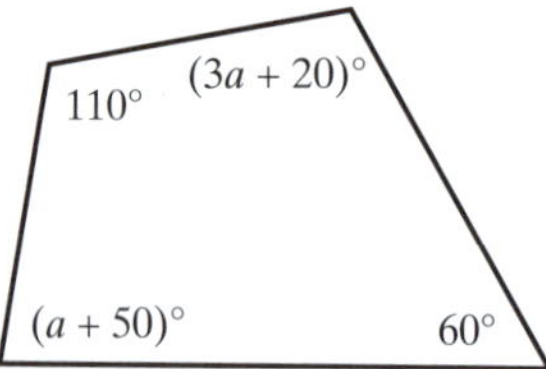

(1 mark)

36 $ABDE$ is a parallelogram and $BD = BC$.
$\angle BAE = 130°$
Find the size of $\angle BCD$.

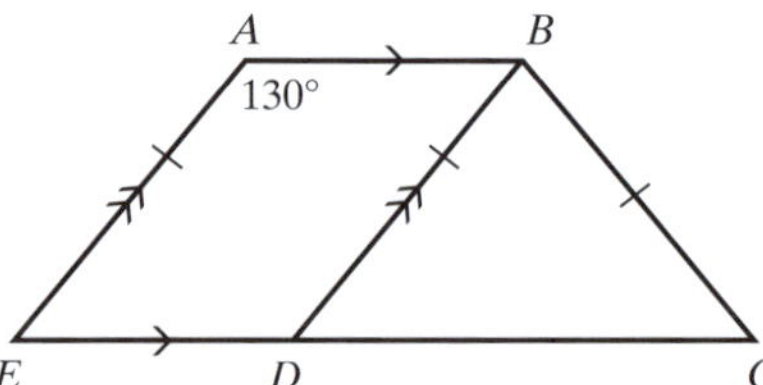

(1 mark)

37 Explain why $\angle ACB = \angle ADB$.

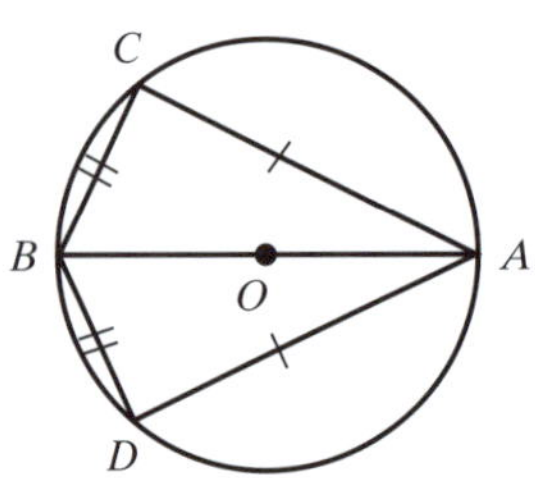

(1 mark)

38 A group of 40 tea drinkers was surveyed. Twenty-three added sugar to their tea while 26 added milk. Nineteen people added both sugar and milk to their tea. If a person is chosen at random, what is the probability that they drink their tea with no added milk or sugar?

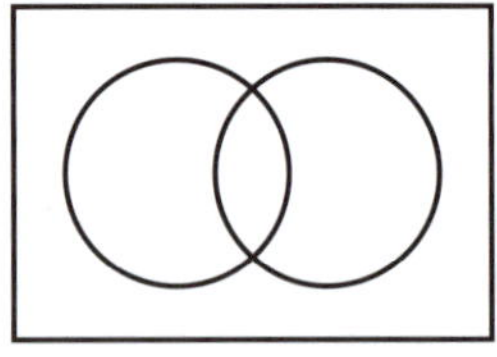

(1 mark)

39 The call-out rate for an electrician is given by the formula $C = 80 + 120h$ where C is the cost in dollars and h is the number of hours. If Min paid \$350 to the electrician, how long did the electrician work? (1 mark)

40 At a school dance there were 40 more girls than boys and the ratio of teachers to boys was 2 : 25. If there were 18 teachers at the dance, what was the total number of students present? (1 mark)

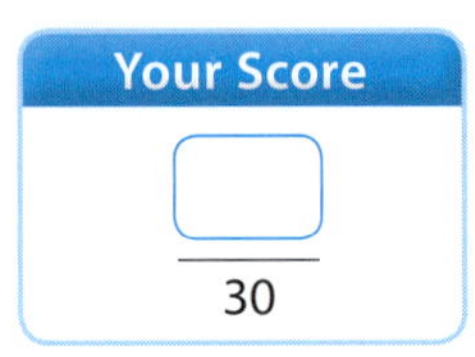

Part C Show All Working (60 marks)

41 Find the value of the pronumerals.

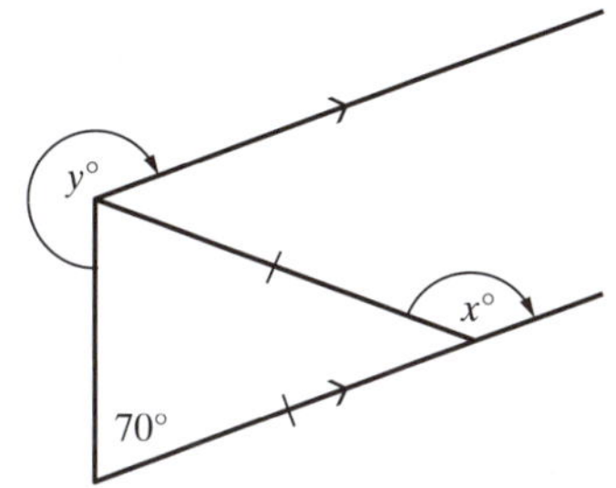

(2 marks)

42 A digital camera is dropped in price by successive discounts of 20% and 5%.

a What single rate of discount is equivalent to these successive discounts? (1 mark)

b If the new price is $380, what was the original price prior to the two discounts? (1 mark)

43 A length of timber measuring 3.2 metres is cut into two pieces where the first is three times as long as the second. Find the length of the longer piece. (2 marks)

44 In a church youth group the ratio of boys to girls is 2 : 3. On a 'bring your friends' night all the boys bring 2 male friends each while the girls bring a female friend each. What is the new ratio of boys to girls? (2 marks)

The following information is used for questions 45 and 46.
In her new car, Fiona uses 91-octane petrol or 95-octane petrol. The car has a 60-litre capacity fuel tank.

Petrol type	Fuel economy	Cost per litre
91-octane	8 L/100 km	142.9 c/L
95-octane	7.5 L/100 km	149.9 c/L

45 How much further can Fiona drive on a tank of petrol when she uses 95-octane petrol instead of the 91-octane petrol? (2 marks)

46 Fiona calculates that the 95-octane is cheaper per kilometre. Do you agree with her? Justify your answer. (2 marks)

47 The spinner is used by a group of friends to choose an activity for the first Tuesday of the holidays. Find the probability that the group:

a goes ice skating. (1 mark)

b either bowls or goes to the beach. (1 mark)

48 A plane leaves Molongo at 11:30 am and travels 2800 km to Jalanga at an average speed of 800 km/h. If Molongo is 3 hours ahead of Jalanga, what is the local time in Jalanga when the plane lands? (2 marks)

49 In a large group, the ratio of boys to girls is 5 : 3.
If there are 24 more boys than girls, how many are in the group? (2 marks)

50 Sean leaves town A and drives towards town B at an average speed of 72 km/h. At the same time, Grace leaves town B and travels at an average speed of 64 km/h towards town B. If the distance between the two towns is 272 km, when and how far from town A will the two motorists meet? (2 marks)

51 Zendra's Jewellery increased all its prices by the same percentage. A watch increased in price from \$160 to \$200. Find the new price of a bangle originally priced at \$380. (2 marks)

52 The diagram shows a large square with an area of $4x^2$ cm^2. The midpoints of the square are joined. What is the area of the shaded region?

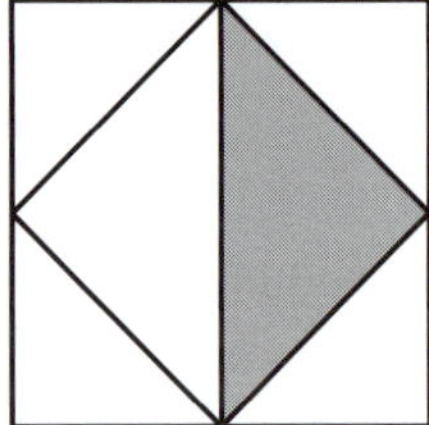

(2 marks)

53 Solve $3 - 4(4 - x) = 2 - (5 - x)$ (2 marks)

54 Solve $\frac{2a}{3} - 4 = 6a$ (2 marks)

55 The length of a rectangle is four times as long as it is wide.
The perimeter is 50 cm. Find the area of the rectangle. (2 marks)

56 Doubling a certain number then adding 6 is the same as four times the same number then subtracting 8. Write an equation in terms of x, and then solve it to find the number. (2 marks)

57 Given $S = \frac{a(r^n - 1)}{r - 1}$, find a, if $S = 400$, $r = 3$ and $n = 4$. (2 marks)

58 The line $y = 2x + 1$ is graphed on the number plane.
On the same number plane, graph $y = 4 - x$, and find the point of intersection of the two lines. (2 marks)

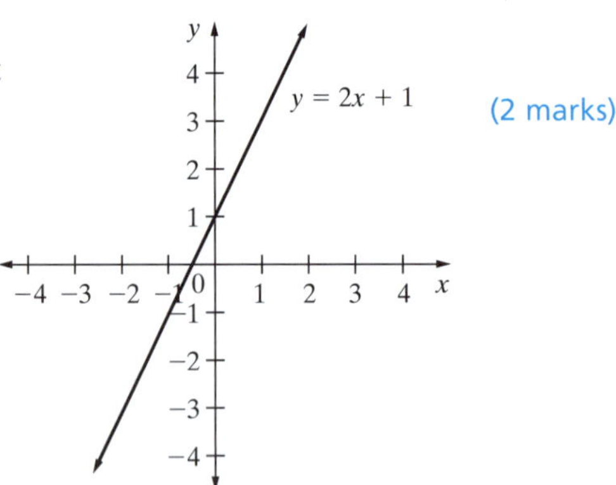

59 Factorise and simplify $\frac{x^2 - 3x - xy + 3y}{3x - 3y}$ (2 marks)

60 Payne's Electrical Repairs charges a call-out fee of \$40 plus \$3 per minute for domestic work. This information is summarised in the table.

Minutes (t)	0	10	20	30	60
Cost in \$ (C)	40	70	100	130	220

a Write a formula linking cost (C) and time (t). (1 mark)

b How long will the repairman be working if he charges \$115? (1 mark)

61 Use the frequency histogram to complete the table to find the values of c and d.

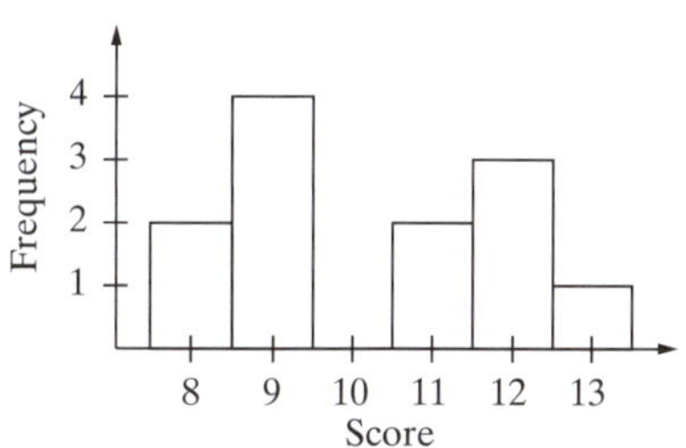

Score (x)	Frequency (f)	fx
8		
9		
10		
11		
12		
13		
Total	c	d

(2 marks)

62 Use the frequency polygon to find the:

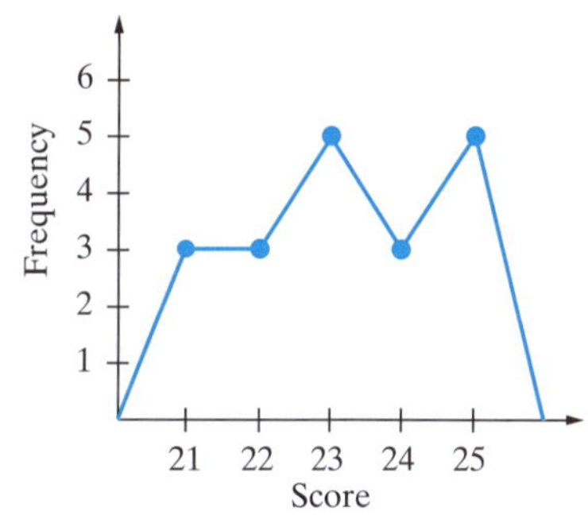

a median (1 mark)

b mean (1 mark)

63 A survey was conducted to find the number of cars owned by people living in our street. The data was recorded in a frequency histogram.

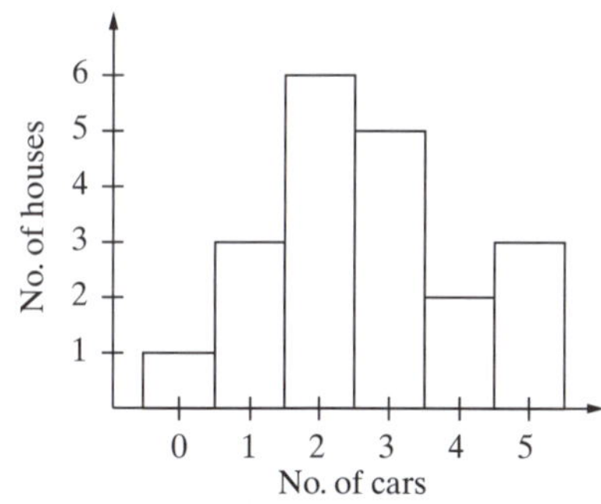

a Find the number of households in the street. (1 mark)

b Find the mean number of cars per household. (1 mark)

64 $ABCD$ is a rhombus, where $AC = 6$ cm and $BD = 8$ cm. Find the perimeter of $ABCD$. (2 marks)

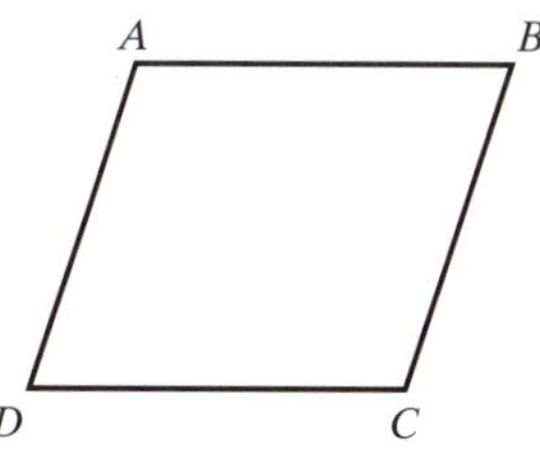

65 The area of the triangle is 24 cm^2. Find the value of x. (2 marks)

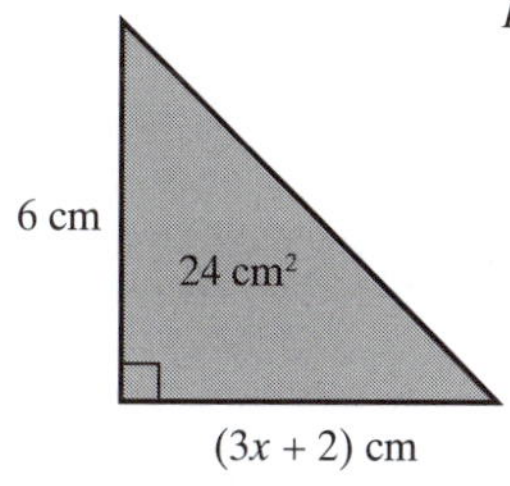

66 Find the perimeter. (2 marks)

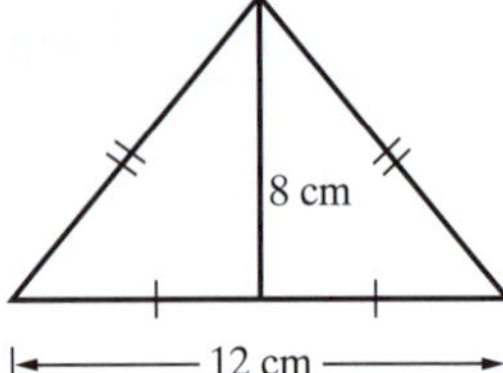

67 The cube has side 4 cm.

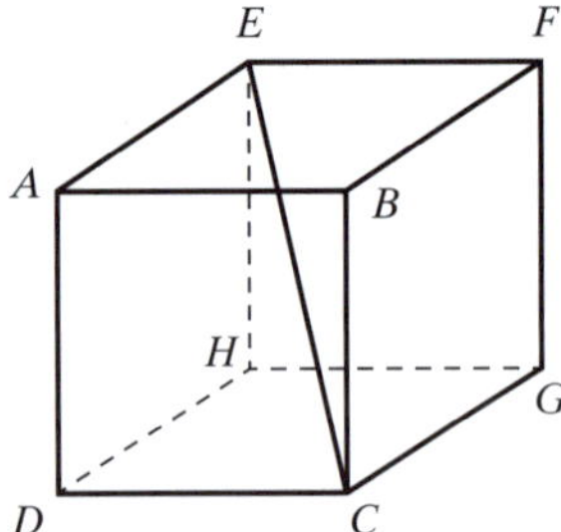

Find the length of EC, correct to 2 decimal places. (2 marks)

68 A cube with side 10 cm is half-filled with water. If all the water is then tipped into a cylinder with diameter 10 cm, what is the depth of water?
Give your answer in terms of π. (2 marks)

69 If a dealer had sold a refrigerator for \$600, she would have made a profit of 20%. Instead, she sold it for a 20% loss. At what price was the refrigerator sold? (2 marks)

70 Lucia owns a fruit shop and bought some boxes of mangoes at a cost of 6 mangoes for \$10 at the local market. Later she sold them in her shop at a price of 2 for \$5. When all of the mangoes were sold, she calculated that she had made a profit of \$180.

a Find her profit as a percentage of the cost price. (1 mark)

b How many boxes of mangoes did she buy, if each box contains a dozen mangoes? (1 mark)

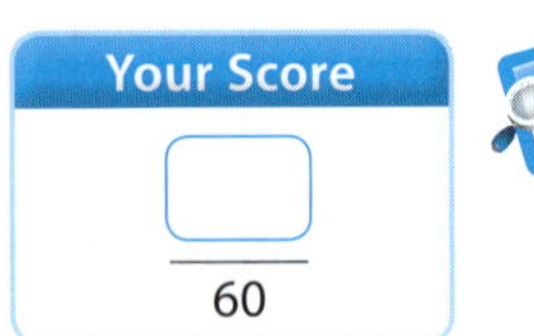

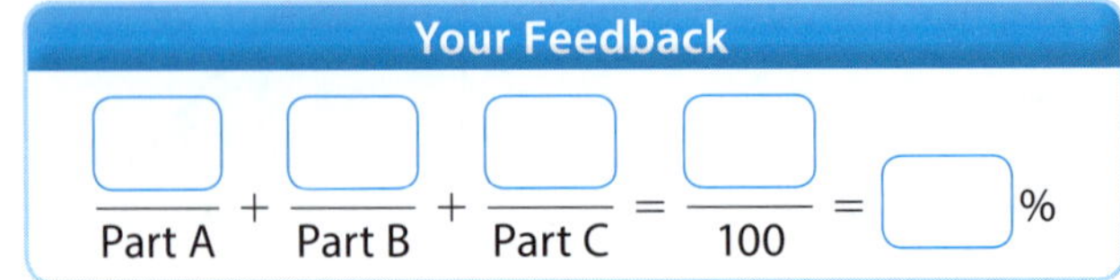

WORKED SOLUTIONS

CHECK YOUR SOLUTIONS

NUMBER, FRACTIONS AND DECIMALS
SKILLS CHECK PAGE 2

1

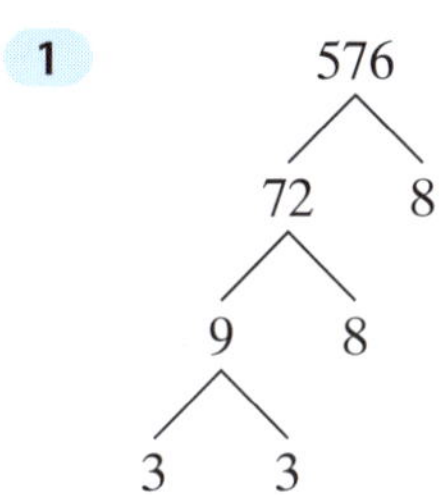

$\therefore \sqrt{576} = \sqrt{3^2 \times 8^2}$
$= 24$

OR

576
2 288
2 144
2 72
2 36

$\therefore \sqrt{576} = \sqrt{(2^2)^2 \times 6^2}$
$= 24$

2 a

$$\begin{array}{r} 42 \\ \times\ 26 \\ \hline 252 \\ 840 \\ \hline 1092 \end{array}$$

$\therefore 1092$

b

$$\begin{array}{r} 31\frac{16}{21} \\ 21\overline{)667} \\ 63 \\ \hline 37 \\ 21 \\ \hline 16 \end{array}$$

$\therefore 31\dfrac{16}{21}$

3 a 23 431 not divisible by 2, $\therefore$ not divisible by 6 (from divisibility tests) $\therefore$ F

b $7 + 6 + 1 + 4 = 18$, which is divisible by 3 $\therefore$ T

c last digit is 5 $\therefore$ T

4 a $12 - 36 \div 9 = 12 - 4$
$= 8$

b $\dfrac{\sqrt{12 + 4}}{5 - 3} = \dfrac{\sqrt{16}}{2} = \dfrac{4}{2}$
$= 2$

c $4(21 - 3 \times 5) = 4(21 - 15)$
$= 4 \times 6$
$= 24$

5 a $\dfrac{16}{5} = \dfrac{15}{5} + \dfrac{1}{5} = 3\dfrac{1}{5}$

b $3\dfrac{9}{11} = \dfrac{33}{11} + \dfrac{9}{11} = \dfrac{42}{11}$

c reciprocal of $\dfrac{a}{b} = \dfrac{b}{a}$

$\therefore$ reciprocal of $\dfrac{5}{3}$ is $\dfrac{3}{5}$

d $\dfrac{75 \div 5}{90 \div 5} = \dfrac{15 \div 3}{18 \div 3} = \dfrac{5}{6}$

6 a $\dfrac{17}{25} = \dfrac{68}{100} = 0.68$

b $8\overline{)5.000}$ with quotient 0.625, $= 0.625$

c $11\overline{)5.00000000}$ with quotient $0.454\,545\ldots$, $= 0.\dot{4}\dot{5}$

7 a $\dfrac{3}{4} - \dfrac{2}{5} = \dfrac{15 - 8}{20} = \dfrac{7}{20}$

b $1\dfrac{2}{3} + 3\dfrac{4}{5} = 4 + \dfrac{10 + 12}{15}$
$= 4 + \dfrac{22}{15} = 5\dfrac{7}{15}$

c $2\dfrac{7}{8} - 1\dfrac{1}{3} = 1 + \dfrac{21 - 8}{24}$
$= 1\dfrac{13}{24}$

d $\dfrac{2}{\cancel{5}_1} \times \dfrac{\cancel{10}^2}{3} = \dfrac{4}{3}$
$= 1\dfrac{1}{3}$

e $\dfrac{3}{8} \times \dfrac{3}{8} = \dfrac{9}{64}$

f $\dfrac{6}{5} \div \dfrac{3}{2} = \dfrac{\cancel{6}^2}{5} \times \dfrac{2}{\cancel{3}_1}$
$= \dfrac{4}{5}$

8 a 3241.5 [decimal point 2 places to →]

b 0.8091 [decimal point 3 places to ←]

c 3210 [decimal point 4 places to →]

9 a $2.000 - 0.034 = 1.966$

b $3.604 - 1.800 = 1.804$

c 8.7 [1 decimal place in question and answer]

d 0.0624 [4 decimal places in question and answer]

e $423.90 \div 2 = 211.95$

f $0.04 \times 0.04 = 0.0016$

10 a $1.8 - 0.4 = 1.4$

b $0.1 \times 3.44 = 0.344$

c $0.08 \div 2 = 0.04$

11 a $11 - 18 = -7$

b $-3 - (-5) = -3 + 5$
$= 2$

c $-3 - 2 \times 4 = -3 - 8$
$= -11$

NUMBER, FRACTIONS AND DECIMALS
INTERMEDIATE TEST PAGE 3

1 Remember divisibility tests.
Factor of 6 means divisible by 2 (last digit is even or zero) and divisible by 3 (digits add up to a number divisible by 3).
Try each of the alternatives.
For 2094, 4 is even and
$2 + 0 + 9 + 4 = 15$
$\therefore$ last digit is even and 15 is divisible by 3
$\therefore$ [C] (1 mark)

2 $28 - 24 \div (4 \times 2 + 4)$
$= 28 - 24 \div 12$
$= 28 - 2$
$= 26$
$\therefore$ [C] (1 mark)

3 To find the number in between, add the given numbers and divide the result by 2.

$\left(\dfrac{1}{3} + \dfrac{1}{5}\right) \div 2 = \dfrac{5 + 3}{15} \times \dfrac{1}{2}$
$= \dfrac{\cancel{8}^4}{15} \times \dfrac{1}{\cancel{2}_1}$
$= \dfrac{4}{15}$

$\therefore$ [A] (1 mark)

4 $\frac{2}{3} \div 4 \times 10 = \frac{\overset{1}{\cancel{2}}}{3} \times \frac{1}{\underset{2_1}{\cancel{4}}} \times \frac{\overset{5}{\cancel{10}}}{1}$

$= \frac{5}{3} = 1\frac{2}{3}$

∴ [A] (1 mark)

5 $2\frac{2}{5} \div \frac{5}{8} = \frac{12}{5} \times \frac{8}{5}$

$= \frac{96}{25}$

$= 3\frac{21}{25}$

∴ [D] (1 mark)

6 Try each of the alternatives.

Reciprocal of $2\frac{1}{2} = 1 \div 2\frac{1}{2}$

$= \frac{1}{1} \div \frac{5}{2}$

$= 1 \times \frac{2}{5}$

$= \frac{2}{5}$

$= 0.4$

∴ [D] (1 mark)

7 Average of 4 numbers = −2

Sum of 4 numbers = −8

Let unknown number be x

$\therefore 4 + (-5) + 2 + x = -8$

$1 + x = -8$

$x = -8 - 1$

$= -9$

∴ the number is −9

∴ [A] (1 mark)

8 a $4 - (2 + 5) = 4 - 7$ ✓

$= -3$ ✓

b $15 - 4 \times 3 = 15 - 12$ ✓

$= 3$ ✓

c $-3 - (3 - 3 \div 3)$

$= -3 - (3 - 1)$ ✓

$= -3 - 2$

$= -5$ ✓ (6 marks)

9 Fraction remaining

$= 1 - \left(\frac{3}{5} + \frac{1}{3}\right)$

$= 1 - \frac{9 + 5}{15}$

$= 1 - \frac{14}{15}$

$= \frac{1}{15}$ ✓

∴ Distance remaining

$= \frac{1}{15} \times 45 = 3$

∴ 3 km yet to run ✓ (2 marks)

10 $\frac{3}{4}$ full = 2700

Full = 2700 ÷ 3 × 4 ✓

= 3600

∴ tank holds 3600 L ✓

(2 marks)

11 a Cost = \$1.60 × 42

= \$67.20 ✓

b No. of 100 km = 540 ÷ 100

= 5.4 ✓

Consumption rate

= 42 ÷ 5.4

= 420 ÷ 54

= 7.78 [2 decimal places]

∴ 7.78 L/100 km ✓

(3 marks)

(Total 20 marks)

NUMBER, FRACTIONS AND DECIMALS
ADVANCED TEST PAGE 4

1 a 78, 120

∴ 2 multiples of 6 ✓

b 120, 184, 368

∴ 3 multiples of 8 ✓

(2 marks)

2 Lowest common multiple of 2, 4, 5: ✓

Multiples of 2: ..., 16, 18, 20, 22,...

Multiples of 4: ..., 16, 20, 24, ...

Multiples of 5: 5, 10, 15, 20, 25, ...

∴ LCM is 20

∴ every 20th bag will have all three items ✓ (2 marks)

3 Highest common factor of 24 and 30: ✓

Factors of 24: 1, 2, 3, 4, 6, 8, 12, 24

Factors of 30: 1, 2, 3, 5, 6, 10, 15, 30

∴ HCF is 6

∴ there are 6 possible groups ✓ (2 marks)

4 a $\frac{10}{20} = \frac{1}{2}$ ✓

b $\frac{6}{20} = \frac{3}{10}$ ✓

c $\frac{8}{20} = \frac{2}{5}$ (2, 3, 5, 7, 11, 13, 17, 19) ✓ (3 marks)

5 a $12 - 4 \times 2 = 12 - 8$

$= 4$ ✓

b $(21 \div 7 + 4 \times 2)^2$

$= (3 + 8)^2$

$= (11)^2$

$= 121$ ✓

c $\frac{16 - 4 \times 2}{2(3 + 1)} = \frac{16 - 8}{2 \times 4}$

$= \frac{8}{8}$

$= 1$ ✓ (3 marks)

6 a $\frac{20}{300} = \frac{1}{15}$ ✓

b $\frac{0.5}{10000} = \frac{1}{20000}$ ✓

c $\frac{2}{2000000} = \frac{1}{1000000}$ ✓

d $\frac{40}{14400} = \frac{1}{360}$ ✓ (4 marks)

7 a $\frac{\frac{2}{3} + \frac{1}{2}}{\frac{2}{3} - \frac{1}{2}} = (\frac{2}{3} + \frac{1}{2}) \div (\frac{2}{3} - \frac{1}{2})$

$= 7$ ✓

b $\frac{4}{5} \times 1\frac{2}{3} - \frac{5}{6} \div \frac{2}{3} = \frac{1}{12}$ ✓

(2 marks)

8 Difference $= \frac{2}{3} - \frac{3}{8}$

$= \frac{7}{24}$ ✓

$\frac{7}{24}$ of tank = 1330

full tank = 1330 ÷ 7 × 24

= 4560

∴ the tank has a capacity of 4560 litres ✓ (2 marks)

9 $\frac{1}{3}$ stamps before sister gift = 48

stamps before sister gift

= 48 × 3 = 144 ✓

$\frac{3}{4}$ stamps before brother gift

= 144

stamps before brother gift

= 144 ÷ 3 × 4 = 192

∴ Jackson originally had 192 stamps ✓ (2 marks)

10 $\frac{3}{4}$ money before savings $= 360$

money before savings $= 360 \div 3 \times 4$

$= 480$ ✓

$\frac{4}{5}$ money before food $= 480$

money before food $= 480 \div 4 \times 5$

$= 600$

$\frac{2}{3}$ money before rent $= 600$

money before rent $= 600 \div 2 \times 3$

$= 900$

∴ Jasmine is originally paid $900 ✓ (2 marks)

11 a $0.35 \div 0.05 + 0.4 \times 0.8 = 7.32$ ✓

b $1 - (0.6)^2 = 0.64$ ✓

c $\frac{2.4 + 0.6}{1.2 - 0.6} = (2.4 + 0.6) \div (1.2 - 0.6)$

$= 5$ ✓ (3 marks)

12 Cost $= 217.2 \div 3$

$= 72.4$

∴ each person paid $72.40 ✓ (1 mark)

13 Growth $= 1.7 - 0.83$

$= 0.87$

∴ Lisa grew 0.87 m ✓ (1 mark)

14 Number $= 94.5 \div 1.5$

$= 63$

∴ there are 63 DVDs in the stack ✓ (1 mark)

15 a Mass $= 32.4 \times 0.72$

$= 23.328$

∴ the mass is 23.328 kg ✓

b No. of litres $= 16.4 \div 0.82$

$= 20$

∴ 20 L has a mass of 16.4 kg ✓

c No. of litres $= 75 \div 1.5$

$= 50$ ✓

Mass $= 50 \times 0.72$

$= 36$

∴ the additional mass is 36 kg ✓

d Difference $= 1\,000\,000 \times (1.02 - 1)$

$= 20\,000$ ✓

As $20\,000 \div 1000 = 20$, then the difference is 20 tonne ✓ (6 marks)

(Total 36 marks)

PERCENTAGES
SKILLS CHECK PAGE 6

1 a $\frac{71}{100} \times \frac{100}{1}\% = 71\%$ b $\frac{3}{100} \times \frac{100}{1}\% = 3\%$

c $\frac{7}{25} \times \frac{100}{1}\% = 28\%$ d $\frac{3}{5} \times \frac{100}{1}\% = 60\%$

e $\frac{17}{20} \times \frac{100}{1}\% = 85\%$

f $\frac{3}{8} \times \frac{100}{1}\% = 37.5\% = 37\frac{1}{2}\%$

g $\frac{2}{3} \times \frac{100}{1}\% = 66.\dot{6}\% = 66\frac{2}{3}\%$

h $1\frac{1}{4} \times \frac{100}{1}\% = 125\%$

i $\frac{7}{1000} \times \frac{100}{1}\% = 0.7\%$ or $\frac{7}{10}\%$

2 a $\frac{16}{100} = \frac{4}{25}$ b $\frac{6}{100} = \frac{3}{50}$

c $\frac{95}{100} = \frac{19}{20}$ d $\frac{12\frac{1}{2}}{100} = \frac{25}{200} = \frac{1}{8}$

e $\frac{5\frac{1}{4}}{100} = \frac{21}{400}$ f $\frac{\frac{3}{5}}{100} = \frac{3}{500}$

3 a $\frac{111}{100} = 1\frac{11}{100}$ b $\frac{186}{100} = 1\frac{86}{100} = 1\frac{43}{50}$

c $\frac{550}{100} = 5\frac{50}{100} = 5\frac{1}{2}$

4 a $0.4 \times 100\% = 40\%$ b $0.07 \times 100\% = 7\%$

c $0.019 \times 100\% = 1.9\%$ d $1.6 \times 100\% = 160\%$

e $1.05 \times 100\% = 105\%$ f $0.125 \times 100\% = 12.5\%$

5 a $32 \div 100 = 0.32$ b $6 \div 100 = 0.06$

c $120 \div 100 = 1.2$ d $8.5 \div 100 = 0.085$

e $12.5 \div 100 = 0.125$ f $7.25 \div 100 = 0.0725$

6 a $0.16 \times 700 = 112$ ∴ $112 b $0.08 \times 72 = 5.76$ ∴ $5.76

c $1.04 \times 280 = 291.2$ ∴ $291.20 d $1.25 \times 4000 = 5000$ ∴ $5000

e $0.035 \times 4900 = 171.5$ ∴ $171.50 f $0.0575 \times 680 = 39.1$ ∴ $39.10

7 a $0.06 \times 300 = 18$ ∴ 18 cm b $0.30 \times 120 = 36$ ∴ 36 seconds

c $1.08 \times 12 = 12.96$ ∴ 12.96 mm d $0.21 \times 14\,000 = 2940$ ∴ 2940 g

e $1.35 \times 42 = 56.7$ ∴ 56.7 km f $0.045 \times 2000 = 90$ ∴ 90 mL

8 a $\frac{14}{56} \times \frac{100}{1}\% = 25\%$

b $\frac{20}{120} \times \frac{100}{1}\% = 16.\dot{6}\% = 16\frac{2}{3}\%$

9 a $\frac{420}{2100} \times \frac{100}{1}\% = 20\%$

b $\frac{15}{120} \times \frac{100}{1}\% = 12.5\%$

WORKED SOLUTIONS

CHECK YOUR SOLUTIONS

PERCENTAGES
INTERMEDIATE TEST PAGE 7

1 $1.06 \times 100\% = 106\%$

$\therefore$ [A] (1 mark)

2 $0.18 \times 51 = 9.18$

$\therefore$ 18% of \$51 = \$9.18

$\therefore$ [A] (1 mark)

3 One revolution = 360°

$\therefore \frac{120}{360} \times 100\% = 33.\dot{3}$

$= 33\frac{1}{3}\%$

$\therefore$ [C] (1 mark)

4 $42\% = \frac{42}{100} = 0.42$

Try each of the alternatives.

$\therefore$ closest to $\frac{43}{100}$

$\therefore$ [B] (1 mark)

5 Measure rectangles.

$\therefore \frac{4.8}{8} \times 100\% = 60\%$

$\therefore$ [B] (1 mark)

6 Males = 50 − 24

= 26

$\therefore$ % male $= \frac{26}{50} \times 100\%$

= 52%

$\therefore$ [D] (1 mark)

7

Students	Votes
Brown	64
Black	**18**
Green	48
White	70

a Black received 18 votes. ✓

b White (70 votes) received the most votes ✓

c % Green $= \frac{48}{200} \times 100\%$

= 24% ✓

(3 marks)

8 a Australian Rules

= 1 cm out of 8 cm ✓

$\frac{1}{8} \times 160 = 20$

$\therefore$ 20 boys play Australian Rules. ✓

b Soccer $= \frac{3}{8} \times 100\%$ ✓

= 37.5%

$\therefore$ 37.5% play soccer. ✓

(4 marks)

9 a Geography angle

= 360 − (40 + 80 + 60 + 120) ✓

= 60

$\therefore$ geography angle is 60°. ✓

b i % maths

$= \frac{120}{360} \times 100\%$ ✓

$= 33.\dot{3}\% = 33\frac{1}{3}\%$

$\therefore$ percentage who selected maths is

$33\frac{1}{3}\%$ ✓

ii % science

$= \frac{80}{360} \times 100\%$ ✓

$= 22.\dot{2}\% = 22\frac{2}{9}\%$

$\therefore$ percentage who selected science is

$22\frac{2}{9}\%$ ✓ (6 marks)

(Total 19 marks)

PERCENTAGES
ADVANCED TEST PAGE 8

1 a $\frac{37}{40} \times 100\% = 92.5\%$ ✓

b $2\frac{21}{25} \times 100\% = 284\%$ ✓

c $\frac{17}{1000} \times 100\% = 1.7\%$ ✓

d $\frac{3}{500} \times 100\% = 0.6\%$ ✓

e $1.003 \times 100\% = 100.3\%$ ✓

f $0.0009 \times 100\% = 0.09\%$ ✓

(6 marks)

2 a $\frac{3}{4} \div 100 = \frac{3}{400}$ ✓

b $7\frac{4}{5} \div 100 = \frac{39}{5} \div 100$

$= \frac{39}{500}$ ✓

c $15.5 \div 100 = 15\frac{1}{2} \div 100$

$= \frac{31}{2} \div 100$

$= \frac{31}{200}$ ✓

(3 marks)

3 a $270 \div 100 = 2.7$ ✓

b $0.03 \div 100 = 0.0003$ ✓

c $5.05 \div 100 = 0.0505$ ✓

d $17\frac{3}{5} \div 100 = 17.6 \div 100$

$= 0.176$ ✓

e $20\frac{17}{20} \div 100 = 20.85 \div 100$

$= 0.2085$ ✓

(5 marks)

4 a $\frac{20}{160} \times 100\% = 12.5\%$ ✓

b $\frac{3}{1000} \times 100\% = 0.3\%$ ✓

c $\frac{15}{40} \times 100\% = 37.5\%$ ✓

d $\frac{1}{2} \div 2 \times 100\% = 25\%$ ✓

e $2\frac{1}{5} \div 10 \times 100\% = 22\%$ ✓

f $\frac{15}{24} \times 100\% = 62.5\%$ ✓

g $\frac{1}{1\,000\,000} \times 100\%$

$= 0.0001\%$ ✓

h $\frac{1}{2} \div 10 \times 100\% = 5\%$ ✓

(8 marks)

5 a $0.23 \times 400 = 92$ $\therefore$ \$92 ✓

b $0.1225 \times 800 = 98$

$\therefore$ \$98 ✓

c $1.2 \times 60 = 72$ ✓

d $0.95 \times 200 = 190$ ✓

e $0.16 \times 3 = 0.48$

$\therefore$ 0.48 mg ✓ (5 marks)

6 $100 - (75 + 16) = 9$

$\therefore$ 9% zinc ✓

Mass $= 0.09 \times 65$

= 5.85

$\therefore$ 5.85 kg zinc ✓ (2 marks)

7 Increase $= 0.04 \times 960$ ✓

= 38.4

$\therefore$ increase of \$38.40 ✓ (2 marks)

8 $100 - 80 = 20$

$\therefore$ 20% of questions incorrect ✓

WORKED SOLUTIONS

No. incorrect $= 0.2 \times 40$
$= 8$

$\therefore$ Hayden got 8 questions incorrect ✓ (2 marks)

9 $100 - 60 = 40$

$\therefore$ 40% of members are male ✓

40% of members $= 24$

100% of members $= 24 \div 40 \times 100$
$= 60$

$\therefore$ there are 60 members ✓ (2 marks)

10 a $20 - (11 + 5) = 4$

$\therefore$ the team drew 4 games ✓

Percentage drawn $= \frac{4}{20} \times 100\% = 20\%$

$\therefore$ team drew 20% of the games ✓

b 3 out of 4 the team did not score

$\therefore$ the team scored in 1 game ✓

Percentage scored $= \frac{1}{4} \times 100\% = 25\%$

$\therefore$ team scored in 25% of the drawn games ✓ (4 marks)

11 a Increase $= 20\%$ of 2.4
$= 0.2 \times 2.4$
$= 0.48$

$\therefore$ Craig increases distance by 0.48 km ✓

b 120% of last week's distance $= 4.8$ ✓

100% of last week's distance $= 4.8 \div 120 \times 100$
$= 4$

$\therefore$ Jess ran 4 km last week ✓

c 20% of this week's distance $= 1.6$

120% of this week's distance $= 1.6 \div 20 \times 120$
$= 9.6$

$\therefore$ Ian will run 9.6 km next week ✓

Increase $= 20\%$ of 9.6
$= 0.2 \times 9.6$
$= 1.92$

Distance week after $= 9.6 + 1.92$
$= 11.52$

$\therefore$ Ian will run 11.52 km the week after ✓ (5 marks)

12 $100 - 11 = 89$

$\therefore$ 89% not in year 12 ✓

11% of school pop $= 132$

89% of school pop $= 132 \div 11 \times 89$
$= 1068$

$\therefore$ there are 1068 students not in year 12 ✓ (2 marks)

13 Total votes $= 2000$ ✓

Percentage $= \frac{450}{2000} \times 100\%$
$= 22.5\%$

$\therefore$ Delaney received 22.5% of the votes ✓ (2 marks)

14 Let Fenton have 10 coins.

$\therefore$ Eloise has 30 coins and Jayden has 60 coins

$\therefore$ Total coins $= 100$ ✓

Percentage $= \frac{60}{100} \times 100\%$
$= 60\%$

$\therefore$ Jayden has 60% of the coins ✓ (2 marks)

(Total 50 marks)

USING THE CALCULATOR
SKILLS CHECK PAGE 10

1 a $75 \div (5 \times 5) = 3$

b $(63 - 27) \div (4 \times 3) = 3$

c $4[3 + 2(2 + 4)] = 60$

d $(12 + 8) \div \sqrt{16} = 5$

e $\sqrt{(40 + 3 \times 3)} \div (12 - 5) = 1$

f $\sqrt{((10 + 2 \times 3) \div (12 \div 3))} = 2$

2 a $\sqrt[3]{12.76} = 2.337$

b $4 \div 6.41^2 = 4 \div 6.41$ $\boxed{x^2}$ $= 0.097$

c $(3.54 - 2.6) \div (2.86 + 1.07) = 0.239$

d $4.13^2 - 3.59^2 = 4.13$ $\boxed{x^2}$ $- 3.59$ $\boxed{x^2}$
$= 4.169$

e $\sqrt{(3.51 \div 2.6)} = 1.162$

f $\sqrt{15} - \sqrt{11} = 0.556$

3 a $1.5^4 = 1.5$ $\boxed{x^y}$ $4 = 5.0625$

b $(3.64 \times 25)^2 = (3.64 \times 25)$ $\boxed{x^2}$ $= 8281$

c $1 \div ((2.5 \div 0.5)$ $\boxed{x^3}$ $) = 0.008$

4 a $2a - 3b = 2 \times 3 - 3 \times 4$
$= -6$

b $b^2 - c^2 = 4^2 - 2^2$
$= 12$

c $\frac{ab - 3c}{c} = (3 \times 4 - 3 \times 2) \div 2$
$= 3$

d $3b^2 - 2a^2 = 3 \times 4^2 - 2 \times 3^2$
$= 30$

e $\sqrt{15 - ac} = \sqrt{(15 - 3 \times 2)}$
$= 3$

f $\frac{bc}{2c + ab} = (4 \times 2) \div (2 \times 2 + 3 \times 4)$
$= 0.5$

5 a $2 - (3 \boxed{a\frac{b}{c}} 5 + 2 \boxed{a\frac{b}{c}} 3) = \frac{11}{15}$ or $0.7\dot{3}$

b $5 \boxed{a\frac{b}{c}} 3 \boxed{a\frac{b}{c}} 4 \times 1 \boxed{a\frac{b}{c}} 1 \boxed{a\frac{b}{c}} 3 = 7\frac{2}{3}$ or $7.\dot{6}$

c $(3 \boxed{a\frac{b}{c}} 1 \boxed{a\frac{b}{c}} 3 - 1 \boxed{a\frac{b}{c}} 1 \boxed{a\frac{b}{c}} 4)$
$\div (3 \boxed{a\frac{b}{c}} 1 \boxed{a\frac{b}{c}} 3 + 1 \boxed{a\frac{b}{c}} 1 \boxed{a\frac{b}{c}} 4)$
$= \frac{5}{11}$ or $0.\dot{4}\dot{5}$

WORKED SOLUTIONS

6 a $(3 \boxed{a\frac{b}{c}} 4 \times 2 \boxed{a\frac{b}{c}} 3)^2 = \frac{1}{4}$ or 0.25

b $3 \boxed{a\frac{b}{c}} 4 \times (2 \boxed{a\frac{b}{c}} 3)^2 = \frac{1}{3}$ or $0.\dot{3}$

c $3(3 \boxed{a\frac{b}{c}} 4 - 2 \boxed{a\frac{b}{c}} 3) = \frac{1}{4}$ or 0.25

7 a 3 (DMS) 4 (DMS) 16 + 2 (DMS) 14 (DMS) 32

$= 5.31\dot{3}$ (2ndF) (DMS)

= 5 h 18 min 48 s

b 6 (DMS) 10 (DMS) 8 − 2 (DMS) 14 (DMS) 9

$= 3.9330\dot{5}$ (2ndF) (DMS)

= 3 h 55 min 59 s

c 2 (DMS) − 1 (DMS) 48 (DMS) 10

$= 0.197\dot{2}$ (2ndF) (DMS)

= 11 min 50 s

d 3 (DMS) 4 (DMS) 16 − 0 (DMS) 28 (DMS) 19

$= 2.5991\dot{6}$ (2ndF) (DMS)

= 2 h 35 min 57 s

8 Total Time

= 0 (DMS) 12 (DMS) 15 + 0 (DMS) 32 (DMS) 18 + 0 (DMS) 27 (DMS) 48

$= 1.2058\dot{3}$ (2ndF) (DMS)

= 1 h 12 min 21 s

Average Time = 1 (DMS) 12 (DMS) 21 ÷ 3

$= 0.4019\dot{4}$ (2ndF) (DMS)

= 0 (DMS) 24 (DMS) 07

∴ Kim's average time is 24 min 7 s

[Here (DMS) has been used—other calculators use (• ˃ ˃˃)]

USING THE CALCULATOR
INTERMEDIATE TEST PAGE 11

1 $(3.4 + 2.5) \div (4.6 - 1.8) = 2.107\,142\,857$
$= 2.11$ [2 decimal places]

∴ [B] (1 mark)

2 Approximate no. seconds:
$= 14 \times 365.25 \times 24 \times 60 \times 60$
$= 441\,806\,400$
$\approx 442\,000\,000$ ∴ [A] (1 mark)

3 $\frac{pq}{(q-2)^2} = \frac{2 \times 4}{(4-2)^2}$
$= \frac{8}{4}$
$= 2$ ∴ [D] (1 mark)

4 As $2 \div 2\frac{1}{4} = \frac{8}{9}$

∴ reciprocal $= \frac{9}{8}$
$= 1\frac{1}{8}$ ∴ [C] (1 mark)

5 a $\frac{20 - 4 \times 3}{6 - 4} = (20 - 4 \times 3) \div (6 - 4)$ ✓
$= 4$ ✓

b $\sqrt{\frac{30 + 6 \times 4}{9 - 3 \times 1}}$
$= \sqrt{((30 + 6 \times 4) \div (9 - 3 \times 1))}$ ✓
$= 3$ ✓

c $\sqrt{3 + 4 \times 3 + 1} = \sqrt{(3 + 4 \times 3 + 1)}$ ✓
$= 4$ ✓ (6 marks)

6 a $\frac{3.057}{\sqrt{2.8 + 1.6}} = 3.057 \div \sqrt{(2.8 + 1.6)}$ ✓
$= 1.457\,367\,568$
$= 1.46$ [2 decimal places] ✓

b $\sqrt{\frac{8.402 - 3.47}{6.05}} = \sqrt{((8.402 - 3.47) \div 6.05)}$ ✓
$= 0.902\,887\,928$
$= 0.90$ [2 decimal places] ✓

c $\left(\frac{3.54}{2.9}\right)^3 = (3.54 \div 2.9)$ (x^3) ✓
$= 1.818\,929\,189$
$= 1.82$ [2 decimal places] ✓

d $\sqrt[3]{4.07 - 2.96} = \sqrt[3]{(4.07 - 2.96)}$ ✓
$= 1.035\,398\,805$
$= 1.04$ [2 decimal places] ✓

e $\frac{1}{3.47} - \frac{3}{2.94} = (1 \div 3.47) - (3 \div 2.94)$ ✓
$= -0.732\,223\,725$
$= -0.73$ [2 decimal places] ✓

f $\frac{6.4 - 2.08}{3.92^2} = (6.4 \div 2.08) \div 3.92$ (x^2) ✓
$= 0.281\,132\,861$
$= 0.28$ [2 decimal places] ✓ (12 marks)

7 a $(a - b + c)^3 = (5 - 2 + 3)^3$ ✓
$= 6^3$
$= 216$ ✓

b $\sqrt{\frac{3a - 2b}{3c + 2}} = \sqrt{\frac{3 \times 5 - 2 \times 2}{3 \times 3 + 2}}$ ✓
$= \sqrt{\frac{11}{11}}$
$= 1$ ✓

c $\sqrt[3]{4ac + 2b} = \sqrt[3]{4 \times 5 \times 3 + 2 \times 2}$ ✓
$= \sqrt[3]{64}$
$= 4$ ✓ (6 marks)

8 3 h 10 min 48 s minus 2 h 28 min 16 s
= 3 (DMS) 10 (DMS) 48 (DMS) –
2 (DMS) 28 (DMS) 16 (DMS)
= $0.70\dot{8}$ (2ndF) (DMS) ✓
= 42 min 32 s
∴ Grant waited 42 min 32 s ✓ (2 marks)

9 a 6.4 (2ndF) (DMS) = 6 h 24 min ✓
b 15.2 (2ndF) (DMS) = 15 min 12 s ✓
c $8\frac{2}{3}$ (2ndF) (DMS) = 8 min 40 s ✓
d $\frac{4}{25}$ (2ndF) (DMS) = 9 min 36 s ✓ (4 marks)
(Total 34 marks)

USING THE CALCULATOR ADVANCED TEST PAGE 12

1 a $70 \div (12 - 2 \times 1) = 7$ ✓
b $24 - [16 - (2 \times 4 + 3)] = 19$ ✓
c $(35 - 5 \times 2) \div (3 + 2) = 5$ ✓
d $27 \div [18 - (6 \times 2 + 3)] = 9$ ✓
e $3 \times [12 \div (9 + 3) + 4] = 15$ ✓ (5 marks)

2 a $\frac{\sqrt{22 - 2 \times 3}}{2 + 2} = 1$ ✓ b $\sqrt{\frac{14 + 10}{15 - 9}} = 2$ ✓
c $\sqrt{\frac{31 - 3 \times 2}{6 - 5 \times 1}} = 5$ ✓ d $\frac{18 + 4 \times 3}{\sqrt{15 - 6}} = 10$ ✓
e $\frac{12}{\sqrt{36}} + \frac{16}{\sqrt{64}} = 4$ ✓ (5 marks)

3 a $(10 - 3 \times 2)^2 = 16$ ✓
b $1^2 + 2^3 + 3^4 = 90$ ✓
c $(16 - 3 \times 2)^5 = 100\,000$ ✓
d $5.2^2 + 2.6^4 = 72.7376$ ✓
e $10^2 - (12 - 4)^2 = 36$ ✓ (5 marks)

4 a $\sqrt[3]{5 \times 3 + 4 \times 3} = 3$ ✓
b $\sqrt[3]{\frac{25 \times 5 + 3}{14 - 12}} = 4$ ✓
c $\frac{14 + 2}{\sqrt[3]{14 - 3 \times 2}} = 8$ ✓
d $\frac{\sqrt{25}}{\sqrt[3]{1000}} = 0.5$ ✓
e $(\sqrt[3]{64})^2 + (\sqrt{64})^3 = 528$ ✓ (5 marks)

5 a $\sqrt{\frac{263.8}{11.45 \times 8.2}} = \sqrt{(263.8 \div (11.45 \times 8.2))}$
$= 1.68$ (2 dec. pl.) ✓

b $\frac{8.3}{\sqrt{6.46 - 3.91}} = 8.3 \div \sqrt{(6.46 - 3.91)}$
$= 5.20$ (2 dec. pl.) ✓

c $\sqrt{\frac{4^2 + 11^2}{243 - 13^2}} = \sqrt{((4^2 + 11^2) \div (243 - 13^2))}$
$= 1.36$ (2 dec. pl.) ✓ (3 marks)

6 a $\frac{2}{3} + \frac{3}{5} \times 1\frac{2}{3} = 1\frac{2}{3}$ ✓
b $2\frac{5}{8} - 1\frac{1}{4} = 1\frac{3}{8}$ ✓ (2 marks)

7 Two-fifths of total = 108 ✓
Five-fifths of total = 108 ÷ 2 × 5
= 270
∴ 270 photos submitted ✓ (2 marks)

8 a Use (DMS) button:
2 (DMS) 58 (DMS) 48 (DMS)
– 2 (DMS) 18 (DMS) 32 (DMS)
= 40 min 16 s ✓
b 3 (DMS) 11 (DMS) 7 (DMS)
– 2 (DMS) 29 (DMS) 16 (DMS)
= 41 min 51 s ✓ (2 marks)

9 No. of red balloons = $\frac{2}{5} \times 40$
= 16
∴ 16 red balloons, 24 blue balloons ✓
After balloons burst, 15 red balloons and 20 blue balloons.
∴ $\frac{15}{35} = \frac{3}{7}$ balloons are red ✓ (2 marks)

10 Green balls = 13
Red balls = 13 + 9
= 22
Total green and red = 13 + 22
= 35 ✓
Five-eighths of bag = 35
Eight-eighths of bag = 35 ÷ 5 × 8
= 56
∴ 56 balls in bag ✓ (2 marks)

11 Average = (6 (DMS) 28 + 5 (DMS) 52) ÷ 2
= 6° 10'
∴ average length is 6 minutes 10 seconds ✓ (1 mark)

12 a $M = \frac{ab}{\sqrt{c^2 + 7a}}$
$= \frac{4 \times 3}{\sqrt{2^2 + 7 \times 4}}$ ✓
$= (4 \times 3) \div \sqrt{(2^2 + 7 \times 4)}$
$= 2.1$ (1 dec. pl.) ✓

b $M = \sqrt{\dfrac{a-b}{a+bc}}$

$= \sqrt{\dfrac{4-3}{4+3\times 2}}$ ✓

$= \sqrt{((4-3) \div (4+3\times 2))}$

$= 0.3$ (1 dec. pl.) ✓ (4 marks)

13 **a** $A = \dfrac{\sqrt{pq-r}}{t}$

$= \dfrac{\sqrt{3\times 6-2}}{7}$ ✓

$= 0.6$ (nearest tenth) ✓

b $A = \dfrac{\sqrt{\frac{1}{2}\times\frac{1}{4}-\frac{1}{10}}}{\frac{1}{5}}$ ✓

$= 0.8$ (nearest tenth) ✓

c $A = \dfrac{\sqrt{3.6\times 1.8-2.1}}{2.5}$ ✓

$= 0.8$ (nearest tenth) ✓

d $A = \dfrac{\sqrt{(-2)\times(-8)-(-12)}}{12}$ ✓

$= 0.4$ (nearest tenth) ✓ (8 marks)

(Total 46 marks)

PATTERNS AND ALGEBRA SKILLS CHECK PAGE 14

1 **a**

x	0	1	2	3
y	**−1**	**1**	**3**	**5**

b

p	0	1	2	3
q	**0**	**2**	**8**	**18**

2 **a** $y = x - 2$ **b** $b = 2a + 3$

3 **a** $(xy)^2 = (4\times 2)^2$
$= 64$

b $x^2 - y^2 = 16 - 4$
$= 12$

c $2x - 5y = 2\times 4 - 5\times 2$
$= -2$

d $\sqrt{3x + 4y \div 2} = \sqrt{3\times 4 + 4\times 2 \div 2}$
$= \sqrt{12 + 4}$
$= 4$

e $\dfrac{5x+4}{3y-2} = \dfrac{5\times 4+4}{3\times 2-2}$
$= 6$

f $\dfrac{3x}{2} - \dfrac{8}{y} = \dfrac{3\times 4}{2} - \dfrac{8}{2}$
$= 2$

4 **a** $3p + 2q = 3\times 0.2 + 2\times 0.5$
$= 0.6 + 1$
$= 1.6$

b $3p^2 = 3\times 0.2\times 0.2$
$= 0.12$

c $pq - (p - q) = 0.2\times 0.5 - (0.2 - 0.5)$
$= 0.1 + 0.3$
$= 0.4$

5 **a** $3\times a\times a\times a\times b\times b = 3a^3b^2$

b $4xy - 2yx = 4xy - 2xy$
$= 2xy$

c $3a - 2b + 4a - b = 7a - 3b$

d $14a \div 2 = 7a$

e $5y\times 2x\times 8x = 80x^2y$

f $\dfrac{12x^2y}{4x} = 3xy$

6 **a** As $100\times 1 = 100$, then
$100\times p = 100p$
$\therefore \$p = 100p$ cents

b As $1000\times 1 = 1000$, then
$1000\times q = 1000q$
$\therefore q$ km $= 1000q$ m

c As $1 \div 1000 = \dfrac{1}{1000}$, then
$y \div 1000 = \dfrac{y}{1000}$,
$\therefore y$ mL $= \dfrac{y}{1000}$ L

7 **a** Cost $= p\times q + x\times y$ $\therefore (pq + xy)$ cents

b Length $= t - m\times n$ $\therefore (t - mn)$ metres

c Average $= \dfrac{a+b+c}{3}$

8 **a** $x - 7 = 12$
$x - 7 + 7 = 12 + 7$
$x = 19$

b $y + 8 = 13$
$y + 8 - 8 = 13 - 8$
$y = 5$

c $a + 4 = 2$
$a + 4 - 4 = 2 - 4$
$a = -2$

d $3x = 39$
$\dfrac{3x}{3} = \dfrac{39}{3}$
$x = 13$

e $2a + 1 = 11$
$2a + 1 - 1 = 11 - 1$
$2a = 10$
$\dfrac{2a}{2} = \dfrac{10}{2}$
$a = 5$

f $\dfrac{y}{3} = 6$
$3\times\dfrac{y}{3} = 3\times 6$
$y = 18$

WORKED SOLUTIONS

CHECK YOUR SOLUTIONS

PATTERNS AND ALGEBRA
INTERMEDIATE TEST PAGE 15

1 $2y^2 = 2 \times 3^2$
$= 18$
$\therefore$ [B] (1 mark)

2 $4 \times x + 5 = 4x + 5$
$\therefore$ [C] (1 mark)

3 $5a + 3 - 2a - 5 = 3a - 2$
$\therefore$ [B] (1 mark)

4 $7 \times b - 3 \times b \times 4 = 7b - 12b$
$= -5b$
$\therefore$ [A] (1 mark)

5 From C, subs $x = 2$ in $4 - x = 2$
$4 - 2 = 2$ … true
$\therefore$ [C] (1 mark)

6 From D, subs $b = -1$ in $3b = 3$
$3 \times -1 = 3$ … false
$\therefore$ [D] (1 mark)

7 a
$2x - 1 = 9$
$2x - 1 + 1 = 9 + 1$
$2x = 10$ ✓
$\frac{2x}{2} = \frac{10}{2}$
$x = 5$ ✓

b
$\frac{t-1}{4} = 3$
$4 \times \frac{t-1}{4} = 4 \times 3$
$t - 1 = 12$ ✓
$t - 1 + 1 = 12 + 1$
$t = 13$ ✓

c
$2 + 3a = 8$
$2 + 3a - 2 = 8 - 2$
$3a = 6$ ✓
$\frac{3a}{3} = \frac{6}{3}$
$a = 2$ ✓

(6 marks)

8 $y = 3x - 1$ ✓✓

x	0	1	2
y	**−1**	**2**	**5**

✓

(3 marks)

9

x	0	1	2	3	4
y	6	5	4	3	2

$\therefore y = 6 - x$ ✓✓ (2 marks)

(Total 17 marks)

PATTERNS AND ALGEBRA
ADVANCED TEST PAGE 16

1 a $y = 3x - 5$ ✓
b $y = x^3 - 11$ ✓ (2 marks)

2 a Adding 45, so that next term is 255
$\therefore$ 255 ✓
b Continue the sequence:
…, 210, 255, 300, 345, … ✓
$\therefore$ it will take 7 hours ✓
c $c = 45n + 30$ ✓
d Subs $n = 12$:
$c = 45n + 30$
$= 45 \times 12 + 30$
$= 570$
$\therefore$ he will receive \$570 ✓
(5 marks)

3 a $\frac{ab-2}{c} = \frac{4 \times 5 - 2}{3}$ ✓
$= 6$ ✓
b $(b - c)(a + c)$
$= (5 - 3)(4 + 3)$ ✓
$= 14$ ✓
c $\frac{\sqrt{a+b}}{c} = \frac{\sqrt{4+5}}{3}$ ✓
$= 1$ ✓
d $\frac{3a - b + 1}{(c+1)^2}$
$= \frac{3 \times 4 - 5 + 1}{(3+1)^2}$ ✓
$= 0.5$ ✓ (8 marks)

4 $c = 110 + 90n$ ✓ (1 mark)

5 a $A = p^2 - 2qr$
$= (-3)^2 - 2(5)(-2)$ ✓
$= 29$ ✓
b $A = \left(\frac{2}{3}\right)^2 - 2\left(\frac{1}{4}\right)\left(\frac{3}{5}\right)$ ✓
$= \frac{13}{90}$ ✓
c $A = (0.9)^2 - 2(-1.6)(-0.5)$ ✓
$= -0.79$ ✓ (6 marks)

6 a $\frac{x}{2} + \frac{2x}{3} < 12$ ✓
b $x(x + 2) = 63$ ✓
c $\frac{10}{3x} \geq 6x$ ✓ (3 marks)

7 Area $= 64y^2$
Side $= \sqrt{64y^2}$
$= 8y$ ✓
Perimeter $= 4 \times 8y$
$= 32y$
$\therefore$ perimeter is $32y$ cm ✓
(2 marks)

8 a

x	−1	0	1	2
y	2	0	−2	−4

✓

b $y = -2x$ ✓ (2 marks)

9 a $5x - 3y - 2x + 7y$
$= 3x + 4y$ ✓
b $8a - 1 - 4 - 9a$
$= -a - 5$ ✓
c $3x^2 - 2xy - 5x^2 - yx$
$= -2x^2 - 3xy$ ✓
d $-3w - q - w + 2q$
$= -4w + q$ ✓
e $12ba + 3a - 2b - 13ab$
$= -ab + 3a - 2b$ ✓
(5 marks)

10 a $4y \times (-7y) = -28y^2$ ✓
b $(-3a)^2 = 9a^2$ ✓
c $18p^2 \div 6p = 3p$ ✓
d $\frac{36g}{9g^2} = \frac{4}{g}$ ✓
e $\frac{-52w^2}{13w} = -4w$ ✓ (5 marks)

11 a $18c \div 3 - 4 \times 5c$
$= 6c - 20c$ ✓
$= -14c$ ✓

b $(8b - 6b \times 3)^2$
$= (8b - 18b)^2$ ✓
$= (-10b)^2$
$= 100b^2$ ✓

c $\dfrac{3a - 4a \times 2}{5a} = \dfrac{3a - 8a}{5a}$ ✓
$= \dfrac{-5a}{5a}$
$= -1$ ✓

d $\sqrt{16a^2} \div 4 = 4a \div 4$ ✓
$= a$ ✓

e $\dfrac{12y \div 3 + 2y \times 3}{14y - 6y \times 2}$
$= \dfrac{4y + 6y}{14y - 12y}$ ✓
$= \dfrac{10y}{2y}$
$= 5$ ✓ (10 marks)

12 The two numbers are x, $x + 5$ ✓
$\therefore x \times (x + 5) = 300$
$\therefore x(x + 5) = 300$ ✓ (2 marks)

13 **a** $2, 8c, 32c^2, \_\_\_$
Multiplying by $4c$:
$32c^2 \times 4c = 128c^3$ ✓

b $9x - 6y, 6x - y, 3x + 4y, \_\_\_$
Adding $-3x + 5y$:
$3x + 4y + (-3x) + 5y$
$= 3x + 4y - 3x + 5y$
$= 9y$ ✓ (2 marks)

(Total 53 marks)

AREA AND VOLUME SKILLS CHECK PAGE 18

1 **a** $342 \div 100 = 3.42$
$\therefore$ 342 cm = 3.42 m

b $1320 \div 1000 = 1.32$
$\therefore$ 1320 mm = 1.32 m

c $685 \div 1000 = 0.685$
$\therefore$ 685 m = 0.685 km

d $3.2 \times 100 = 320$
$\therefore$ 3.2 m = 320 cm

e $12.9 \times 1000 = 12\,900$
$\therefore$ 12.9 m = 12 900 mm

f $9.04 \times 1000 = 9040$
$\therefore$ 9.04 km = 9040 m

g $3 \times 10\,000 = 30\,000$
$\therefore$ 3 ha = 30 000 m^2

h $90\,000 \div 10\,000 = 9$
$\therefore$ 90 000 m^2 = 9 ha

i $1200 \div 10\,000 = 0.12$
$\therefore$ 1200 m^2 = 0.12 ha

j $5 \times 1000 = 5000$
$\therefore$ 5 L = 5000 mL

k $4600 \div 1000 = 4.6$
$\therefore$ 4600 L = 4.6 kL

l $65 \div 1000 = 0.065$
$\therefore$ 65 kL = 0.065 ML

2 **a** $P = 6 \times 12.3$
$= 73.8$
$\therefore$ perimeter is 73.8 mm

b $P = 2(15 + 14)$
$= 2 \times 29$
$= 58$
$\therefore$ perimeter is 58 cm

c $P = 2(1.2 + 0.7)$
$= 2 \times 1.9$
$= 3.8$
$\therefore$ perimeter is 3.8 m

3 **a** Area $= 4.2 \times 5$
$= 21.0$
$\therefore$ area is 21 cm^2

b Area $= 4.5 \times 3$
$= 13.5$
$\therefore$ area is 13.5 mm^2

c Area $= 20 \times 20$
$= 400$
$\therefore$ area is 400 cm^2

4 **a** Area $= \frac{1}{2} \times 14 \times 12$
$= 84$
$\therefore$ area is 84 cm^2

b Area $= \frac{1}{2} \times 6.4 \times 8$
$= 25.6$
$\therefore$ area is 25.6 cm^2

c Area $= \frac{1}{2} \times 5 \times 5$
$= 12.5$
$\therefore$ area is 12.5 cm^2

5 **a** Area $= 11 \times 7$
$= 77$
$\therefore$ area is 77 cm^2

b Area $= 12 \times 10$
$= 120$
$\therefore$ area is 120 cm^2

c Area $= 6 \times 4$
$= 24$
$\therefore$ area is 24 cm^2

6 **a** Area $= 12 \times 10 + \frac{1}{2} \times 6 \times 10$
$= 150$
$\therefore$ area is 150 cm^2

b Area $= 12 \times 4 + \frac{1}{2} \times 12 \times 6$
$= 84$
$\therefore$ area is 84 cm^2

7 Area $= 120 \times 85$
$= 10\,200$
Cost $= 10\,200 \div 10 \times 1.8$
$= 1836$
$\therefore$ cost is \$1836

8 length $= 326.34 \div 12.6$
$= 25.9$
$\therefore$ the length is 25.9 cm

9 Volume $= 12 \times 8 \times 7$
$= 672$
$\therefore$ the volume is 672 cm^3

AREA AND VOLUME INTERMEDIATE TEST PAGE 19

1 As 1 m = 100 cm,
$0.04 \times 100 = 4$
$\therefore$ 0.04 m = 4 cm
$\therefore$ [C] (1 mark)

2 Area $= 30 \times 20$
$= 600$
$\therefore$ area is 600 mm^2
$\therefore$ [B] (1 mark)

3

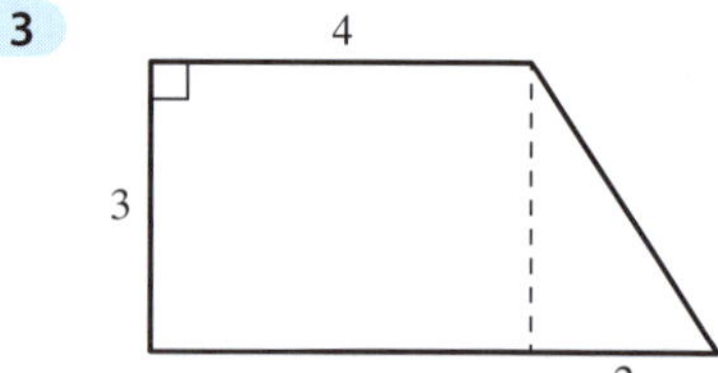

shape = rectangle + triangle
Area $= 4 \times 3 + \frac{1}{2} \times 2 \times 3$
$\therefore$ [C] (1 mark)

4 Volume = length $\times$ breadth $\times$ height
$120 = \text{length} \times 4 \times 6$
length $= 120 \div 24$
$= 5$ $\therefore$ 5 cm
$\therefore$ [B] (1 mark)

5 As 10 000 m^2 = 1 ha,
then $12 \times 10\,000 = 120\,000$
$\therefore$ 120 000 m^2
$\therefore$ [C] (1 mark)

6 As 100 cm = 1 m, and 1000 m = 1 km, then 100 000 cm = 1 km
$4.05 \times 100\,000 = 405\,000$
$\therefore$ [D] (1 mark)

7 a Area $= bh$
$= 12.6 \times 8$ ✓
$= 100.8$
$\therefore 100.8\text{ cm}^2$ ✓

b Area $= \frac{1}{2}bh$
$= \frac{1}{2} \times 5.1 \times 4$ ✓
$= 10.2$
$\therefore 10.2\text{ cm}^2$ ✓

c Area $= 6 \times 5$ ✓
$= 30$
$\therefore 30\text{ units}^2$ ✓ (6 marks)

8 a Area $= 16 \times 9 - 11 \times 4$ ✓✓
$= 100$
$\therefore 100\text{ cm}^2$ ✓

b Area $= 12 \times 10 - 6 \times 4$ ✓✓
$= 96$
$\therefore 96\text{ cm}^2$ ✓ (6 marks)

9 Area $= 8.6 \times 3$
$= 25.8$
$\therefore$ area is 25.8 cm^2 ✓
As 2 coats, the total area is 51.6 cm^2. ✓
Amount of paint $= 51.6 \div 8$
$= 6.45$
$\therefore$ John needs 6.45 L of paint. ✓ (3 marks)

10 Volume $= 20 \times 25 \times 10$ ✓
$= 5000$
$\therefore$ the volume is 5000 cm^3. ✓
$\therefore$ the capacity is 5000 mL, or 5 L. ✓ (3 marks)

(Total 24 marks)

AREA AND VOLUME ADVANCED TEST PAGE 21

1 a Area $= 53 \times 37$
$= 1961$
$\therefore$ area is 1961 cm^2 ✓

b Area $= 3.7 \times 2.03$
$= 7.511$
$\therefore$ area is 7.511 cm^2 ✓

c Area $= 1\frac{5}{8} \times \frac{3}{4}$
$= 1\frac{7}{32}$
$\therefore$ area is $1\frac{7}{32}\text{ cm}^2$ ✓ (3 marks)

2 a Area $= 27^2$
$= 729$
$\therefore$ area is 729 cm^2 ✓

b Area $= (0.15)^2$
$= 0.0225$
$\therefore$ area is 0.0225 cm^2 ✓

c Area $= (3\frac{1}{4})^2$
$= 10\frac{9}{16}$
$\therefore$ area is $10\frac{9}{16}\text{ cm}^2$ ✓ (3 marks)

3 a Area $= 23 \times 18$
$= 414$
$\therefore$ area is 414 cm^2 ✓

b Area $= 5.09 \times 2.7$
$= 13.743$
$\therefore$ area is 13.743 cm^2 ✓

c Area $= 3\frac{4}{5} \times 2\frac{7}{10}$
$= 10\frac{13}{50}$
$\therefore$ area is $10\frac{13}{50}\text{ cm}^2$ ✓ (3 marks)

4 a Area $= 0.5 \times 17 \times 12$ ✓
$= 102$
$\therefore$ area is 102 cm^2 ✓

b Area $= 0.5 \times 15.04 \times 11.7$ ✓
$= 87.984$
$\therefore$ area is 87.984 cm^2 ✓

c Area $= 0.5 \times 3\frac{3}{5} \times \frac{7}{8}$ ✓
$= 1.575$
$\therefore$ area is 1.575 cm^2 ✓ (6 marks)

5 a $560 = \text{length} \times 16$ ✓
Length $= 560 \div 16$
$= 35$
$\therefore$ length is 35 cm ✓

b $33\frac{16}{25} = \text{side}^2$ ✓
side $= \sqrt{33\frac{16}{25}}$
$= 5\frac{4}{5}$
$\therefore$ side is $5\frac{4}{5}$ cm ✓

c $23\frac{5}{6} = 6\frac{1}{2} \times \text{height}$ ✓
height $= 23\frac{5}{6} \div 6\frac{1}{2}$
$= 3\frac{2}{3}$
$\therefore$ perpendicular height is $3\frac{2}{3}$ cm ✓

d $66.12 = 0.5 \times \text{base} \times 5.8$ ✓
$66.12 = 2.9 \times \text{base}$
base $= 66.12 \div 2.9$
$= 22.8$
$\therefore$ base is 22.8 cm ✓ (8 marks)

6 Cost $= 7 \times 6 \times 29.9$ ✓
$= 1255.8$
$\therefore$ cost is \$1255.80 ✓ (2 marks)

7 Number of bottles
$= 24 \times 16 \div 64$
$= 6$
$\therefore$ need 6 bottles ✓
Cost $= 5.10 \times 6$
$= 30.6$
$\therefore$ total cost of \$30.60 ✓ (2 marks)

8 8 m = 800 cm and 6 m = 600 cm
As, $800 \div 40 = 20$ and $600 \div 40 = 15$,
No. of tiles $= 20 \times 15$
$= 300$ ✓
Total cost $= 300 \times 3.9$
$= 1170$
$\therefore$ total cost of \$1170 ✓ (2 marks)

9 Perimeter $= 205.2 \div 2.7$
$= 76$
$\therefore$ rectangle has perimeter of 76 m. ✓
Now, a square will give the largest area.
Side length $= 76 \div 4$
$= 19$
$\therefore$ square with side 19 m. ✓
Area $= 19^2$
$= 361$
$\therefore$ largest area is 361 m^2 ✓ (3 marks)

10 Volume $= \frac{3}{4} \times 24 \times 7 \times 30$ ✓
$= 3780$
$\therefore$ volume is 3780 cm^3 ✓ (2 marks)

WORKED SOLUTIONS

11 As $20 \div 2.5 = 8$, $16 \div 0.5 = 32$ and $8 \times 32 = 256$, then 256 rolls of lawn is required. ✓

Cost $= 5.2 \times 256$
$= 1331.2$

$\therefore$ cost is \$1331.20 ✓ (2 marks)

12 Amount $= 22 \times 3 \times 0.085$ ✓
$= 5.61$

$\therefore$ requires 5.61 kg of fertiliser ✓ (2 marks)

13 $32 + 2 \times 6.5 = 45$ and $24 + 2 \times 6.5 = 37$

$\therefore$ the cardboard is 45 cm × 37 cm ✓

Border Area $= 45 \times 37 - 32 \times 24$
$= 897$

$\therefore$ the area of border is 897 cm^2 ✓ (2 marks)

14 Side length $= \sqrt{1156}$
$= 34$

$\therefore$ the cube has side length of 34 cm ✓

Volume $= 34^3$
$= 39\,304$

$\therefore$ volume is 39 304 cm^3

As $39\,304 \div 1000 = 39.304$, then the capacity is 39.304 L. ✓ (2 marks)

15 One-ninth $= 60$

Nine-ninths $= 60 \times 9$
$= 540$

$\therefore$ the height is 540 m. ✓

Volume $= 12 \times 8 \times 0.54$
$= 51.84$

$\therefore$ the volume is 51.84 km^3 ✓ (2 marks)

(Total 44 marks)

SHAPE AND GEOMETRIC REASONING
SKILLS CHECK PAGE 24

1

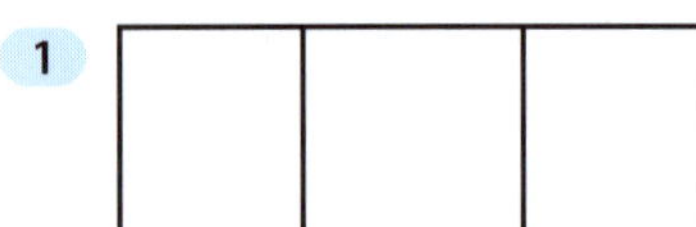

2 a rectangle: 2

b parallelogram: 2 (except if it is a square and it has 4)

c kite: 1

d scalene triangle: 1

e isosceles triangle: 1

f equilateral triangle: 3

3 a $90 - 42 = 48$

$\therefore$ the complement is 48°

b $90 - x$

$\therefore$ the complement is $(90 - x)°$

4 a $x = 180 - 135$ (straight angle)
$= 45$

b $y = 130$ (vertically opposite angles)

c $x + 60 = 130$

(exterior angle of a triangle equals the sum of the two opposite interior angles)

$x + 60 - 60 = 130 - 60$

$x = 70$

d $x + 65 + 90 = 180$ (angle sum of triangle)

$x + 155 = 180$

$x + 155 - 155 = 180 - 155$

$x = 25$

e $x + 70 + 100 + 140 = 360$ (angle sum of quadrilateral)

$x + 310 = 360$

$x + 310 - 310 = 360 - 310$

$x = 50$

f

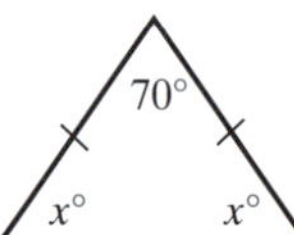

$x + x + 70 = 180$ (base angles of isosceles triangle, angle sum of triangle)

$2x + 70 = 180$

$2x + 70 - 70 = 180 - 70$

$2x = 110$

$\frac{2x}{2} = \frac{110}{2}$

$x = 55$

g $3x = 180 - 90$ (straight angle)

$3x = 90$

$\frac{3x}{3} = \frac{90}{3}$

$x = 30$

h $2x + 90 = 180$ (straight angle)

$2x + 90 - 90 = 180 - 90$

$2x = 90$

$\frac{2x}{2} = \frac{90}{2}$

$x = 45$

5 a $x = 130, y = 130$ b $x = 50, y = 50, z = 50$

6 a

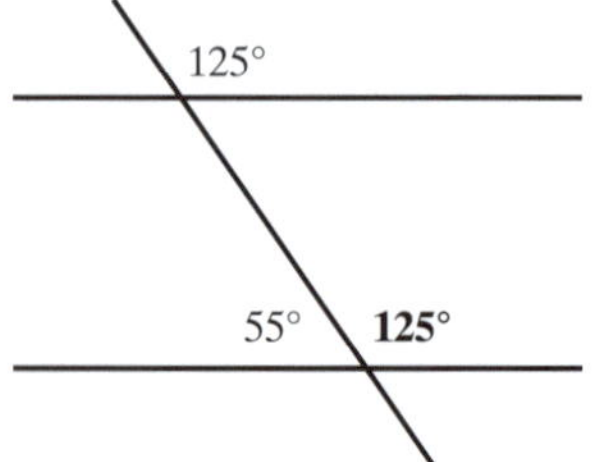

Parallel, because corresponding angles are equal.

b Not parallel as the co-interior angles are equal (they should add to 180°).

WORKED SOLUTIONS

CHECK YOUR SOLUTIONS

SHAPE AND GEOMETRIC REASONING
INTERMEDIATE TEST PAGE 25

1 As $360 - (150 + 120) = 90$
$\therefore$ shaded angle is right angle $\therefore$ **[B]** (1 mark)

2

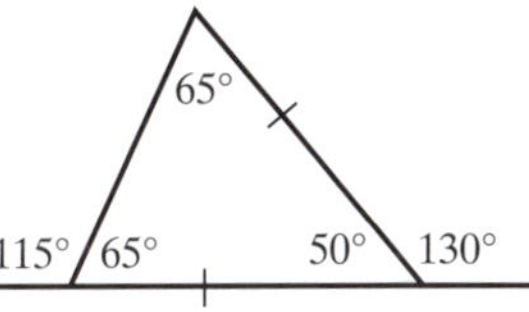

$\therefore x = 115$ $\therefore$ **[D]** (1 mark)

3

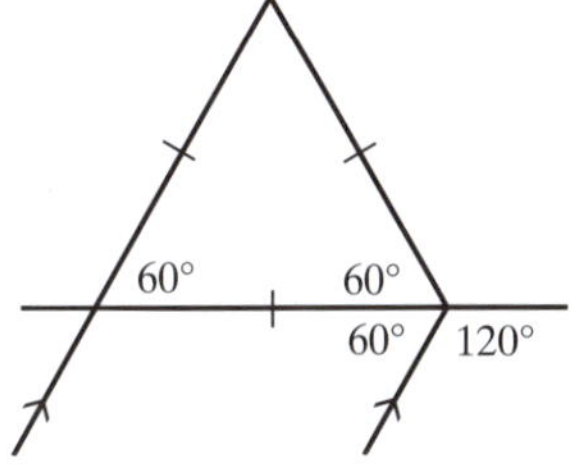

$\therefore x = 120$ $\therefore$ **[C]** (1 mark)

4

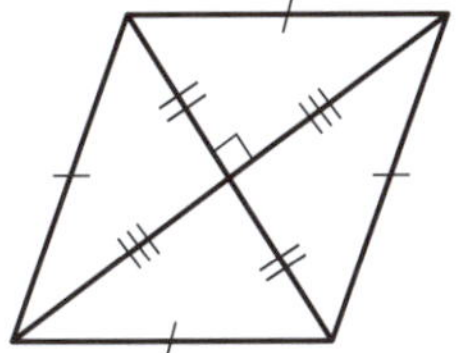

'Opposite angles complementary' is not true
$\therefore$ **[D]** (1 mark)

5 As $14 > 5 + 6$, then
5 cm, 6 cm, 14 cm is impossible, $\therefore$ **[D]** (1 mark)

6

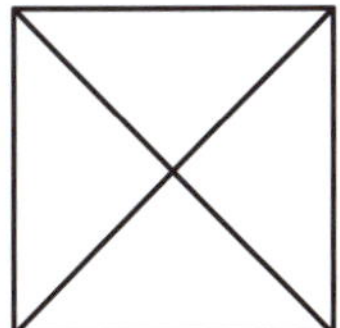

$\therefore$ **[A]** (1 mark)

7

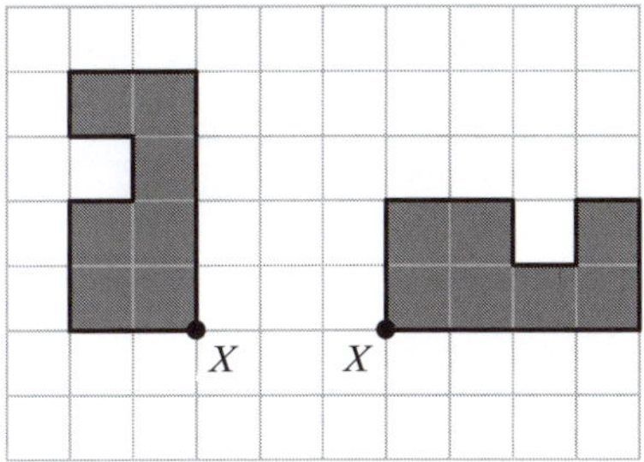

(3 marks)

8

Front Right Top (3 marks)

9 a alternate angles ✓
b corresponding angles ✓ (2 marks)

10 a

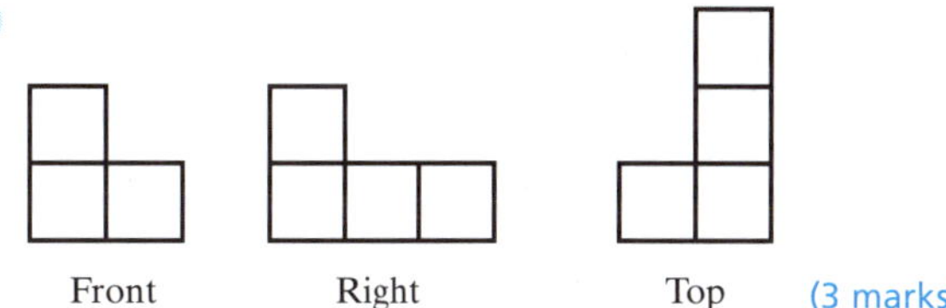

$\therefore x = 120$ ✓
$y = 80$ ✓

b

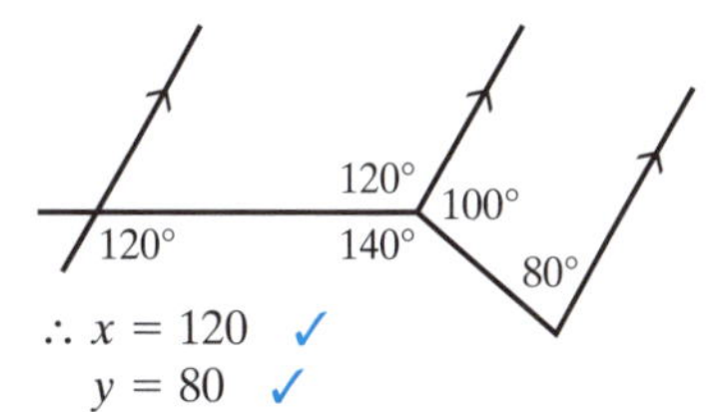

$x = 110$ ✓
$y = 110$ ✓ (4 marks)

11 a

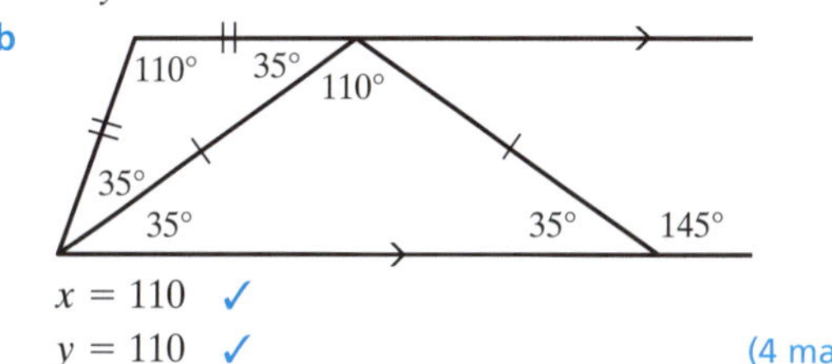

$x = 75$ ✓✓

b

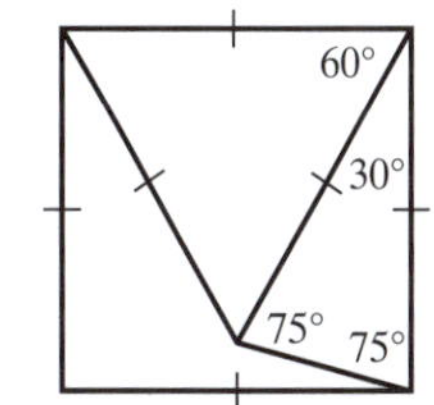

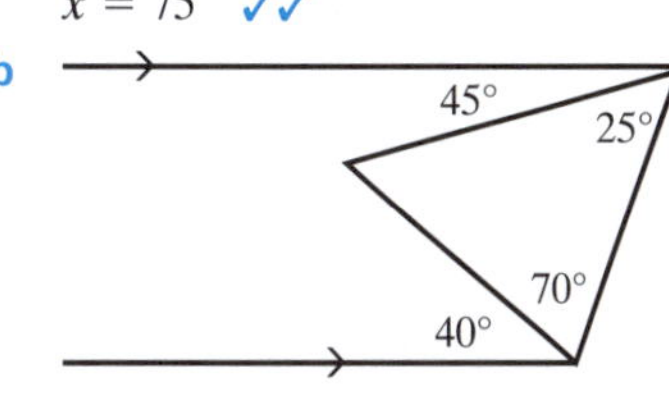

$x = 25$ ✓✓ (4 marks)

12 a Angles are equal because corresponding angles in parallel lines are equal.
$\therefore 2x + 20 = x + 40$ ✓
$2x - x = 40 - 20$
$x = 20$ ✓✓

b Base angles of an isosceles triangle are equal and angles in a triangle add to 180°.
$\therefore 2x + 10 + 2x + 10 + 40 = 180$ ✓
$4x + 60 = 180$
$4x = 180 - 60$
$4x = 120$
$\frac{4x}{4} = \frac{120}{4}$
$x = 30$ ✓✓ (6 marks)

(Total 28 marks)

WORKED SOLUTIONS

CHECK YOUR SOLUTIONS

SHAPE AND GEOMETRIC REASONING
ADVANCED TEST PAGE 27

1 **a**

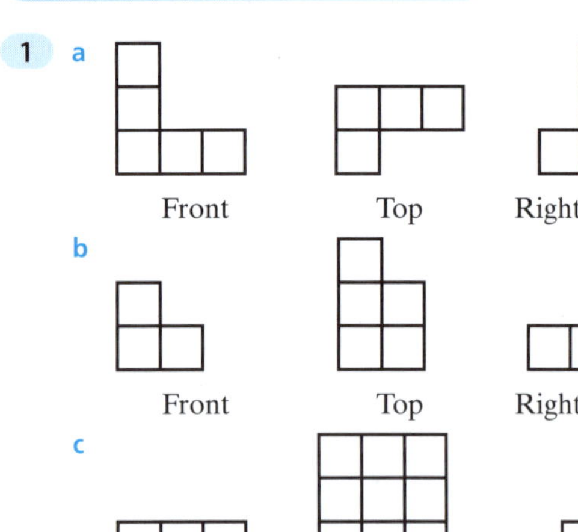

Front Top Right ✓✓✓

b

Front Top Right ✓✓✓

c

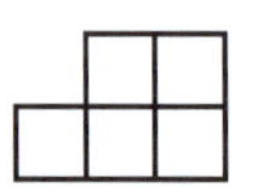

Front Top Right ✓✓✓

d

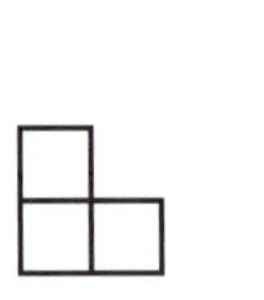

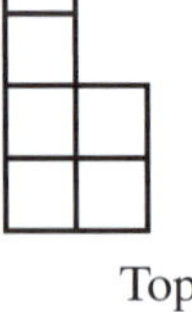

Front Top Right ✓✓✓

e

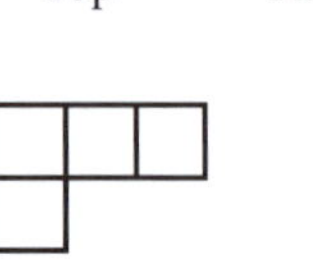

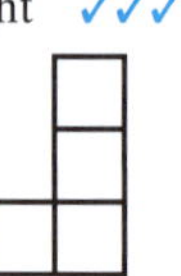

Front Top Right ✓✓✓

f

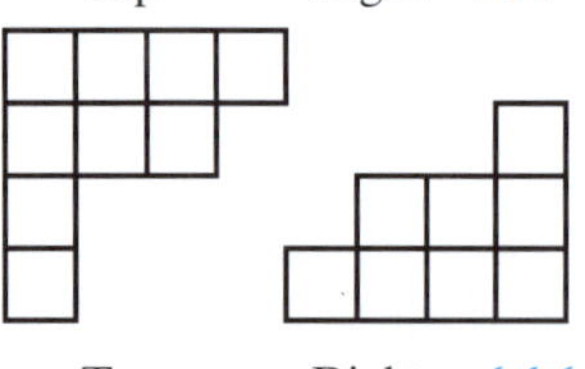

Front Top Right ✓✓✓

(18 marks)

2 **a** $90 - 47 = 43$
$\therefore 43^\circ$ ✓
b $(90 - y)^\circ$ ✓
c $90 - (90 - x) = x$
$\therefore x^\circ$ ✓ (3 marks)

3 **a** $180 - 47 = 133 \quad \therefore 133^\circ$ ✓
b $(180 - y)^\circ$ ✓
c $180 - (180 - x) = x$
$\therefore x^\circ$ ✓ (3 marks)

4 $2x - 20 + x + 50 = 90$
$3x + 30 = 90$
$3x = 90 - 30$
$3x = 60$
$x = 20$ ✓
As $2(20) - 20 = 20$ and $20 + 50 = 70$, then the angles are 20° and 70° ✓ (2 marks)

5 $x + 30 + 2x - 20 + 3x + 20 = 180$
$6x + 30 = 180$
$6x = 180 - 30$
$6x = 150$
$x = 25$ ✓
As $25 + 30 = 55$ and $2(25) - 20 = 30$ and $3(25) + 20 = 95$, then the angles are 55°, 30° and 95°. ✓ (2 marks)

6 $3x + 40 = x + 80$ ✓
$3x - x = 80 - 40$
$2x = 40$
$x = 20$
As $20 + 80 = 100$, then the angles are both 100°. ✓ (2 marks)

7 **a** $3x + 10 + 110 = 180$ ✓
$3x + 120 = 180$
$3x = 180 - 120$
$3x = 60$
$x = 20$ ✓
b $4x - 10 + 160 + 90 = 360$ ✓
$4x + 240 = 360$
$4x = 360 - 240$
$4x = 120$
$x = 30$ ✓
c $2x + 2x + 2x + 30 = 360$ ✓
$6x + 30 = 360$
$6x = 360 - 30$
$6x = 330$
$x = 55$ ✓
d $3x + 50 = x + 80$ ✓
$3x - x = 80 - 50$
$2x = 30$
$x = 15$ ✓
e $2x + 2x + 10 = 90$ ✓
$4x + 10 = 90$
$4x = 90 - 10$
$4x = 80$
$x = 20$ ✓
f $x + 20 + x + 10 = 90$ ✓
$2x + 30 = 90$
$2x = 90 - 30$
$2x = 60$
$x = 30$ ✓

g $6x + 7x + 2x + 30 = 360$ ✓
$15x + 30 = 360$
$15x = 360 - 30$
$15x = 330$
$x = 22$ ✓

h $3x + x + 20 + 280 = 360$ ✓
$4x + 300 = 360$
$4x = 360 - 300$
$4x = 60$
$x = 15$ ✓

i $3x + x - 10 + x + 10 + x = 180$ ✓
$6x = 180$
$x = 30$ ✓ (18 marks)

8 a $3x + 20 + 5x + 40 = 180$ ✓
$8x + 60 = 180$
$8x = 180 - 60$
$8x = 120$
$x = 15$ ✓

b $5a = 3a + 20$ ✓
$5a - 3a = 20$
$2a = 20$
$a = 10$ ✓

c $4a = 2a + 50$ ✓
$4a - 2a = 50$
$2a = 50$
$a = 25$ ✓
(6 marks)

9 a $x = 50, y = 10$ ✓✓
b $x = 30, y = 80, z = 110$ ✓✓✓
c $x = 40$ ✓
d $x = 30, y = 30$ ✓✓
e $3x + 20 = x + 50 + 40$ ✓
$3x + 20 = x + 90$
$3x - x = 90 - 20$
$2x = 70$
$x = 35$ ✓

f $x + 50 + 2x + 10 + 2x + 10 = 180$ ✓
$5x + 70 = 180$
$5x = 180 - 70$
$5x = 110$
$x = 22$ ✓ (12 marks)

10 a $x = 360 - (30 + 40 + 220)$
$= 360 - 290$
$= 70$ ✓

b $3x + 2x + 90 + 90 = 360$ ✓
$5x + 180 = 360$
$5x = 360 - 180$
$5x = 180$
$x = 36$ ✓

c $x + 25 + 2x + 20 + 130 + 80 = 360$ ✓
$3x + 255 = 360$
$3x = 360 - 255$
$3x = 105$
$x = 35$ ✓ (5 marks)

(Total 71 marks)

DATA REPRESENTATION AND CHANCE
SKILLS CHECK PAGE 30

1 a mean $= (4 + 7 + 2 + 6 + 11 + 5 + 3 + 6 + 1) \div 9$
$= 5$
$\therefore$ mean $= 5$

b median: 1, 2, 3, 4, 5, 6, 6, 7, 11
$\therefore$ median $= 5$

c mode $= 6$

d range $= 11 - 1 = 10$

2 a mean $= (12 + 16 + 12 + 13 + 20 + 11) \div 6$
$= 14$
$\therefore$ mean $= 14$

b median: 11, 12, 12, 13, 16, 20
$\therefore$ median $= 12.5$

c mode $= 12$

d range $= 20 - 11 = 9$

3

Score	Tally	Frequency
1	||	2
2	卌 ||	7
3	卌 ||	7
4	卌	5
5	|||	3

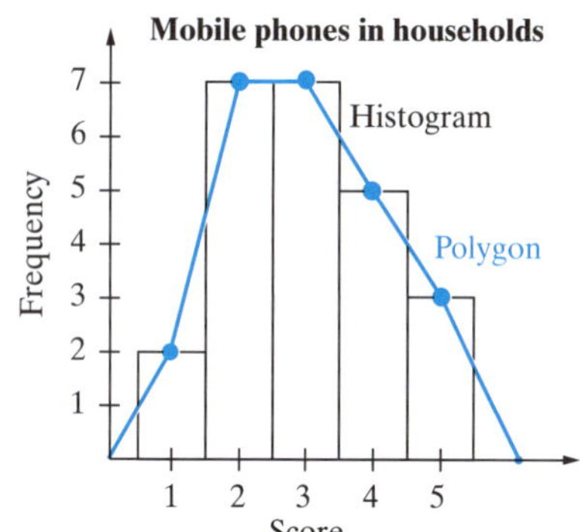

4

Score	Tally	Frequency
12	|||	3
13	|||	3
14	卌 |	6
15	||||	4
16	|||	3
17	|	1

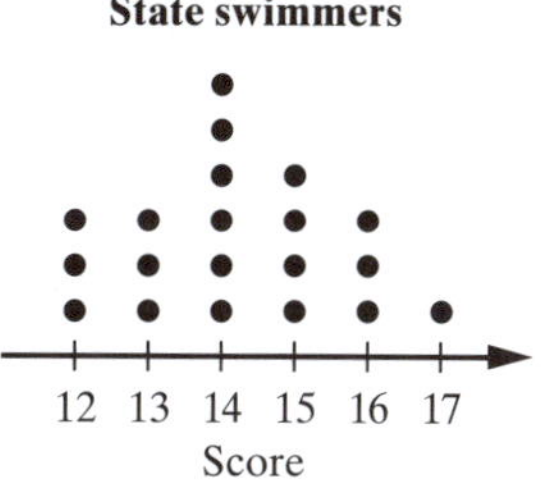

WORKED SOLUTIONS

5 Sales of bottles

Stem	Leaf
4	8
5	2 7 8 8
6	5 5 8 9
7	0 3 4 5 7 9
8	1 3 5 7 9

6 a $\Pr(\text{green}) = \frac{3}{10}$ b $\Pr(\text{blue}) = \frac{1}{10}$

c $\Pr(\text{red or green}) = \frac{9}{10}$

7 a $\Pr(\text{even}) = \frac{4}{8} = \frac{2}{4} = \frac{1}{2}$

b $\Pr(6) = \frac{1}{8}$

c $\Pr(\text{prime}) = \frac{4}{8} = \frac{2}{4} = \frac{1}{2}$

d $\Pr(\text{composite}) = \frac{3}{8}$

e $\Pr(\text{less than } 7) = \frac{6}{8} = \frac{3}{4}$

f $\Pr(\text{greater than } 8) = 0$

g $\Pr(\text{multiple of } 3) = \frac{2}{8} = \frac{1}{4}$

h $\Pr(\text{divisible by } 2) = \frac{4}{8} = \frac{1}{2}$

i $\Pr(\text{factor of } 12) = \frac{5}{8}$

DATA REPRESENTATION AND CHANCE
INTERMEDIATE TEST PAGE 31

1 Mean = (3 + 8 + 4 + 0 + 5) ÷ 5
= 4

∴ the mean is 4.

∴ [A] (1 mark)

2 Range: highest score − lowest score

Range = 12 − (−10)
= 12 + 10
= 22

∴ the range is 22.

∴ [C] (1 mark)

3 Mode: most common score 3, 4, 8 all occur twice.

∴ 5 is not a mode.

∴ [A] (1 mark)

4 Mean = (6 + 7 + 3 + 8 + 8 + 4 + 1) ÷ 7
= 5.3 (1 dec. pl.)

Mode = 8

Range = 8 − 1 = 7

Median: 1, 3, 4, 6, 7, 8, 8

∴ the median is 6.

∴ [D] (1 mark)

5 At least 4 means 4, 5, 6.

$\Pr(\text{at least } 4) = \frac{3}{6} = \frac{1}{2}$

∴ [B] (1 mark)

6 Two black 7s: 7 of clubs and 7 of spades in a pack of 52 cards

$\Pr(\text{black 7s}) = \frac{2}{52} = \frac{1}{26}$

∴ [C] (1 mark)

7 a

Score	Frequency
57	1
58	3
59	4
60	5
61	4
62	1
63	2

(2 marks)

b

(2 marks)

8 a 0, 2, 4, 4, 5, 7, 7, 7, 10

∴ median = 5 ✓

b mean = (4 + 0 + 2 + 7 + 10 + 5 + 7 + 4 + 7) ÷ 9
= $5.\dot{1}$ ✓

c mode: 7 ✓

d range = 10 − 0
= 10 ✓ (4 marks)

9

Stem	Leaf
4	3 5 5 9
5	3 7 9
6	0 0 3 4 5 8 9
7	3 8
8	1 3 7 7

(3 marks)

10 a $\Pr(5, 10, 15, 20, 25, 30) = \frac{6}{30} = \frac{1}{5}$ ✓

b $\Pr(12, 13, \ldots, 30) = \frac{19}{30}$ ✓

c $\Pr(1, 2, 5, 10) = \frac{4}{30} = \frac{2}{15}$ ✓

d $Pr(2, 3, 5, 7, 11, 13, 17, 19, 23, 29) = \frac{10}{30} = \frac{1}{3}$ ✓

e $Pr(5, 15, 25) = \frac{3}{30} = \frac{1}{10}$ ✓

f $Pr(2, 4, 6, 8) = \frac{4}{30} = \frac{2}{15}$ ✓ (6 marks)

11

Stem	Leaf
14	9
15	3 8
16	0 5 7

(2 marks)

(Total 25 marks)

DATA REPRESENTATION AND CHANCE ADVANCED TEST PAGE 32

1 a % swimming $= \frac{2}{10} \times 100\%$
$= 20\%$ ✓

b Using 2 hours = 120 minutes,

i Time in class $= \frac{4}{10} \times 120$
$= 48$
$\therefore$ 48 minutes in a class ✓

ii Time with weights $= \frac{1}{10} \times 120$
$= 12$
$\therefore$ 12 minutes using weights ✓

c 3 parts = 15
1 part = 5

i 2 parts = 10
$\therefore$ 10 minutes swimming ✓

ii 4 parts = 20
$\therefore$ 20 minutes in class ✓ (5 marks)

2 a **Waiting Time at Surgery**

More than 25	Less than 5	Between 15 and 25	Between 5 and 15

✓✓

b i Less than 5 $= \frac{90}{360} \times 40$
$= 10$
$\therefore$ 10 people waited less than 5 min ✓

ii More than 25 $= \frac{45}{360} \times 40$
$= 5$
$\therefore$ 5 people waited more than 25 min ✓

c 45 degrees = 12
180 degrees $= 12 \times 4$
$= 48$
$\therefore$ 48 people waited between 5 and 15 minutes ✓
(5 marks)

3

Men		Women
9	1	8
9 8 5	2	2 5 6 8
7 5 4 1	3	1 3 5
3	4	0

✓✓
(2 marks)

4 Mean mass = 55
Total mass $= 55 \times 4$
$= 220$ ✓
Garry's mass $= 220 - (47 + 2 \times 60)$
$= 53$
$\therefore$ Garry's mass is 53 kg ✓ (2 marks)

5 Start with two numbers 3 away from 6:
$\therefore 3, x, y, 9$
Then, middle numbers are equal distance from 6:
$\therefore 3, 4, 8, 9$ ✓
[Could be others, including 3, 5, 7, 9] (1 mark)

6 Start with median:
$\therefore a, 6, 7, b$
Then, another 7 as it is the mode:
$\therefore a, 6, 7, 7$
Then subtract 3 from 7:
$\therefore 4, 6, 7, 7$ ✓ (1 mark)

7 a Already two 6s and 8s, so need another 6:
4, 6, 6, 6, 8, 8, 12
$\therefore$ new score = 6 ✓

b As $7 \times 7 = 49$, then total of new set has to be 49:
4, 5, 6, 6, 8, 8, 12
$\therefore$ new score = 5 ✓

c The median is already 7:
4, 6, 6, 7, 8, 8, 12
$\therefore$ new score = 7 ✓

d The range is presently 8, so either:
0, 4, 6, 6, 8, 8, 12
or
4, 6, 6, 8, 8, 12, 16
$\therefore$ new score = 0 or 16 ✓ (4 marks)

8 Existing mean = 9
Existing total $= 9 \times 5 = 45$ ✓
New mean = 11
New total $= 11 \times 5 = 55$
Difference $= 55 - 45 = 10$
$\therefore$ one score increased by 10 ✓ (2 marks)

9 Mean of 4 tests = 70
Total of 4 tests $= 70 \times 4 = 280$ ✓
Mean of 5 tests = 75
Total of 5 tests $= 75 \times 5 = 375$
Difference $= 375 - 280 = 95$
$\therefore$ Lachlan needs to score 95% ✓ (2 marks)

10 a If mean = 5, then total = 30 ✓

$1 + 3 + 4 + x + 8 + 8 = 30$

$x + 24 = 30$

$x = 30 - 24$

$= 6$ ✓

b 1, 3, 4, 8, 8, 8

$\therefore x = 8$ ✓ (3 marks)

11 Outcomes are 1, 2, 3, 1, 5, 6

a $\Pr(1) = \frac{2}{6} = \frac{1}{3}$ ✓

b $\Pr(\text{even}) = \frac{2}{6} = \frac{1}{3}$ ✓

c $\Pr(\text{less than } 3) = \frac{3}{6} = \frac{1}{2}$ ✓ (3 marks)

12 a $\Pr(\text{red}) = 1 - (0.25 + 0.3 + 0.1)$

$= 0.35$ ✓

b blue $= 0.25 \times 40 = 10$

green $= 0.3 \times 40 = 12$

red $= 0.35 \times 40 = 14$

yellow $= 0.1 \times 40 = 4$

$\therefore$ 10 blue, 12 green, 14 red, 4 yellow ✓

c As $0.25 \times 10 = 2.5$, and there cannot be 2.5 blue balls, so there cannot be a total of 10 balls in the bag. ✓

d Rewrite the probabilities as simplified fractions: $\frac{1}{4}, \frac{3}{10}, \frac{7}{20}, \frac{1}{10}$. As the lowest common denominator is 20, then the smallest possible total is 20 balls. ✓ (4 marks)

(Total 34 marks)

DIRECTED NUMBERS AND INDEX NOTATION SKILLS CHECK PAGE 34

1 a $4 - 7 = -3$ b $-3 + 5 = 2$

c $2 - (+7) = 2 - 7 = -5$

d $-4 - (-6) = -4 + 6 = 2$

e $-6 - 8 = -14$ f $-2 + 5 - 3 = 0$

g $-5 + (-3) = -5 - 3 = -8$

h $-1 - 1 - 1 = -3$ i $-5 - (-5) + 5 = 5$

2 a $-3 \times -4 = 12$ b $6 \times -7 = -42$

c $-12 \times -4 = 48$ d $4 \times (-3) = -12$

e $-1 \times -1 \times -1 = -1$

f $(-3)^2 = -3 \times -3 = 9$

g $-10 \times -10 \times -10 = -1000$

h $-5 \times -2 \times -3 = -30$

i $(-1)^{99} = -1$

3 a $-12 \div -4 = 3$ b $-16 \div -8 = 2$

c $(-81) \div 9 = -9$ d $-100 \div -5 = 20$

e $12 \div -2 \div -2 = 3$

f $(-24) \div (-3) \div (-4) = -2$

g $\frac{-36}{4} = -9$ h $\frac{-120}{-30} = 4$

i $\frac{63}{-7} = -9$

4 a $12 - 4 \times 2 = 12 - 8$

$= 4$

b $16 \div (-4) + 3 \times (-2) = -4 + (-6)$

$= -10$

c $(5 \times -2)^2 = (-10)^2$

$= 100$

d $\sqrt{-4 + 13} = \sqrt{9}$

$= 3$

e $\frac{-6 \times 3}{15 \div -5} = \frac{-18}{-3}$

$= 6$

f $-8 \times -3 \div 12 = 24 \div 12$

$= 2$

5 a $5 \times 5 \times 5 \times 5 = 5^4$

b $8 \times 8 \times 8 \times 8 \times 8 = 8^5$

c $2 \times 2 \times 2 = 2^3$

d $7 \times 7 \times 4 \times 4 \times 4 = 7^2 \times 4^3$

e $3 \times 3 \times 3 \times 2 = 3^3 \times 2$

f $9 \times 9 \times 5 \times 5 \times 5 \times 5 = 9^2 \times 5^4$

6 a $6^3 = 6 \times 6 \times 6$

b $5^2 \times 3^4 = 5 \times 5 \times 3 \times 3 \times 3 \times 3$

c $4^3 \times 2^5 = 4 \times 4 \times 4 \times 2 \times 2 \times 2 \times 2 \times 2$

7 a $2^3 \times 2^4 = 2^7$ b $4^2 \times 4^4 = 4^6$

c $10^5 \times 10^4 = 10^9$

8 a $5^6 \div 5^2 = 5^4$ b $3^{11} \div 3^{10} = 3^1 = 3$

c $7^4 \div 7 = 7^4 \div 7^1$

$= 7^3$

9 a $(2^6)^2 = 2^{12}$ b $(3^4)^5 = 3^{20}$

c $(5^2)^{12} = 5^{24}$

10 a $5^0 = 1$ b $2^0 + 3^0 = 1 + 1$

$= 2$

c $(3^0 + 5^0)^0 = 1$

DIRECTED NUMBERS AND INDEX NOTATION INTERMEDIATE TEST PAGE 35

1 Check each option:

$(-2)^2 \times (-3)^2 = 4 \times 9$

$= 36$

$-6 + 2 \times 3 = -6 + 6$

$= 0$

$\frac{-48}{-6 + 2} = \frac{-48}{-4}$

$= 12$ $\therefore$ [C] (1 mark)

2 As $4^2 = 16$ and $(-4)^2 = 16$, then the answer is -4.
$\therefore$ [B] (1 mark)

3 The average is -4, then the total is -12.
$\therefore\ 3 + (-5) + \text{number} = -12$
$-2 + \text{number} = -12$
$\therefore$ the number is -10
$\therefore$ [D] (1 mark)

4 $3^2 \times 2^3 = 3 \times 3 \times 2 \times 2 \times 2$
$\therefore$ [D] (1 mark)

5 $72 = 8 \times 9$
$= 2^3 \times 3^2$
$\therefore$ [D] (1 mark)

6 $3^0 \times 2^0 = 1 \times 1$
$= 1$
$\therefore$ [D] (1 mark)

7 a $-3 + 4 + 3 = 4$ ✓
b $(-121) \div 11 = -11$ ✓
c $\sqrt{(-3)^2 + (-4)^2} = 5$ ✓ (3 marks)

8 a $4 - 2 \times 3 = 4 - 6$ ✓
$= -2$ ✓
b $12 \div (6 \div 3) = 12 \div 2$ ✓
$= 6$ ✓
c $(-4 - 2) - 12 \times (3 - 4) = -6 - 12 \times (-1)$ ✓
$= -6 + 12$
$= 6$ ✓ (6 marks)

9 a $2^1 \times 2^2 \times 2^3 = 2^{1+2+3}$
$= 2^6$ ✓
b $12^8 \div 12^4 = 12^{8-4}$
$= 12^4$ ✓
c $(3^5)^2 = 3^{5 \times 2}$
$= 3^{10}$ ✓ (3 marks)

10 a $5^0 + 4 = 1 + 4$ ✓
$= 5$ ✓
b $(6 + 2)^0 - 6^0 = 1 - 1$ ✓
$= 0$ ✓
c $(3^4 \times 3^2 \div 3^5)^2 = 3^2$ ✓
$= 9$ ✓ (6 marks)

11 $\text{Average} = \dfrac{(-9) + (-6) + (-3) + 2}{4}$ ✓
$= \dfrac{-16}{4}$
$= -4$ ✓ (2 marks)

12 The numbers are 4 and -6 because
$4 + (-6) = -2$ and $4 \times -6 = -24$. (2 marks)
(Total 28 marks)

DIRECTED NUMBERS AND INDEX NOTATION
ADVANCED TEST PAGE 36

1 Depth $= -120 - 75 + 56$
$= -139$
$\therefore$ it is at a depth of 139 metres ✓ (1 mark)

2 a $46 - (-23) = 69$
$\therefore$ the difference is 69° ✓
b $57 - (-89) = 146$
$\therefore$ the difference is 146° ✓
c $-23 - (-89) = 66$
$\therefore$ the difference is 66° ✓ (3 marks)

3 a $30 - [15 \div (3 - 6)] = 30 - [15 \div (-3)]$ ✓
$= 30 - [-5]$
$= 35$ ✓
b $-5(2 - 8 \times 3) = -5(2 - 24)$ ✓
$= -5(-22)$
$= 110$ ✓
c $-18 \div (3 + 6) - (2 - 3)^3 = -18 \div 9 - (-1)^3$ ✓
$= -2 - (-1)$
$= -2 + 1$
$= -1$ ✓
d $\sqrt{18 - 7 \times 2} \times \sqrt{5 \times 8 + 6 \times 4}$
$= \sqrt{18 - 14} \times \sqrt{40 + 24}$ ✓
$= \sqrt{4} \times \sqrt{64}$
$= 2 \times 8$
$= 16$ ✓
e $\dfrac{-4 - 12}{2 - 6} = \dfrac{-16}{-4}$ ✓
$= 4$ ✓
f $\dfrac{5 - 20}{5} - \dfrac{20 - 5}{-5} = \dfrac{-15}{5} - \dfrac{15}{-5}$ ✓
$= -3 + 3 = 0$ ✓
g $\dfrac{(4 - 10)^2}{(3 - 6)^2} = \dfrac{(-6)^2}{(-3)^2}$ ✓
$= \dfrac{36}{9} = 4$ ✓
h $\dfrac{15 - 30 \div 6}{(6 + 24) \div (-6)} = \dfrac{15 - 5}{30 \div (-6)}$ ✓
$= \dfrac{10}{-5} = -2$ ✓
i $\dfrac{12 - 4 \times 8}{(12 - 4) \div 8} = \dfrac{12 - 32}{8 \div 8}$ ✓
$= \dfrac{-20}{1} = -20$ ✓

j $\dfrac{(-20) \div (5 \times 2) + 3 \times (6 - 2)}{(-20) \div 5 \times 2 + 3 \times 6 - 2}$

$= \dfrac{(-20) \div 10 + 3 \times 4}{-8 + 18 - 2}$ ✓

$= \dfrac{-2 + 12}{8} = \dfrac{10}{8} = 1\dfrac{1}{4}$ ✓ (20 marks)

4 a i $12 - 2 \times 6.5 = -1$

$\therefore$ temperature is $-1°$ ✓

ii $12 - 7 \times 6.5 = -33.5$

$\therefore$ temperature is $-33.5°$ ✓

iii $12 - 9.5 \times 6.5 = -49.75$

$\therefore$ temperature is $-49.75°$ ✓

b i $-24 + 2 \times 6.5 = -11$

$\therefore$ temperature is $-11°$ ✓

ii $-24 - 4 \times 6.5 = -50$

$\therefore$ temperature is $-50°$ ✓

iii $-24 + 6 \times 6.5 = 15$

$\therefore$ temperature is $15°$ ✓ (6 marks)

5 a $(3^5 \div 3^3) \times (3^4 \div 3^3) = 3^2 \times 3$
$= 3^3$ ✓

b $5^4 \times 5^2 \div 5^7 = 5^6 \div 5^7$
$= 5^{-1}$ ✓

c $(2^{0.5})^4 = 2^{0.5\times4}$
$= 2^2$ ✓

d $(7^4)^{\frac{1}{2}} = 7^2$ ✓

e $\dfrac{5^5 \div 5}{5^0} = 5^5 \div 5^1$
$= 5^4$ ✓

f $\dfrac{3^3 \times 3^4}{3^5} = 3^7 \div 3^5$
$= 3^2$ ✓

g $\dfrac{2^8 \div 2^5}{2^7 \div 2^2} = 2^3 \div 2^5$
$= 2^{-2}$ ✓ (7 marks)

6 Evaluate

a $9^2 \div 3^2 = (3^2)^2 \div 3^2$
$= 3^4 \div 3^2$
$= 3^2$ ✓

b $2^2 \times 4^3 = 2^2 \times (2^2)^3$
$= 2^2 \times 2^6$
$= 2^8$ ✓

c $\dfrac{(4^3)^4}{2^{10}} = (4^3)^4 \div 2^{10}$
$= 4^{12} \div 2^{10}$
$= (2^2)^{12} \div 2^{10}$
$= 2^{24} \div 2^{10}$
$= 2^{14}$ ✓ (3 marks)

7 a

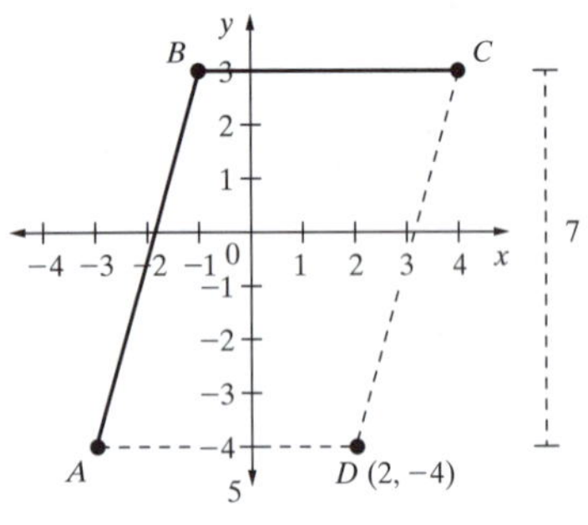

$\therefore D(2, -4)$ ✓

b Area $= 5 \times 7 = 35$

$\therefore$ area is 35 units^2 ✓ (2 marks)

8 a

t	0	1	2	3	4
T	3	1	−1	**−3**	**−5**

✓

b $T = 3 - 2t$ ✓

c Initial means at the start, when $t = 0$

$T = 3 - 2 \times 0 = 3$

$\therefore$the temperature is initially 3° ✓

d Subs $t = 6$:

$T = 3 - 2 \times 6 = -9$

$\therefore$the temperature will be $-9°$ ✓

e Subs $T = -13$:

$-13 = 3 - 2t$ ✓

$2t = 3 + 13$

$2t = 16$

$t = 8$

$\therefore$ it will take 8 hours ✓ (6 marks)

9 a $ab^2 - c = -3 \times (-4)^2 - (-5)$ ✓
$= -3 \times 16 + 5$
$= -48 + 5$
$= -43$ ✓

b $2a - 9b + 4c = 2 \times (-3) - 9 \times (-4) + 4 \times (-5)$ ✓
$= -6 + 36 - 20$
$= 10$ ✓

c $(ac + 7c)^2 = (-3 \times -5 + 7 \times -5)^2$ ✓
$= (15 - 35)^2$
$= (-20)^2$
$= 400$ ✓

d $2b^2 - 4a^2 = 2 \times (-4)^2 - 4 \times (-3)^2$ ✓
$= 32 - 36$
$= -4$ ✓

e $c(3 - ab) = -5(3 - (-3) \times (-4))$ ✓
$= -5(3 - 12)$
$= -5 \times -9$
$= 45$ ✓

f $\dfrac{cb + 2a + 2}{b + 8}$

$= \dfrac{(-5) \times (-4) + 2 \times (-3) + 2}{(-4) + 8}$ ✓

$= \dfrac{20 - 6 + 2}{4}$

$= 4$ ✓

g $\sqrt{\dfrac{-b^3}{(2a - b)^2}} = \sqrt{\dfrac{(-4)^3}{(2 \times (-3) - (-4))^2}}$ ✓

$= \sqrt{\dfrac{64}{(-6 + 4)^2}}$

$= \sqrt{\dfrac{64}{4}}$

$= 4$ ✓ (14 marks)

(Total 62 marks)

WORKED SOLUTIONS

CHECK YOUR SOLUTIONS

FINANCIAL MATHEMATICS
SKILLS CHECK PAGE 38

1 a $1.2 \times 70 = 84$
$\therefore$ \$84

b $1.08 \times 320 = 345.6$
$\therefore$ \$345.60

c $1.075 \times 9400 = 10\,105$
$\therefore$ \$10 105

2 a $0.88 \times 390 = 343.2$
$\therefore$ \$343.20

b 0.91×4.2 million
$= 3.822$ million
$\therefore$ \$3.822 million or \$3 822 000

c $0.8775 \times 4000 = 3510$
$\therefore$ \$3510

3 a $SP = 125\%$ of \$420
$\therefore SP = 1.25 \times 420$
$= 525$
$\therefore$ selling price of \$525

b $SP = 140\%$ of \$6500
$\therefore SP = 1.4 \times 6500$
$= 9100$
$\therefore$ selling price of \$9100

c $SP = 78\%$ of \$12 000
$\therefore SP = 0.78 \times 12\,000$
$= 9360$
$\therefore$ selling price of \$9360

d $SP = 84.5\%$ of \$350
$\therefore SP = 0.845 \times 350$
$= 295.75$
$\therefore$ selling price of \$295.75

4 Profit = \$576 000 − \$360 000
= \$216 000
$\therefore$ Profit % $= \frac{216\,000}{360\,000} \times \frac{100\%}{1}$
$= 60\%$

5 a Savings $= 0.15 \times 320$
$= 48$
$\therefore$ \$48

b Cost $= 0.85 \times 470$
$= 399.5$
$\therefore$ \$399.50

6 Cost $= 62 \times 5 \times 0.9 \times 0.95$
$= 265.05$
$\therefore$ paint costs \$265.05

7 GST $= 0.1 \times 175$
$= 17.5$
$\therefore$ GST of \$17.50

8 GST $= 198 \div 11 = 18$
$\therefore$ GST of \$18

9 Total cost $= 1.1 \times 320 = 352$
$\therefore$ total cost of \$352

10 Price including GST $= 4.95$
Amount of GST $= 4.95 \div 11$
$= 0.45$
Price without GST
$= 4.95 - 0.45 = 4.5$
$\therefore$ price before GST added was \$4.50

11 a 55% of amount $= 12\,100$
1% of amount
$= 12\,100 \div 55 = 220$
$\therefore$ \$220

b 1% of amount $= 220$
100% of amount
$= 220 \times 100 = 22\,000$
$\therefore$ \$22 000

12 a 1% of amount
$= 690 \div 30 = 23$
100% of amount $= 23 \times 100$
$= 2300$
$\therefore$ whole amount is 2300 kg

b Spending $= 2700 \div 45 \times 55$
$= 3300$
$\therefore$ Sarah has spent \$3300

c Robyn paid 75% of the original price
$\therefore$ original price
$= 36 \div 75 \times 100 = 48$
$\therefore$ original price is \$48

13 selling price
= 140% of cost price
140% of cost price $= 560$
1% of cost price $= 560 \div 140$
$= 4$
100% of cost price $= 4 \times 100$
$= 400$
$\therefore$ the cost price of the bracelet was \$400.

FINANCIAL MATHEMATICS
INTERMEDIATE TEST PAGE 39

1 As $100 - 12\frac{1}{2} = 87\frac{1}{2}$,
then price $= 0.875 \times 780$
$= 682.5$
$\therefore$ new price is \$682.50
$\therefore$ [B] (1 mark)

2 As an increase of 8% means 108%,
then price $= 1.08 \times 1470$
$= 1587.6$
$\therefore$ new price is \$1587.60
$\therefore$ [D] (1 mark)

3 Amount of GST $= 22 \div 11$
$= 2$
$\therefore$ \$2 GST
Original cost $= 22 - 2$
$= 20$
$\therefore$ \$20
$\therefore$ [C] (1 mark)

4 % discount $= \frac{4}{80} \times 100\%$
$= 5\%$
$\therefore$ [B] (1 mark)

5 Increase by 10% means
$110\% = 1.1$
Decrease by 10% means
$90\% = 0.9$
$\therefore$ New amount
$= 400 \times 1.1 \times 0.9$
$= 396$
$\therefore$ new amount is \$396
$\therefore$ [D] (1 mark)

6 70% of total price $= 16\,800$
Total price $= 16\,800 \div 7 \times 10$
$= 24\,000$
$\therefore$ \$24 000
$\therefore$ [C] (1 mark)

7 a Sale price $= 1.22 \times 315\,000$
$= 384\,300$
$\therefore$ Harry sells for \$384 300 ✓

b Profit $= 384\,300 - 315\,000$
$= 69\,300$
$\therefore$ Harry's profit is \$69 300. ✓ (2 marks)

8 15% of price $= 102$
100% of price
$= 102 \div 15 \times 100$ ✓
= \$680
$\therefore$ 680 ✓ (2 marks)

9 a Loss % $= \frac{360}{1200} \times 100\%$ ✓
$= 30\%$ ✓

b Sale price $= 0.95 \times 360$ ✓
$= 342$
$\therefore$ sale price is \$342 ✓

c Selling price = 115% of cost price
∴ Cost price = 230 ÷ 115 × 100 ✓
= 200
∴ television cost $200 ✓ (6 marks)

10 a Price = 0.8 × 0.9 × 120 ✓
= 86.4
∴ Chen paid $86.40 ✓

b Discount = $120 − $86.40
= $33.60 ✓

$\% \text{ discount} = \frac{33.6}{120} \times 100\%$
= 28%
∴ Chen received 28% discount. ✓ (4 marks)

11 As 100 − 60 = 40, then
40% of original price = 150
1% of original price = 150 ÷ 40
= 3.75 ✓
100% of original = 3.75 × 100
= 375
∴ it originally cost $375. ✓ (2 marks)

12 a New price = 72 ÷ 1.1 ÷ 1.15 ✓
= 91.08
∴ new price of $91.08 ✓

b Existing price = 84 ÷ 1.15 ÷ 1.1 ✓
= 80.35 (2 dec. pl.)
∴ existing price of $80.35 ✓ (4 marks)

(Total 26 marks)

FINANCIAL MATHEMATICS ADVANCED TEST PAGE 40

1 a New amount = 5000 × 1.2 × 0.85
= 5100
∴ new amount is $5100 ✓

b New amount = 5000 × 0.85 × 1.2
= 5100
∴ new amount is $5100 ✓ (2 marks)

2 Friday price = 0.75 × 18
= 13.5
Price decrease = 18 − 13.5
= 4.5
∴ price dropped $4.50 to $13.50 ✓

$\% \text{ increase} = \frac{4.5}{13.5} \times 100\%$

$= 33\frac{1}{3}\%$

∴ percentage increase of $33\frac{1}{3}\%$ ✓ (2 marks)

3 100 − 35 = 65
65% of original price = 71.5 ✓
100% of original price = 71.5 ÷ 65 × 100
= 110
∴ the original price was $110 ✓ (2 marks)

4 40 − 25 = 15
15% of original price = 24 ✓
100% of original price = 24 ÷ 15 × 100
= 160
∴ the original price was $160 ✓ (2 marks)

5 a 100 − 60 = 40
40% of original price = 48 ✓
100% of original price = 48 ÷ 40 × 100
= 120
∴ the original price was $120 ✓

b Savings = 120 − 48
= 72
∴ savings of $72 ✓ (3 marks)

6 Normal cost = 22 + 18
= 40
Savings = 9 ✓

$\text{Percentage} = \frac{9}{40} \times 100\%$
= 22.5% ✓ (2 marks)

7

Cost P	Selling P	Profit % of Cost	Profit % of Selling
$36	$45	**25%** ✓	**20%** ✓
$20	**$23** ✓	15%	**13.04%** ✓
$45 ✓	$90	**100%** ✓	50%
$150	**$180** ✓	20%	$\mathbf{16\frac{1}{6}\%}$ ✓
$60 ✓	$80	$\mathbf{33\frac{1}{3}\%}$ ✓	25%

(10 marks)

8

Item	0%	10%	15%
A	$32	**$35.20** ✓	**$36.80** ✓
B	**$70** ✓	$77	**$80.50** ✓
C	**$24** ✓	**$26.40** ✓	$27.60

(6 marks)

9 100 − 30 = 70
70% of cost price = 630 ✓
100% of cost price = 630 ÷ 70 × 100 = 900
∴ the bike cost $900 ✓ (2 marks)

10

Object	Cost P	Markup	Selling P
table	$120	160%	**$312** ✓
vase	$290	**65%** ✓	$478.50
lamp	**$38** ✓	120%	$83.60

(3 marks)

WORKED SOLUTIONS

CHECK YOUR SOLUTIONS

11 Discount in Shop A $= 0.35 \times 28$
$= 9.8$ ✓
Discount in Shop B $= 10$
As \$10 − \$9.80 = \$0.20, then Shop B is selling the book cheaper by 20c. ✓ (2 marks)

12 Let the original price be \$100 ✓
New cost $= 100 \times 0.80 \times 0.90$
$= 72$
Discount $= 100 - 72$
$= 28$
% discount $= \frac{28}{100} \times 100\%$
$= 28\%$
∴ total discount of 28% ✓ (2 marks)

13 **a** Value in 2 years (in 2015)
$= 820\,000 \times 1.025 \times 1.025$
$= 820\,000 \times 1.025^2$
$= 861\,512.5$
∴ the value will be \$861 512.50 ✓

b Value in 2013 = 820 000
Value in 2012 $= 820\,000 \div 1.025$
$= 800\,000$
∴ the value was \$800 000 ✓ (2 marks)

14 **a** Bella's tax $= 0.15 \times 17\,500$
$= 2625$
∴ Bella pays tax of \$2625 ✓

b As $45\,750 - 20\,000 = 25\,750$,
Travis's tax $= 0.15 \times 20\,000 + 0.22 \times 25\,750$ ✓
$= 8665$
∴ Travis pays tax of \$8665 ✓ (3 marks)

15 $1.75 - 1.5 = 0.25$
0.25% of taxable income = 156 ✓
100% of taxable income $= 156 \div 0.25 \times 100$
$= 62\,400$
∴ Conrad's taxable income is \$62 400 ✓ (2 marks)

16 Day 1 price $= 0.99 \times 200$
$= 198$ ∴ \$198 ✓
Day 2 price $= 0.98 \times 198$
$= 194.04$ ∴ \$194.04
And so on ...
∴ $200 \times 0.99 \times 0.98 \times ... \times 0.88 = 88.55$
∴ on the 12th day the price is under \$100 ✓✓
(3 marks)

(Total 48 marks)

RATIO AND RATES
SKILLS CHECK PAGE 42

1 **a** $12:16 = \frac{12}{4}:\frac{16}{4} = 3:4$

b $4:40:400 = \frac{4}{4}:\frac{40}{4}:\frac{400}{4} = 1:10:100$

c $\$2:\$12 = 2:12 = \frac{2}{2}:\frac{12}{2} = 1:6$

d $\frac{2}{3}:\frac{3}{5} = \frac{2}{3} \times \frac{5}{5}:\frac{3}{5} \times \frac{3}{3} = \frac{10}{15}:\frac{9}{15} = 10:9$

e $\frac{3}{4}:1 = \frac{3}{4}:\frac{4}{4} = 3:4$

f $1\frac{1}{2}:2\frac{1}{4} = \frac{3}{2}:\frac{9}{4} = \frac{3}{2} \times \frac{2}{2}:\frac{9}{4} = \frac{6}{4}:\frac{9}{4}$
$= 6:9$
$= 2:3$

2 **a** $0.6:1 = 6:10 = 3:5$

b $0.3:0.25 = 0.30 \times 100:0.25 \times 100$
$= 30:25 = 6:5$

c 20 s : 3 min = 20 s : 180 s
$= \frac{20}{20}:\frac{180}{20} = 1:9$

d 4.5 L : 200 mL = 4500 mL : 200 mL
$= 4500:200 = 45:2$

e $3x^2:15x = \frac{3x^2}{x}:\frac{15x}{x} = 3x:15 = \frac{3x}{3}:\frac{15}{3} = x:5$

f 350 g : 2 kg : 0.6 t = 350 g : 2000 g : 600 000 g
$= 350:2000:600\,000$
$= 7:40:12\,000$

3 **a** 6 parts = 180
1 part $= \frac{180}{6} = 30$
4 parts $= 30 \times 4 = 120$
∴ smallest piece is 120 cm in length

b Total parts $= 4 + 5 + 6$
$= 15$
15 parts $= 15 \times 30$
$= 450$
∴ original piece was 450 cm in length

4 Total parts $= 4 + 3$
$= 7$
$\frac{3}{7} \times 3829 = 1641$
∴ 1641 children

5 **a** 1 cm = 10 metres
1 cm = 1000 cm
∴ 1 : 1000

b 1000 parts = 275 metres
1 part = 0.275 m
∴ 27.5 cm

6 Total parts $= 3 + 2 + 4$
$= 9$
9 parts = 180
1 part = 20
4 parts = 80 ∴ 80°

7 a $x : 5 = 18 : 15$

From 15 down to 5 is dividing by 3.

This means 18 divided by 3 gives 6.

$\therefore x = 6$

b $\frac{1}{2} : 4 = x : 16$

From 4 up to 16 is multiplying by 4.

This means $\frac{1}{2}$ multiplied by 4 gives 2.

$\therefore x = 2$

c $\frac{x}{3} = \frac{8}{12}$

From 12 down to 3 is dividing by 4.

This means 8 divided by 4 gives 2.

$\therefore x = 2$

8

Distance	Speed	Time
200 km	25 km/h	**8 h**
600 km	150 km/h	4 h
150 m	20 m/min	**7 min 30 s**
396 km	**72 km/h**	5 h 30 min
240 km	64 km/h	3 h 45 min
352 km	66 km/h	**5 h 20 min**

9 As $300\,000 \times 60 = 18\,000\,000$, $\therefore$ 18 000 000 km

10 Time = 10:40 minus 7:20

= 3 h 20 min

$= 3\frac{1}{3}$ h

Distance $= 90 \times 3\frac{1}{3} = 300$

$\therefore$ Sandy travels 300 km

11 a As $4800 \div 600 = 8$,

$\therefore$ 8 minutes to discharge

b As 4800 L = 4.8 kL,

$\therefore$ Cost = $1350 × 4.8

= $6480

$\therefore$ petrol cost $6480

12 Wastage $= 8 \times 15 \times 60 \times 24$

$= 172\,800$

$\therefore$ 172.8 L of water is wasted per day.

RATIO AND RATES
INTERMEDIATE TEST PAGE 43

1 $3 : \frac{2}{3} = \frac{9}{3} : \frac{2}{3}$

= 9 : 2 [multiply by 3]

$\therefore$ [C] (1 mark)

2 4 km : 200 m = 4000 : 200

= 20 : 1

$\therefore$ [C] (1 mark)

3 Try each of the alternatives.

Not A, as 18 not divisible by 4

Not B, as 2 not divisible by 4

Not D, as 28 not divisible by 11

$\therefore$ correct answer is 35, as it is divisible by 7

$\therefore$ [C] (1 mark)

4 Angles are $\frac{2}{9} \times 180° = 40°$

$\frac{3}{9} \times 180° = 60°$ and

$\frac{4}{9} \times 180° = 80°$

The only correct answer is 80°

$\therefore$ [B] (1 mark)

5 Time = 9 : 20 minus 7 : 40

= 1 h 40 min

Distance

= speed × time

= 24 × 1 (DMS) 40 (DMS)

= 40

$\therefore$ distance is 40 km

$\therefore$ [B] (1 mark)

6 Pay rate $= 360 \div 25$

= 14.4

Hourly rate is $14.40

No. of hours $= 259.20 \div 14.4$

= 18

$\therefore$ Last week Marcus worked 18 h.

$\therefore$ [D] (1 mark)

7 a $2.40 : $6 = 240c : 600c

= 240 : 600 = 2 : 5 ✓

b 1 hectare : 1000 m^2

= 10 000 m^2 : 1000 m^2

= 10 000 : 1000 = 10 : 1 ✓

c 100 mL : 0.2 kL

= 100 mL : 200 000 mL

= 100 : 200 000 =

1 : 2000 ✓ (3 marks)

8 2 parts = 340

1 part = 170 ✓

5 parts = 5 × 170 = 850

$\therefore$ 850 DVDs ✓ (2 marks)

9 a jobs : cars = 3 : 2

3 parts = 600

1 part = 200 ✓

2 parts = 400

$\therefore$ 400 car ads ✓

b cars : property = 4 : 3

Car ads $= \frac{4}{7} \times 959$ ✓

= 548

$\therefore$ 548 car ads ✓

c To combine the ratios make the value of the common element (cars) the same for both.

jobs : cars = 3 : 2

= 6 : 4

cars : property = 4 : 3

$\therefore$ jobs : cars : property

= 6 : 4 : 3 ✓✓

d Using c above, 3 parts = 930

1 part = 310

6 parts = 1860

$\therefore$ 1860 job ads ✓✓

(8 marks)

10 Time $= 372 \div 72$

= 5.166 666 66 (2ndF) (DMS)

= 5 h 10 min ✓

So time of arrival = 11:40 am plus 5 h 10 min

= 16:50

= 4:50 pm

$\therefore$ Ross arrived at 4:50 pm. ✓(2 marks)

11 a Time = 23:30 − 20:10

= 3 h 20 min ✓

b Distance = 78 × 3 (DMS) 20 (DMS) ✓

= 260

$\therefore$ 260 km ✓

c Rate $= \frac{32}{260} \times 100$ ✓

= 12.307 692 31

= 12.31 [2 decimal places]

$\therefore$ fuel rate is 12.31 L/100 km ✓

WORKED SOLUTIONS

CHECK YOUR SOLUTIONS

d Cost $= 1.629 \times 32$ ✓
$= 52.128$
$= 52.13$ [2 decimal places]
$\therefore$ petrol cost \$52.13 ✓ (7 marks)

(Total 28 marks)

RATIO AND RATES
ADVANCED TEST PAGE 44

1 **a** $12:16:20 = 3:4:5$ ✓
b $0.7:0.35:0.05 = 0.70:0.35:0.05$
$= 70:35:5$
$= 14:7:1$ ✓
c $2:2\frac{3}{4}:3 = 2:2.75:3$
$= 200:275:300$
$= 8:11:12$ ✓
d 20 mm : 3 cm : 0.6 m = 20 mm : 30 mm : 600 mm
$= 20:30:600$
$= 2:3:60$ ✓
e 350 s : 10 min : 1 h = 350 s : 600 s : 3600 s
$= 350:600:3600$
$= 35:60:360$
$= 7:12:72$ ✓
f 120 mL : 2 L : 0.006 kL
= 120 mL : 2000 mL : 6000 mL
$= 120:2000:6000$
$= 12:200:600$
$= 3:50:150$ ✓ (6 marks)

2 **a** 5 parts = 400
7 parts $= 400 \div 5 \times 7$
$= 560$
$\therefore$ increased amount is \$560 ✓
b 9 parts = 162
2 parts $= 162 \div 9 \times 2$
$= 36$
$\therefore$ decreased amount is \$36 ✓
c 5 parts = 600
8 parts $= 600 \div 5 \times 8$
$= 960$
$\therefore$ increased amount is \$960 ✓
3 parts = 960
2 parts $= 960 \div 3 \times 2$
$= 640$
$\therefore$ decreased amount is \$640 ✓ (4 marks)

3 **a** $x:3 = 12:18$
As $18 \div \mathbf{6} = 3$, then $12 \div \mathbf{6} = 2$
$\therefore x = 2$ ✓
b $5:6 = x:30$
As $6 \times \mathbf{5} = 30$, then $5 \times \mathbf{5} = 25$
$\therefore x = 25$ ✓
c Firstly, $24:36 = 2:3$
$14:x = 2:3$
As $2 \times \mathbf{7} = 14$, then $3 \times \mathbf{7} = 21$
$\therefore x = 21$ ✓ (3 marks)

4 Loss $= 600 - 450$
$= 150$
$\therefore$ loss of \$150
a selling price : cost price = 450 : 600
$= 3:4$ ✓
b selling price : loss = 450 : 150
$= 3:1$ ✓
c loss : cost price : selling price = 150 : 600 : 450
$= 1:4:3$ ✓ (3 marks)

5 Males $= \frac{3}{4}$, females $= \frac{1}{4}$
a females : total $= \frac{1}{4}:1$
$= 1:4$ ✓
b males : females $= \frac{3}{4}:\frac{1}{4}$
$= 3:1$ ✓ (2 marks)

6 Perimeter = 56 cm,
length + breadth = 28 cm
Length: $\frac{4}{7} \times 28 = 16$
Breadth: $\frac{3}{7} \times 28 = 12$
Dimensions are 16 cm, 12 cm ✓
Area $= 16 \times 12$
$= 192$
$\therefore$ area is 192 cm^2 ✓ (2 marks)

7 $180 - 40 = 140$
Angles are 140° and 40° ✓
Ratio $= 140:40$
$= 7:2$ ✓ (2 marks)

8 Two lengths are 120 cm and 80 cm
a 80 cm : 120 cm = 80 : 120
$= 2:3$ ✓
b 120 cm : 2 m = 120 : 200
$= 3:5$ ✓ (2 marks)

9 footballs : basketballs = 6 : 5
$= 24:20$
basketballs : netballs = 4 : 3
$= 20:15$
$\therefore$ footballs : basketballs : netballs = 24 : 20 : 15 ✓
24 parts = 48
1 part = 2
20 parts = 40
15 parts = 30
$\therefore$ 40 basketballs and 30 netballs ✓ (2 marks)

10 **a** $\$0.54 \times 100 = \$54$
$\therefore$ 54c/10 mL = \$54 /L ✓

b $48 \times 60 \times 60 \div 1000$
$\therefore$ 48 m/s = 172.8 km/h ✓

c $100 \div 9.2 = 10.9$ (1 dec. pl.)
$\therefore$ 9.2 L/100 km = 10.9 km/L ✓ (3 marks)

11 Time = Distance ÷ Speed
First-half time = $15 \div 20 = 0.75$
$\therefore$ first half takes 0.75 h
Second-half time = $15 \div 15 = 1$
$\therefore$ second half takes 1 h ✓
Speed = Distance ÷ Time
= $30 \div 1.75$
= 17.14 (2 dec. pl.)
$\therefore$ average speed is 17.14 km/h ✓ (2 marks)

12 $90 + 100 = 190$
Time = Distance ÷ Speed
= $760 \div 190$
= 4 ✓
$\therefore$ after 4 hours the cars meet.
This is 360 km from Brisbane and 400 km from Charleville. ✓ (2 marks)

13 Time = 8 h 45 min
= 8.75 h ✓
Speed = $700 \div 8.75$
= 80
$\therefore$ average speed of 80 km/h ✓ (2 marks)

14 $8.5 \times 200\,000 = 1\,700\,000$
Distance is 1 700 000 cm ✓
Now, $1\,700\,000 \div 100\,000 = 17$
$\therefore$ distance is 17 km ✓(2 marks)

15 $11.4 \times 0.75 = 8.55$
$8.6 \times 0.5 = 4.30$
Total cost of $12.85 for 1.25 kg ✓
As $12.85 \div 1.25 = 10.28$
$\therefore$ Cost is $10.28/kg ✓ (2 marks)

16 Time = Distance ÷ Speed
Time at 60 km/h
= $1 \div 60$
= 0.016 666 6... h
= 1 min
= 60 s ✓
Time at 100 km/h = $1 \div 100$
= 0.01 h
= 0.6 min
= 36 s
$\therefore$ it takes 24 seconds more ✓ (2 marks)

17 a Distance = Speed × Time
= 40×0.5
= 20
$\therefore$ the distance is 20 km ✓

b Time = Distance ÷ Speed
= $20 \div 50$
= 0.4
$\therefore$ the drive to work took 0.4 h, or 24 min ✓ (2 marks)

18 Distance = $5 \times 60 \times 10$
= 3000 m
= 3 km
$\therefore$ Mim ran 3 km in 10 minutes ✓ (1 mark)

19 Existing mixture has 4 L blue, 6 L white.
If 5 L of blue paint is added, then new mixture will have 9 L blue, 6 L white. ✓
$\therefore$ % blue $= \frac{9}{15} \times 100\%$
$= 60\%$
$\therefore$ need to add 5 litres of blue paint ✓ (2 marks)

(Total 46 marks)

ALGEBRA SKILLS CHECK PAGE 46

1 a $5x - 3y - 2x + 7y$
$= 3x + 4y$

b $8ab - 10ba = -2ab$

c $5a^2 - 6a^2 = -a^2$

d $7 - a - 10 + 2a = -3 + a$

e $3x - 9y - x + 2y = 2x - 7y$

f $9y^3 - 10y^3 = -y^3$

g $6a \times (-3a) = -18a^2$

h $(-2c) \times (-3d) = 6cd$

i $(-3y)^2 = (-3y) \times (-3y)$
$= 9y^2$

j $10m \div (-5m) = -2$

k $\frac{-4x}{2} = -2x$

l $(-24x^2) \div (-4x) = 6x$

2 a $p^2 - q^2 = (-3)^2 - (-4)^2$
$= 9 - 16$
$= -7$

b $(p + q)^2 = (-3 + -4)^2$
$= (-3 - 4)^2$
$= (-7)^2$
$= 49$

c $q(p - 1) = -4 \times (-3 - 1)$
$= -4 \times -4$
$= 16$

3 a $\frac{c - b}{a} = \frac{6 - -4}{-2}$
$= \frac{10}{-2}$
$= -5$

b $\sqrt{1 - bc} = \sqrt{1 - (-4) \times 6}$
$= \sqrt{1 + 24}$
$= \sqrt{25}$
$= 5$

c $(3a)^0 = (3 \times (-2))^0$
$= (-6)^0$
$= 1$

4 a $4(x + 7) = 4x + 28$

b $(4y - 2)6 = 24y - 12$

c $5(3a - 6) = 15a - 30$

d $6(3a - 9) = 18a - 54$

e $2(9 - a) = 18 - 2a$

f $7(2a - 3b + 1)$
$= 14a - 21b + 7$

5 a $-7(2z + 1) = -14z - 7$

b $-2(a + 4b) = -2a - 8b$

c $-4(3c - 4d) = -12c + 16d$

d $-(3x - y) = -3x + y$

e $-(3x - y + z)$
$= -3x + y - z$

f $-(-a + b) = a - b$

6 a $x(x - 3) = x^2 - 3x$

b $3a(4a - 5) = 12a^2 - 15a$

c $-6y(2y + 5) = -12y^2 - 30y$

d $g(3 - g) = 3g - g^2$

e $y(-3 - 4x) = -3y - 4xy$

f $-3w(w - 2) = -3w^2 + 6w$

7 a $6(2a + 5) + 3(3a - 1)$
$= 12a + 30 + 9a - 3$
$= 21a + 27$

b $5(y - 3) + 7(2y + 1)$
$= 5y - 15 + 14y + 7$
$= 19y - 8$

c $4(2y + 5) - 2(5y + 1)$
$= 8y + 20 - 10y - 2$
$= -2y + 18$

d $2(3a - 1) - (5 - a)$
$= 6a - 2 - 5 + a$
$= 7a - 7$

8 a $2 + 3(2x - 3) = 2 + 6x - 9$
$= 6x - 7$

b $9 - 2(3a + 4) = 9 - 6a - 8$
$= 1 - 6a$

c $1 - (a - 7) = 1 - a + 7$
$= 8 - a$

d $y - (4 - y) = y - 4 + y$
$= 2y - 4$

9 a $3x - 6 = 3(x - 2)$

b $10y - 12 = 2(5y - 6)$

c $60x - 40xy = 20x(3 - 2y)$

d $12ab + 9a = 3a(4b + 3)$

e $\pi r^2 - 2\pi r = \text{pr}(r - 2)$

f $36p - 30pq = 6p(6 - 5q)$

10 a $x(x + y) - 7(x + y)$
$= (x + y)(x - 7)$

b $a(a - b) - b(a - b)$
$= (a - b)(a - b)$
$= (a - b)^2$

c $c(c - 4) - (c - 4)$
$= (c - 4)(c - 1)$

ALGEBRA
INTERMEDIATE TEST PAGE 47

1 $5m - 12 - 3m + 2 = 2m - 10$
$\therefore$ [A] (1 mark)

2 $ab^2 = 2 \times (-3)^2$
$= 2 \times 9$
$= 18$
$\therefore$ [C] (1 mark)

3 $(3x - 1)5 = 5(3x - 1)$
$= 15x - 5$
$\therefore$ [C] (1 mark)

4 $-4(5c - 4) = -20c + 16$
$\therefore$ [B] (1 mark)

5 $4a^2 - 12a = 4a(a - 3)$
$\therefore$ [C] (1 mark)

6 $ax - ay + bx - by$
$= a(x - y) + b(x - y)$
$= (x - y)(a + b)$
$\therefore$ [B] (1 mark)

7 a $4y - 2 \times 7y = 4y - 14y$
$= -10y$ ✓

b $3a - 2 + a^2 - 3$
$= a^2 + 3a - 5$ ✓

c $20r \div -5r = -4$ ✓
(3 marks)

8 a $2(5x - 2y + z)$
$= 10x - 4y + 2z$ ✓

b $-3(4 - 2xy)$
$= -12 + 6xy$ ✓

c $xy(2x - 3y)$
$= 2x^2y - 3xy^2$ ✓

d $-(4 - a + 2b)$
$= -4 + a - 2b$ ✓

e $-y(2y - 1)$
$= -2y^2 + y$ ✓

f $-(a - b - 2c)$
$= -a + b + 2c$ ✓ (6 marks)

9 a $2(3a + 5) + 3(a - 1)$
$= 6a + 10 + 3a - 3$ ✓
$= 9a + 7$ ✓

b $2 + 3(a - 1)$
$= 2 + 3a - 3$ ✓
$= 3a - 1$ ✓

c $3k + 2(k - 3)$
$= 3k + 2k - 6$ ✓
$= 5k - 6$ ✓

d $8 - 3(2g - 5)$
$= 8 - 6g + 15$ ✓
$= 23 - 6g$ ✓

e $2(a - b) - (b - a)$
$= 2a - 2b - b + a$ ✓
$= 3a - 3b$ ✓

f $4a - 3a(1 - 2a)$
$= 4a - 3a + 6a^2$ ✓
$= a + 6a^2$ ✓ (12 marks)

10 a $18xy - 6x = 6x(3y - 1)$ ✓

b $m^4 - 3m^3 = m^3(m - 3)$ ✓

c $12a^2b + 8ab^2$
$= 4ab(3a + 2b)$ ✓ (3 marks)

(Total 30 marks)

ALGEBRA
ADVANCED TEST PAGE 48

1 a $3(2 - 7y) + 2(y - 8)$
$= 6 - 21y + 2y - 16$ ✓
$= -19y - 10$ ✓

b $6(5a - 2) - 3(a + 1)$
$= 30a - 12 - 3a - 3$ ✓
$= 27a - 15$ ✓

c $-(a - 2b + 3c) - a + b$
$= -a + 2b - 3c - a + b$ ✓
$= -2a + 3b - 3c$ ✓

d $5(a - b) - 5(b - a)$
$= 5a - 5b - 5b + 5a$ ✓
$= 10a - 10b$ ✓

e $a(a - 1) - 2a(2 - 5a)$
$= a^2 - a - 4a + 10a^2$ ✓
$= 11a^2 - 5a$ ✓

f $a^2(a - 1) + 2a(a^2 - 1)$
$= a^3 - a^2 + 2a^3 - 2a$ ✓
$= 3a^3 - a^2 - 2a$ ✓

g $6x(3x - 3) - (2x^2 - 5x - 1)$
$= 18x^2 - 18x - 2x^2 + 5x + 1$ ✓
$= 16x^2 - 13x + 1$ ✓
(14 marks)

2 a $-3(3x - 6) = -9x + 18$ ✓

b $-5(2x - 7) = -10x + 35$ ✓

c $-2(-7t - 3) = 14t + 6$ ✓

d $3a(2a - 7) = 6a^2 - 21a$ ✓
(4 marks)

3 a $3a - 6 + 2 - 8a$
$= -5a - 4$ ✓

b $2x^2 + 3x - 1 + 4x - 3x^2 - 1$
$= -x^2 + 7x - 2$ ✓

c $1 - 3x - x^2 + 5 + 2x + 2x^2$
$= x^2 - x + 6$ ✓ (3 marks)

4 a $7x - 1 - (5x - 2)$ ✓
$= 7x - 1 - 5x + 2$
$= 2x + 1$ ✓

b $2a + 8 - (2 - 6a)$ ✓
$= 2a + 8 - 2 + 6a$
$= 8a + 6$ ✓

c $-4a - 9 - (-2a + 3)$ ✓
$= -4a - 9 + 2a - 3$
$= -2a - 12$ ✓

d $2x^2 - x + 5 - (x^2 + 6x + 9)$ ✓
$= 2x^2 - x + 5 - x^2 - 6x - 9$
$= x^2 - 7x - 4$ ✓

e $4 - 2m - m^2 - (9 + 4m - 5m^2)$ ✓
$= 4 - 2m - m^2 - 9 - 4m + 5m^2$
$= -5 - 6m + 4m^2$ ✓
(10 marks)

5 a $4(3a - 2) = 12a - 8$
$\therefore$ perimeter is $(12a - 8)$ cm ✓

b $3(15 - 2x) = 45 - 6x$
$\therefore$ perimeter is $(45 - 6x)$ cm ✓

c $2(3b + 2) + 2(2b - 5)$
$= 6b + 4 + 4b - 10$
$= 10b - 6$
$\therefore$ perimeter is $(10b - 6)$ cm ✓

WORKED SOLUTIONS

CHECK YOUR SOLUTIONS

d $6(4x - 2) = 24x - 12$

$\therefore$ perimeter is $(24x - 12)$ cm ✓ (4 marks)

6 **a** $\frac{1}{2} \times 12 \times (3g - 2) = 6(3g - 2)$
$= 18g - 12$

$\therefore$ area is $(18g - 12)$ cm^2 ✓

b $7(5y - 2) = 35y - 14$

$\therefore$ area is $(35y - 14)$ cm^2 ✓

c $10(2 - 3w) = 20 - 30w$

$\therefore$ area is $(20 - 30w)$ cm^2 ✓

d $4x(2x - 1) = 8x^2 - 4x$

$\therefore$ area is $(8x^2 - 4x)$ cm^2 ✓ (4 marks)

7 **a** $A = (2x - 5)^2$ cm^2 ✓

b $A = (3x - 1)(x + 2)$ cm^2 ✓

c $A = \frac{1}{2}(3p - 1)(2p + 1)$ cm^2 ✓ (3 marks)

8 $3x(2x - 1) - (4 - 2x) = 6x^2 - 3x - 4 + 2x$ ✓
$= 6x^2 - x - 4$ ✓ (2 marks)

9 **a** $2 - 3(p - 3) = 2 - 3p + 9$ ✓
$= 11 - 3p$ ✓

b $5a + 4(a - 1) = 5a + 4a - 4$ ✓
$= 9a - 4$ ✓

c $2y - (8 - 3y) = 2y - 8 + 3y$ ✓
$= 5y - 8$ ✓

d $2a^2 - 3a(a + 2) = 2a^2 - 3a^2 - 6a$ ✓
$= -a^2 - 6a$ ✓

e $3y^2 - (4y^2 + y - 2) = 3y^2 - 4y^2 - y + 2$ ✓
$= -y^2 - y + 2$ ✓ (10 marks)

10 **a** $5ab - 30b = 5b(a - 6)$ ✓

b $12xy - 18x = 6x(2y - 3)$ ✓

c $x^2 + 5xy = x(x + 5y)$ ✓

d $-2a - 8a^2 = -2a(1 + 4a)$ ✓

e $-5ab + 30b = -5b(a - 6)$ ✓

f $-x^3 - x^2 - x = -x(x^2 + x + 1)$ ✓ (6 marks)

11 **a** $a(a - b) + 3(a - b) = (a - b)(a + 3)$ ✓

b $2y(x + y) - x(x + y) = (x + y)(2y - x)$ ✓

c $5w(a - b) - 2(b - a) = 5w(a - b) + 2(a - b)$
$= (a - b)(5w + 2)$ ✓

(3 marks)

12 **a** $a^2 + 3a + ab + 3b = a(a + 3) + b(a + 3)$ ✓
$= (a + 3)(a + b)$ ✓

b $pq - 5q - 2p + 10 = q(p - 5) - 2(p - 5)$ ✓
$= (p - 5)(q - 2)$ ✓

c $2x + 8y - 3xz - 12yz$
$= 2(x + 4y) - 3z(x + 4y)$ ✓
$= (x + 4y)(2 - 3z)$ ✓

d $3a + 2b + ab + 6 = 3a + ab + 2b + 6$
$= a(3 + b) + 2(b + 3)$ ✓
$= (b + 3)(a + 2)$ ✓ (8 marks)

13 $6a^2 + 21a = 3a(2a + 7)$

$\therefore$ the other expression is $(2a + 7)$ ✓ (1 mark)

14 $6ab + 10a = 2a(3b + 5)$

$\therefore$ the length is $(3b + 5)$ cm ✓ (1 mark)

15 $6x^2 - 4x = 2x(3x - 2)$

$\therefore$ the perpendicular height is $2x$ cm ✓ (1 mark)

16 **a** $\frac{4x^2 - 12x}{2x - 6} = \frac{4x(x - 3)}{2(x - 3)}$ ✓
$= 2x$ ✓

b $\frac{xy - x^2 - x + y}{2y - 2x} = \frac{x(y - x) - 1(x - y)}{2(y - x)}$ ✓
$= \frac{x(y - x) + 1(y - x)}{2(y - x)}$
$= \frac{(y - x)(x + 1)}{2(y - x)}$ ✓
$= \frac{x + 1}{2}$ ✓

c $\frac{4x}{4x - 8} \times \frac{3x^2 - 6x}{x^2 - x}$
$= \frac{4x}{4(x - 2)} \times \frac{3x(x - 2)}{x(x - 1)}$ ✓
$= \frac{3x}{x - 1}$ ✓

d $\frac{3a + 6b}{x - 4y} \times \frac{2x - 8y}{2a + 4b}$
$= \frac{3(a + 2b)}{x - 4y} \times \frac{2(x - 4y)}{2(a + 2b)}$ ✓
$= 3$ ✓

(9 marks)

(Total 83 marks)

BASIC EQUATIONS
SKILLS CHECK PAGE 50

1 **a** $a - 7 = 3$
$a = 3 + 7$
$\therefore a = 10$

b $4 + a = 9$
$a = 9 - 4$
$\therefore a = 5$

c $12 = p - 6$
$p = 12 + 6$
$\therefore p = 18$

2 **a** $4y = 16$
$\frac{4y}{4} = \frac{16}{4}$
$\therefore y = 4$

b $-3y = 9$

$\frac{-3y}{-3} = \frac{9}{-3}$

$\therefore y = -3$

c $8p = -12$

$\frac{8p}{8} = \frac{-12}{8}$

$\therefore p = -1.5$

3 **a** $\frac{a}{2} = 7$

$2 \times \frac{a}{2} = 2 \times 7$

$\therefore a = 14$

b $\frac{x}{-5} = 3$

$-5 \times \frac{x}{-5} = -5 \times 3$

$\therefore x = -15$

c $\frac{y}{3} = -4$

$3 \times \frac{y}{3} = 3 \times -4$

$\therefore y = -12$

4 **a** $\frac{3g}{4} = 6$

$4 \times \frac{3g}{4} = 4 \times 6$

$\frac{3g}{3} = \frac{24}{3}$

$\therefore g = 8$

b $\frac{-a}{3} = 4$

$3 \times \frac{-a}{3} = 3 \times 4$

$\frac{-a}{-1} = \frac{12}{-1}$

$\therefore a = -12$

c $\frac{2p}{5} = 12$

$5 \times \frac{2p}{5} = 5 \times 12$

$\frac{2p}{2} = \frac{60}{2}$

$\therefore p = 30$

5 **a** $3a - 4 = 8$

$3a = 8 + 4$

$\frac{3a}{3} = \frac{12}{3}$

$\therefore a = 4$

b $3 = 4y - 2$

$4y - 2 = 3$

$4y = 3 + 2$

$\frac{4y}{4} = \frac{5}{4}$ $\therefore y = 1.25$

c $2a = a - 1$

$2a - a = -1$

$\therefore a = -1$

6 **a** $4y - 2 = y + 4$

$4y - y = 4 + 2$

$\frac{3y}{3} = \frac{6}{3}$ $\therefore y = 2$

b $3(a - 1) = 9$

$3a - 3 = 9$

$3a = 9 + 3$

$\frac{3a}{3} = \frac{12}{3}$ $\therefore a = 4$

c $2(3t + 5) = 2t$

$6t + 10 = 2t$

$6t - 2t = -10$

$\frac{4t}{4} = \frac{-10}{4}$

$\therefore t = -2.5$

7 **a** $5(2a - 1) = 3(3a + 4)$

$10a - 5 = 9a + 12$

$10a - 9a = 12 + 5$

$\therefore a = 17$

b $6y - 2(y + 1) = 0$

$6y - 2y - 2 = 0$

$4y - 2 = 0$

$\frac{4y}{4} = \frac{2}{4}$

$\therefore y = 0.5$

c $5 - (a + 1) = a + 3$

$5 - a - 1 = a + 3$

$4 - a = a + 3$

$-a - a = 3 - 4$

$\frac{-2a}{-2} = \frac{-1}{-2}$

$\therefore a = 0.5$

8 **a** $4(b-2) - 3(b+1) = -7$

$4b - 8 - 3b - 3 = -7$

$b - 11 = -7$

$b = -7 + 11$

$b = 4$

b $3(r - 2) - 4(3 - r) = 4(2r + 5)$

$3r - 6 - 12 + 4r = 8r + 20$

$7r - 18 = 8r + 20$

$-r = 20 + 18$

$-r = 38$

$r = -38$

9 **a** $\frac{3y - 4}{2} = 7$

$2 \times \frac{3y - 4}{2} = 7 \times 2$

$3y - 4 = 14$

$3y = 14 + 4$

$\frac{3y}{3} = \frac{18}{3}$

$\therefore y = 6$

b $\frac{5 - 2y}{3} = 8$

$3 \times \frac{5 - 2y}{3} = 8 \times 3$

$5 - 2y = 24$

$-2y = 24 - 5$

$\frac{-2y}{-2} = \frac{19}{-2}$

$\therefore y = -9.5$

c $\frac{2a + 5}{2} = -4$

$2 \times \frac{2a + 5}{2} = -4 \times 2$

$2a + 5 = -8$

$2a = -8 - 5$

$\frac{2a}{2} = \frac{-13}{2}$

$\therefore a = -6.5$

10 $\frac{5(2a - 1) - (a + 3)}{2} = 5$

$2 \times \frac{5(2a - 1) - (a + 3)}{2} = 2 \times 5$

$10a - 5 - a - 3 = 10$

$9a - 8 = 10$

$9a = 10 + 8$

$9a = 18$

$\frac{9a}{9} = \frac{18}{9}$

$a = 2$

BASIC EQUATIONS
INTERMEDIATE TEST PAGE 51

1 Try each of the alternatives.
i.e. substitute $a = 6$ in equation

$3(6) - 4 = 6 + 8$

$14 = 14$

[or you could solve the equation] $\therefore$ **[C]** (1 mark)

WORKED SOLUTIONS

CHECK YOUR SOLUTIONS

2 Line 4 should be $x = -1$ $\therefore$ **[D]** (1 mark)

3 Try each of the alternatives.

i.e. substitute $b = -1$ in $3b + 1 = b - 1$

$$\therefore 3(-1) + 1 = -1 - 1$$
$$-2 = -2$$

[or you could solve the equation] $\therefore$ **[A]** (1 mark)

4 Try each of the alternatives.

i.e. substitute $x = 2$ in $3x = 2x + 2$

$$3(2) = 2(2) + 2$$
$$6 = 6$$

[or you could solve the equation] $\therefore$ **[D]** (1 mark)

5 Try each of the alternatives.

i.e. substitute $a = 1$ in $2 + a = 1$

$$2 + 1 \neq 1$$

This means $a = 1$ is not solution.

[or you could solve the equations] $\therefore$ **[B]** (1 mark)

6 $3(x - 1) - 2(x + 1) = 2$

$3x - 3 - 2x - 2 = 2$

The error is in Line 1 $\therefore$ **[A]** (1 mark)

7 **a**
$$3p - 7 = 2p + 11$$
$$3p - 2p = 11 + 7 \checkmark$$
$$p = 18 \checkmark$$

b
$$5(a - 2) = 3a + 4$$
$$5a - 10 = 3a + 4$$
$$5a - 3a = 4 + 10 \checkmark$$
$$\frac{2a}{2} = \frac{14}{2}$$
$$a = 7 \checkmark$$

c
$$\frac{2x - 7}{3} = 5$$
$$3 \times \frac{2x - 7}{3} = 5 \times 3$$
$$2x - 7 = 15 \checkmark$$
$$2x = 15 + 7$$
$$\frac{2x}{2} = \frac{22}{2}$$
$$x = 11 \checkmark$$

d
$$\frac{x}{2} - \frac{x}{3} = 4$$
$$\frac{x}{2} \times 6 - \frac{x}{3} \times 6 = 4 \times 6 \checkmark$$
$$3x - 2x = 24$$
$$x = 24 \checkmark$$

(8 marks)

8 **a**
$$5 - 2(x + 1) = 3$$
$$5 - 2x - 2 = 3 \checkmark$$
$$3 - 2x = 3 \checkmark$$
$$-2x = 0$$
$$x = 0 \checkmark$$

b
$$\frac{2(3a - 1) - (2a + 1)}{4} = 1$$
$$\frac{6a - 2 - 2a - 1}{4} = 1$$
$$\frac{4a - 3}{4} = 1 \checkmark$$
$$4 \times \frac{4a - 3}{4} = 4 \times 1 \checkmark$$
$$4a - 3 = 4$$
$$4a = 4 + 3$$
$$4a = 7$$
$$\frac{4a}{4} = \frac{7}{4}$$
$$a = 1.75 \checkmark$$

c
$$\frac{3p - 2}{5} - 2 = 6$$
$$\frac{3p - 2}{5} = 6 + 2$$
$$\frac{3p - 2}{5} = 8 \checkmark$$
$$5 \times \frac{3p - 2}{5} = 8 \times 5$$
$$3p - 2 = 40 \checkmark$$
$$3p = 40 + 2$$
$$3p = 42$$
$$\frac{3p}{3} = \frac{42}{3}$$
$$p = 14 \checkmark$$

d
$$\frac{4a - 1}{3} - \frac{2a - 1}{2} = 4$$
$$\frac{6(4a - 1)}{3} - \frac{6(2a - 1)}{2} = 6 \times 4 \checkmark$$
$$2(4a - 1) - 3(2a - 1) = 24$$
$$8a - 2 - 6a + 3 = 24 \checkmark$$
$$2a + 1 = 24$$
$$2a = 24 - 1$$
$$2a = 23$$
$$\frac{2a}{2} = \frac{23}{2}$$
$$a = 11.5 \checkmark$$

(12 marks)

(Total 26 marks)

BASIC EQUATIONS ADVANCED TEST PAGE 52

1 **a**
$$3x - 2 = 2x + 5$$
$$3x - 2x = 5 + 2 \checkmark$$
$$x = 7 \checkmark$$

b
$$5m + 3 = 4m - 6$$
$$5m - 4m = -6 - 3 \checkmark$$
$$m = -9 \checkmark$$

c $5 + 2a = 8 - a$
$2a + a = 8 - 5$ ✓
$3a = 3$
$a = 1$ ✓

d $14 + 5x = 7 - 2x$
$5x + 2x = 7 - 14$ ✓
$7x = -7$
$x = -1$ ✓

e $11 - 2c = c + 5$
$-2c - c = 5 - 11$ ✓
$-3c = -6$
$c = 2$ ✓

f $7 - 3k = k + 3$
$-3k - k = 3 - 7$ ✓
$-4k = -4$
$k = 1$ ✓

g $3b = 8 - b$
$3b + b = 8$ ✓
$4b = 8$
$b = 2$ ✓

h $6q = 16 - 2q$
$6q + 2q = 16$ ✓
$8q = 16$
$q = 2$ ✓

i $12 = 4x - 8$
$4x - 8 = 12$
$4x = 12 + 8$ ✓
$4x = 20$
$x = 5$ ✓

j $-10 = 3p + 2$
$3p + 2 = -10$
$3p = -10 - 2$ ✓
$3p = -12$
$p = -4$ ✓ (20 marks)

2 a $3(2x - 1) = 5x - 6$
$6x - 3 = 5x - 6$ ✓
$6x - 5x = -6 + 3$
$x = -3$ ✓

b $5(2a - 2) = 9a - 6$
$10a - 10 = 9a - 6$ ✓
$10a - 9a = -6 + 10$
$a = 4$ ✓

c $2(4y + 2) = 2(3y - 1)$
$8y + 4 = 6y - 2$ ✓
$8y - 6y = -2 - 4$
$2y = -6$
$y = -3$ ✓

d $3(5x - 1) = 4(x + 7)$
$15x - 3 = 4x + 28$ ✓
$15x - 4x = 28 + 3$
$11x = 31$
$x = 2\frac{9}{11}$ ✓

e $3 - 2(x + 1) = 2(1 - 3x)$
$3 - 2x - 2 = 2 - 6x$ ✓
$1 - 2x = 2 - 6x$
$-2x + 6x = 2 - 1$
$4x = 1$
$x = \frac{1}{4}$ ✓

f $6 - 5(2n + 3) = 4(2 - 5n)$
$6 - 10n - 15 = 8 - 20n$ ✓
$-9 - 10n = 8 - 20n$
$-10n + 20n = 8 + 9$
$10n = 17$
$n = 1\frac{7}{10}$ ✓

g $10 - (w - 4) = 3w - (2 - w)$
$10 - w + 4 = 3w - 2 + w$ ✓
$14 - w = 4w - 2$
$4w - 2 = 14 - w$
$4w + w = 14 + 2$
$5w = 16$
$w = 3\frac{1}{5}$ ✓

h $2 - (3t + 1) = 4t - (6 - 4t)$
$2 - 3t - 1 = 4t - 6 + 4t$ ✓
$1 - 3t = 8t - 6$
$8t - 6 = 1 - 3t$
$8t + 3t = 1 + 6$
$11t = 7$
$t = \frac{7}{11}$ ✓

i $4a - 3(a + 5) = 2 - (a - 1)$
$4a - 3a - 15 = 2 - a + 1$ ✓
$a - 15 = 3 - a$
$a + a = 3 + 15$
$2a = 18$
$a = 9$ ✓

j $8p - 2(3p + 1) = 7p - (2 - 5p)$
$8p - 6p - 2 = 7p - 2 + 5p$ ✓
$2p - 2 = 12p - 2$
$12p - 2 = 2p - 2$
$12p - 2p = -2 + 2$
$10p = 0$
$p = 0$ ✓ (20 marks)

3 a $\frac{3y - 4}{2} = y$
$2 \times \frac{3y - 4}{2} = 2 \times y$
$3y - 4 = 2y$ ✓

$3y - 2y = 4$
$y = 4$ ✓

b $\frac{5a - 2}{3} = 2a$
$3 \times \frac{5a - 2}{3} = 3 \times 2a$
$5a - 2 = 6a$ ✓
$6a = 5a - 2$
$6a - 5a = -2$
$a = -2$ ✓

c $\frac{5x - 2}{3} = x - 1$
$3 \times \frac{5x - 2}{3} = 3(x - 1)$
$5x - 2 = 3x - 3$ ✓
$5x - 3x = -3 + 2$
$2x = -1$
$x = -\frac{1}{2}$ ✓

d $\frac{4c + 1}{5} = 2c - 3$
$5 \times \frac{4c + 1}{5} = 5(2c - 3)$
$4c + 1 = 10c - 15$ ✓
$10c - 15 = 4c + 1$
$10c - 4c = 1 + 15$
$6c = 16$
$c = 2\frac{2}{3}$ ✓

e $\frac{3 - a}{2} = 4a + 3$
$2 \times \frac{3 - a}{2} = 2(4a + 3)$
$3 - a = 8a + 6$ ✓
$8a + 6 = 3 - a$
$8a + a = 3 - 6$
$9a = -3$
$a = -\frac{1}{3}$ ✓

f $\frac{7 - 3y}{4} = 2 - 4y$
$4 \times \frac{7 - 3y}{4} = 4(2 - 4y)$
$7 - 3y = 8 - 16y$ ✓
$-3y + 16y = 8 - 7$
$13y = 1$
$y = \frac{1}{13}$ ✓

g $\frac{3a + 7}{-2} = 6a - 3$
$-2 \times \frac{3a + 7}{-2} = -2(6a - 3)$
$3a + 7 = -12a + 6$ ✓
$3a + 12a = 6 - 7$
$15a = -1$
$a = -\frac{1}{15}$ ✓ (14 marks)

4 **a** $\frac{3y - 2}{y} = 2$
$y \times \frac{3y - 2}{y} = y \times 2$
$3y - 2 = 2y$ ✓
$3y - 2y = 2$
$y = 2$ ✓

b $\frac{3 - 5m}{m} = 4$
$m \times \frac{3 - 5m}{m} = m \times 4$
$3 - 5m = 4m$ ✓
$4m = 3 - 5m$
$4m + 5m = 3$
$9m = 3$
$m = \frac{1}{3}$ ✓

c $\frac{5 - 2p}{3p} = 2$
$3p \times \frac{5 - 2p}{3p} = 3p \times 2$
$5 - 2p = 6p$ ✓
$6p = 5 - 2p$
$6p + 2p = 5$
$8p = 5$
$p = \frac{5}{8}$ ✓

d $\frac{3a + 2}{-5a} = -3$
$-5a \times \frac{3a + 2}{-5a} = -5a \times -3$
$3a + 2 = 15a$ ✓
$15a = 3a + 2$
$15a - 3a = 2$
$12a = 2$
$a = \frac{1}{6}$ ✓ (8 marks)

5 **a** $\frac{m + 4}{2} - 3m = 5$
$2 \times \frac{m + 4}{2} - 2 \times 3m = 2 \times 5$
$m + 4 - 6m = 10$ ✓

$$-5m + 4 = 10$$
$$-5m = 10 - 4$$
$$-5m = 6$$
$$m = -1\frac{1}{5} \checkmark$$

b
$$2w - \frac{3 - w}{3} = 4$$
$$3 \times 2w - 3 \times \frac{3 - w}{3} = 3 \times 4$$
$$6w - (3 - w) = 12 \checkmark$$
$$6w - 3 + w = 12$$
$$7w - 3 = 12$$
$$7w = 12 + 3$$
$$7w = 15$$
$$w = 2\frac{1}{7} \checkmark$$

c
$$3p - \frac{p + 2}{5} = 2$$
$$5 \times 3p - 5 \times \frac{p + 2}{5} = 5 \times 2$$
$$15p - (p + 2) = 10 \checkmark$$
$$15p - p - 2 = 10$$
$$14p - 2 = 10$$
$$14p = 10 + 2$$
$$14p = 12$$
$$p = \frac{6}{7} \checkmark$$

(6 marks)

6 a
$$\frac{2a + 1}{4} - \frac{3a - 2}{3} = 1$$
$$12 \times \frac{2a + 1}{4} - 12 \times \frac{3a - 2}{3} = 12 \times 1$$
$$3(2a + 1) - 4(3a - 2) = 12 \checkmark$$
$$6a + 3 - 12a + 8 = 12 \checkmark$$
$$-6a + 11 = 12$$
$$-6a = 12 - 11$$
$$-6a = 1$$
$$a = -\frac{1}{6} \checkmark$$

b
$$\frac{3x + 2}{2} - \frac{2 - x}{5} = 2$$
$$10 \times \frac{3x + 2}{2} - 10 \times \frac{2 - x}{5} = 10 \times 2$$
$$5(3x + 2) - 2(2 - x) = 20 \checkmark$$
$$15x + 10 - 4 + 2x = 20 \checkmark$$
$$17x + 6 = 20$$
$$17x = 20 - 6$$
$$17x = 14$$
$$x = \frac{14}{17} \checkmark$$

(6 marks)

7 a
$$x^2 + 3 = 12$$
$$x^2 = 12 - 3 \checkmark$$
$$x^2 = 9$$
$$x = \pm 3 \checkmark$$

b
$$y^2 - 11 = 25$$
$$y^2 = 25 + 11 \checkmark$$
$$y^2 = 36$$
$$y = \pm 6 \checkmark$$

c
$$4a^2 = 100$$
$$a^2 = 25 \checkmark$$
$$a = \pm 5 \checkmark$$

d
$$\frac{4}{x} = x$$
$$x \times \frac{4}{x} = x \times x$$
$$4 = x^2 \checkmark$$
$$x^2 = 4$$
$$x = \pm 2 \checkmark$$

(8 marks)

8 a
LHS $= 3m + 2$
$= 3(-4) + 2$
$= -10$ ✓

RHS $= m - 6$
$= -4 - 6$
$= -10$

$\therefore m = -4$ is solution ✓

b
LHS $= 2(3y - 1)$
$= 2(3 \times 6 - 1)$
$= 2 \times 17$
$= 34$ ✓

RHS $= 1 + 3(y + 5)$
$= 1 + 3(6 + 5)$
$= 34$

$\therefore y = 6$ is solution ✓

c
LHS $= 2g - 3(2g + 5)$
$= 2 \times (-11) - 3(2 \times (-11) + 5)$
$= -22 + 51$
$= 29$ ✓

RHS $= 7 - 2g$
$= 7 - 2 \times (-11)$
$= 29$

$\therefore g = -11$ is solution ✓

d
LHS $= \frac{2a - 5}{3}$
$= \frac{2(-17) - 5}{3}$
$= -13$ ✓

RHS $= a + 4$
$= -17 + 4$
$= -13$

$\therefore a = -17$ is solution ✓

e
LHS $= \frac{7 - 4p}{3p}$
$= \frac{7 - 4 \times 1}{3 \times 1}$
$= 1$ ✓

RHS $= p$
$= 1$

$\therefore p = 1$ is solution ✓

f $\text{LHS} = \frac{2a - 3}{3} - \frac{a + 1}{4}$
$= \frac{2 \times 3 - 3}{3} - \frac{3 + 1}{4}$
$= 1 - 1$
$= 0$ ✓
$\text{RHS} = a - 1$
$= 3 - 1$
$= 2$
$\text{LHS} \neq \text{RHS}$
$\therefore a = 3$ is NOT a solution ✓ (12 marks)

(Total 94 marks)

FORMULAE AND USING EQUATIONS
SKILLS CHECK PAGE 54

1 **a** $y = 3 \times 2 + 5$
$\therefore y = 11$

b $y = -2 \times 3 + (-4)$
$= -6 - 4$
$\therefore y = -10$

2 **a** $A = \frac{4 + 7 + 10}{3}$
$= \frac{21}{3}$
$\therefore A = 7$

b $A = \frac{-4 + 0 + 7}{3}$
$= \frac{3}{3}$
$\therefore A = 1$

3 **a** $C = \frac{5(68 - 32)}{9}$
$= \frac{5 \times \overset{4}{\cancel{36}}}{\underset{1}{\cancel{9}}}$
$= 5 \times 4$
$\therefore C = 20$

b $100 = \frac{5(F - 32)}{9}$
$5(F - 32) = 100 \times 9$
$5(F - 32) = 900$
$F - 32 = 900 \div 5$
$F - 32 = 180$
$F = 180 + 32$
$\therefore F = 212$

4 **a** $A = \frac{(20)(5)}{2} = 50$
$\therefore A = 50$

b $16 = \frac{\overset{2}{\cancel{4}} \times h}{\underset{1}{\cancel{2}}}$
$2h = 16$
$\therefore h = 8$

5 **a** $S = \frac{15}{1 - 0.8}$
$S = \frac{15}{0.2}$
$\therefore S = 75$

b $36 = \frac{a}{1 - 0.5}$
$\frac{a}{0.5} = 36$
$a = 36 \times 0.5$
$\therefore a = 18$

6 **a** $p = b - 2$
(or $b = p + 2$)

b $p = 20 - 2$
$\therefore p = 18$

c $48 = b - 2$
$b = 48 + 2$
$\therefore b = 50$

7 **a** Let the number be x.
$2(x + 4) = 12$
$2x + 8 = 12$
$2x = 12 - 8$
$2x = 4$
$x = 2$
$\therefore$ the number is 2

b Let the numbers be x, $x + 1, x + 2$.
$x + (x + 1) + (x + 2) = 36$
$3x + 3 = 36$
$3x = 36 - 3$
$3x = 33$
$x = 11$
$\therefore$ the numbers are 11, 12, 13

c Let the numbers be $x, x + 2$.
$4x = 3(x + 2)$
$4x = 3x + 6$
$4x - 3x = 6$
$x = 6$
$\therefore$ the numbers are 6 and 8

d Let the number be x.
$\frac{x + 2x + 3}{3} = 5$
$x + 2x + 3 = 15$
$3x + 3 = 15$
$3x = 12$
$x = 4$
$\therefore$ the number is 4

8 **a**

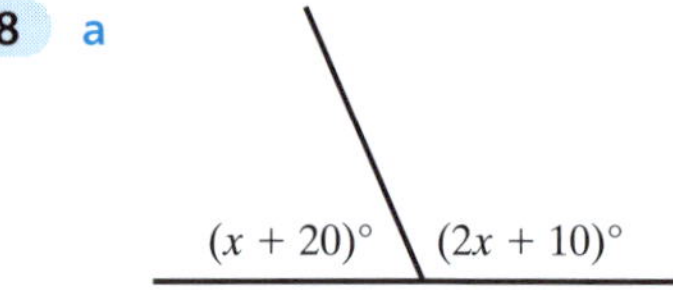

$(x + 20) + (2x + 10) = 180$
[straight $\angle = 180°$]
$3x + 30 = 180$
$3x = 150$
$\therefore x = 50$

b

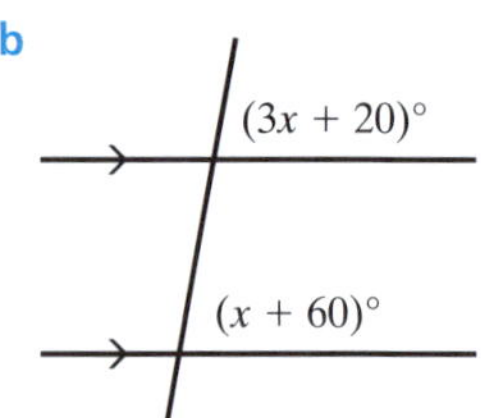

$3x + 20 = x + 60$
[corresponding $\angle$s of $\parallel$ lines]
$3x - x = 60 - 20$
$2x = 40$
$\therefore x = 20$

c

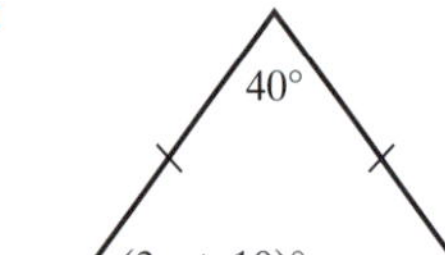

$2(3x + 10) + 40 = 180$
[base $\angle$s of isosceles $\triangle$ equal, angle sum of $\triangle$ is 180°]
$6x + 20 + 40 = 180$
$6x + 60 = 180$
$6x = 120$
$\therefore x = 20$

d

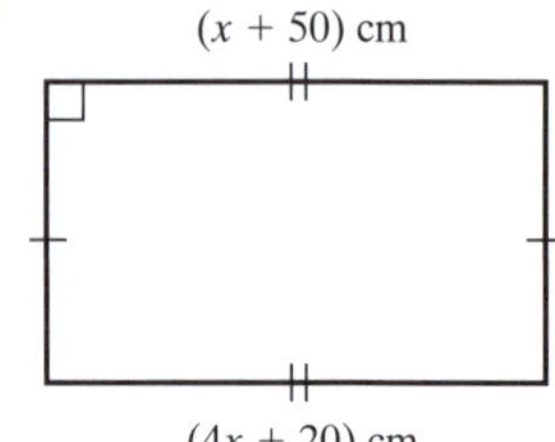

$4x + 20 = x + 50$
[opposite sides of rectangle equal]
$4x - x = 50 - 20$
$3x = 30$
$\therefore x = 10$

WORKED SOLUTIONS

CHECK YOUR SOLUTIONS

FORMULAE AND USING EQUATIONS
INTERMEDIATE TEST PAGE 55

1 $X = \frac{a + b + c}{3}$

$X = \frac{4 + 2 + 6}{3} = \frac{12}{3} = 4 \quad \therefore$ **[B]** (1 mark)

2 $V = \pi r^2 h$

$= 3.1 \times 4^2 \times 5$

$= 248 \quad \therefore$ **[A]** (1 mark)

3 $S = \frac{n}{2}(a + l)$

$120 = \frac{16}{2}(a + 10)$

$120 = 8(a + 10)$

$120 = 8a + 80$

$8a = 120 - 80$

$8a = 40$

$a = 5 \quad \therefore$ **[A]** (1 mark)

4 $T = a + (n - 1)d$

$64 = 14 + (6 - 1)d$

$64 = 14 + 5d$

$5d = 64 - 14$

$5d = 50$

$d = 10 \quad \therefore$ **[D]** (1 mark)

5 As $\angle$ sum of $\triangle = 180°$ and base $\angle$s equal, then angles are 40°, 70°, 70°.
This means $(x + 45) + 40 \neq (2x + 20)$
$\therefore$ **[C]** (1 mark)

6 **a** Let the numbers be $x, x + 2, x + 4, x + 6$.
$x + (x + 2) + (x + 4) + (x + 6) = 64$
$\therefore 4x + 12 = 64$ ✓

b $4x + 12 = 64$

$4x = 64 - 12$

$4x = 52$

$x = 13$ ✓

$\therefore$ the numbers are 13, 15, 17, 19 ✓ (3 marks)

7 Area $= \frac{1}{2} \times$ base $\times$ height

$4(10x + 4) = 136$ ✓

$40x + 16 = 136$ ✓

$40x = 136 - 16$

$40x = 120$

$\therefore x = 3$ ✓ (3 marks)

8 **a** Let the number be x.
$\therefore 2x + 3 = 4x - 7$ ✓

b $4x - 7 = 2x + 3$

$4x - 2x = 3 + 7$

$2x = 10$ ✓

$x = 5$

$\therefore$ the number is 5 ✓ (3 marks)

9 **a** Sum of all angles = 360°, so

$(4x + 10) + (3x + 50) = 270$ ✓

$7x + 60 = 270$

$7x = 270 - 60$

$7x = 210$

$\therefore x = 30$ ✓

b Sum of all angles = 180°, so

$(4x + 20) + 50 + 50 = 180$ ✓

$4x + 120 = 180$

$4x = 60$

$\therefore x = 15$ ✓

c Sum of angles = 180°, so

$(3x + 40) + (2x + 20) = 180$ ✓

$5x + 60 = 180$

$5x = 180 - 60$

$5x = 120$

$\therefore x = 24$ ✓ (6 marks)

10 **a** $3x + 20 = 2x + 50$ ✓

b $3x - 2x = 50 - 20$

$\therefore x = 30$ ✓

c Length $= 3(30) + 20$
$= 110$

$\therefore$ 110 cm ✓

Width $= 2(30) = 60$

$\therefore$ 60 cm ✓

$\therefore$ dimensions are 110 cm by 60 cm

$\therefore$ Area $= 110 \times 60$
$= 6600$

$\therefore$ Area is 6600 cm^2 ✓

Perimeter $= 2(110 + 60)$
$= 340$

$\therefore$ Perimeter is 340 cm ✓ (6 marks)

(Total 26 marks)

FORMULAE AND USING EQUATIONS
ADVANCED TEST PAGE 56

1 **a** $C = \frac{5}{9}(F - 32) = \frac{5}{9}(68 - 32)$ ✓

$= 20$ ✓

b $V - E + F = 2$

$V - 30 + 20 = 2$ ✓

$V - 10 = 2$

$V = 12$ ✓

c $c^2 = a^2 + b^2$
$c^2 = (1.05)^2 + (2.08)^2$ ✓
$= 5.4289$
$c = 2.33$ ✓ $(c > 0)$ (6 marks)

2 **a** $d = \sqrt{(x_2 - x_1)^2 + (y_2 - y_1)^2}$
$= \sqrt{(4 - 2)^2 + (-5 - 3)^2}$ ✓
$= \sqrt{4 + 64}$
$= \sqrt{68}$ ✓

b $m = \dfrac{y_2 - y_1}{x_2 - x_1}$
$= \dfrac{-5 - 3}{4 - 2}$ ✓
$= \dfrac{-8}{2}$
$= -4$ ✓ (4 marks)

3 Let the numbers be $x, x + 2, x + 4$
$x + x + 2 + x + 4 = 45$ ✓
$3x + 6 = 45$
$3x = 45 - 6$
$3x = 39$
$\therefore x = 13$
$\therefore$ the numbers are 13, 15, 17 ✓ (2 marks)

4 Let Aidan's age be x
$\therefore$ Lucas $= x - 3$, Jayden $= x + 2$
$x + x - 3 + x + 2 = 47$ ✓
$3x - 1 = 47$
$3x = 47 + 1$
$3x = 48$
$x = 16$
$\therefore$ Aiden is 16, Lucas is 13 and Jayden is 18 ✓
(2 marks)

5 **a** Let x = Stella's age
$\therefore 34 - x$ = Mia's age
Also, 4 years ago, Stella was $(x - 4)$
$\therefore 34 - x = 4(x - 4)$ ✓
$34 - x = 4x - 16$
$4x - 16 = 34 - x$
$4x + x = 34 + 16$
$5x = 50$
$x = 10$
$\therefore$ Stella is 10 and Mia is 24 ✓ (2 marks)

6 Let x = price paid
$2x + 40 = 1620$ ✓
$2x = 1620 - 40$
$2x = 1580$
$x = 790$
$\therefore$ Dylan bought the bat for \$790 ✓ (2 marks)

7 Let x = number of males
$\therefore 1772 - x$ = number of females
$3x + 8 = 1772 - x$ ✓
$3x + x = 1772 - 8$
$4x = 1746$
$x = 441$
$\therefore$ there are 441 males at the concert ✓ (2 marks)

8 Let x = lowest mark
$\therefore 118 - x$ = highest mark
$2x + 22 = 118 - x$ ✓
$2x + x = 118 - 22$
$3x = 96$
$x = 32$
As $118 - 32 = 86$, the highest mark is 86 ✓ (2 marks)

9 Let x = amount Zoe earned
$3x + 60$ = amount Claire earned ✓
$x + 3x + 60 = 2420$ ✓
$4x + 60 = 2420$
$4x = 2420 - 60$
$4x = 2360$
$x = 590$
$\therefore$ Zoe earned \$590, Claire earned \$1830 ✓ (3 marks)

10 Let x = cost of skirt
$135 - x$ = cost of shoes
$\therefore 135 - x = 2x - 18$ ✓
$2x - 18 = 135 - x$
$2x + x = 135 + 18$
$3x = 153$
$x = 51$
As $135 - 51 = 84$, then the cost of the shoes was \$84 ✓ (2 marks)

11 Let x = first person's amount
$\therefore x - 60$ = second person's amount
$x + 20$ = third person's amount
$\therefore x + x - 60 + x + 20 = 2600$ ✓
$3x - 40 = 2600$
$3x = 2600 + 40$
$3x = 2640$
$x = 880$
$\therefore$ amounts are \$880, \$820, \$900 ✓ (2 marks)

12 Let x = size of first angle
$\therefore 3x$ = size of second angle
$6x$ = size of third angle
$\therefore x + 3x + 6x = 10x$ ✓
$10x = 180$
$x = 18$
$\therefore$ angles are 18°, 54°, 108° ✓ (2 marks)

13 Let x = price of maths guide
$\therefore 84 - x$ = price of science text

$84 - x = 2x + 12$ ✓
$2x + 12 = 84 - x$
$2x + x = 84 - 12$
$3x = 72$
$x = 24$
∴ maths guide is \$24, science text is \$60 ✓ (2 marks)

14 Let x = degrees in angle
∴ $90 - x$ = degrees in complement
$180 - x$ = degrees in supplement
$180 - x = 2(90 - x) + 40$ ✓
$180 - x = 180 - 2x + 40$
$180 - x = 220 - 2x$
$-x + 2x = 220 - 180$
$x = 40$
∴ the angle is 40° ✓ (2 marks)

15 Let x = one side of triangle
∴ $3x$ = another side
∴ $3x + x + 14 = 42$ ✓
$4x + 14 = 42$
$4x = 42 - 14$
$4x = 28$
$x = 7$
∴ the shortest side is 7 cm ✓ (2 marks)

16 Let x = smaller number
∴ $40 - x$ = larger number
$6x = 4(40 - x)$ ✓
$6x = 160 - 4x$
$6x + 4x = 160$
$10x = 160$
$x = 16$
∴ the numbers are 16 and 24 ✓ (2 marks)

17 Let x = Maryanne's age
∴ $x + 5$ = Dino's age
$3x$ = Billy's age
$x - 4$ = Rick's age
∴ $x + x + 5 + 3x + x - 4 = 49$ ✓
$6x + 1 = 49$
$6x = 49 - 1$
$6x = 48$
$x = 8$
Maryanne is 8, Dino is 13, Billy is 24 and Rick is 4 ✓ (2 marks)

18 Let x = number of student tickets
∴ $600 - x$ = number of adult tickets
$8x + 12(600 - x) = 5640$ ✓
$8x + 7200 - 12x = 5640$
$7200 - 4x = 5640$
$7200 - 5640 = 4x$
$4x = 1560$
$x = 390$
∴ 390 student tickets and 210 adult tickets ✓ (2 marks)

(Total 43 marks)

COORDINATE GEOMETRY
SKILLS CHECK PAGE 58

1 a

x	0	1	2
y	**1**	**3**	**5**

b

x	0	1	2
y	**4**	**3**	**2**

c

x	0	1	2
y	**2**	**1**	**0**

2 a $y = 2x - 3$
For $x = 1, y = 2(1) - 3 \neq 3$
∴ (1, 3) not on line
∴ False

b $y = 2x - 7$
For $x = 3, y = 2(3) - 7 = -1$
∴ (3, −1) is on line
∴ True

c $y = 4x - 3$
For $x = 1, y = 4(1) - 3 = 1$
∴ The line passes through (1, 1)
∴ True

d $y = 4 - x$
For $x = 2, y = 4 - 2 \neq -1$
∴ The line does not pass through (2, −1)
∴ False

3 a

Hours (h)	0	2	4	6
Cost (c)	**50**	**130**	**210**	**290**

b $c = 50 + 40h$

c

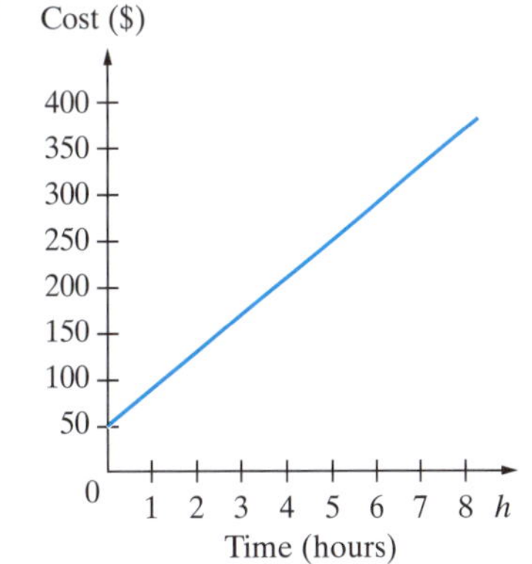

d i $c = 50 + 40(3)$
$= 170$
∴ \$170

ii $330 = 50 + 40h$
$40h = 280$
$h = 7$
∴ 7 hours

4 **a**

x	0	1	2
y	−4	−1	2

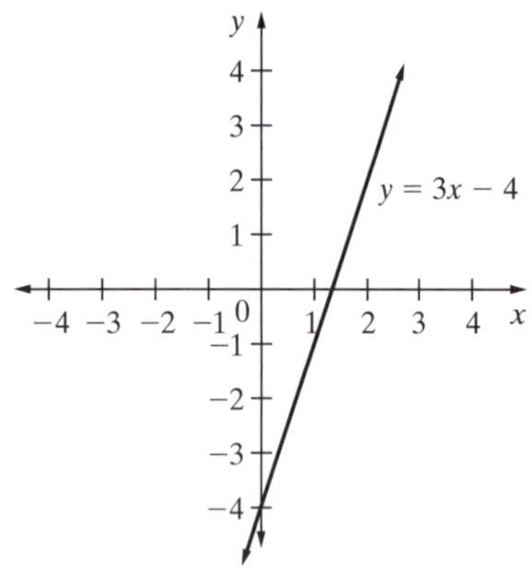

b

x	0	1	2
y	3	2	1

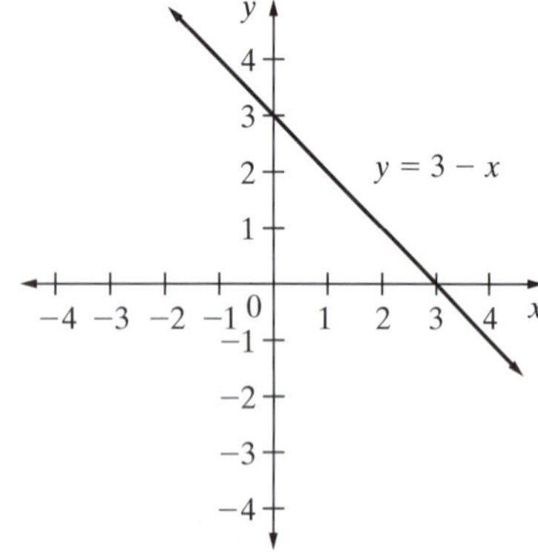

5

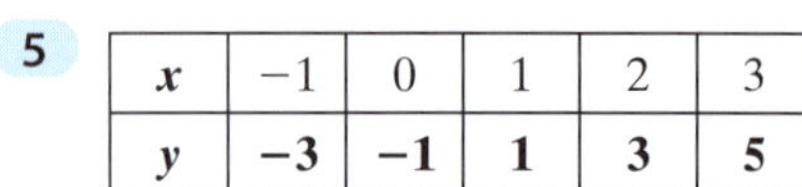

x	−1	0	1	2	3
y	**−3**	**−1**	**1**	**3**	**5**

$y = 2x - 1$

6 **a** i l ii n iii m

b (0, 3)

7

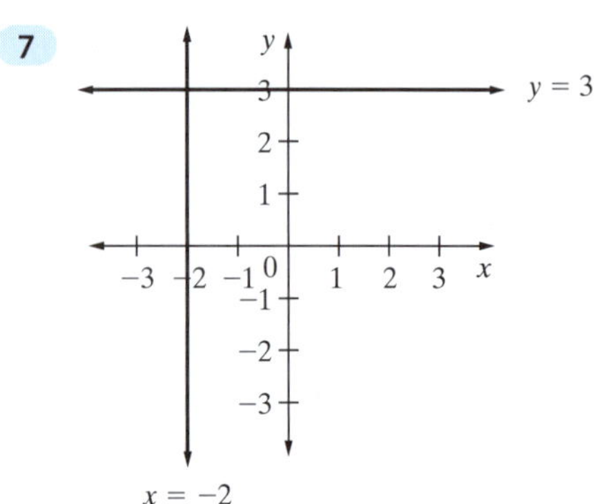

COORDINATE GEOMETRY
INTERMEDIATE TEST PAGE 59

1 Try each of the alternatives.

Substitute $(2, -4)$ in $y = 2 - 3x$

i.e. $-4 = 2 - 3(2)$

$-4 = 2 - 6$? Yes!

$\therefore$ $y = 2 - 3x$ passes through $(2, -4)$

$\therefore$ **[D]** (1 mark)

2 Try each of the alternatives.

Substitute $(-1, 3)$ in $y = x + 4$

i.e. $3 = -1 + 4$? Yes!

$\therefore$ **[B]** (1 mark)

3 Line cuts through (0, 3).

Try each of the alternatives.

Substitute $(0, 3)$ in $y = x + 3$

i.e. $3 = 0 + 3$? Yes!

$\therefore$ **[A]** (1 mark)

4 $y = 3 - 2x$ passes through $(a, 5)$.

Substitute $x = a$, $y = 5$ in equation

$5 = 3 - 2a$

$2a = 3 - 5$

$2a = -2$

$a = -1$ $\therefore$ **[A]** (1 mark)

5 The vertical line is $x = 3$ and the horizontal line is $y = -1$. The point of intersection is $(3, -1)$.

$\therefore$ **[C]** (1 mark)

6 **a** ✓

x	0	1	2
y	**−4**	**−2**	**0**

b ✓✓

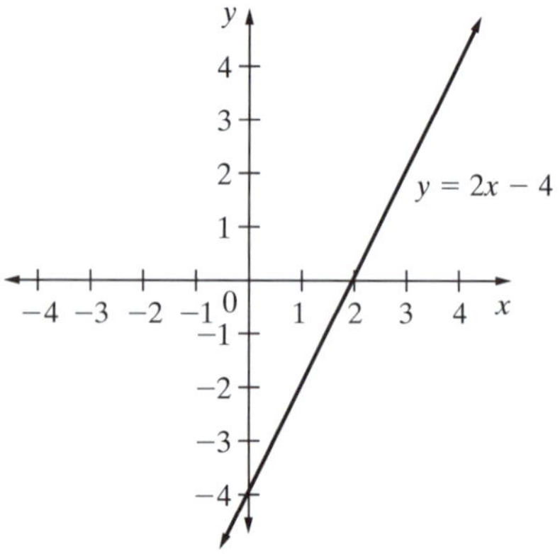

y = 2x − 4

c As $y = 2x - 4$

$2 = 2(3) - 4$

$= 6 - 4$? Yes!

$\therefore$ (3, 2) lies on line ✓

WORKED SOLUTIONS

d Substitute in $x = a, y = 0$ into line

$0 = 2a - 4$

$2a = 4$

$a = 2$ ✓ [or use the graph] (5 marks)

7 **a**

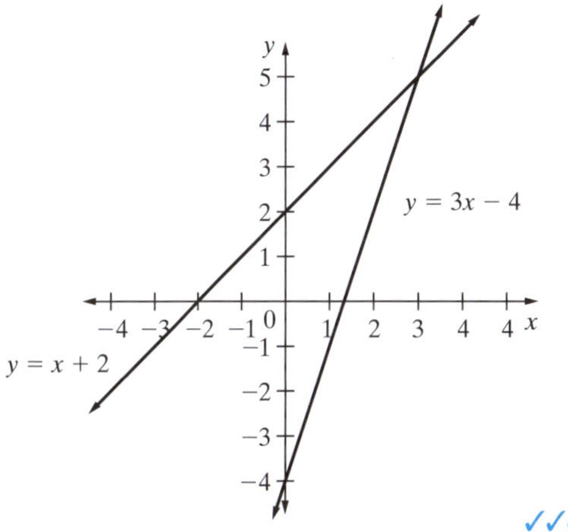

✓✓✓✓

b At point of intersection

$x + 2 = 3x - 4$

$0 = 2x - 6$

$2x = 6$

$\therefore x = 3$

Substitute $x = 3$ into one of the equations:

$y = (3) + 2$

$= 5$

$\therefore (3, 5)$

Or consult number plane, $(3, 5)$ ✓ (5 marks)

8 **a**

h	0	2	4	6
c	**40**	**80**	**120**	**160**

✓

b $c = 20h + 40$ ✓

c

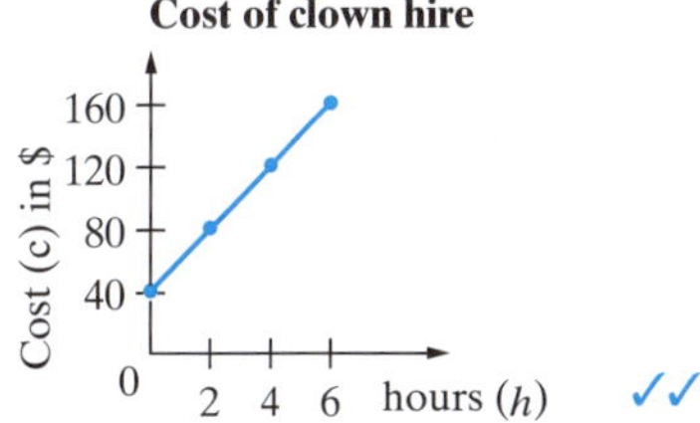

✓✓

d $140 = 20h + 40$

$20h = 140 - 40$

$20h = 100$

$h = 5$

$\therefore$ Krustie worked for 5 hours ✓ (5 marks)

(Total 20 marks)

COORDINATE GEOMETRY
ADVANCED TEST PAGE 60

1 7 units right adds 7 to the x-values;
6 units up adds 6 to the y-values:
$\therefore (2, 4), (2, 1), (5, 1)$ and $(5, 4)$ ✓✓ (2 marks)

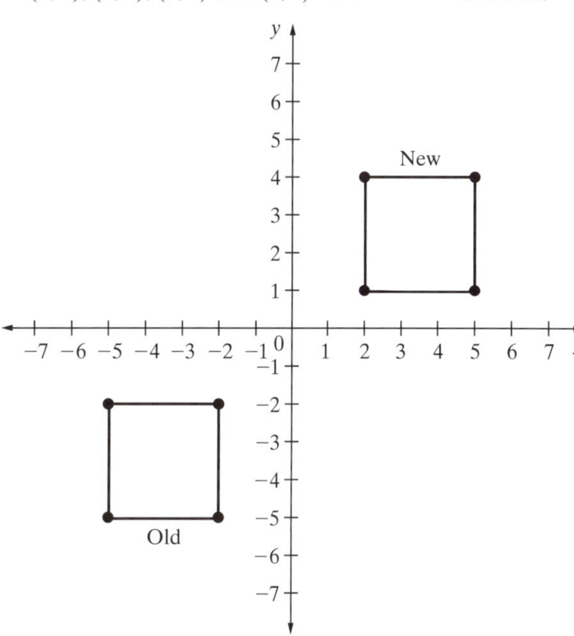

2 When reflecting over the x-axis, any y-value changes its sign.
$\therefore (4, -2), (-1, -5)$ and $(-4, -3)$ ✓✓ (2 marks)

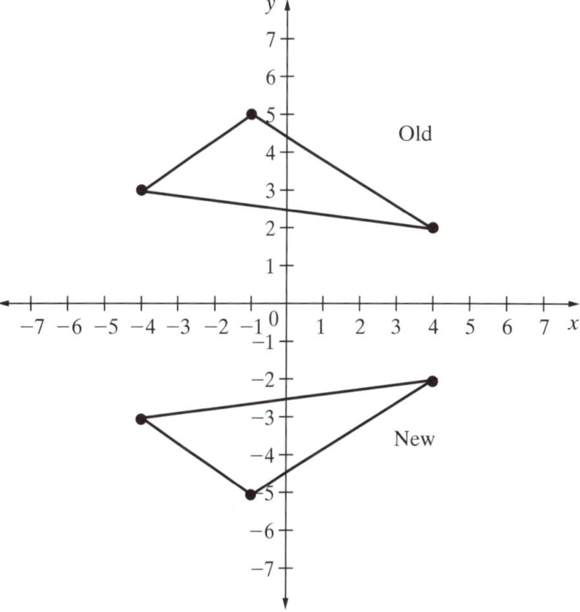

WORKED SOLUTIONS

3 a

x	0	1	2
y	**0**	**1**	**2**

✓

$\therefore y = x$ ✓

b

x	0	2	4
y	**0**	**1**	**2**

✓

$\therefore y = \frac{x}{2}$ ✓

c

x	0	1	2
y	**3**	**0**	**−3**

✓

$\therefore y = 3 - 3x$ ✓

d

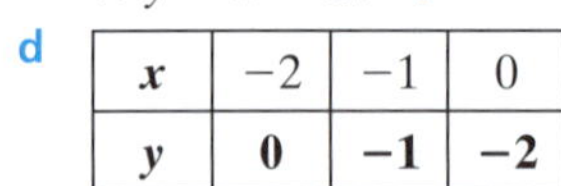

x	−2	−1	0
y	**0**	**−1**	**−2**

✓

$\therefore y = -x - 2$ ✓ (8 marks)

4 $y = 2x - 1$

x	0	1	2
y	−1	1	3

$y = 2 - x$

x	0	1	2
y	2	1	0

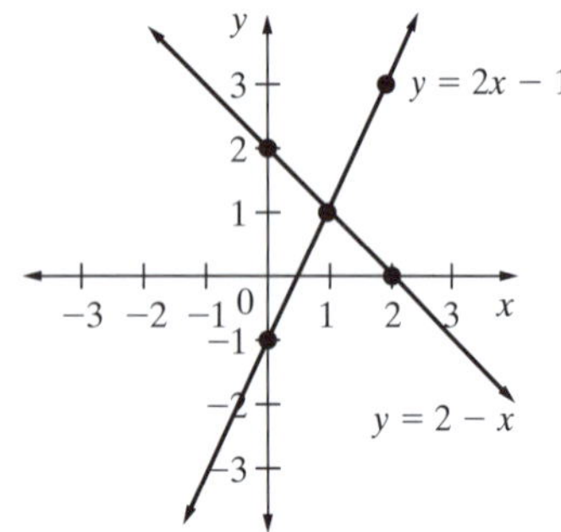

✓✓

$\therefore x = 1$ ✓ (3 marks)

5 $y = x - 5$ (1 mark)

6 a different slopes (gradients)
$\therefore$ 1 point of intersection ✓

b different slopes (gradients)
$\therefore$ 1 point of intersection ✓

c same slopes (gradients)
$\therefore$ lines are parallel
$\therefore$ no point of intersection ✓ (3 marks)

7 a

n	0	5	10	15
V	1200	1000	800	600

✓✓

b $V = 1200 - 40n$ ✓

c

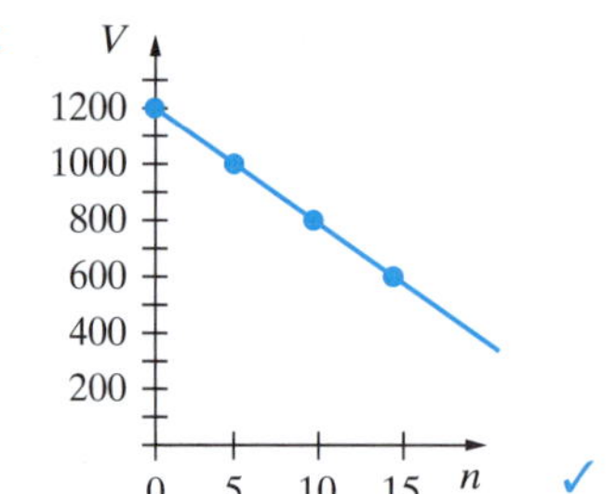

✓

d Subs. $n = 12$ in $V = 1200 - 40n$

$V = 1200 - 40 \times 12$
$= 720$

After 12 minutes, 480 litres has escaped ✓

(5 marks)

8 a

c	0	1	2	3
v	4800	**4000**	**3200**	**2400**

✓✓

b $v = 4800 - 800c$ ✓

c Subs. $v = 0$ in $v = 4800 - 800c$

$0 = 4800 - 800c$ ✓
$800c = 4800$
$c = 6$

$\therefore$ the toll would be \$6 ✓

d

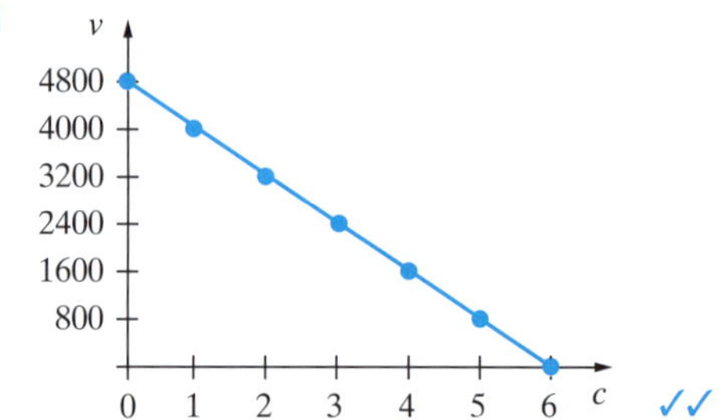

✓✓

e

Cost (c)	Vehicles (v)	$c \times v$
0	4800	0
1	4000	4000
2	3200	6400
3	2400	7200
4	1600	6400
5	800	4000
6	0	0

The maximum return occurs when 2400 cars pay \$3 and the return is \$7200

$\therefore$ the toll is \$3 ✓✓ (9 marks)

(Total 33 marks)

WORKED SOLUTIONS

CHECK YOUR SOLUTIONS

LENGTH, AREA AND VOLUME
SKILLS CHECK PAGE 62

1 a $4.72 \times 1000 = 4720$
$\therefore$ 4720 mm

b $3.86 \times 10 = 38.6$
$\therefore$ 38.6 mm

c $264 \div 100 = 2.64$
$\therefore$ 2.64 m

2 a $300 \div 100 = 3$
$\therefore$ 3 mm^2

b $90\,000 \div 10\,000 = 9$
$\therefore$ 9 m^2

c $5.3 \times 10\,000 = 53\,000$
$\therefore$ 53 000 cm^2

d $900 \div 10\,000 = 0.09$
$\therefore$ 0.09 m^2

e $2\,000\,000 \div 1\,000\,000 = 2$
$\therefore$ 2 km^2

f $0.5 \times 1\,000\,000 = 500\,000$
$\therefore$ 500 000 mm^2

3 a $3 \times 10\,000 = 30\,000$
$\therefore$ 30 000 m^2

b $65000 \div 10\,000 = 6.5$
$\therefore$ 6.5 ha

c $0.078 \times 10\,000 = 780$
$\therefore$ 780 m^2

4 a $7000 \div 1000 = 7$
$\therefore$ 7 cm^3

b $60\,000\,000 \div 1\,000\,000 = 60$
$\therefore$ 60 m^3

5 Perimeter = 2(length + width)
$48 = 2(18 + \text{width})$
$24 = 18 + \text{width}$
$\text{Width} = 24 - 18$
$= 6$
$\therefore$ width is 6 cm

6 a Area $= 16 \times 11$
$= 176$
$\therefore$ 176 cm^2

b Area $= 12.2^2$
$= 148.84$
$\therefore$ 148.84 cm^2

c Area $= \frac{1}{2} \times 16 \times 13$
$= 104$
$\therefore$ 104 cm^2

d Area $= 15 \times 12$
$= 180$
$\therefore$ 180 cm^2

e Area $= \frac{1}{2} \times 18 \times (21 + 36)$
$= 513$
$\therefore$ 513 cm^2

f Area $= \frac{1}{2} \times 18 \times 14$
$= 126$
$\therefore$ 126 cm^2

g Area $= \frac{1}{2} \times 20 \times 24$
$= 240$
$\therefore$ 240 cm^2

7 a Volume $= 8 \times 7 \times 9$
$= 504$
$\therefore$ 504 cm^3

b Volume $= \frac{1}{2} \times 12 \times 10 \times 8$
$= 480$
$\therefore$ 480 cm^3

c Volume $= 14 \times 6$
$= 84$
$\therefore$ 84 cm^3

d Volume
$= \frac{1}{2} \times 10 \times (12 + 21) \times 6$
$= 990$
$\therefore$ 990 cm^3

8 a Volume $= 65 \times 45 \times 40$
$= 117\,000$
$\therefore$ 117 000 cm^3
Capacity = 117 000 mL
= 117 L $\therefore$ 117 L

LENGTH, AREA AND VOLUME
INTERMEDIATE TEST PAGE 63

1 Area $= 400 \times 300$
$= 120\,000$
$\therefore$ [D] (1 mark)

2 Area $= \frac{1}{2}h(a + b)$
$= \frac{1}{2} \times 4(6 + 3)$
$\therefore$ [B] (1 mark)

3 Perimeter $= 2 \times (6 + 5)$
$= 22$
$\therefore$ perimeter is 22 cm
$\therefore$ [C] (1 mark)

4 1 hectare = 10 000 m^2
6 hectares = 60 000 m^2
$\therefore$ [A] (1 mark)

5

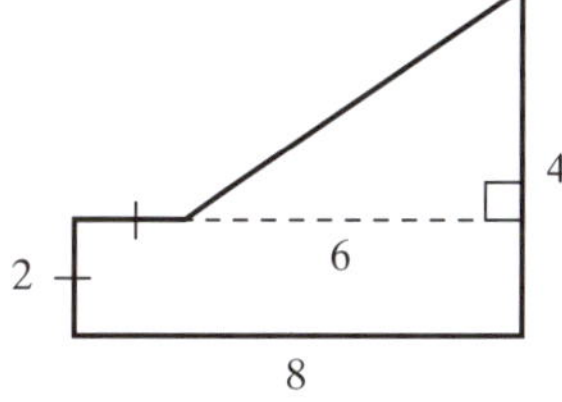

Area $= 8 \times 2 + \frac{1}{2} \times 6 \times 4$
$= 28$
$\therefore$ area is 28 cm^2
$\therefore$ [A] (1 mark)

6 As 24 L = 24 000 mL = 24 000 cm^3, and
Volume = length × breadth × height
$24\,000 = 40 \times 20 \times \text{height}$
$24\,000 = 800 \times \text{height}$
$\text{height} = 24\,000 \div 800$
$= 30$
$\therefore$ height is 30 cm
$\therefore$ [B] (1 mark)

7 a Area $= bh$
$= 12.4 \times 11.2$ ✓
$= 138.88$
$\therefore$ area is 138.88 cm^2 ✓

b Area $= \frac{1}{2}h(a + b)$
$= \frac{1}{2} \times 8.4 \times (12 + 17)$ ✓
$= 121.8$
$\therefore$ area is 121.8 cm^2 ✓

c Area
$= \frac{1}{2} \times$ product of diagonals
$= \frac{1}{2} \times 4.8 \times 7.6$ ✓
$= 18.24$
$\therefore$ area is 18.24 cm^2 ✓

d Area
$= \frac{1}{2} \times$ product of diagonals
$= \frac{1}{2} \times 18 \times 15$ ✓
$= 135$
$\therefore$ area is 135 cm^2 ✓
(8 marks)

8 a Perimeter $= 2(6.8 + 4.5)$
$= 22.6$
$\therefore$ the perimeter is 22.6 m ✓

Cost $= \$2.60 \times 22.6$
$= \$58.76$
$\therefore$ cost is \$58.76 ✓

b Area $= 6.8 \times 4.5$
$= 30.6$
$\therefore$ the area is 30.6 m^2 ✓
Cost $= \$0.70 \times 30.6$
$= \$21.42$
$\therefore$ cost is \$21.42 ✓

c Volume
$= 6.8 \times 4.5 \times 0.2$ ✓
$= 6.12$
$\therefore$ the volume is 6.12 m^3 ✓
(6 marks)

9 a Dimensions are 8 cm by 6 cm ✓

b Area $= \frac{1}{2} \times 4 \times 3$
$= 6$
$\therefore$ each area is 6 cm^2 ✓

c Shaded area $= 48 - 4 \times 6$
$= 24$
(or can use area of rhombus)
$\therefore$ the area is 24 cm^2 ✓
(3 marks)
(Total 23 marks)

LENGTH, AREA AND VOLUME ADVANCED TEST PAGE 65

1 a Dimensions are 120 m by 60 m ✓
$\therefore$ Perimeter $= 2(120 + 60)$
$= 360$
$\therefore$ perimeter is 360 metres ✓

b Required wire $= 360 \times 4$
$= 1440$
$\therefore$ need 1440 metres of wire ✓
As $1440 \div 400 = 3.6$
$\therefore$ need 4 rolls of wire
Cost $= 105 \times 4$
$= 420$
$\therefore$ it will cost \$420 ✓
(4 marks)

2 $60 + 2 \times 4 = 68$,
$40 + 2 \times 4 = 48$ ✓
Dimensions of frame:
68 cm by 48 cm
Length $= 2(68 + 48) = 232$
$\therefore$ need 232 cm, or 2.32 m ✓
(2 marks)

3 a Area
$= \frac{1}{2}$ product of diagonals
$= 0.5 \times 0.45 \times 0.1$ ✓
$= 0.0225$
$\therefore$ area is 0.0225 m^2 ✓

b Area
$= \frac{1}{2}h(a + b)$
$= 0.5 \times 9.2 \times (12 + 18)$ ✓
$= 138$
$\therefore$ area is 138 cm^2 ✓

c Area
$= \frac{1}{2}$ product of diagonals
$= \frac{1}{2} \times \frac{4}{5} \times 1\frac{1}{2}$ ✓
$= \frac{3}{5}$
$\therefore$ area is $\frac{3}{5}$ cm^2 ✓

d Area $= 1.5 \times 0.097$
$= 0.1455$ ✓
$\therefore$ area is 0.1455 m^2 ✓

e It is a square—we use the rhombus formula:
Area
$= \frac{1}{2}$ product of diagonals ✓
$= \frac{1}{2} \times 16 \times 16$
$= 128$
$\therefore$ area is 128 cm^2 ✓
(10 marks)

4 $A = \frac{1}{2}h(a + b)$
$68 = \frac{1}{2} \times h \times (9 + 11)$ ✓
$68 = \frac{1}{2} \times h \times 20$
$10h = 68$
$h = 6.8$
$\therefore$ the height is 6.8 cm ✓
(2 marks)

5 a 1 cm^2 = 100 mm^2
$\therefore 3.6 \times 100 = 360$
$\therefore$ 3.6 cm^2 = 360 mm^2 ✓

b 1 m^2 = 10 000 cm^2
$\therefore 430 \div 10\,000 = 0.043$
$\therefore$ 430 cm^2 = 0.043 m^2 ✓

c 1 cm^3 = 1000 mm^3
$\therefore 183 \div 1000 = 0.183$
$\therefore$ 183 mm^3 = 0.183 cm^3 ✓

d 1 m^3 = 1 000 000 cm^3
$\therefore 5300 \div 1\,000\,000 = 0.0053$
$\therefore$ 5300 cm^3 = 0.0053 m^3 ✓
(4 marks)

6 Volume
$= 0.5 \times 50 \times 40 \times 120$ ✓
$= 120\,000$
$\therefore$ volume is 120 000 cm^3
$\therefore$ capacity is 120 000 mL, or 120 L ✓
(2 marks)

7 a The dimensions of the prism are 10 cm, 8 cm and 6 cm. ✓
As $8 \times 6 = 48$, the area of the other two faces is 48 cm^2. ✓

b Volume $= 10 \times 8 \times 6$
$= 480$
$\therefore$ volume is 480 cm^3
$\therefore$ capacity is 480 mL ✓
(3 marks)

8 The area of a square can be found using the formula for the area of a rhombus.
Area
$= \frac{1}{2}$ product of diagonals ✓
$= \frac{1}{2} \times \sqrt{18} \times \sqrt{18}$
$= \frac{1}{2} \times 18$
$= 9$
$\therefore$ area is 9 cm^2 ✓
$\therefore$ length of each side is 3 cm
$\therefore$ perimeter is 12 cm ✓
(3 marks)

9 180 mL = 180 cm^3
Volume = area of base $\times$ height
180 = area of base $\times$ 5
$\therefore$ area of base $= 180 \div 5$
$= 36$
$\therefore$ length of side $= 6$ ✓
$\therefore$ base is a square with side length 6 cm.
Depth of 180 mL = 5 cm
Depth of 900 mL
$= 5 \div 180 \times 900$
$= 25$ ✓
$\therefore$ Water level rises another 25 cm
As $5 + 25 = 30$, the height is 30 cm

∴ the vase has dimensions 6 cm, 6 cm, 30 cm ✓ (3 marks)

10 1 ha = 10 000 m^2
3.5 × 10 000 = 35 000
∴ the area is 35 000 m^2 ✓
Also, 25 cm = 0.25 m
Volume = 35 000 × 0.25
= 8750
∴ volume is 8750 m^3
Using 1 m^3 = 1 kL, the volume is 8750 kL ✓ (2 marks)

11 The shape is a trapezoidal prism.

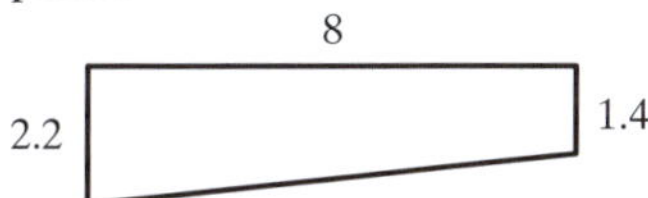

Area of trapezium
$= \frac{1}{2} \times 8 \times (1.4 + 2.2)$
= 14.4 ✓
Volume = 14.4 × 4
= 57.6
∴ volume is 57.6 m^3
Using 1 m^3 = 1 kL, the volume is 57.6 kL ✓ (2 marks)

12

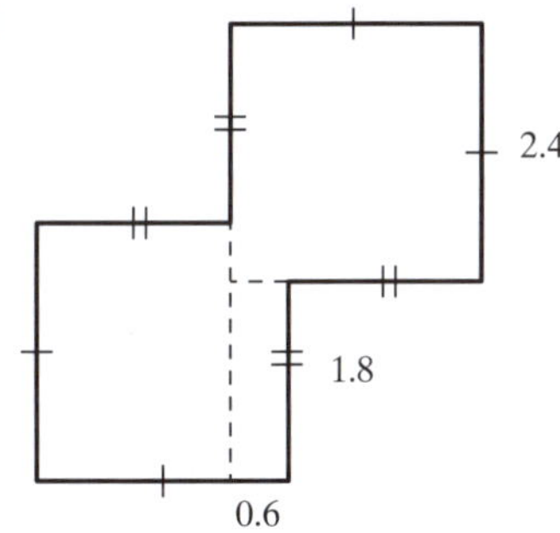

Area
$= 2.4^2 + 1.8 \times 0.6 + 2.4 \times 1.8$ ✓
= 11.16
∴ the area is 11.16 cm^2 ✓
Alternatively,

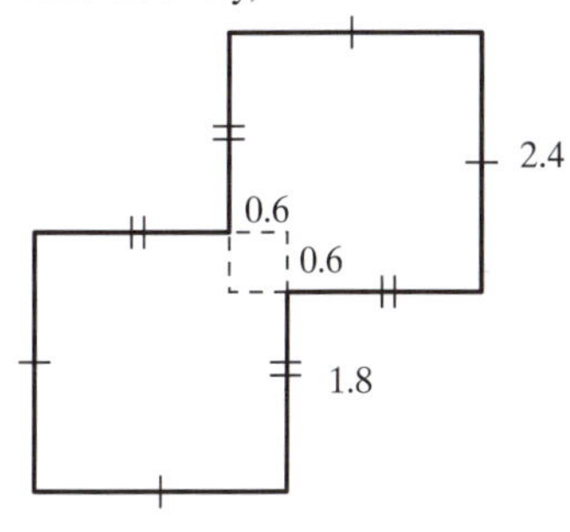

Area $= 2 \times 2.4^2 - 0.6^2$
= 11.16 (2 marks)

13 Volume of Solid A = 24^3
= 13 824
∴ the volume is 13 824 cm^3 ✓
Let x = width/height of Solid B
$54 \times x \times x = 13\,824$
$54x^2 = 13\,824$
$x^2 = 256$
$x = 16$
∴ the height is 16 cm ✓ (2 marks)

14 For rectangle, length × 8 = 96
length = 12
∴ the base of trapezium is 12 cm ✓

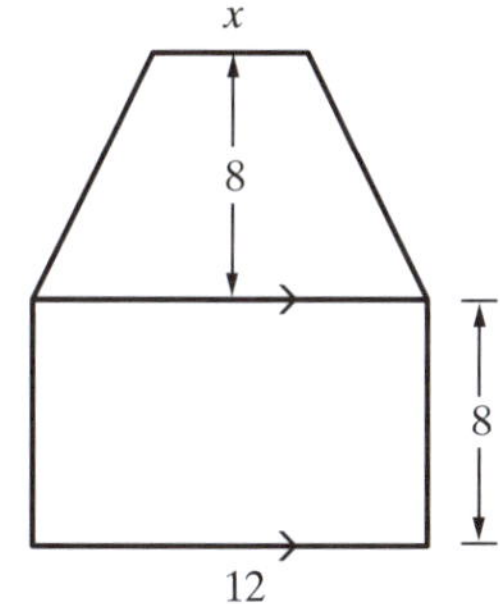

If 40% is trapezium, then 60% is rectangle.
60% of entire shape = 96
40% of entire shape
= 96 ÷ 60 × 40
= 64
∴ area of trapezium is 64 cm^2 ✓
$64 = \frac{1}{2} \times 8 \times (x + 12)$
$4(x + 12) = 64$
$4x + 48 = 64$
$4x = 64 - 48$
$4x = 16$
$x = 4$ ✓ (3 marks)

(Total 44 marks)

CIRCLES AND CYLINDERS SKILLS CHECK PAGE 67

1 **a** $C = 2 \times \pi \times 4$
= 25.13 [2 decimal places]
∴ 25.13 cm

b $C = 2 \times \pi \times 5$
= 31.42 [2 decimal places]
∴ 31.42 cm

c $C = 2 \times \pi \times 3.7$
= 23.25 [2 decimal places]
∴ 23.25 mm

d $C = 2 \times \pi \times 1.25$
= 7.85 [2 decimal places]
∴ 7.85 cm

e $C = 2 \times \pi \times 3.5$
= 21.99 [2 decimal places]
∴ 21.99 mm

f $C = 2 \times \pi \times 160$
= 1005.31 [2 decimal places]
∴ 1005.31 cm

2 **a** $A = \pi \times 6^2 = 36\pi$
∴ 36π cm^2

b $A = \pi \times 5^2 = 25\pi$
∴ 25π m^2

c $A = \pi \times \left(\frac{7}{2}\right)^2 = \frac{49\pi}{4}$
∴ $\frac{49\pi}{4}$ cm^2

d $A = \pi \times 1^2 = \pi$
∴ π m^2

e $A = \pi \times \left(\frac{2}{5}\right)^2 = \frac{4\pi}{25}$
∴ $\frac{4\pi}{25}$ mm^2

f $A = \pi \times \left(\frac{9}{8}\right)^2 = \frac{81\pi}{64}$
∴ $\frac{81\pi}{64}$ cm^2

3 **a** $V = \pi \times 4^2 \times 8$
= 402.124 [3 decimal places]
∴ 402.124 cm^3

b $V = \pi \times 2^2 \times 8$
= 100.531 [3 decimal places]
∴ 100.531 cm^3

c $V = \pi \times 8^2 \times 5$
= 1005.310 [3 decimal places]
∴ 1005.310 cm^3

d $V = \pi \times 9^2 \times 4.5$
= 1145.111 [3 decimal places]
∴ 1145.111 cm^3

4 **a** Sector is 240° out of 360°

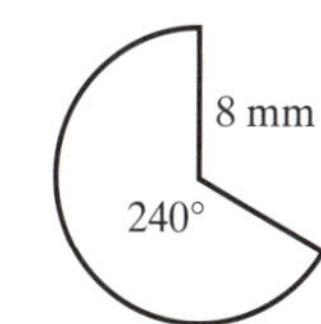

WORKED SOLUTIONS

$A = \frac{240}{360} \times \pi \times 8^2$
$= 134$ [nearest whole]
$\therefore$ 134 mm^2

b

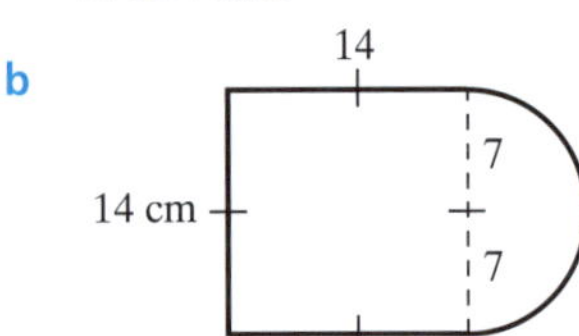

Rectangle plus semi-circle

$A = 14 \times 14 + \frac{1}{2} \times \pi \times 7^2$
$= 273$
$\therefore$ 273 cm^2 [nearest whole]

5 a $V = \pi \times 7.5^2 \times 20$
$= 3534.29$ [2 decimal places]
$\therefore$ 3534.29 cm^3

b $V = \frac{1}{2} \times \pi \times 7^2 \times 20$
$= 1539.38$ [2 decimal places]
$\therefore$ 1539.38 cm^3

6 Vol $= \pi \times 6^2 \times 18$
$= 2036$ cm^3 [nearest cm^3]
$\therefore$ capacity = 2036 mL

7 a $C = 2\pi r$
$16 = 2\pi r$
$\therefore \frac{2\pi r}{2\pi} = \frac{16}{2\pi}$
$r = 2.5$ [1 decimal place]
$\therefore$ radius is 2.5 cm

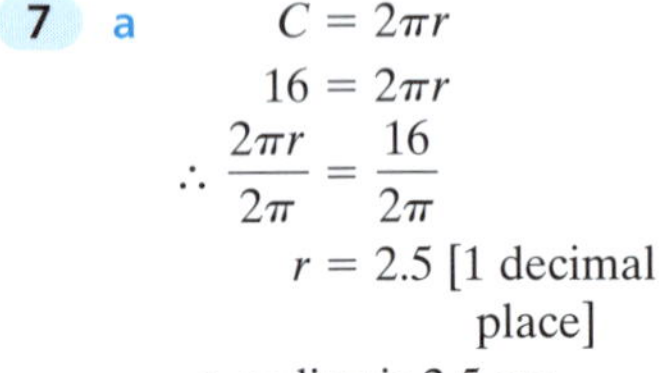

b $A = \pi r^2$
$14 = \pi r^2$
$\therefore \frac{\pi r^2}{\pi} = \frac{14}{\pi}$
$r^2 = \frac{14}{\pi}$
$r = \sqrt{\frac{14}{\pi}} = 2.1$
[1 decimal place]
$\therefore$ radius is 2.1 cm
[note: only need +ve case, not ±]

8 a

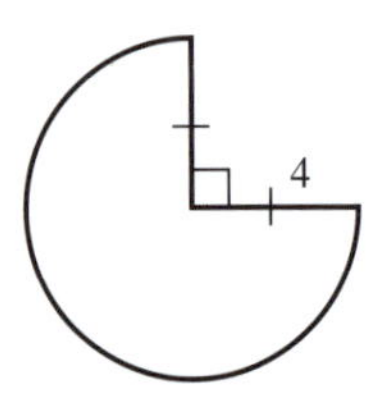

$P = 4 + 4 + \frac{3}{4} \times 2 \times \pi \times 4$
$= 8 + 6\pi$
i.e. perimeter is $(8 + 6\pi)$ cm

b

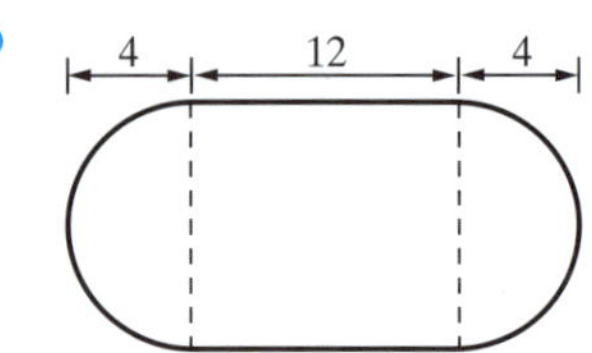

$P = 12 + 12 + 2 \times \pi \times 4$
$= 24 + 8\pi$
i.e. perimeter is $(24 + 8\pi)$ cm

CIRCLES AND CYLINDERS
INTERMEDIATE TEST PAGE 68

1 Distance = $50 \times$ circumference
$= 50 \times 2 \times \pi \times 10$
$= 3141.592\,654$
$\therefore$ distance is 3142 cm [nearest whole]
i.e. distance is 31 m [nearest m]
$\therefore$ **[A]** (1 mark)

2 Shaded region
= area of large circle − area of small circle
$= \pi \times 8^2 - \pi \times 4^2$
$= 64\pi - 16\pi$
$= 48\pi$
$\therefore$ area is 48π cm^2
$\therefore$ **[D]** (1 mark)

3 Area $= \pi r^2$
$\pi r^2 = \pi$
$\therefore r^2 = 1$
$r = \pm 1$
i.e. radius is 1 cm
$\therefore C = 2\pi r$
$= 2 \times \pi \times 1$
$= 2\pi$
i.e. circumference is 2π cm
$\therefore$ **[C]** (1 mark)

4 Perimeter
$= 10 + \frac{1}{2} \times 2 \times \pi \times 5$
$= 25.707\,096\,327$
$= 25.7$ [1 decimal place]
i.e. perimeter 25.7 mm
$\therefore$ **[C]** (1 mark)

5 a Perimeter
$= 2(2.4) +$ circle
$= 2(2.4) + 2 \times \pi \times 0.4$ ✓
$= 7.313\,274\,123$
$= 7.313$ [3 decimal places]
$\therefore$ distance is 7.313 km ✓

b Laps $= 100 \div 7.313$
$= 13.674\,278\,68$
$\therefore$ cyclist to complete 14 laps ✓ (3 marks)

6 a Let d = diameter
$\therefore d^2 = 3^2 + 4^2$
$= 9 + 16$
$= 25$
$d = \sqrt{25}$
$= 5$ ✓
$\therefore$ area
= triangle + semi-circle
$= \frac{1}{2} \times 3 \times 4 + \frac{1}{2} \times \pi \times 2.5^2$ ✓
$= 15.817\,477\,04$
$= 15.82$ [2 decimal places]
$\therefore$ area is 15.82 cm^2 ✓

b

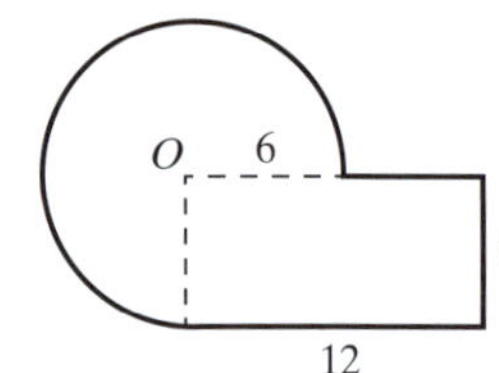

Figure
$= \frac{3}{4}$ of circle + rectangle
$= \frac{3}{4} \times \pi \times 6^2 + 12 \times 6$ ✓✓
$= 156.823\,0016$
$= 156.82$ [2 decimal places]
$\therefore$ area is 156.82 cm^2 ✓
(6 marks)

7 a $V = \left[80 \times 70 + \frac{1}{2} \times \pi \times 40^2\right] \times$ ✓
$= 486\,796.4474$
$= 486\,796$ [nearest whole]
$\therefore$ volume is 486 796 cm^3 ✓

b
$V = \left[\frac{1}{2} \times \pi \times 4.5^2 - \frac{1}{2} \times \pi \times 1.5^2\right] \times 15$
$= 424.115\,0082$
$= 424$ [nearest whole]
$\therefore$ volume is 424 cm^3 ✓ (4 mark

WORKED SOLUTIONS

8 $V = \pi \times 1.2^2 \times 2$
$= 9.047\,868\,42$ ✓
$= 9.048$ [3 decimal places]
$\therefore$ Capacity $= 9.048 \times 1000$
$= 9048$
i.e. capacity is 9048 L ✓
(2 marks)
(Total 19 marks)

CIRCLES AND CYLINDERS
ADVANCED TEST PAGE 69

1 Radii are 41 m and 47 m
$C = 2\pi r$
$C_{\text{inside}} = 2 \times \pi \times 41$
$= 257.61$ (2 dec. pl.) ✓
$C_{\text{outside}} = 2 \times \pi \times 47$
$= 295.31$ (2 dec. pl.) ✓
$295.31 - 257.61 = 37.7$
$= 38$ (nearest whole)
$\therefore$ the extra distance is 38 m ✓
(3 marks)

2 Radii are 0.75 m and 0.175 m
$C = 2\pi r$
$C_{\text{front}} = 2 \times \pi \times 0.75$
$= 4.71$ (2 dec. pl.)
Revolutions of large wheel
$= 1000 \div 4.71$ ✓
$= 212.206\,5908...$
$C_{\text{rear}} = 2 \times \pi \times 0.175$
$= 1.10$ (2 dec. pl.)
Revolutions of large wheel
$= 1000 \div 1.10$ ✓
$= 909.456\,8177...$
$909.46 - 212.21$
$= 697.25$
$= 700$ (nearest hundred)
$\therefore$ the rear wheel has about 700 more revolutions ✓ (3 marks)

3 **a** $C = 2\pi r$
$28 = 2\pi r$
$r = \dfrac{28}{2\pi}$
$= \dfrac{14}{\pi}$ ✓
$A = \pi r^2$
$= \pi \times \left(\dfrac{14}{\pi}\right)^2$
$= 62.39$ (2 dec. pl.)
$\therefore$ area is 62.39 cm^2 ✓

b $C = 2\pi r$
$16\pi = 2\pi r$
$r = \dfrac{16\pi}{2\pi}$
$= 8$ ✓
$A = \pi r^2$
$= \pi \times 8^2$
$= 64\pi$
$\therefore$ area is 64π cm^2 ✓
(4 marks)

4 Area of square $= 12^2$
$= 144$
$\therefore$ area of square is 144 cm^2 ✓
Diameter of circle is 12 cm, radius is 6 cm
$A = \pi r^2$
$= \pi \times 6^2$
$= 113.10$ (2 dec. pl.)
$\therefore$ area is 113.10 cm^2 ✓
Percentage $= \dfrac{113.10}{144} \times 100\%$
$= 78.54$
$\therefore$ the circle covers 78.54% of the square ✓ (3 marks)

5 **a** Using $C = \pi d$
Diameters are 8 cm and 12 cm. ✓
As $12 - 8 = 4$, then YZ is 4 cm ✓
b Radii are 4 cm and 6 cm
$A_{\text{large}} = \pi \times 6^2$
$= 36\pi$ ✓
$A_{\text{small}} = \pi \times 4^2$
$= 16\pi$
Area not covered
$= 36\pi - 16\pi$
$= 20\pi$
$\therefore$ the area not covered is 20π cm^2 ✓ (4 marks)

6 **a**

$P = 2 \times \pi \times 4 + \dfrac{1}{2} \times 2 \times \pi \times 8$
$= 50.27$
$\therefore$ the perimeter is 50.27 cm ✓
$A = \dfrac{1}{2} \times \pi \times 8^2$
$= 100.53$ (2 dec. pl.)
$\therefore$ the area is 100.53 cm^2 ✓

b $P = 2 \times 5 + \dfrac{3}{4} \times 2 \times \pi \times 5$
$= 33.56$
$\therefore$ the perimeter is 33.56 cm ✓
$A = \dfrac{3}{4} \times \pi \times 5^2$
$= 58.90$ (2 dec. pl.)
$\therefore$ the area is 58.90 cm^2 ✓
(4 marks)

7

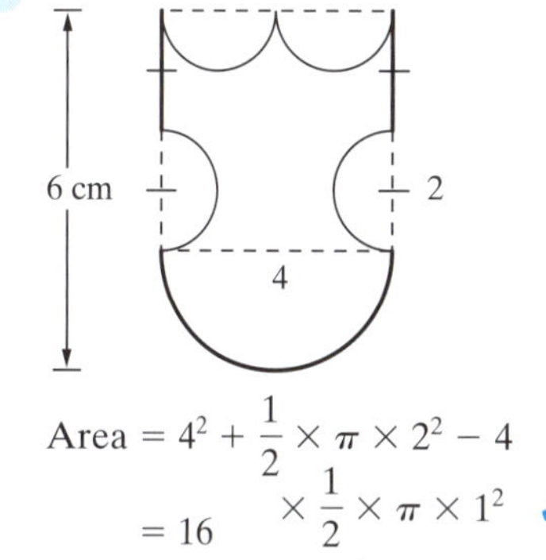

Area $= 4^2 + \dfrac{1}{2} \times \pi \times 2^2 - 4 \times \dfrac{1}{2} \times \pi \times 1^2$ ✓
$= 16$
$\therefore$ the area is 16 cm^2 ✓ (2 marks)

8 5 litres $= 5000$ cm^3
$V = \pi r^2 h$
$5000 = \pi \times 10^2 \times h$ ✓
$5000 = 100\pi\, h$
$h = \dfrac{5000}{100\pi}$
$= 15.915\,494\,31...$
$= 16$ (nearest whole)
$\therefore$ the height is 16 cm ✓
(2 marks)

9 Volume $= 12^3$
$= 1728$
$\therefore$ the volume is 1728 cm^3
$V = \pi r^2 h$
$1728 = \pi \times 6^2 \times h$ ✓
$1728 = 36\pi h$
$h = \dfrac{1728}{36\pi}$
$= 15.278\,874\,54...$
$= 15$ (nearest whole)
$\therefore$ the height is 15 cm ✓
(2 marks)

10 Let $x = AC$
Area of kite $= \dfrac{1}{2}$ product of diagonals
$48 = \dfrac{1}{2} \times 8 \times x$
$4x = 48$
$x = 12$ ✓
$\therefore$ the diameter of circle is 12 cm, radius is 6 cm

WORKED SOLUTIONS

CHECK YOUR SOLUTIONS

Area of circle $= \pi \times 6^2$
$= 113$ (nearest whole) ✓

Area of shaded region
$= 113 - 48$
$= 65$
$\therefore$ the shaded area is 65 cm^2 ✓
(3 marks)

11 Volume
$= \frac{72}{360} \times \pi \times 6^2 \times 5$ ✓
$= 113.10$ (2 dec. pl.)
$\therefore$ the volume is 113.10 cm^3 ✓
(2 marks)

12 **a** Radius of pool is 3.2 m
$V = \pi \times 3.2^2 \times 1.4$ ✓
$= 45.04$ (2 dec places)
$\therefore$ the volume is 45.04 m^3 ✓

b

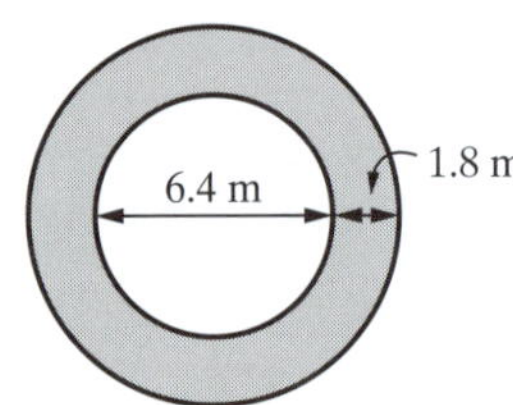

$A = \pi \times 5^2 - \pi \times 3.2^2$ ✓
$= 46.37$
$\therefore$ the area is 46.37 m^2 ✓
(4 marks)

13 Volume of each ice cube $= 4^3$
$= 64$
$\therefore$ each ice cube has a volume of 64 cm^3 ✓

Total volume of cubes $= 64 \times 6$
$= 384$
$\therefore$ six ice cubes have volume of 384 cm^3

$V = \pi r^2 h$
$384 = \pi \times 4^2 \times h$ ✓
$16\pi h = 384$
$h = \frac{384}{16\pi}$
$= 7.638\,437\,268...$
$= 8$ (nearest whole)
$\therefore$ the height is 8 cm ✓
(3 marks)

(Total 39 marks)

TIME AND PYTHAGORAS' THEOREM

SKILLS CHECK PAGE 71

1 **a** 0920 = 9:20 am
b 2120 = 9:20 pm
c 2355 = 11:55 pm

2 **a** 6:40 am = 0640
b 12:50 pm = 1250
c 12:50 am = 0050

3 **a** 2:15 pm minus 1 h 30 min
= 12:45 pm
b 2:15 pm plus 2 h 30 min
= 4:45 pm

4 4:30 pm Monday plus 15 h = 7:30 am Tuesday in Newcastle

5 **a** $4^2 = 16$
$2^2 + 3^2 = 13$
$16 \neq 13$
$\therefore$ not a Pythagorean triad

b $13^2 = 169$
$5^2 + 12^2 = 25 + 144$
$169 = 169$
$\therefore$ is a Pythagorean triad

c $15^2 = 225$
$9^2 + 12^2 = 81 + 144$
$225 = 225$
$\therefore$ is a Pythagorean triad

6 $17^2 = 289$
$8^2 + 15^2 = 64 + 225$
$289 = 289$
$\therefore \triangle ABC$ is right-angled as Pythagoras' theorem holds

7 **a** $x^2 = 3^2 + 5^2$
$= 9 + 25$
$= 34$
$\therefore x = \sqrt{34}$

b $x^2 = 5^2 + 8^2$
$= 25 + 64$
$= 89$
$\therefore x = \sqrt{89}$

c $x^2 = 7^2 + 9^2$
$= 49 + 81$
$= 130$
$\therefore x = \sqrt{130}$

8 **a** $10^2 = x^2 + 7^2$
$x^2 = 10^2 - 7^2$
$= 100 - 49$
$= 51$
$x = \sqrt{51}$
$\therefore x = 7.14$ (2 dec. pl.)

b $(3.2)^2 = y^2 + (1.8)^2$
$y^2 = (3.2)^2 - (1.8)^2$
$= 10.24 - 3.24$
$= 7$
$y = \sqrt{7}$
$\therefore y = 2.65$ (2 dec. pl.)

c $4^2 = c^2 + (3.1)^2$
$c^2 = 4^2 - (3.1)^2$
$= 16 - 9.61$
$= 6.39$
$c = \sqrt{6.39}$
$\therefore c = 2.53$ (2 dec. pl.)

9

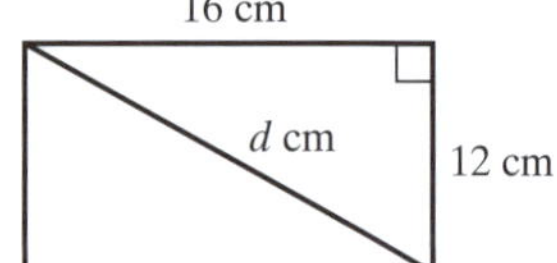

Let diagonal be d cm.
$d^2 = 12^2 + 16^2$
$= 144 + 256$
$= 400$
$d = \sqrt{400}$
$= 20$
$\therefore$ diagonal is 20 cm in length

10 **a** Let missing side be x cm.

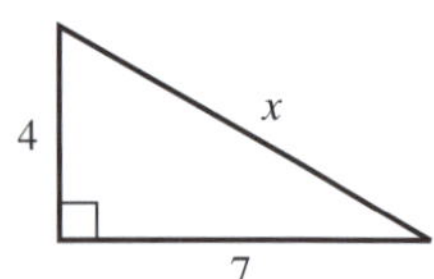

$x^2 = 4^2 + 7^2$
$= 16 + 49$
$= 65$
$x = \sqrt{65}$
$= 8.062$
Perimeter = 4 + 7 + 8.062
$\therefore$ perimeter is 19.062 cm

b Let missing side be x cm.

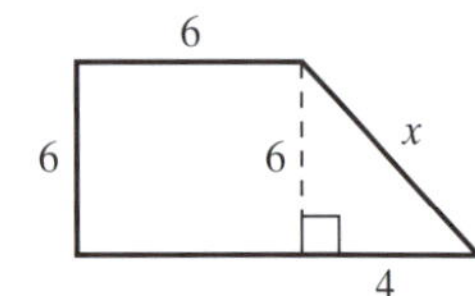

$x^2 = 4^2 + 6^2$
$= 16 + 36$
$= 52$
$x = \sqrt{52}$
$= 7.211$
Perimeter
$= 7.211 + 10 + 6 + 6$
$\therefore$ perimeter is 29.211 cm

TIME AND PYTHAGORAS' THEOREM
INTERMEDIATE TEST PAGE 72

1 The analog is showing 6:17. Adding 15 min gives 6:32.
$\therefore$ 0632
$\therefore$ [A] (1 mark)

2 New Delhi is 5 h 30 min behind Melbourne.
It will be 8:40 pm in New Delhi.
$\therefore$ [B] (1 mark)

3 0548 to 0600 is 12 min. 0600 to 1700 is 11 h. 1700 to 1742 is 42 min. The total time is 11 h 54 min.
$\therefore$ [A] (1 mark)

4 Use the DMS key on your calculator, or start with 2 h 42 min: add 18 min gives 3 h then another 14 min. As 18 + 14 = 32 then the difference is 32 min.
$\therefore$ [A] (1 mark)

5 Try each of the alternatives.
$25^2 = 7^2 + 24^2$?
$625 = 49 + 576$? Yes!
$\therefore$ {7, 24, 25} is a Pythagorean triad.
$\therefore$ [C] (1 mark)

6 If a right triangle, then Pythagoras' theorem can be applied. Try each of the alternatives.
In D, $62^2 = 11^2 + 60^2$?
i.e. 3844 = 121 + 3600? No!
$\therefore$ 11 cm, 60 cm, 62 cm do not form a right-angled triangle.
$\therefore$ [D] (1 mark)

7 a Lowest tide of 0.36 m occurs at 1352 Tuesday. ✓

b Sam's tide is at 0751. Using subtraction, he has to wait 1 h 31 min. ✓

c The low tides are at 0133, 1420, 0215 and 1352. The three differences are 12 h 47 min, 11 h 55 min, 11 h 37 min. The longest time is 12 h 47 min. ✓✓ (4 marks)

8 a $x^2 = 4^2 + 7^2$
$= 16 + 49$ ✓
$= 65$
$x = \sqrt{65}$
$\therefore x = 8.06$ [2 decimal places] ✓

b $12.7^2 = x^2 + 5.4^2$
$x^2 = 12.7^2 - 5.4^2$ ✓
$= 161.29 - 29.16$
$= 132.13$
$x = \sqrt{132.13}$
$\therefore x = 11.49$ [2 decimal places] ✓

c $14.3^2 = x^2 + 11.7^2$
$x^2 = 14.3^2 - 11.7^2$ ✓
$= 204.49 - 136.89$
$= 67.6$
$x = \sqrt{67.6}$
$\therefore x = 8.22$ [2 decimal places] ✓
(6 marks)

9 a $x^2 = 20^2 - 12^2$ ✓
$= 400 - 144$
$= 256$
$x = \sqrt{256}$
$= 16$
i.e. height is 17.5 metres ✓

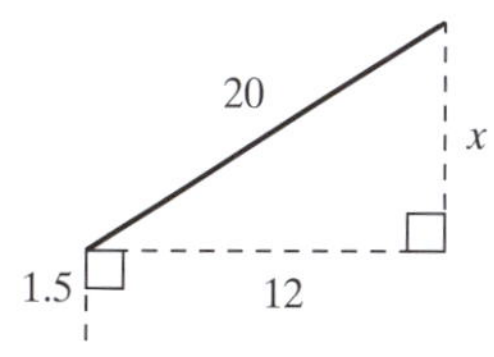

b $d^2 = 16^2 + 12^2$ ✓
$= 256 + 144$
$= 400$
$d = \sqrt{400}$
$= 20$
$\therefore$ distance is 20 km ✓

c $h^2 = 10^2 - 5^2$
$= 100 - 25$
$= 75$ ✓
$h = \sqrt{75}$
$= 8.66$
$\therefore$ height is 8.66 cm [2 decimal places] ✓

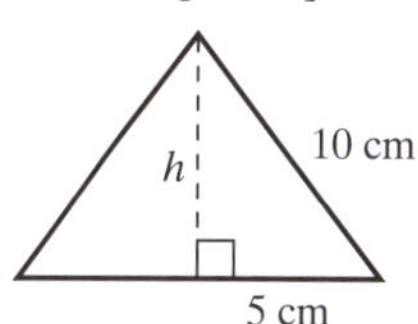

(6 marks)
(Total 22 marks)

TIME AND PYTHAGORAS' THEOREM
ADVANCED TEST PAGE 73

1 Using the calculator,
5 DMS 35 × 9 = 27 DMS 55
$\therefore$ it will take 50 min 15 sec ✓✓
(2 marks)

2 Time = Distance ÷ Speed
= 316 ÷ 60
= 5.266 666 66…
= 5 h 16 min ✓
11:45 plus 5 h 16 min is 17:01
$\therefore$ Erin arrives at 5:01 pm ✓
(2 marks)

3 7 am plus 10 h 50 min is 5:50 pm. ✓
5:50 pm minus 8 hours is 9:50 am
$\therefore$ the plane arrives at 9:50 am ✓ (2 marks)

4 80 + 100 = 180 ✓
Need to find the distance travelled in 20 minutes, or $\frac{1}{3}$ hour, travelling 180 km/h.
Distance = Speed × Time
$= 180 \times \frac{1}{3}$
$= 60$
$\therefore$ the cars are 60 km apart ✓
(2 marks)

5 11 + 6 = 17
Dallas is 17 hours behind Hobart. ✓
13:00 on 25 Dec minus 17 hours is 8 pm on 24 Dec ✓
(2 marks)

6 a Using the calculator,
19 DMS 15 − 5 DMS 48
= 13 DMS 27
$\therefore$ 13 hours 27 minutes ✓✓

b Two mins earlier is 0546
1915 to midnight is
4 h 45 min
4 (DMS) 45 + 5 (DMS) 46
= 10 (DMS) 31
∴ 10 hours 31 minutes ✓✓
(4 marks)

7 She arrives at 10:40 am.

40 minutes $= \frac{2}{3}$h

Time = 20 ÷ 40
= 0.5 ✓

∴ the trip took 30 minutes
∴ She left home at
10:10 am. ✓ (2 marks)

8 Check whether $17^2 = 2.6^2 + 16.8^2$

LHS $= 17^2$
$= 289$ ✓

RHS $= 2.6^2 + 16.8^2$
$= 289$

∴ the triangle is right-angled ✓ (2 marks)

9 Let x = unknown side

$x^2 = 65^2 - 33^2$
$= 3136$
$x = 56$ ✓

Perimeter = 65 + 33 + 56
= 154

∴ the perimeter is 154 cm ✓

Area $= \frac{1}{2} \times 33 \times 56$
$= 924$

∴ the area is 924 cm^2 ✓
(3 marks)

10 Let x = length of unknown side

$x^2 + x^2 = 16^2$ ✓
$2x^2 = 256$
$x^2 = 128$
$x = \sqrt{128}$ ✓
$= 11.31$ (2 dec. pl.)

Perimeter = 2 × 11.31 + 16
= 39 (nearest whole)

∴ the perimeter is 39 cm ✓
(3 marks)

11 Let x = distance between the boyfriends

$x^2 = 7^2 + 5^2$ ✓
$= 74$
$x = \sqrt{74}$
$= 8.602325267...$
$= 9$ (nearest whole)

∴ the boyfriends are
9 metres apart ✓ (2 marks)

12 Let x = height of window ledge

$x^2 = 8^2 - 2^2$ ✓
$= 60$
$x = \sqrt{60}$
$= 7.75$ (2 decimal places)

∴ the ledge is 775 cm high ✓
(2 marks)

13 **a** Let x = length BD

$x^2 = 4^2 + 4^2$ ✓
$= 16 + 16$
$= 32$
$x = \sqrt{32}$

∴ BD is $\sqrt{32}$ cm long ✓

b $EH = \frac{\sqrt{32}}{4}$

∴ area of square

$= \frac{\sqrt{32}}{4} \times \frac{\sqrt{32}}{4}$ ✓

$= \frac{32}{16}$

$= 2$

∴ area of square $EHRF$ is
2 cm^2 ✓

c $A = \frac{1}{2} \times \frac{\sqrt{32}}{4} \times \left(\frac{\sqrt{32}}{4} + 2 \times \frac{\sqrt{32}}{4}\right)$ ✓

$= \frac{1}{2} \times \frac{\sqrt{32}}{4} \times 3 \times \frac{\sqrt{32}}{4}$

$= 3$

∴ area of trapezium $DSFE$
is 3 cm^2 ✓

d Twice area of trapezium in part c.

∴ area of trapezium $DSRB$
is 6 cm^2 ✓ (7 marks)

14

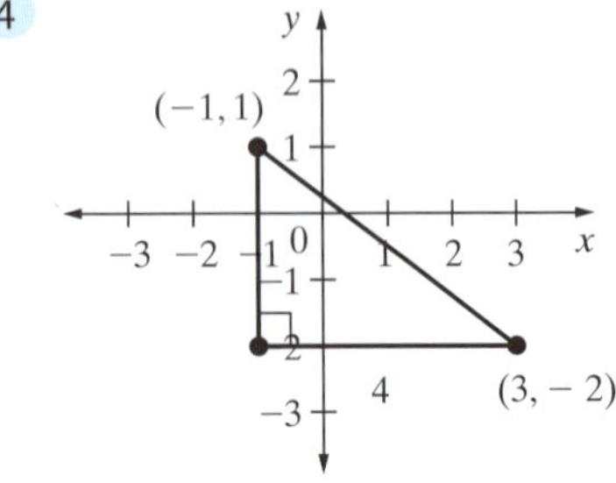

Let x = distance

$x^2 = 3^2 + 4^2$ ✓
$= 25$
$x = 5$

∴ the distance is 5 units ✓
(2 marks)

15

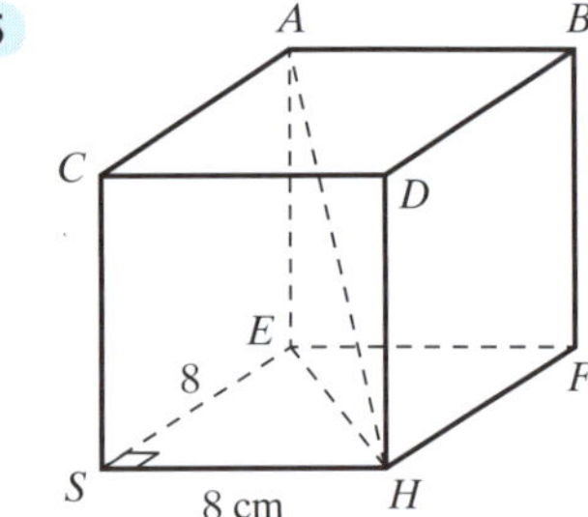

Let x = length EH

$x^2 = 8^2 + 8^2$
$= 64 + 64$
$= 128$
$x = \sqrt{128}$

∴ EH is $\sqrt{128}$ cm long ✓

Let y = length AH

$y^2 = 8^2 + (\sqrt{128})^2$ ✓
$= 64 + 128$
$= 192$
$y = \sqrt{192}$
$= 13.854640646...$
$= 13.9$ (1 dec. pl.)

∴ AH is 139 mm long ✓
(3 marks)

(Total 40 marks)

CONGRUENT TRIANGLES AND TRANSFORMATIONS

SKILLS CHECK PAGE 75

1 **a**

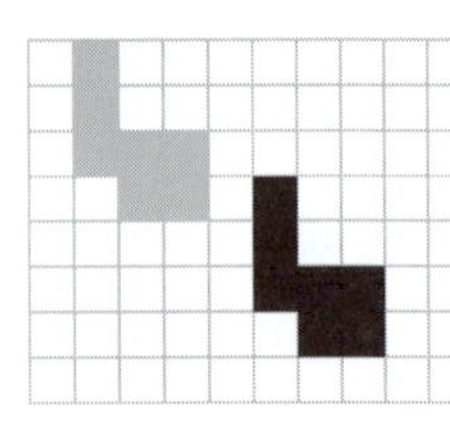

b

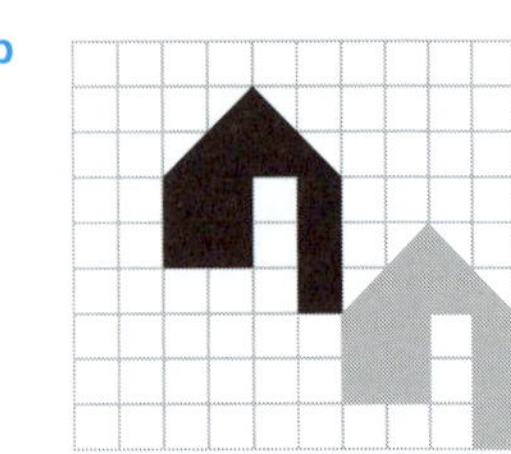

c
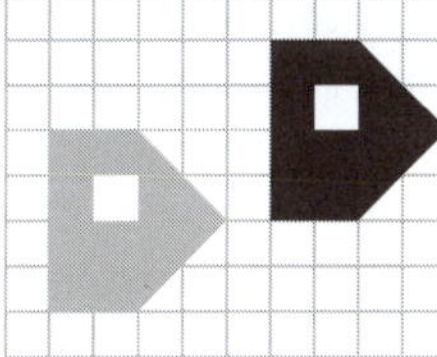

2 a
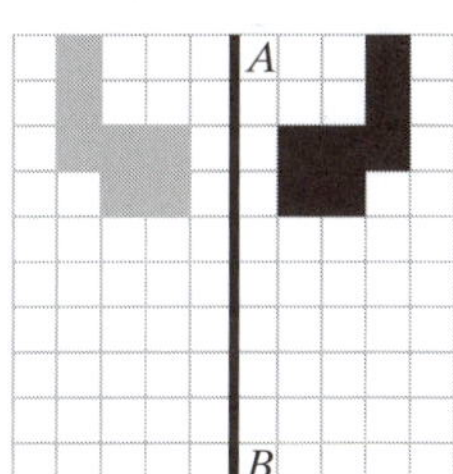

b
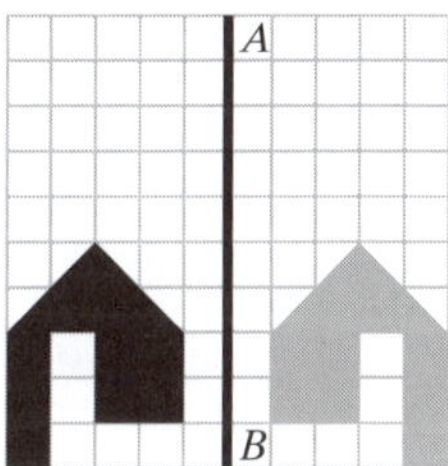

c
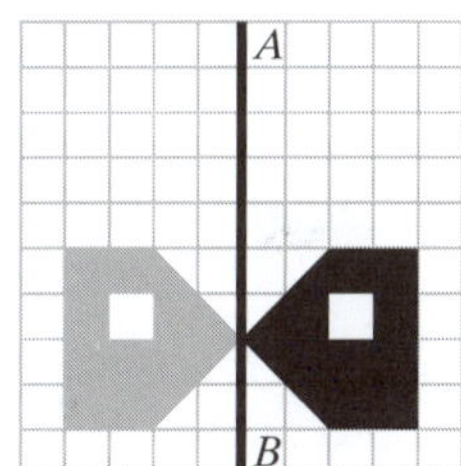

3 a
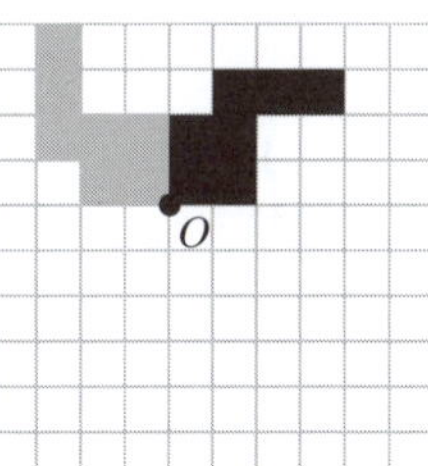

b
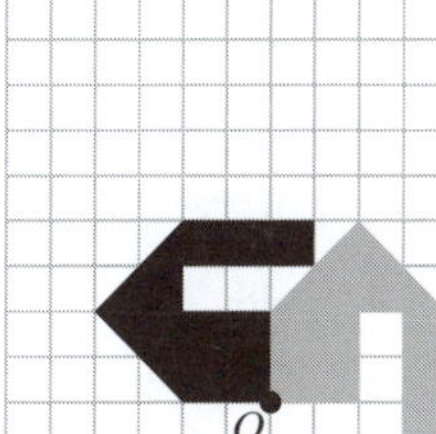

c
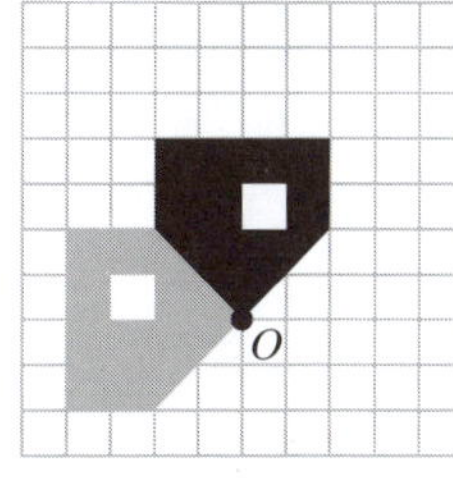

4 a congruent, AAS test
b not congruent
c congruent, RHS test
d congruent, AAS test (angles are 40°, 80° and 60°)

5 a $AB = LM$
b $AC = LN$
c $MN = BC$
d $\angle ABC = \angle LMN$
e $\angle MLN = \angle BAC$
f $\angle LNM = \angle ACB$

6 a $x = 5, y = 70, z = 50$
b $x = 5, y = 55$

CONGRUENT TRIANGLES AND TRANSFORMATIONS
INTERMEDIATE TEST PAGE 76

1 $DF = CB$
$\therefore$ [C] (1 mark)

2 $PR = 5$ cm because this is the matching side opposite the 80° angle.
$\therefore$ [B] (1 mark)

3 Using SAS,

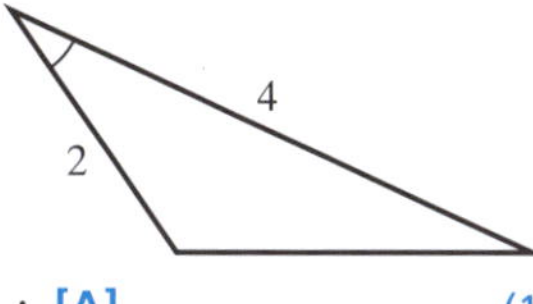

$\therefore$ [A] (1 mark)

4 The triangle has been rotated about the point B.
$\therefore$ [D] (1 mark)

5 a $x = 40, y = 30, z = 7$ ✓✓✓
b $a = 50, b = 6, c = 70$ ✓✓✓
(6 marks)

6 a AC is a common side for both triangles: the test used is SSS. ✓
b i $\angle ADC = \angle CBA$ ✓
ii $\angle BAC = \angle DCA$ ✓
c $\angle BAC, \angle DCA$ ✓✓
Also, $\angle BCA = \angle DAL$
d parallelogram ✓ (6 marks)

7 a SSS ✓
b $\angle PST = \angle RST$ ✓
c SAS ✓
d As $\triangle PST \equiv \triangle RST$ then $\angle PTS = \angle RTS$.
As $\angle PTR = 180°$ then $\angle PTS = 90°$. ✓ (4 marks)
(Total 20 marks)

CONGRUENT TRIANGLES AND TRANSFORMATIONS
ADVANCED TEST PAGE 78

1 a translation ✓
b reflection ✓
c rotation ✓ (3 marks)

2 a $\triangle ABC \equiv \triangle DEF$ ✓
b $\triangle GHI \equiv \triangle GJI$ ✓
c $\triangle PSR \equiv \triangle RQP$ ✓
(3 marks)

3

Abbreviations	Explanation
$\triangle ABC \equiv \triangle PQR$	triangle ABC is congruent to triangle PQR ✓
corr. $\angle$s equal, $BC \parallel ST$	corresponding angles equal, BC parallel to ST ✓
alt. $\angle$s equal, $\parallel$ lines	alternate angles equal, parallel lines ✓
co-int. $\angle$s supp., $XY \parallel MN$	co-interior angles supplementary, XY parallel to MN ✓
vert. opp. $\angle$s equal	vertically opposite angles equal ✓
$\angle$ sum of $\triangle$	angle sum of triangle ✓
matching $\angle$s of cong. $\triangle$s	matching angles of congruent triangles ✓
base $\angle$s of isos. $\triangle$s equal	base angles of isosceles triangle are equal ✓
opp. $\angle$s of parallelogram	opposite angles of a parallelogram ✓

(9 marks)

4 a
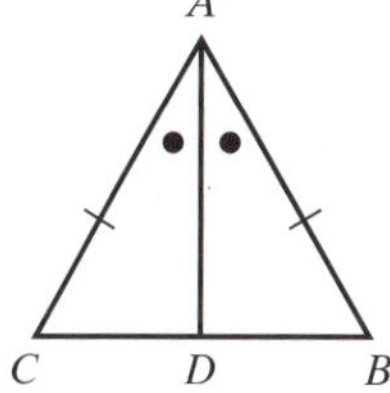

AD is common ✓
$\angle CAD = \angle BAD$ (given) ✓
$AC = AB$ (given) ✓
$\therefore \triangle ADC \equiv \triangle ABC$
(SAS test) ✓

WORKED SOLUTIONS

b

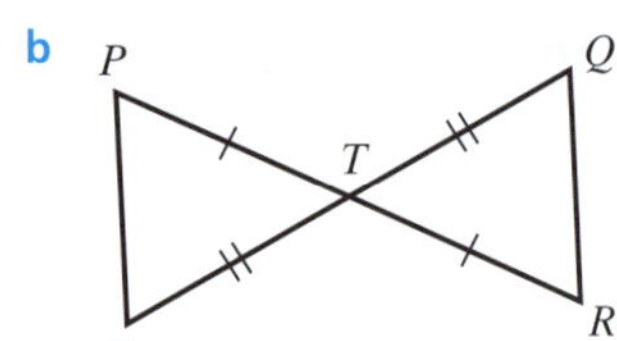

$PT = RT$ (given) ✓
$\angle PTS = \angle RTQ$ (vert opp ∠s equal) ✓
$ST = QT$ (given) ✓
$\therefore \triangle PTS \equiv \triangle RTQ$ (SAS test) ✓

c

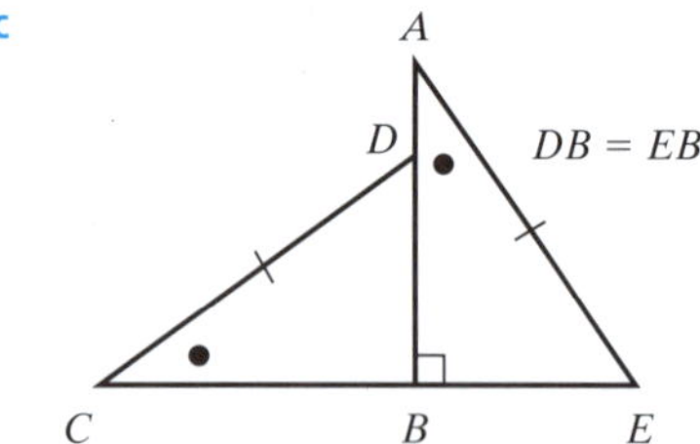

$DC = EA$ (given) ✓
$\angle DBC = \angle EBA$ (given) ✓
$\angle DCB = \angle EAB$ (given) ✓
$\therefore \triangle DBC \equiv \triangle EBA$ (AAS test) ✓ (12 marks)

5 **a**

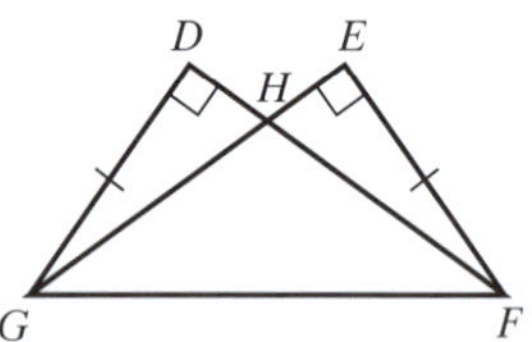

$DG = EF$ (given) ✓
$\angle GDF = \angle FEG$ (given) ✓
GF is common ✓
$\therefore \triangle GDF \equiv \triangle FEG$ (RHS test) ✓

b

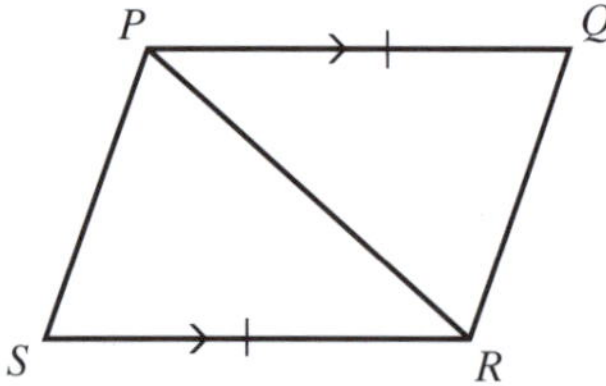

$SR = QP$ (given) ✓
$\angle SRP = \angle QPR$ (alt ∠s equal, $SR \| PQ$) ✓
PR is common ✓
$\therefore \triangle SPR \equiv \triangle RQP$ (SAS test) ✓

c

A E B
F
D C

$ABCD$ is square
$AE = DF$

$AD = DC$ (sides of square) ✓
$\angle DAE = \angle CDF$ (∠s of square) ✓
$AE = DF$ (given) ✓
$\therefore \triangle DAE \equiv \triangle CDF$ (SAS test) ✓ (12 marks)
(Total 39 marks)

PROBABILITY
SKILLS CHECK PAGE 80

1 **a** Pr(born on Tuesday) $= \frac{1}{7}$

b Pr(born on Sat, Sun) $= \frac{2}{7}$

c Pr(not born Monday) $= 1 - \frac{1}{7} = \frac{6}{7}$

2 **a** Pr(yellow) $= \frac{5}{10} = \frac{1}{2}$

b Pr(white) $= 0$

c Pr(not blue) $= 1 - \frac{3}{10} = \frac{7}{10}$

d Pr(not yellow or green) $= 1 - \frac{7}{10} = \frac{3}{10}$

3 **a** Pr(BBB) $= \frac{1}{8}$

b Pr(GGB or GBG or BGG) $= \frac{3}{8}$

c Pr(at least 1 boy) $= 1 -$ Pr(no boy)
$= 1 - \frac{1}{8} = \frac{7}{8}$

d Pr(no boy or 1 boy)
$=$ Pr(GGG or GGB or GBG or BGG)
$= \frac{4}{8} = \frac{1}{2}$

4 **a** Pr(queen of diamonds) $= \frac{1}{52}$

b Pr(red) $= \frac{26}{52} = \frac{1}{2}$

c Pr(five) $= \frac{4}{52} = \frac{1}{13}$

d Pr(spade) $= \frac{13}{52} = \frac{1}{4}$

e Pr(not a spade) $= 1 - \frac{13}{52} = \frac{39}{52} = \frac{3}{4}$

f Pr(not a nine) $= 1 - \frac{4}{52} = \frac{48}{52} = \frac{12}{13}$

5 **a** rolling a die and not getting a three
b not selecting a prime from the numbers less than ten

6 **a** total of 22 students
Pr(dog, not cat) $= \frac{4}{22} = \frac{2}{11}$

b Pr(cat and dog) $= \frac{7}{22}$

WORKED SOLUTIONS

CHECK YOUR SOLUTIONS

7

English

		A	B	C	Total
Maths	A	**5**	**1**	3	9
	B	1	2	2	**5**
	C	3	**2**	**1**	**6**
	Total	9	**5**	6	**20**

a Pr(both A) $= \frac{5}{20} = \frac{1}{4}$

b Pr(at least one A) $= \frac{13}{20}$

c Pr(no A) $= \frac{7}{20}$

8

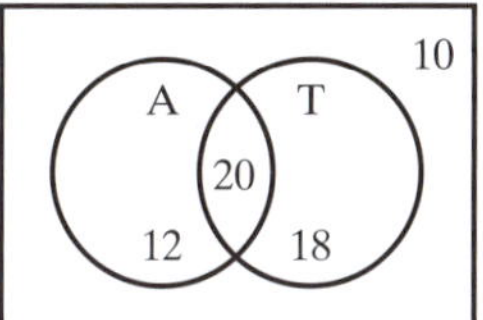

a Pr(liked Avocado but not Tiramisu) $= \frac{12}{60}$

$= \frac{1}{5}$

b Pr(liked neither flavour) $= \frac{10}{60} = \frac{1}{6}$

9

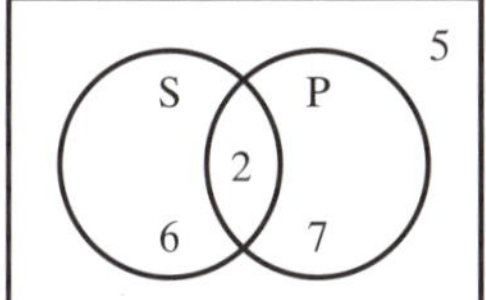

	Surf	**Not surf**
Piano	2	7
Not piano	6	5

PROBABILITY INTERMEDIATE TEST PAGE 81

1 There are three 4s out of six.

$\therefore$ Pr(4) $= \frac{3}{6} = \frac{1}{2}$ $\therefore$ [C] (1 mark)

2 Pr(not rolling a 2) = 1 − Pr(2)

$= 1 - \frac{1}{10}$

$= \frac{9}{10}$ $\therefore$ [D] (1 mark)

3 As $\frac{2}{3}$ of 24 = 16, then there must be 16 yellow marbles in the bag.

$\therefore$ [A] (1 mark)

4 Pr(Tigers win) $= \frac{1}{2}$

This means Pr(other teams win) $= \frac{1}{2}$.

As other teams equally likely and $\frac{1}{2} \div 3 = \frac{1}{6}$,

then Pr(Cats win) $= \frac{1}{6}$.

$\therefore$ [D] (1 mark)

5 Primes: 2, 3, 5 and Evens: 2, 4, 6.
Jess wins and Jay loses: 3, 5

Pr(Jess wins and Jay loses) $= \frac{2}{6} = \frac{1}{3}$

$\therefore$ [B] (1 mark)

6 If Novak is three times more likely, then

Pr(Rafael) $= \frac{1}{4}$ and Pr(Novak) $= \frac{3}{4}$.

$\therefore$ [C] (1 mark)

7 a

	Car	**Bus**	**Walk**	**Train**	**Total**
Boys	8	12	6	10	**36**
Girls	6	14	2	12	**34**
Total	**14**	**26**	**8**	**22**	**70**

✓✓

b i Pr(girl) $= \frac{34}{70} = \frac{17}{35}$ ✓

ii Pr(train traveller) $= \frac{22}{70} = \frac{11}{35}$ ✓

iii Pr(girl on bus) $= \frac{14}{70} = \frac{1}{5}$ ✓

iv Pr(boy walker) $= \frac{6}{70} = \frac{3}{35}$ ✓

v Pr(girl no bus) $= \frac{20}{70} = \frac{2}{7}$ ✓ (7 marks)

8

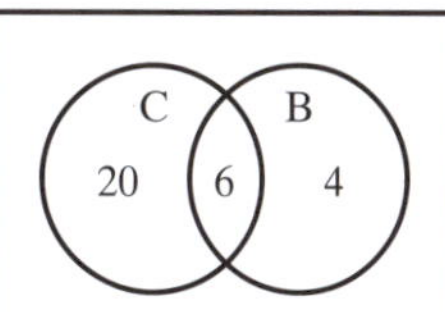

$\frac{4}{30} = \frac{2}{15}$ ✓✓✓

(3 marks)

9 a

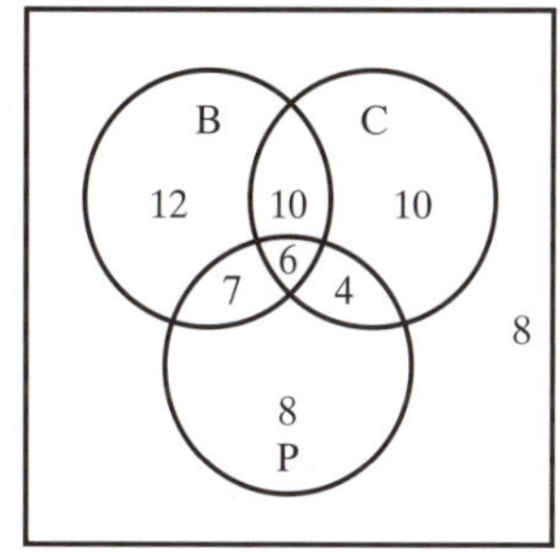

✓✓

b 8 students ✓

c $\frac{10}{65} = \frac{2}{13}$ ✓ (4 marks)

(Total 20 marks)

WORKED SOLUTIONS

CHECK YOUR SOLUTIONS

PROBABILITY
ADVANCED TEST PAGE 82

1 a

	1	**2**	**3**	**4**
1	2	3	4	5
2	4	**4**	**5**	**6**
4	**5**	**6**	**7**	**8**

✓✓

b 5 ✓

c i Pr(odd) $= \frac{6}{12} = \frac{1}{2}$ ✓

ii Pr(< 7) $= \frac{10}{12} = \frac{5}{6}$ ✓

iii Pr(square number) $= \frac{2}{12} = \frac{1}{6}$ ✓

iv Pr(prime) $= \frac{7}{12}$ ✓

v Pr(divisible by 3) $= \frac{4}{12} = \frac{1}{3}$ ✓

vi Pr(multiple of 4) $= \frac{3}{12} = \frac{1}{4}$ ✓

vii Pr(factor of 12) $= \frac{7}{12}$ ✓ (10 marks)

2 a

	1	**2**	**3**	**4**
1	0	1	2	3
2	1	**0**	**1**	**2**
4	**3**	**2**	**1**	**0**

✓✓

b 1 ✓

c i Pr(odd) $= \frac{5}{12}$ ✓

ii Pr(prime) $= \frac{5}{12}$ ✓

iii Pr(not prime) $= 1 - \frac{5}{12} = \frac{7}{12}$ ✓ (6 marks)

3 a i $1 - (\frac{1}{2} + \frac{1}{3}) = \frac{1}{6}$

$\therefore$ Pr(1) $= \frac{1}{6}$ ✓

ii Pr(< 3) = 1 − Pr(3)

$= 1 - \frac{1}{3}$

$= \frac{2}{3}$ ✓

b As Pr(1) $= \frac{1}{6}$, Pr(2) $= \frac{1}{2}$, Pr(3) $= \frac{1}{3}$, the smallest number of balls is 6. ✓

As $\frac{1}{2}$ of 6 is 3, then the smallest number of balls with the digit 2 is 3. ✓ (4 marks)

4 a

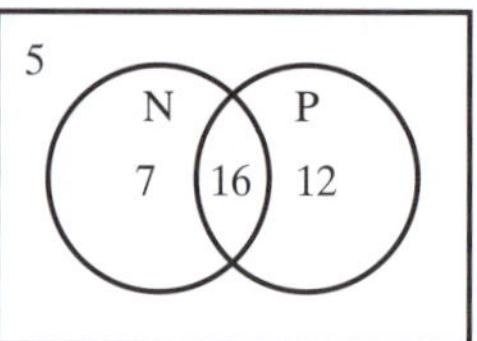

✓

b

	Petrol	**No Petrol**	**Total**
Newspaper	16	7	23
No Newspaper	12	5	17
Total	28	12	40

✓

c i Pr(petrol and newspaper) $= \frac{16}{40} = \frac{2}{5}$ ✓

Pr(newspaper, no petrol) $= \frac{7}{40}$ ✓

d % newspaper $= \frac{23}{40} \times 100\%$

$= 57.5\%$ ✓ (5 marks)

5 a $360 - (90 + 40 + 30 + 60 + 80) = 60$

$\therefore$ '1' has an angle of 60°

$\therefore$ Pr(1) $= \frac{60}{360} = \frac{1}{6}$ ✓

b Pr(even) $= \frac{120}{360} = \frac{1}{3}$ ✓

c Pr(composite) = Pr(4)

$= \frac{90}{360} = \frac{1}{4}$ ✓

d Pr(4 or 5) $= \frac{130}{360} = \frac{13}{36}$ ✓

e Pr(factor of 6) = Pr(1, 2, 3)

$= \frac{150}{360} = \frac{5}{12}$ ✓

f Pr(not 7) = 1 − Pr(7)

$= 1 - \frac{80}{360}$

$= \frac{280}{360}$

$= \frac{7}{9}$ ✓

g Pr(not prime) = 1 − Pr(prime)

= 1 − Pr(2, 3, 5, 7)

$= 1 - \frac{210}{360}$

$= \frac{150}{360} = \frac{5}{12}$ ✓

h Pr(more than 3) = Pr(4, 5, 7)

$= \frac{210}{360} = \frac{7}{12}$ ✓ (8 marks)

6 a Let there be 1 green ball. This means 3 pink balls, 2 red balls and 6 orange balls.

This means in a bag of 12 balls, there are 6 orange, 3 pink, 2 red and 1 green.

$\therefore \text{Pr(orange)} = \frac{6}{12} = \frac{1}{2}$

$\text{Pr(pink)} = \frac{3}{12} = \frac{1}{4}$

$\text{Pr(red)} = \frac{2}{12} = \frac{1}{6}$

$\text{Pr(green)} = \frac{1}{12}$ ✓✓

b The smallest possible number is 12. ✓

c As $\frac{1}{6} \times 60 = 10$, then there will be 10 red balls in the bag. ✓

d From part **a** there are now 3 pink balls, 1 green ball and 6 orange balls.

$\therefore \text{Pr(orange or green)} = \frac{7}{10}$ ✓ (5 marks)

7 Consider the chance of each athlete like tickets in a raffle. Suppose Dee has 1 ticket; then Bree will have 3 tickets and Lee will have 6 tickets. There are no other tickets, so there is a total of 10 tickets in the raffle. The probability of each person winning the raffle is the same as the probability of winning the race.

$\text{Pr(Dee)} = \frac{1}{10}, \text{Pr(Bree)} = \frac{3}{10},$

$\text{Pr(Lee)} = \frac{6}{10} = \frac{3}{5}$ ✓✓ (2 marks)

(Total 40 marks)

INTERPRETING DATA
SKILLS CHECK PAGE 85

1 **a**

0	4
1	2 5 6 7 9 9 9
2	2 2 3 5 6 6 7 8 9
3	0 1 2 3

b median = 23, mode = 19, range = 33 − 8 = 25

c 4

2 **a** mean = (21 + 19 + 17 + 1 + 27) ÷ 5 = 17

median: 1, 17, 19, 21, 27

∴ median is 19

b The outlier is 1.

mean = (21 + 19 + 17 + 27) ÷ 4 = 21

median: 17, 19, 21, 27

∴ median is 20

The mean increases by 4 and the median by 1.

3 **a**

Score (x)	Frequency (f)	$f \times x$
5	1	5
6	2	12
7	2	14
8	6	48
9	4	36
10	2	20
11	1	11
Total	18	146

b median = 8, mode = 8, range = 6

$\text{mean} = \frac{146}{18} = 8.11$ (2 dec. pl.)

c

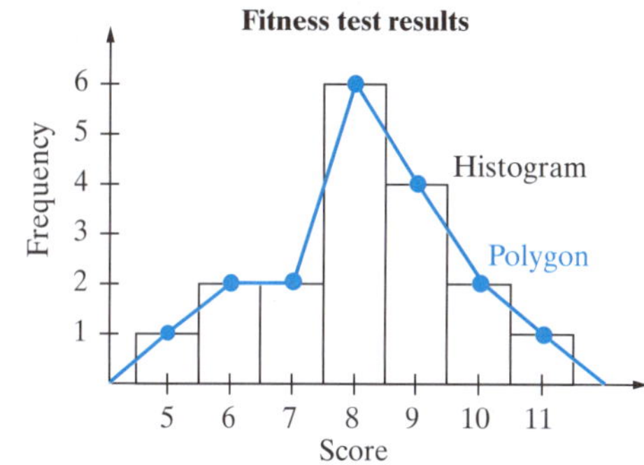

4 **a**

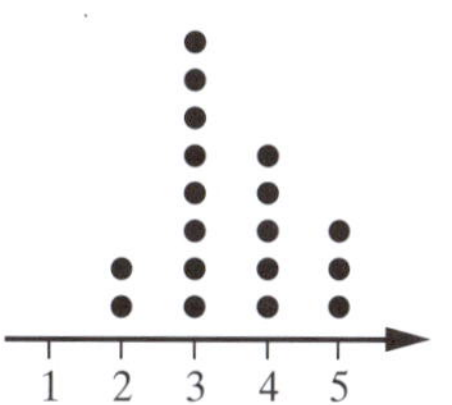

b median = 3, mode = 3, range = 3

5 Originally: mean = 2, mode = 2, median: 0, 1, 2, 2, 3, 4 ∴ median = 2, range = 4

New scores: 0, 4, 2, 1, 3, 2, 2 ∴ mean = 2, mode = 2, median: 0, 1, 2, 2, 2, 3, 4 ∴ median = 2, range = 4

∴ no measure changes

6 **a** categorical **b** mode is pies

c No. Canteen food consumed by adults as well—not just young people.

7

Class	Class centre	Frequency
132–138	135	2
139–145	142	1
146–152	149	5
153–159	156	4
160–166	163	4

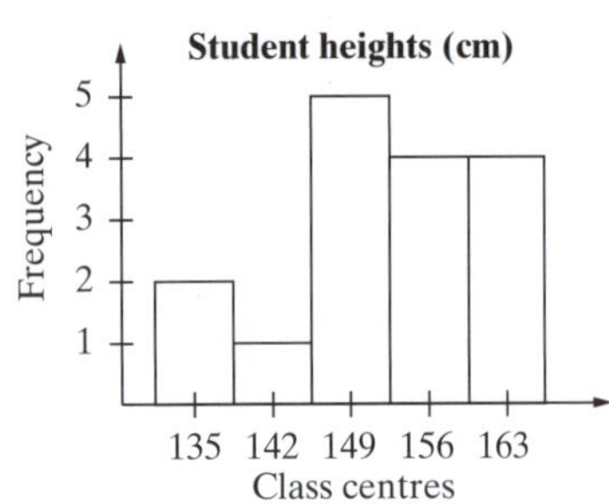

8 a i mean = 70.4 [using STAT mode on calculator]
ii median = 8th score
$\therefore$ median = 72
iii mode = 78
iv range = 89 − 50
$\therefore$ range = 39

b Mean is 70.4, so 7 scores are less than the mean. There are 15 scores in total, so

$\frac{7}{15} \times \frac{100}{1}\% = 46.\dot{6}\% \quad \therefore 46.7\%$

INTERPRETING DATA
INTERMEDIATE TEST PAGE 86

1 Mean age of 4 boys = 8
Total age of 4 boys = 32
Mean age of 2 girls = 14
Total age of 2 girls = 28
Total age of 6 children = 32 + 28
= 60
Mean age of 6 children = 10
$\therefore$ [A] (1 mark)

2 Range = 8 − 5 = 3
Mode = 8
$\therefore$ [D] (1 mark)

3 The survey captures categorical data. The only measure possible is the mode.
$\therefore$ [A] (1 mark)

4 Total of frequencies is 20
Relative frequency = $\frac{3}{20}$ = 0.15
$\therefore$ [C] (1 mark)

5 No. of families with 2 or more children
= 6 + 4 + 2 + 1
= 13
Percentage = $\frac{13}{20} \times 100\%$
= 65%
$\therefore$ [C] (1 mark)

6 Complete a table to help answer questions:

Score (x)	Frequency (f)	$f \times x$
0	2	0
1	5	5
2	6	12
3	4	12
4	2	8
5	1	5
	20	42

a 42 ✓✓
b i Range = 5 − 0
= 5 ✓
ii Mode = 2 ✓
iii Median: 0, 0, 1, 1, 1, 1, 1, 2, 2, 2, …
Of the 20 scores, the middle of the 10th and 11th scores is 2.
$\therefore$ the median is 2. ✓
c Mean = $\frac{42}{20}$
= 2.1 ✓✓ (7 marks)

7 Mean of 5 scores = $\frac{4 + 2 + 8 + 0 + 6}{5}$
= 4 ✓
Mean of 6 scores = 6 ✓
New score = new total − old total
= 36 − 20
= 16
$\therefore$ the new score is 16. ✓ (3 marks)

8 Mode = 8 (and still will be after another mark).
As 14 − 8 = 6, then the new mark is 6.
(N.B. 8 + 8 = 16 which is an impossible test result.)
$\therefore$ the new mark is 6. (2 marks)

9 a Range is 8:
$x = 12 - 8 = 4$, or $x = 5 + 8 = 13$
$\therefore x = 4$ or 13 ✓✓
b If mean of 6 scores is 8, then the total is 48.
But, 12 + 9 + 6 + 11 + 5 = 43, so the missing score is 5.
$\therefore x = 5$ ✓✓
c 5, 6, 9, 11, 12
If median is 8 then the scores are 5, 6, 7, 9, 11, 12
$\therefore x = 7$ ✓ (5 marks)

10 Range = 92 − 37
= 55 ✓
If median = 55, then $y = 60$, as the scores are 37, 48, 50, 60 81, 92.
$\therefore y = 60$ ✓ (2 marks)
(Total 24 marks)

WORKED SOLUTIONS

INTERPRETING DATA
ADVANCED TEST PAGE 87

1 a $69 - 37 = 32 \quad \therefore a = 2$ ✓

b 16 scores.

Median of 50.5 is middle of '$4b$' and 52.

$\therefore$ lower number is 49

$\therefore b = 9$ ✓ (2 marks)

2 a Total students

$= 3 + 5 + 5 + 5 + 6 + 3$

$= 27$ ✓

b Total girls

$= 2 + 3 + 2 + 3 + 2 + 1$

$= 13$ ✓

c 3 girls have 3 mobiles in their homes ✓

d Total mobiles

$= 3 \times 0 + 5 \times 1 + 5 \times 2 + 5 \times 3 + 6 \times 4 + 3 \times 5$ ✓

$= 0 + 5 + 10 + 15 + 24 + 15$

$= 69$ ✓

e i

x	f	fx
0	3	0
1	5	5
2	5	10
3	5	15
4	6	24
5	3	15
Total	**27**	**69**

mode 4, median 3,

mean $= \frac{69}{27} = 2\frac{5}{9}$ ✓✓✓

ii

x	f	fx
0	2	0
1	3	3
2	2	4
3	3	9
4	2	8
5	1	5
Total	**13**	**29**

mode 3, median 2,

mean $= \frac{29}{13} = 2\frac{3}{13}$ ✓✓✓

(11 marks)

3 Females:

x	f	fx
0	2	0
1	4	4
2	5	10
3	3	9
4	1	4
Total	**15**	**27**

Males:

x	f	fx
0	3	0
1	5	5
2	6	12
3	5	15
4	4	16
Total	**23**	**48**

The mean for the males at 2.1 is higher than the mean for the females at 1.8. ✓✓

The mode for males and females is the same at 2. ✓✓

The median for males and females is the same at 2. ✓✓

(6 marks)

4 Boys:

x	f	fx
7	3	21
8	4	32
9	2	18
Total	**9**	**71**

Girls:

x	f	fx
7	1	7
8	4	32
9	4	36
Total	**9**	**75**

The mean for the girls at 8.3 is higher than the mean for the boys at 7.9. ✓✓

The mode for the boys is 8 and the girls are bi-modal at 8 and 9. ✓✓

The median for girls and boys is the same at 8. ✓✓ (6 marks)

5

4
L T
10 12 14

✓

		Tablet		
		Yes	No	Total
L/Top	Yes	**12**	**10**	**22**
	No	**14**	**4**	**18**
	Total	26	**14**	40

✓

(2 marks)

6

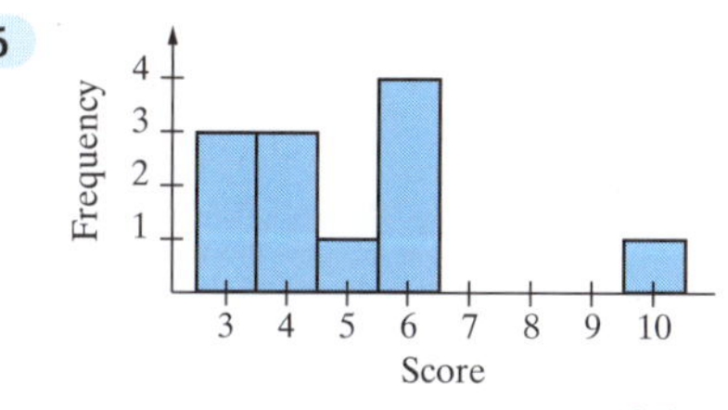

✓✓

(2 marks)

7 Average for 4 games = 3

Sum for 4 games = 12

Average for 5 games = 4

Sum for 5 games = 20 ✓

$\therefore$ the team scored 8 goals

$\therefore$ the score was 8 – 3 ✓

(2 marks)

8 1, 3, 4

$\therefore$ the missing scores are 1 and 3 ✓ (1 mark)

(Total 32 marks)

WORKED SOLUTIONS

CHECK YOUR SOLUTIONS

SAMPLE EXAM PAPER 1
Part A: Multiple Choice PAGE 89

1 $\frac{7}{8} \times 100 = 87.5\%$
$\therefore$ [D] (1 mark)

2 $\frac{1}{3} = 33\frac{1}{3}\%, \frac{1}{2} = 50\%$
$\therefore$ 40% is between $\frac{1}{3}$ and $\frac{1}{2}$.
$\therefore$ [C] (1 mark)

3 6 possible outcomes:
1, 2, 3, 4, 5, 6
$\therefore \text{Pr}(2) = \frac{1}{6}$
$\therefore$ [B] (1 mark)

4 Factors of $6x^2$: $1, 2, 3, 6, x, 2x, 3x, 6x, x^2, 2x^2, 3x^2, 6x^2$
$\therefore$ 4 is not a factor
$\therefore$ [D] (1 mark)

5 Solve the equation (or substitute in each alternative).
$$3x - 2 = x + 6$$
$$3x - x = 6 + 2$$
$$\frac{2x}{2} = \frac{8}{2}$$
$$x = 4$$
$\therefore$ [D] (1 mark)

6 $2a - b = 2 \times 3 - 4$
$= 6 - 4$
$= 2$
$\therefore$ [B] (1 mark)

7 Each alternative has $x = 1$:
$\therefore$ Substitute $x = 1$ in
$y = 2x + 1$
$= 2(1) + 1$
$= 2 + 1$
$= 3 \quad \therefore (1, 3)$
$\therefore$ [C] (1 mark)

8 There are 2 Bs in the 11 letters of the word PROBABILITY
Now try each of the alternatives.
As $\text{Pr(letter I)} = \frac{2}{11}$
$= \text{Pr(letter B)}$
$\therefore$ [D] (1 mark)

9 20% of number = 40
100% of number = 40×5
$= 200$
$\therefore$ [D] (1 mark)

10 Try each of the alternatives.
Range = $10 - 6 = 4$
$\therefore$ range is not 8
$\therefore$ [D] (1 mark)

(Total Part A 10 marks)

SAMPLE EXAM PAPER 1
Part B: Short Answer PAGE 90

11 $140\% = \frac{140}{100}$
$= 1\frac{40}{100}$
$= 1\frac{2}{5}$ (1 mark)

12 $8\frac{1}{2}\% = 0.085$ (1 mark)

13 $0.35 \times 3000 = 1050$
$\therefore$ \$1050 (1 mark)

14 As 8 L = 8000 mL,
$0.05 \times 8000 = 400$
$\therefore$ 400 mL (1 mark)

15 $12 : 16 = 3 : 4$ (1 mark)

16 50c : \$2 = 50 : 200
$= 1 : 4$ (1 mark)

17 Time = distance ÷ speed
$= 480 \div 80$
$= 6$
$\therefore$ 6 hours (1 mark)

18 $3(2x + 1) = 6x + 3$ (1 mark)

19 $12x^2 \times 3xy = 36x^3y$ (1 mark)

20 $\frac{\overset{1}{\cancel{3}}\overset{1}{\cancel{a}}b}{\underset{4}{\cancel{12}}\underset{1}{\cancel{a}}} = \frac{b}{4}$ (1 mark)

21 $2y - 3 = 2 \times 4 - 3$
$= 8 - 3$
$= 5$ (1 mark)

22 $2p + q = 2 \times 6 + 3$
$= 12 + 3$
$= 15$ (1 mark)

23 $3ab - 6a = 3a(b - 2)$ (1 mark)

24 2150 = 9:50 pm (1 mark)

25 $2a - 1 = 9$
$2a = 9 + 1$
$\frac{2a}{2} = \frac{10}{2}$
$a = 5$ (1 mark)

26 $-4(2 - 3y) = -8 + 12y$ (1 mark)

27 $a \times a \times a \times a \times a \times b \times b \times b \times b = a^5b^4$ (1 mark)

28 Crosses y-axis when $x = 0$
As $y = 3x - 2$
$y = 3 \times 0 - 2 = -2$
i.e. $(0, -2)$ (1 mark)

29 Substitute $(3, 1)$ into $y = 2x - 5$
$\therefore 1 = 2 \times 3 - 5$
$= 6 - 5$
$= 1$
Yes! $\therefore (3, 1)$ on the line (1 mark)

30 Range = highest score − lowest score
$= 30 - (-1)$
$= 31$ (1 mark)

31 $4.2^2 + 2.3^2 = 22.93$ (1 mark)

32 $\sqrt{3.74} = 1.933\,907\,961$
$= 1.93$ [2 decimal places]
(1 mark)

33 $3^0 + (2 \times y)^0 = 1 + 1$
$= 2$ (1 mark)

34 $C = 2\pi r$
$= 2 \times \pi \times 9$
$= 56.548\,667\,76$
$= 56.55$ [2 decimal places]
$\therefore$ circumference is 56.55 cm
(1 mark)

35 $A = \pi r^2$
$= \pi \times 6^2$
$= 36\pi$
$\therefore$ area is 36π cm^2 (1 mark)

36 $x = 360 - (100 + 110 + 120)$
$= 360 - 330$
$= 30$ (1 mark)

37 $2x + x = 180$
$3x = 180$
$\frac{3x}{3} = \frac{180}{3}$
$x = 60$ (1 mark)

38 The line is $x = 3$. (1 mark)

39 Triangle ACB: $A = 70°$, $C = 60°$, $B = 50°$, CB = 5 cm. Triangle NLM: $L = 60°$, $N = 70°$, $M = 50°$, LM = 5 cm.
$\therefore \triangle ACB \equiv \triangle NLM$ (1 mark)

40 Matching sides equal (SSS)
(1 mark)

(Total Part B 30 marks)

WORKED SOLUTIONS

SAMPLE EXAM PAPER 1
Part C PAGE 92

41 12.5% of $640 = 0.125 \times 640$ ✓
$= 80$
$\therefore$ \$80 ✓ (2 marks)

42 Profit $= \$60 - \$45$
$= \$15$ ✓
% profit $= \frac{15}{45} \times 100\%$
$= 33\frac{1}{3}\%$
$\therefore$ percentage profit is
$33\frac{1}{3}\%$ ✓ (2 marks)

43 Discounted amount $= 85\%$
$\therefore$ New price $= 0.85 \times 18\,990$ ✓
$= 16\,141.50$
$\therefore$ price is \$16 141.50 ✓
(2 marks)

44 Area $= 64$ cm^2
Length of each side $= 8$ cm ✓
Perimeter $= 4 \times 8$
$= 32$
$\therefore$ perimeter is 32 cm ✓
(2 marks)

45 25% of price $= 120$
100% of price $= 120 \times 4$ ✓
$= 480$
$\therefore$ whole price is \$480 ✓
(2 marks)

46 8 parts $= 56$ ✓
As $\frac{3}{8} \times 56 = 21$
and $\frac{5}{8} \times 56 = 35$
$\therefore$ \$21, \$35 ✓ (2 marks)

47 Speed $= \frac{510}{6}$ ✓
$= 85$
$\therefore$ speed is 85 km/h ✓ (2 marks)

48 Average yield $= \frac{80 \times 120}{2400}$ ✓
$= 4$
$\therefore$ 4 kg of wool per sheep ✓
(2 marks)

49 Bag: 2B, 5W, 3G
a Pr(white) $= \frac{5}{10}$
$= \frac{1}{2}$ ✓
b Pr(not black)
$= 1 - $ Pr(black)
$= 1 - \frac{2}{10}$
$= \frac{8}{10}$
$= \frac{4}{5}$ ✓ (2 marks)

50 $3(a + 2) + 4(2a + 6)$
$= 3a + 6 + 8a + 24$ ✓
$= 11a + 30$ ✓ (2 marks)

51 $3a - 2 = 2a + 5$
$3a - 2a = 5 + 2$ ✓
$a = 7$ ✓ (2 marks)

52 $2(3x - 1) = 5x + 8$
$6x - 2 = 5x + 8$ ✓
$6x - 5x = 8 + 2$
$x = 10$ ✓ (2 marks)

53 Area $= 600 \times 400$
$= 240\,000$
$\therefore$ area is $240\,000$ m^2 ✓
Now, $10\,000$ m^2 $= 1$ ha, and
$240\,000 \div 10\,000 = 24$
$\therefore$ area is 24 ha ✓ (2 marks)

54

x	0	1	2	3
y	4	7	10	13

a $y = 3x + 4$ ✓
b $y = 3 \times 5 + 4$
$= 19$ ✓ (2 marks)

55 $A = xy$
$= 12.8 \times 0.04$ ✓
$= 0.512$ ✓ (2 marks)

56 **a** $P = 2 \times (5 + 3x + 4)$
$= 2(3x + 9)$
i.e. perimeter is
$2(3x + 9)$ cm ✓
b $2(3x + 9) = 48$
$6x + 18 = 48$
$6x = 48 - 18$
$\frac{6x}{6} = \frac{30}{6}$
$x = 5$ ✓ (2 marks)

57 $x + 3x + 20 = 180$ ✓
$4x + 20 = 180$
$4x = 180 - 20$
$\frac{4x}{4} = \frac{160}{4}$
$x = 40$ ✓ (2 marks)

58

x	0	1	2
y	**−1**	**1**	**3**

✓

$y = 2x - 1$

✓
(2 marks)

59

d	0	5	10	20	40
C	**50**	**70**	**90**	**130**	**210**

✓

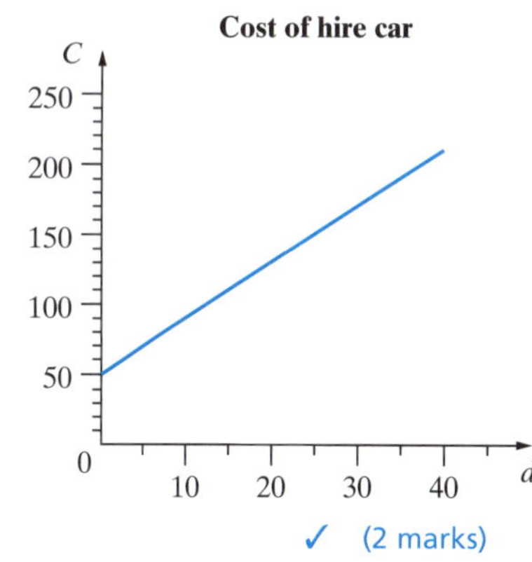

✓ (2 marks)

60

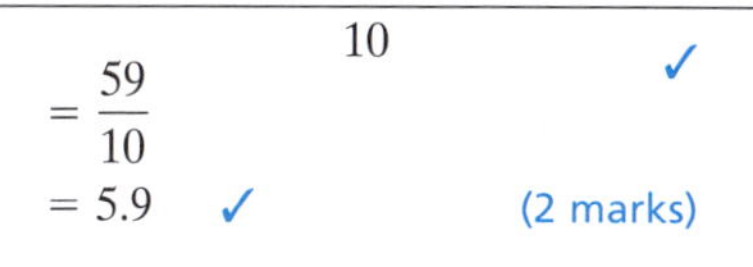

✓✓ (2 marks)

61 3, 5, 2, −1, 6, 8, 9, 2
a mode: 2 ✓
b median:
−1, 2, 2, 3, 5, 6, 8, 9
$\therefore$ middle of 3 and 5
$\therefore$ median $= 4$ ✓ (2 marks)

62 Mean $=$
$\frac{5 + 2 + 3 + 10 + 6 + 8 + 2 + 4 + 8 + 11}{10}$ ✓
$= \frac{59}{10}$
$= 5.9$ ✓ (2 marks)

WORKED SOLUTIONS

63

Stem	Leaf
2	3 7
3	2 8 9
4	2 2 4 5 7
5	3 8
6	x

Median = 42 ✓

As range = highest score − lowest score

42 = highest score − 23

highest score = 42 + 23

= 65

$\therefore x = 5$ ✓ (2 marks)

64 **a**

Score (x)	Frequency (f)	fx
6	2	12
7	4	28
8	7	56
9	6	**54**
10	3	**30**
Total	**22**	**180**

b Mean $= \frac{180}{22}$ ✓

$= 8\frac{2}{11}$ ✓ (2 marks)

65 $x^2 = 8^2 + 15^2$

$= 64 + 225$

$= 289$ ✓

$x = \sqrt{289}$

$= 17$ ✓ (2 marks)

66

10 cm, 8 cm, 16 cm

Area $= \frac{1}{2} \times 8(10 + 16)$ ✓

$= 104$

$\therefore$ area is 104 cm^2 ✓ (2 marks)

67 Loss = 360 − 240

= 120 ✓

% loss $= \frac{120}{360} \times 100\%$

$= 33\frac{1}{3}\%$

$\therefore$ a loss of $33\frac{1}{3}\%$ ✓ (2 marks)

68 $V = \pi r^2 h$

$= \pi \times 8^2 \times 20$ ✓

$= 4021.238\,597$

$= 4021.24$ [2 decimal places]

$\therefore$ volume is 4021.24 cm^3 ✓

(2 marks)

69 $x = 180 - (60 + 53)$ [∠ sum of △]

$= 180 - 113$

$= 67$ ✓

$y = 67$ [alternate ∠s, ∥ lines] ✓

(2 marks)

70 $3 - (2 - x) - 4(x + 1)$

$= 3 - 2 + x - 4x - 4$ ✓

$= -3 - 3x$ ✓ (2 marks)

(Total Part C 60 marks)

SAMPLE EXAM PAPER 2
Part A: Multiple Choice PAGE 95

1 18% of 600 = 0.18 × 600

= 108

$\therefore$ $108

$\therefore$ [D] (1 mark)

2 Change both to cents:

$\therefore \frac{50}{400} \times 100\% = 12.5\%$

$\therefore$ [C] (1 mark)

3 Side = 8 mm

= 0.8 cm

Area = 0.8 × 0.8

= 0.64

$\therefore$ the area is 0.64 cm^2

$\therefore$ [D] (1 mark)

4 Convert each to weekly pay:

$845/wk

$1695 ÷ 2 = $847.50/wk

$3655 × 12 ÷ 52 = $843.46/wk

$43 946 ÷ 52 = $845.12/wk

$\therefore$ best pay rate is $1695/fortnight

$\therefore$ [B] (1 mark)

5 $3(x + 4) = 18$

$3x + 12 = 18$

$3x = 18 - 12$

$\frac{3x}{3} = \frac{6}{3}$

$x = 2$

$\therefore$ mistake in Line 2

$\therefore$ [B] (1 mark)

6 For two-and-a-quarter hours use 0215:

Time = 1340 − 0215

= 1125

$\therefore$ he left home at 11:25 am

$\therefore$ [B] (1 mark)

7 $xy - z = -4 \times 2 - 3$

$= -8 - 3$

$= -11$ $\therefore$ [B] (1 mark)

8 Correct point will have an x-value of −2 and y-value of 3

i.e. (−2, 3) $\therefore$ [A] (1 mark)

9 Arranging in order:

16, 24, 26, x, 38, 40

[x must be more than 26 and less than 38 to give a median of 29]

$\therefore$ median = middle of 26 and x

i.e. 29 = middle of 26 and x

$\therefore x = 32$

$\therefore$ [D] (1 mark)

10 Pythagoras' theorem must hold.

Try each of the alternatives.

$7^2 + 24^2 = 25^2$?

49 + 576 = 625?

625 = 625 Yes!

$\therefore$ must be right-angled triangle

$\therefore$ [B] (1 mark)

(Total Part A 10 marks)

SAMPLE EXAM PAPER 2
Part B: Short Answer PAGE 96

11 $3\frac{1}{2}\%$ of 940 = 0.035 × 940

= 32.9

$\therefore$ $32.90 (1 mark)

12 Hours awake = 24 − 9

= 15

% hours awake $= \frac{15}{24} \times 100$

$= 62.5\%$

$\therefore$ Dominic was awake 62.5%

(1 mark)

13 New amount $= 112\frac{3}{4}\%$ of 110

= 1.1275 × 110

= 124.025

= 124.03 [2 decimal places]

$\therefore$ $124.03 (1 mark)

14 New price = 85% of 48
$= 0.85 \times 48$
$= 40.8$
$\therefore$ \$40.80 (1 mark)

15 Cost of 7 = $10.20 \div 12 \times 7$
$= 5.95$
$\therefore$ \$5.95 (1 mark)

16 \$3.75 : \$4 = 375 : 400
= 15 : 16 (1 mark)

17 $\frac{3}{4}:\frac{2}{3} = \frac{9}{12}:\frac{8}{12}$
= 9 : 8 (1 mark)

18 As 6 h 20 min = $6\frac{1}{3}$h,
speed = $475 \div 6\frac{1}{3}$
$= 75$
i.e. 75 km/h (1 mark)

19 99 tickets remain after the first ticket is drawn
$\therefore$ Pr(John's ticket) = $\frac{1}{99}$
(1 mark)

20 7 odd numbers out of 12
$\therefore$ Pr(odd number) = $\frac{7}{12}$
(1 mark)

21 $3(2a - 1) - 2(a + 6)$
$= 6a - 3 - 2a - 12$
$= 4a - 15$ (1 mark)

22 $\pi r^2 - 2\pi r = \pi r(r - 2)$ (1 mark)

23 $12 \div 80 \div 24 \times 100 = 0.625$
$\therefore$ 0.625 cm/h (1 mark)

24 $3x - 2 = x + 6$
$3x - x = 6 + 2$
$2x = 8$
$x = 4$ (1 mark)

25 $4(g + 1) = 16$
$4g + 4 = 16$
$4g = 16 - 4$
$4g = 12$
$\frac{4g}{4} = \frac{12}{4}$
$g = 3$ (1 mark)

26 $3pq - p^2 - qp + 2p^2$
$= 2pq + p^2$ (1 mark)

27 $(2x)^2 - 2x^2 = (2 \times 5)^2 - 2 \times 5^2$
$= 10^2 - 50$
$= 100 - 50$
$= 50$ (1 mark)

28 $p^2 - q^2 = (-2)^2 - (-3)^2$
$= 4 - 9$
$= -5$ (1 mark)

29 If $x = -2$, subs. into $y = x + 4$
$y = -2 + 4$
$= 2$
$\therefore (-2, 2)$

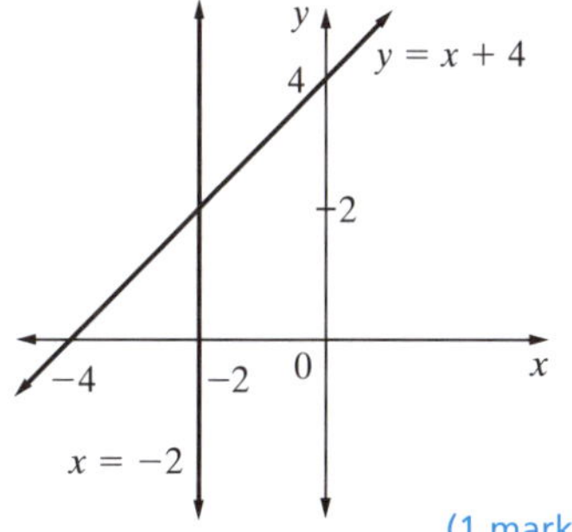

(1 mark)

30 Sum of goals in 6 games = 18
Sum of goals in 7 games = 28
Goals scored in 7th game = 10
$\therefore$ 10 goals scored in 7th game
(1 mark)

31 Mode = 10
As 14 − 10 = 4, or
8 + 10 = 18
$\therefore$ score could be 4 or 18
(1 mark)

32 Mean = $\frac{2x + 5x + 2x + 3x}{4}$
$= \frac{12x}{4}$
$= 3x$
$\therefore$ mean is $3x$ (1 mark)

33 $AB^2 = 61^2 - 60^2$
$= 3721 - 3600$
$= 121$
$AB = \sqrt{121}$
$= 11$
$\therefore AB$ is 11 units (1 mark)

34 Area = $20 \times 12 - 14 \times 6$
$= 240 - 84$
$= 156$
$\therefore$ area is 156 cm^2

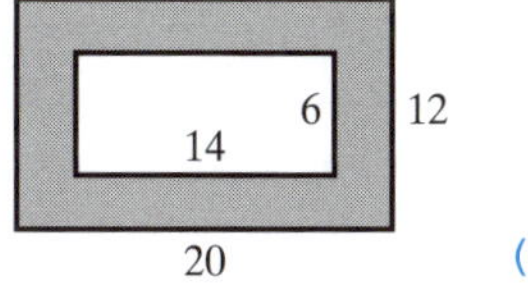

(1 mark)

35 Volume = $4 \times 4 \times 4$
$= 64$
$\therefore$ volume is 64 cm^3

Mass = 64×50
$= 3200$
The mass is 3200 g, or 3.2 kg.
(1 mark)

36 $C = 2 \times \pi \times 8.2$
$= 51.522\,119\,52$
$= 51.52$ [2 decimal places]
$\therefore$ circumference is 51.52 cm
(1 mark)

37 $A = \pi r^2$
$36\pi = \pi r^2$
$r^2 = 36$
$r = 6$ [note $r \neq -6$, as r is radius]
$\therefore$ radius is 6 cm (1 mark)

38

72°
120° **60°** **72°**
110° x°

$x = 360 - (60 + 110 + 72)$
$= 360 - 242$
$= 118$ (1 mark)

39 Area = $\frac{1}{2} \times 28 \times 18$
$= 252$
$\therefore$ area is 252 cm^2 (1 mark)

40 $CD = BD$ [matching sides of congruent triangles equal]
(1 mark)

(Total Part B 30 marks)

SAMPLE EXAM PAPER 2
Part C PAGE 99

41 $\frac{\sqrt{3.6 \times 2.05}}{1.4 - 0.07}$
$= 2.042\,568\,76\ldots$ ✓
$= 2.04$ (2 dec. pl.) ✓ (2 marks)

42 $5 + 3 + 2 = 10$ parts
$\therefore$ smallest $\angle = \frac{2}{10} \times 180$ ✓
$= 36$
$\therefore$ smallest angle is 36° ✓
(2 marks)

43 4 parts = 8
1 part = 2
5 parts = 10 ✓
$\therefore$ 10 boys
$\therefore$ 2 more boys than girls ✓
(2 marks)

44 Time = distance ÷ speed
$= 660 \div 75 = 8.8$
$= 8$ h 48 min ✓
[using 2ndF DMS]
∴ Arrival
= 4:20 am plus 8 h 48 min
= 1:08 pm
∴ Dean arrives at 1:08 pm ✓
(2 marks)

45 1, 2, 3, 4, 5, 6, 7, 8, 9

a $\Pr(\text{even}) = \frac{4}{9}$ ✓

b As 3, 6, 9 are divisible by 3,
Pr(not divisible by 3)
$= 1 - \Pr(\text{divisible by 3})$
$= 1 - \frac{3}{9}$
$= \frac{6}{9}$
$= \frac{2}{3}$ ✓ (2 marks)

46 $T = b^2 - ac$
$= (-2)^2 - (-1)(3)$ ✓
$= 4 + 3$
$= 7$ ✓ (2 marks)

47 $1.05x = 84$ ✓
$x = \frac{84}{1.05} = 80$
∴ height was 80 cm ✓(2 marks)

48 $3(2x - 1) = 2(2x + 8)$
$6x - 3 = 4x + 16$
$6x - 4x = 16 + 3$ ✓
$2x = 19$
$\frac{2x}{2} = \frac{19}{2}$
$x = 9.5$ ✓ (2 marks)

49 $A = \frac{1}{2}h(a + b)$
$75 = \frac{1}{2} \times 10 \times (6 + b)$
$75 = 5(6 + b)$
$75 = 30 + 5b$ ✓
$5b = 75 - 30$
$5b = 45$
$\frac{5b}{5} = \frac{45}{5}$
$b = 9$ ✓ (2 marks)

50 $4a + 65 = 3a + 90$ ✓
[exterior ∠ of △ equals sum of 2 opposite interior ∠s]
$4a - 3a = 90 - 65$
$a = 25$ ✓ (2 marks)

51 Let the numbers be $x, x + 2, x + 4$
$\therefore x + x + 2 + x + 4 = 9$ ✓
$3x + 6 = 9$
$3x = 9 - 6$
$3x = 3$
$\frac{3x}{3} = \frac{3}{3}$
$x = 1$
∴ the numbers are 1, 3, 5 ✓
(2 marks)

52 a

n	2	3	5	7	10
C	11	15	23	31	43

$\therefore C = 4n + 3$ ✓

b $4n + 3 = 195$
$4n = 195 - 3$
$4n = 192$
$\frac{4n}{4} = \frac{192}{4}$
$n = 48$ ✓ (2 marks)

53

x	0	1	2
y	3	1	−1

✓

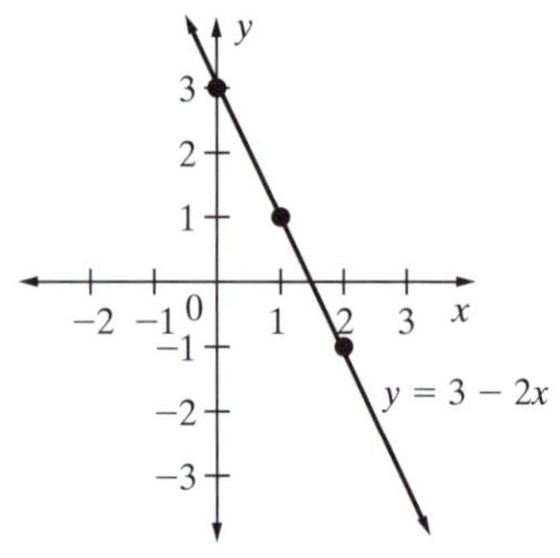

✓ (2 marks)

54

Score (x)	Frequency (f)	fx
16	4	**64**
17	**7**	119
18	10	180
19	**8**	**152**
20	6	**120**
Total	35	635

$\therefore a = 8$ ✓ $b = 152$ ✓
(2 marks)

55 a Students
$= 1 + 4 + 5 + 4 + 1$
$= 15$ ✓

b $7 \times 1 + 8 \times 4 + 9 \times 5 + 10 \times 4 + 11 \times 1$
$= 7 + 32 + 45 + 40 + 11$
$= 135$
$\therefore \text{Mean} = \frac{135}{15}$
$= 9$ ✓ (2 marks)

56 a Mode = 12 ✓

b Median: 25 scores
$\therefore \left(\frac{25 + 1}{2}\right)$th score
i.e. 13th score
i.e. 12
∴ median is 12 ✓ (2 marks)

57 a Median = 28 ✓

b Mean
$= 463 \div 19$
$= 24.368\,421\,05$
$= 24.37$ [2 decimal places] ✓
(2 marks)

58 a Range = 4

Score (x)	Frequency (f)
4	a
8	10

If median = 4, the value of a must be larger than 10
$\therefore a = 11, 12, 13$, etc. ✓

b Mode = 4 ✓ (2 marks)

59

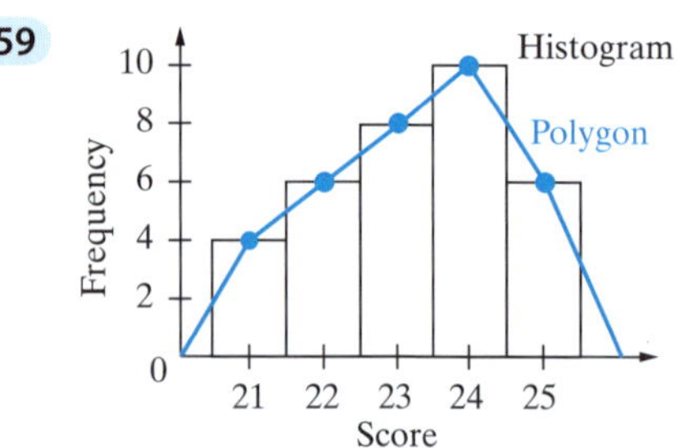

✓✓ (2 marks)

60 $x^2 = 4.1^2 - 3.2^2$
$= 16.81 - 10.24 = 6.57$ ✓
$x = \sqrt{6.57}$
$= 2.563\,201\,124$
$= 2.56$ [2 decimal places] ✓
(2 marks)

61 $x^2 = 3^2 + 4^2$
$= 9 + 16$
$= 25$
$x = \sqrt{25}$
$= 5$

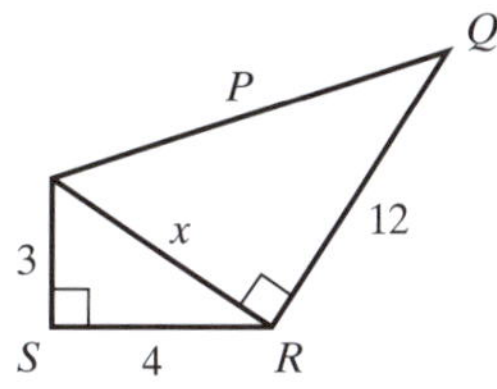

Now, $PQ^2 = 5^2 + 12^2$ ✓
$= 25 + 144$
$= 169$
$PQ = \sqrt{169}$
$= 13$
∴ PQ is 13 mm ✓ (2 marks)

62 $x^2 = 17^2 - 15^2$
$= 289 - 225$
$= 64$
$x = \sqrt{64}$
$= 8$ ✓

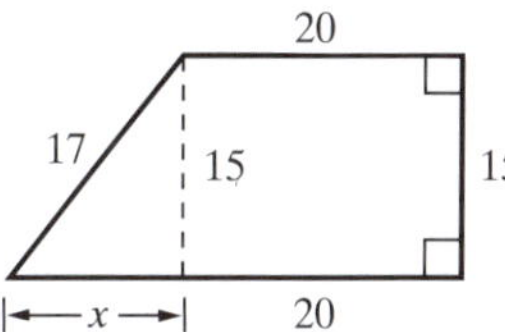

∴ $P = 20 + 15 + 28 + 17$
$= 80$
∴ perimeter is 80 cm ✓ (2 marks)

63 $PS^2 = 5^2 - 4^2$
$= 25 - 16$
$= 9$
$PS = \sqrt{9}$
$= 3$ ✓

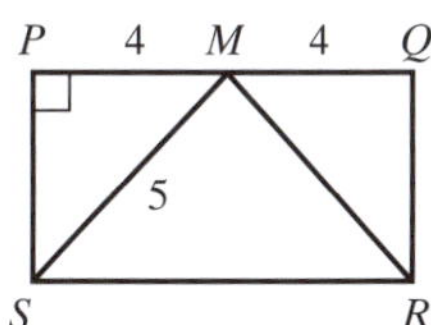

∴ perimeter $= 3 + 4 + 5$
$= 12$
∴ perimeter is 12 cm ✓ (2 marks)

64 GST $= 167.20 \div 11$
$= 15.2$
GST of \$15.20 ✓
Cost without GST
$= 167.20 - 15.20$
$= 152$
∴ the cost would be \$152 ✓ (2 marks)

65 $P = \frac{1}{2} \times 2 \times \pi \times 8 + 16$
$= 8\pi + 16$ ✓
∴ perimeter is
$(8\pi + 16)$ cm ✓ (2 marks)

66 Shape is one full circle
∴ Area $= \pi \times 5^2$ ✓
$= 78.539\,816\,34$
$= 78.54$ [2 decimal places]
∴ area is 78.54 cm^2 ✓ (2 marks)

67 red to blue $= 3:4$,
blue to green $= 2:5 = 4:10$
∴ red to blue to green
$= 3:4:10$ ✓
∴ red balls $= \frac{3}{17} \times 340$
$= 60$ ✓
∴ 60 red balls (2 marks)

68 $V = \frac{1}{2} \times \pi \times 7^2 \times 20$ ✓
$= 1539.3804$
$= 1539.38$ [2 decimal places]
∴ volume is 1539.38 mm^3 ✓ (2 marks)

69 $x = 180 - (70 + 70)$
$= 180 - 140$
$= 40$ ✓

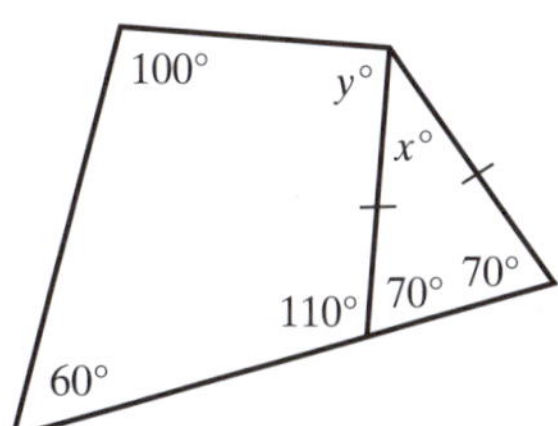

$y = 360 - (60 + 100 + 110)$
$= 360 - 270$
$= 90$ ✓ (2 marks)

70

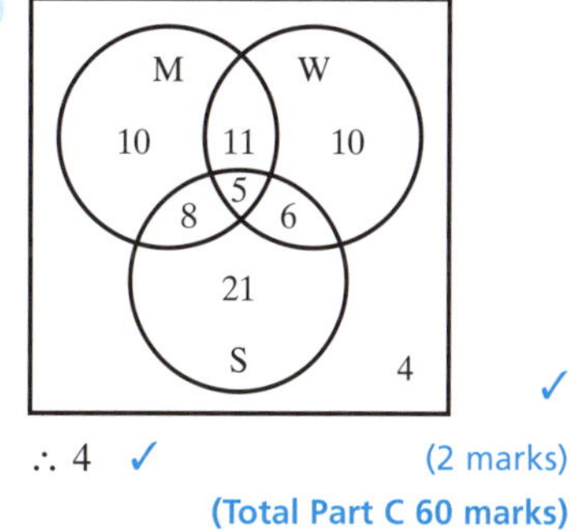

✓

∴ 4 ✓ (2 marks)

(Total Part C 60 marks)

SAMPLE EXAM PAPER 3
Part A: Multiple Choice PAGE 103

1 Try each of the alternatives.
8% of 80 $= 0.08 \times 80$
$= 6.4$
∴ \$6.40 is greatest
[other answers: 40c, \$1.60, \$3.60]
∴ [D] (1 mark)

2 $\angle DBA = 180° - 36°$
$= 144°$
Percentage $= \frac{144}{180} \times 100\%$
$= 80\%$
∴ [D] (1 mark)

3 Price $= 160 \times 115\% \times 85\%$
$= 160 \times 1.15 \times 0.85$
$= 156.4$
∴ dress cost \$156.40
∴ [C] (1 mark)

4 As $2000 - 375 = 1625$
∴ concentrate : water
$= 375 : 1625$
$= 3 : 13$
∴ [C] (1 mark)

5 Doubling the number always gives an even result. Then subtracting 1 always gives an odd result.
∴ impossible to get even result
∴ Pr(even) $= 0$
∴ [A] (1 mark)

6 Mean of 4 numbers $= 10$
Total of 4 numbers $= 40$
Mean of 6 numbers $= 11$
Total of 6 numbers $= 66$
Difference $= 66 - 40$
$= 26$
Missing number $= 26 - 8$
$= 18$
∴ [D] (1 mark)

7 If point is on the line $y = 2$,
∴ substitute $y = 2$ into
$y = x + 3$
$2 = x + 3$
$x = 2 - 3$
$= -1$
∴ point of intersection is $(-1, 2)$
∴ [A] (1 mark)

8 The line k crosses the y-axis at a positive value.
Try each of the alternatives.
Subs $x = 0$ in $y = 2x + 4$
$\therefore y = 4$
$\therefore$ line is $y = 2x + 4$
$\therefore y = 2x + 4 \quad \therefore$ **[A]** (1 mark)

9 Try each of the alternatives.
For 2, 6, 7, 9
Median = 6.5
$$\text{Mean} = \frac{2+6+7+9}{4} = \frac{24}{4} = 6$$
$\therefore$ median $\neq$ mean $\quad \therefore$ **[C]** (1 mark)

10 Let Shae's share $= x$
$\therefore$ Liam's share $= x - 40$
Jackson's share $= x + 60$
$$\therefore x + x - 40 + x + 60 = 440$$
$$3x + 20 = 440$$
$$3x = 440 - 20$$
$$3x = 420$$
$$\frac{3x}{3} = \frac{420}{3}$$
$$x = 140$$
$\therefore$ Jackson's share is $140 + 60 = \$200$
$\therefore$ **[A]** (1 mark)
(Total Part A 10 marks)

SAMPLE EXAM PAPER 3
Part B: Short Answer PAGE 104

11 $\frac{7}{9} \times 100\% = 77\frac{7}{9}\%$ (1 mark)

12 $0.1275 \times 680 = 86.7$
$\therefore \$86.70$ (1 mark)

13 No. $= 60 - (23 + 18 + 7)$
$= 60 - 48$
$= 12$
$$\therefore \text{Percentage} = \frac{12}{60} \times 100\% = 20\%$$
$\therefore$ 20% preferred Town Square. (1 mark)

14 New pay = 112% of existing pay
$\therefore$ 112% of existing pay = 2072
Existing pay $= 2072 \div 112 \times 100 = 1850$
$\therefore$ Helen currently receives \$1850 per fortnight.
(1 mark)

15 5 hectares $= 50\,000\ \text{m}^2$
$$\therefore \frac{750}{50\,000} \times 100\% = 1.5\%$$
$\therefore$ Darcy keeps 98.5% of property (1 mark)

16 Substitute $x = 3$ in $2x - y = 5$:
$$2 \times 3 - y = 5$$
$$6 - 5 = y$$
$$y = 1$$
$\therefore$ point of intersection at (3, 1) (1 mark)

17 Time $= 100\,000 \div 60 \div 60$
$= 27.777\,777\,7777$
$= 27$ h 46 min 40 s
[using (2ndF) (DMS)]
$\therefore$ 100 000 seconds is 27 h 46 min 40 s (1 mark)

18 As $1\ \text{m}^2 = 10\,000\ \text{cm}^2$
$\therefore 25\ \text{m}^2 : 50\ \text{cm}^2 = 250\,000 : 50$
$= 5000 : 1$ (1 mark)

19 Ratio of contributions = \$2 : \$2.50 : \$1.50
$= 4 : 5 : 3$
$$\therefore \text{Kim's winnings} = \frac{5}{12} \times 7200 = 3000$$
i.e. Kim receives \$3000. (1 mark)

20 Time $= 360 \div 75$
$= 4.8$
$\therefore$ travelling time is 4.8 hours i.e. 4 h 48 min
$\therefore$ Jason arrives at 2:08 pm. (1 mark)

21 From 16 cards, Adam reveals first card with picture of a dog. 15 cards remain, 1 with the matching picture.
$\therefore \text{Pr(next card is dog)} = \frac{1}{15}$ (1 mark)

22 $3 - (3 - 3y) - 3y = 3 - 3 + 3y - 3y$
$= 0$ (1 mark)

23 $a(a + b) - 2(a + b) = (a + b)(a - 2)$ (1 mark)

24
$$M = \frac{3}{4}(N - 24)$$
$$84 = \frac{3}{4}(N - 24)$$
$$336 = 3(N - 24)$$
$$3N - 72 = 336$$
$$\frac{3N}{3} = \frac{408}{3}$$
$$N = 136$$
(1 mark)

25 $x^2 = 10^2 - 8^2$
$= 100 - 64$
$= 36$
$x = \sqrt{36}$
$= 6$

WORKED SOLUTIONS

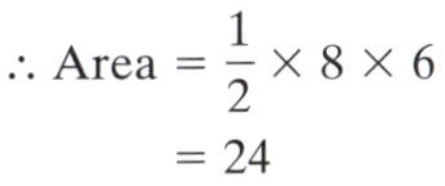

$\therefore$ Area $= \frac{1}{2} \times 8 \times 6$

$= 24$

$\therefore$ area is 24 cm^2 (1 mark)

26 $x^2 = 6^2 + 8^2$

$= 36 + 64$

$= 100$

$x = \sqrt{100}$

$= 10$

$\therefore$ perimeter $= 6 + 8 + 10$

$= 24$

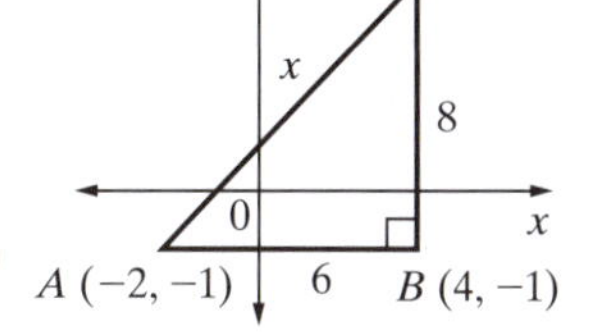

$\therefore$ perimeter is 24 units (1 mark)

27 Area $= 36$

$= \frac{1}{2} \times 12 \times h$

$6h = 36$

$h = 6$

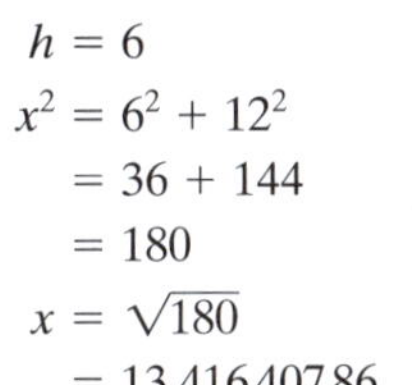

$x^2 = 6^2 + 12^2$

$= 36 + 144$

$= 180$

$x = \sqrt{180}$

$= 13.416\,407\,86$

$= 13.42$ [2 decimal places]

$\therefore$ perimeter $= 6 + 12 + 13.42 = 31.42$

$\therefore$ perimeter is 31.42 cm (1 mark)

28 $AE^2 = 5^2 - 3^2$

$= 25 - 9$

$= 16$

$AE = \sqrt{16}$

$= 4$

i.e. AE is 4 cm

Now as $AC = 10$ cm

$\therefore EC = 6$ cm (1 mark)

29 Let the number be x.

$3x + 18 - 12 = 30$

$3x + 6 = 30$

$3x = 30 - 6$

$3x = 24$

$\frac{3x}{3} = \frac{24}{3}$

$x = 8$

$\therefore$ the number is 8 (1 mark)

30 Capacity is 100 000 L = 100 kL

$\therefore$ volume $= 100$ m^3

and area $= 2500$ m^2

$\therefore 2500 \times h = 100$

$h = \frac{100}{2500}$

$= 0.04$

$\therefore$ depth of water is 4 cm (1 mark)

31

	Females	Males	Total
Requires glasses	7	**5**	**12**
Does not require glasses	**39**	**29**	68
Total	46	**34**	**80**

Pr(male not glasses) $= \frac{29}{80}$ (1 mark)

32 $C = 2 \times \pi \times \frac{9}{2} \times \frac{1}{2} = \frac{9\pi}{2}$

$\therefore$ circumference is $\frac{9\pi}{2}$ cm (1 mark)

33 Diameter = 2.4 cm, by measurement

$\therefore$ radius $= 1.2$ cm

$\therefore$ Area $= \pi \times 1.2^2$

$= 4.523\,893\,21$

$= 4.52$ [2 decimal places]

$\therefore$ area is 4.52 cm^2 (1 mark)

34 First, find circumference of the reel:

$C = 2 \times \pi \times 1.5$

$= 9.424\,777\,961$

$= 9.425$ [3 decimal places]

i.e. circumference is 0.094 25 m

No. of times $= 50 \div 0.094\,25$

$= 530.503\,9788$

$= 500$ [nearest 100]

$\therefore$ cotton is wrapped around 500 times (1 mark)

35 $3a + 20 + 60 + a + 50 + 110 = 360$

$4a + 240 = 360$

$4a = 360 - 240$

$4a = 120$

$a = 30$ (1 mark)

36

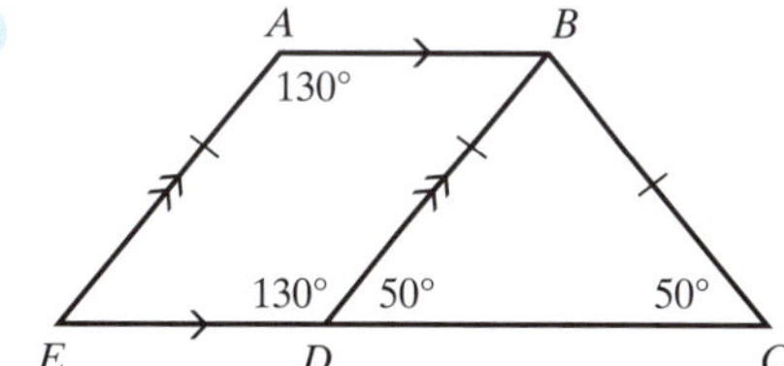

$\angle BCD = 50°$

Here's the proof:

$\angle BDE = 130°$ [opposite $\angle$s of parallelogram]

$\angle BDC = 50°$ [$\angle$ in straight line]

As $BD = BC$ [given]

$\angle BCD = \angle BDC$ [base $\angle$s of isosceles $\triangle$]

$\therefore \angle BCD = 50°$ (1 mark)

37 As:

$AC = AD$

$BC = BD$

AB is common to both triangles

$\therefore \triangle ACB \equiv \triangle ADB$ [matching sides equal] [SSS]

So, $\angle ACB = \angle ADB$

[matching $\angle$s of congruent $\triangle$s] (1 mark)

38

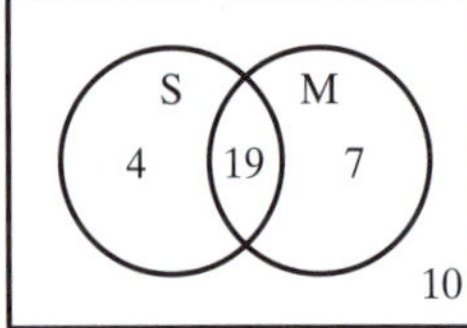

Pr(no milk or sugar) $= \frac{10}{40} = \frac{1}{4}$ (1 mark)

39 Subs. $C = 350$ in $C = 80 + 120h$

$$350 = 80 + 120h$$
$$120h + 80 = 350$$
$$120h = 350 - 80$$
$$120h = 270$$
$$\frac{120h}{120} = \frac{270}{120}$$
$$h = 2.25$$

$\therefore$ the electrician worked for 2 h 15 min (1 mark)

40 teachers : boys = 2 : 25

2 parts = 18

1 part = 9

25 parts = 225

$\therefore$ there were 225 boys at the dance

As 40 + 225 = 265, there were 265 girls at the dance.

Total students = 225 + 265
= 490

$\therefore$ there were 490 students at the dance. (1 mark)

(Total Part B 30 marks)

SAMPLE EXAM PAPER 3

Part C PAGE 107

41 $x = 140$ ✓
$y = 250$ ✓

(2 marks)

42 **a** Let camera be valued at $100.

$\therefore$ price = $100 \times 0.80 \times 0.95$
= 76

i.e. a single discount of 24% ✓

b 76% of price = 380

100% of price = $380 \div 76 \times 100$
= 500

i.e. original price was $500 ✓ (2 marks)

43 Ratio of new lengths = 3 : 1 ✓

Longer piece $= \frac{3}{4} \times 3.2 = 2.4$

$\therefore$ longer piece of 2.4 m ✓ (2 marks)

44 Suppose existing youth group is 20 boys and 30 girls. On the special night, there would be 60 boys and 60 girls.

$\therefore$ boys : girls = 1 : 1 ✓✓ (2 marks)

45 Distance on 91-octane = $60 \div 8 \times 100$
= 750 i.e. 750 km ✓

Distance on 95-octane = $60 \div 7.5 \times 100$
= 800 km i.e. 800 km

$\therefore$ Fiona can drive a further 50 km. ✓ (2 marks)

46 Cost/tank:

91-octane: $1.429 × 60 = $85.74

95-octane: $1.499 × 60 = $89.94

$\therefore$ Cost/km:

91-octane: 85.74 ÷ 750 = 0.114 32

i.e. $0.114 32/km

95-octane: 89.94 ÷ 800 = 0.112 425

i.e. $0.112 425/km ✓

$\therefore$ Fiona is correct. It is slightly cheaper per kilometre to use high octane petrol in her car. ✓ (2 marks)

47 **a** Pr(ice skating) $= \frac{2}{12} = \frac{1}{6}$ ✓

b Pr(bowls or beach) $= \frac{2}{12} + \frac{3}{12}$
$= \frac{5}{12}$ ✓ (2 marks)

48 Time of travel $= \frac{2800}{800}$
= 3.5 ✓

i.e. plane took 3 h 30 min $\therefore$ it is 3 pm (Molongo time) when the plane arrives in Jalanga

$\therefore$ it is noon in Jalanga ✓ (2 marks)

49 As 5 − 3 = 2

$\therefore$ 2 parts = 24 ✓

1 part = 12

8 parts = 96

$\therefore$ 96 in the group ✓ (2 marks)

50 As 72 + 64 = 136, find time to travel 272 km at 136 km/h

Time = Distance ÷ Speed
= 272 ÷ 136
= 2

$\therefore$ motorists meet after 2 hours ✓

Sean's Distance = Speed × Time
= 72 × 2
= 144

$\therefore$ meet 144 km from town A after 2 hours ✓

(2 marks)

51 Increase $= 200 - 160$
$= 40$

% increase $= \frac{40}{160} \times 100\%$
$= 25\%$ ✓

New price $= 1.25 \times 380$
$= 475$

$\therefore$ the bangle will cost \$475 ✓ (2 marks)

52 Area of square $= 4x^2$
Length of square $= 2x$
Triangle has base $2x$ cm and height of x cm. ✓

Area of triangle $= \frac{1}{2} \times 2x \times x$
$= x^2$

$\therefore$ area of triangle is x^2 cm^2 ✓ (2 marks)

53 $3 - 4(4 - x) = 2 - (5 - x)$
$3 - 16 + 4x = 2 - 5 + x$
$-13 + 4x = -3 + x$ ✓
$4x - x = -3 + 13$
$3x = 10$
$\frac{3x}{3} = \frac{10}{3}$
$x = 3\frac{1}{3}$ ✓ (2 marks)

54 $\frac{2a}{3} - 4 = 6a$
$3 \times \frac{2a}{3} - 3 \times 4 = 6a \times 3$
$2a - 12 = 18a$ ✓
$2a - 18a = 12$
$-16a = 12$
$\frac{-16a}{-16} = \frac{12}{-16}$
$a = -\frac{3}{4}$ ✓ (2 marks)

55 Let width $= x$ cm
$\therefore$ the length $= 4x$ cm
$P = 2(4x + x) = 50$
$10x = 50$
$x = 5$
Dimensions are 20 cm by 5 cm ✓
Area $= 20 \times 5$
$= 100$
$\therefore$ the area is 100 cm^2 ✓ (2 marks)

56 Let the number be x.
$2x + 6 = 4x - 8$
$4x - 8 = 2x + 6$
$4x - 2x = 6 + 8$ ✓
$2x = 14$
$\frac{2x}{2} = \frac{14}{2}$
$x = 7$
$\therefore$ the number is 7 ✓ (2 marks)

57 $S = \frac{a(r^n - 1)}{r - 1}$
$400 = \frac{a(3^4 - 1)}{3 - 1}$
$400 = \frac{a(81 - 1)}{2}$ ✓
$800 = 80a$
$80a = 800$
$\frac{80a}{80} = \frac{800}{80}$
$a = 10$ ✓ (2 marks)

58 $y = 4 - x$

x	0	1	2
y	4	3	2

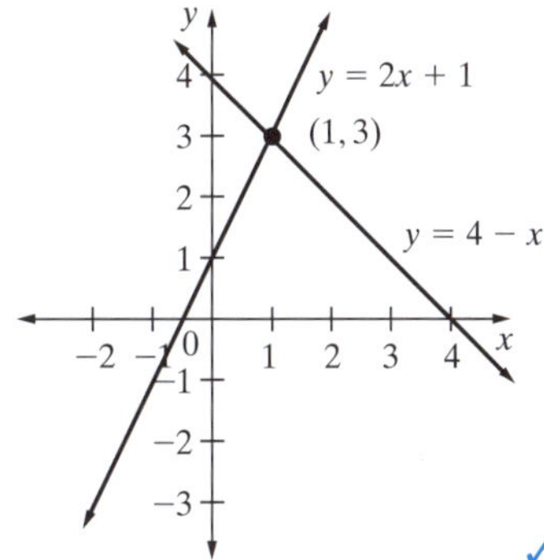

✓

$\therefore$ point of intersection is (1, 3) ✓ (2 marks)

59 $\frac{x^2 - 3x - xy + 3y}{3x - 3y}$
$= \frac{x(x - 3) - y(x - 3)}{3(x - y)}$ ✓
$= \frac{(x - y)(x - 3)}{3(x - y)}$
$= \frac{x - 3}{3}$ ✓ (2 marks)

60 **a** $C = 3t + 40$ ✓

b $115 = 3t + 40$
$3t + 40 = 115$
$3t = 115 - 40$
$3t = 75$
$\frac{3t}{3} = \frac{75}{3}$
$t = 25$
$\therefore$ 25 minutes ✓ (2 marks)

61

Score (x)	Frequency (x)	fx
8	**2**	**16**
9	**4**	**36**
10	**0**	**0**
11	**2**	**22**
12	**3**	**36**
13	**1**	**13**
Total	**12**	**123**

$\therefore c = 12; d = 123$ ✓✓ (2 marks)

62 The scores can be displayed in a frequency table:

Score (x)	Frequency (x)	fx
21	3	63
22	3	66
23	5	115
24	3	72
25	5	125
Total	19	441

a median: 23 ✓

b mean: $\frac{441}{19}$
$= 23.210\,526\,32$
$= 23.21$ [2 decimal places] ✓ (2 marks)

63 **a** Number of households
$= 1 + 3 + 6 + 5 + 2 + 3$
$= 20$
$\therefore$ 20 households ✓

b Number of cars:
$= 0 \times 1 + 1 \times 3 + 2 \times 6 + 3 \times 5 + 4 \times 2 + 5 \times 3$
$= 0 + 3 + 12 + 15 + 8 + 15$
$= 53$
$\therefore$ 53 cars
$\therefore$ Mean $= \frac{53}{20} = 2.65$
i.e. mean number of cars is 2.65 ✓ (2 marks)

64

$AB^2 = 3^2 + 4^2$
$= 9 + 16$
$= 25$

$AB = 5$ ✓

∴ perimeter is 20 cm ✓ (2 marks)

65 Area $= \frac{1}{2} \times 6 \times (3x + 2)$

$= 3(3x + 2)$ ✓

i.e. $3(3x + 2) = 24$

$9x + 6 = 24$
$9x = 24 - 6$
$9x = 18$
$\frac{9x}{9} = \frac{18}{9}$
$x = 2$ ✓ (2 marks)

66 $x^2 = 8^2 + 6^2$
$= 64 + 36$
$= 100$

$x = 10$ ✓

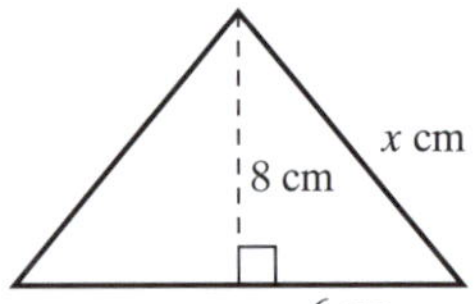

∴ perimeter $= 10 + 10 + 12$
$= 32$

i.e. perimeter is 32 cm ✓ (2 marks)

67

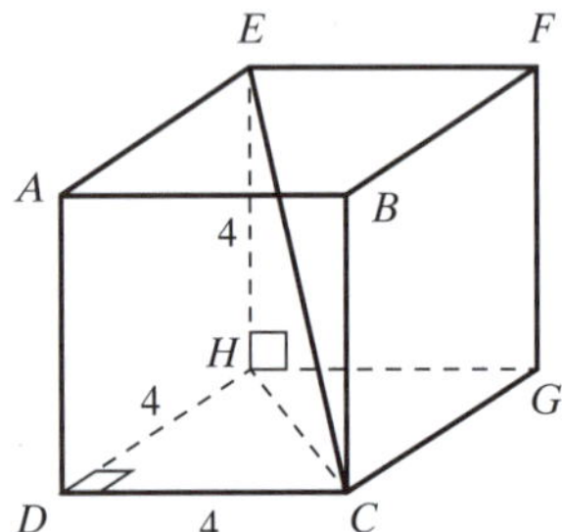

In $\triangle DHC$

$HC^2 = HD^2 + CD^2$
$= 4^2 + 4^2$
$= 16 + 16$
$= 32$

$HC = \sqrt{32}$ ✓

Now, in $\triangle EHC$,

$EC^2 = EH^2 + HC^2$
$= 4^2 + (\sqrt{32})^2$
$= 16 + 32$
$= 48$

$EC = \sqrt{48}$
$= 6.928\,203\,23$
$= 6.93$

∴ the length of EC is 6.93 cm (2 dec. pl.) ✓ (2 marks)

68 Volume $= 10 \times 10 \times 5$
$= 500$

∴ volume of water is 500 cm^3

$V = \pi r^2 h$
$500 = \pi \times 5^2 \times h$ ✓
$500 = 25\pi h$
$h = \frac{500}{25\pi}$
$= \frac{20}{\pi}$

∴ the height is $\frac{20}{\pi}$ cm ✓ (2 marks)

69 Let cost price = 100%

120% of cost price = 600

1% of cost price = 5 ✓

80% of cost price = 400

∴ it sold for $400 ✓ (2 marks)

70 **a** Cost: 6 for $10

Sold: 2 for $5, or 6 for $15

Profit (for 6) = $5

% profit $= \frac{5}{10} \times 100\%$
$= 50\%$

∴ the profit is 50% ✓

b Number of mangoes $= 180 \div 5 \times 6$
$= 216$

Number of boxes $= 216 \div 12$
$= 18$

∴ Lucia bought 18 boxes. ✓ (2 marks)

(Total Part C 60 marks)

TEST & EXAM RESULTS

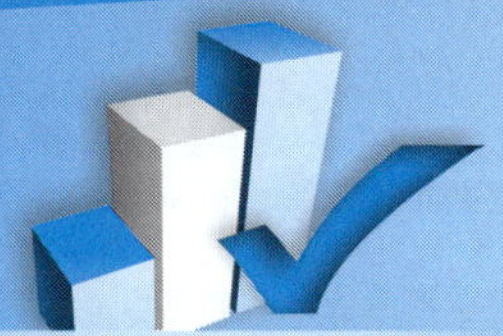

Transfer your **percentage score** that you calculated in the **Your Feedback** box at the end of each **test** and **exam** to the table below. This will help you work out your areas of strength and weakness.

Test Topic	Intermediate Test Score	Advanced Test Score
Review: Number, Fractions and Decimals	%	%
Review: Percentages	%	%
Review: Using the Calculator	%	%
Review: Patterns and Algebra	%	%
Review: Area and Volume	%	%
Review: Shape and Geometric Reasoning	%	%
Review: Data Representation and Chance	%	%
Number and Algebra: Directed Numbers and Index Notation	%	%
Number and Algebra: Financial Mathematicss	%	%
Number and Algebra: Ratio and Rates	%	%
Number and Algebra: Algebra	%	%
Number and Algebra: Basic Equations	%	%
Number and Algebra: Formulae and Using Equations	%	%
Number and Algebra: Coordinate Geometry	%	%
Measurement and Geometry: Length, Area and Volume	%	%
Measurement and Geometry: Circles and Cylinders	%	%
Measurement and Geometry: Time and Pythagoras's Theorem	%	%
Measurement and Geometry: Congruent Triangles and Transformations	%	%
Statistics and Probability: Probability	%	%
Statistics and Probability: Interpreting Data	%	%
Sample Exam Papers		
Sample Exam Paper 1		%
Sample Exam Paper 2		%
Sample Exam Paper 3		%

FEEDBACK CHECKLIST TO IMPROVE YOUR TEST & EXAM RESULTS

Do you want to improve your scores in the Sample Exams? Check that:

You are ready.

This is a revision workbook designed specifically for the revision of work already done. It is not a replacement for your textbook or class notes. Cover the topic in class or in your own time by reading your textbook or the ***Excel*** *Year 8 Mathematics Study Guide*, before using this book for further practice on the topic.

You are revising in the right order.

Maths is a subject that builds on previous knowledge. Often you will need to have a good grasp of an early topic in order to fully understand a later topic.

Your standards are realistic.

You cannot expect to score 100% all the time. Remember that this book has been designed to help you identify your strengths as well as your weaknesses, so it is OK to make mistakes. The key to success is learning from those mistakes.

You are not rushing through the questions.

Many Maths students fail to read questions properly. This accounts for a large number of the mistakes made in tests and exams. Although your time is limited, you must still take enough time to read each question carefully. If necessary, read the question a second (or even third) time. Don't start your answer until you are sure that you understand the question. For the longer questions, take a moment or two to plan your answer.

You are allowing yourself enough time to study.

Preparation for any test or exam requires a sufficient investment of time to be undertaken successfully. This means that you have to plan ahead. Don't wait until a week or so before an exam, for example, to ask yourself the question: How much time will I need to devote to this subject to revise it thoroughly? Don't forget to allow sufficient time for your other subjects—Maths isn't the only subject you will have to sit an exam for!

You are OK.

You may be having some problems unrelated to your schoolwork. It is wise to sort out such problems as quickly as possible. Speak to your teacher, a parent or your school counsellor if you think you need help.

INDEX

NOTES

NOTES